CW00970177

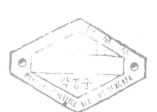

MINISTRY OF CULTURE THE DEP. OF KOREA

FEB 25 2001
Z 92

9.00

Z A
SALIDA

MIGRACION

DEPARTMENT OF IMMIGRATION
PERMITTED TO ENTER
AUSTRALIA.

on 24 APR 1996

For stay of 12 Month

SYDNEY AIRPORT 54

IMMIGRATION DIVISION BANGKOK THAILAND
A
72
DEPARTED
- 6 FEB 1998
SIGNED

IMMIGRATION & ETHNIC AFFAIRS
.... Person
30 OCT 1999
DEPARTED
AUSTRALIA
SYDNEY 32

中华人民共和国
入
东省公安厅

上陸許可
ADMITTED
15. FEB. 1996
Status:4-1- 4
Duration: 90 days
NARITA(N)
Immigration Inspector
日本国

ADMITTED
20 OCT. 1998
Status: 4-1-16
Duration 180 days
Port: HANEDA
Signature

Nº 011278

THE UNITED STATES
OF AMERICA
NONIMMIGRANT VISA
ISSUED AT
PASSED
Air Port

U.S. IMMIGRATION
170 HHW 1710
JUL 20 1998

HONG KONG
(1038)
- 7 JUN 1997
IMMIGRATION
OFFICER

T R A V E L E R ' S
ECUADOR
C O M P A N I O N

The 2001–2002 Traveler's Companions

ARGENTINA • AUSTRALIA • BALI • CALIFORNIA • CANADA • CHILE • CHINA • COSTA RICA • CUBA • EASTERN CANADA • ECUADOR • FLORIDA • HAWAII • HONG KONG • INDIA • INDONESIA • JAPAN • KENYA • MALAYSIA & SINGAPORE • MEDITERRANEAN FRANCE • MEXICO • NEPAL • NEW ENGLAND • NEW ZEALAND • PERU • PHILIPPINES • PORTUGAL • RUSSIA • SOUTH AFRICA • SOUTHERN ENGLAND • SPAIN • THAILAND • TURKEY • VENEZUELA • VIETNAM, LAOS AND CAMBODIA • WESTERN CANADA

Traveler's Ecuador Companion

First published 1998
Second edition 2001
The Globe Pequot Press
246 Goose Lane, PO Box 480,
Guilford, CT 06437 USA
www.globe.pequot.com

© 2001 by The Globe Pequot Press, Guilford, CT, USA

ISBN: 0-7627-1006-3

Distributed in the European Union by
World Leisure Marketing Ltd, Unit 11
Newmarket Court, Newmarket Drive,
Derby, DE24 8NW, United Kingdom
www.map-guides.com

Created, edited and produced by
Allan Amsel Publishing, 53 rue Beaudouin,
27700 Les Andelys, France.
E-mail: aamsel@aol.com
Editor in Chief: Allan Amsel
Editor: Anne Trager
Original design concept: Hon Bing-wah
Picture editor and designer: David Henry

ACKNOWLEDGMENTS:
The publisher would like to thank several people and organizations for valuable
assistance and advice which helped the authors in their research for this edition.
In Quito: Beatriz Andrade of the Ministerio de Turismo, the Ministerio del Ambiente,
the South American Explorers, Safari Tours, Hotel Café Cultura and Yaca-Amu Rafting.
In the Galápagos, Latin Tour and the Red Mangrove Inn. In the north, Hacienda Cusín,
Hostería Hacienda Pinsaquí and Hostería Ali Shingu; in the south, Canodros S.A.,
Hotel Crespo and Hacienda La Ciénega; on the coast, Playa Escondida,
Bahía Dolphin Tours and Hostería Alandaluz.

Printed by Samhwa Printing Co. Ltd., Seoul, South Korea

TRAVELER'S
ECUADOR
COMPANION

by Derek Davies and Dominic Hamilton

photographs by Robert Holmes

Second Edition

The Globe Pequot Press

GUILFORD
CONNECTICUT

Contents

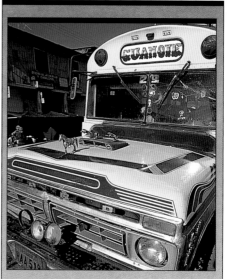

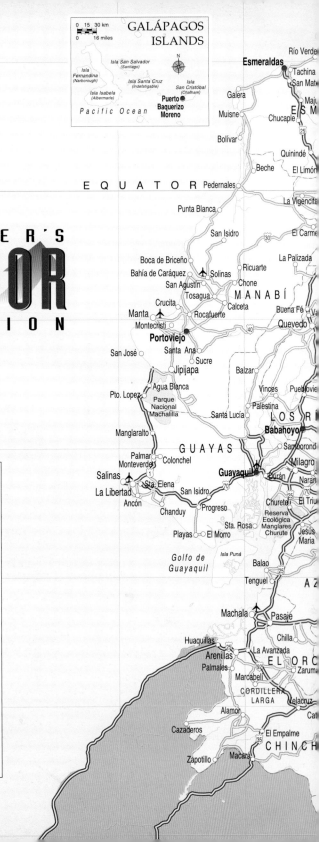

GALÁPAGOS ISLANDS

0   15   30 km
0   16 miles

Isla San Salvador (Santiago)

Isla Fernandina (Narborough)

Isla Santa Cruz (Indefatigable)

Isla San Cristóbal (Chatham)

Isla Isabela (Albermarle)

N

Puerto Baquerizo Moreno

Pacific Ocean

T R A V E L E R ' S

ECUADOR

C O M P A N I O N

LEGEND

Populations

◎ QUITO	Capital
● Guayaquil	Provincial Capital
○ Atenas	Large Town
○ Lagarto	Small Town

Transportation

═══21═══ Main Routes

Primary Routes

Secondary and Unpaved Roads

━ ╳ ━ ╳ ━ Railways

Physical Features

Bordering Countries

National and Provincial Boundaries

Forests, Reserves and National Parks

Lakes and Rivers

3030 Aquatic Parks

Mountains and Volcanoes

Río Verde
Esmeraldas
Tachina
San Mate
Galera
Maju
Muisne
E S M
Chucaple
Bolívar
25
Quinindé
Beche
El Limón
E Q U A T O R   Pedernales
La Vigencia
Punta Blanca
San Isidro
El Carme
30
La Palizada
Boca de Briceño
Ricuarte
Bahía de Caráquez
Solinas
Chone
San Agustín
M A N A B Í
Crucita
Tosagua
Calceta
Buena Fé
Manta
Rocafuerte
Quevedo
40
Montecristi
Portoviejo
San José
Santa Ana
Sucre
Jipijapa
Balzar
Pto. Lopez
Agua Blanca
Vinces
Pueblovie
Parque Nacional Machalilla
Palestina
Santa Lucía
L O S R
Manglaralto
Babahoyo
G U A Y A S
Samborond
Palmar
Colonchel
Milagro
Monteverde
Salinas
Guayaquil
Burán
Naran
La Libertad
Sta. Elena
70
Ancón
San Isidro
70
Chanduy
Progreso
Churete
El Triu
Reserva Ecológica Manglares Churute
Sta. Rosa
Jesús Maria
Playas
El Morro
Golfo de Guayaquil
Isla Puná
Balao
25
Tenguel
A Z
Machala
Pasaje
Chilla
Huaquillas
25
La Avanzada
Arenillas
Palmales
Zaruma
E L O R C
Marcabelí
CORDILLERA LARGA
Velacruz
Alamor
Cat
Cazaderos
El Empalme
35
C H I N C H
Zapotillo
Macará

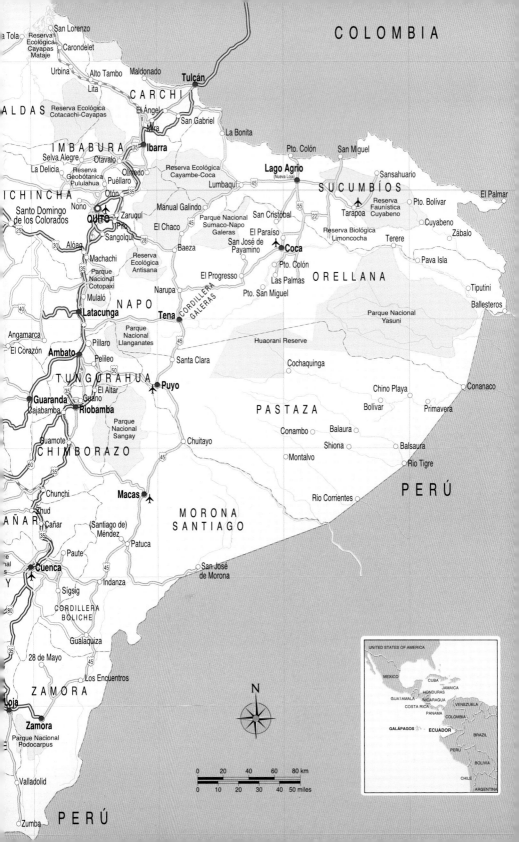

TOP SPOTS

Cruise the Galápagos Islands

A typical Galápagos day begins with music piped into your cabin and a breakfast of delicious, unfamiliar fruits and juices. A *panga* awaits you and the dozen or so other passengers. This small dingy ferries you from the cruise ship to a long, low headland of twisted volcanic rock, or else to a pristine sandy beach, where a strong-armed boat boy helps those laden with cameras, binoculars, large sun hats and suntan lotion through the "wet landing."

Here, prehistoric marine iguanas, which Charles Darwin called "Imps of Darkness," lounge on black rocks while sleek and slithery sea lions bask in the sun on the beach, their whiskery noses smudged with sand. Both play starring roles on the islands, supported by blue-footed and masked boobies. Galápagos doves, mockingbirds, hawks, lava herons, night herons, oystercatchers, swallowtail gulls, various finches, lava lizards and the occasional snake take cameo roles.

Surprisingly, the animals don't scurry away when approached. Even the birds appear quite tame, pecking about at your feet and perhaps even landing on your shoulders. For hundreds of years human visitors have commented on the abundance and tameness of the wildlife in these remote and isolated islands that straddle the equator in the Pacific Ocean, about 1,000 km (625 miles) off the coast of Ecuador. In fact, the word tame isn't quite accurate, since it implies domesticated wildlife. For the most part animals of the Galápagos have evolved and lived without fear of predators common in other parts of the world, neither human nor four-legged. This absence of fear on the part of the birds and animals makes human visitors feel an extraordinary, uplifting harmony with nature difficult to find elsewhere on earth. It's for good reasons the Galápagos Islands have often been called the Garden of Eden.

For equally good reasons, the archipelago is also known as the world's greatest natural laboratory of evolution. Ever since Charles Darwin's visit in 1835, scientists have been drawn to the islands to study creatures that evolved in isolation from their cousins on the mainland. In 1959, responding to a growing awareness of the environmental and scientific importance of the archipelago, Ecuador designated 97 percent of the 8,000 sq km (3,088 sq miles) land area of Galápagos as a national park. In 1986, the water around the archipelago was also protected, UNESCO recognizing the islands as a World Heritage Site, and a Man and Biosphere Reserve soon thereafter. Today, over 130,000 sq km (51,793 sq miles) of the islands and surrounding waters are protected by the

OPPOSITE: Multi-chromatic sunrises and sunsets are a feature of the Galápagos Islands. Here dawn breaks over Santa Fé, home to a unique species of land iguana. ABOVE: A red-footed booby, on the Galápagos Islands.

Galápagos National Park and the Galápagos Marine Resources Reserve.

After lunch back on the cruise ship, passengers prepare for an afternoon snorkel in waters glinting and flickering with millions of tropical fish. You may spot a turtle or two. Or perhaps a white-tipped shark will cruise silently past you underwater, like a policeman of the deep keeping an eye on things. Often a school of curious sea lions will approach, ducking and diving about you, zooming right up to your mask only to pull away at the last moment. The cheekier ones will grab your flipper.

On other days, an afternoon stroll on a neighboring island beckons. About a kilometer's walk (just over a half mile) from the port at Punta Suárez on Española, for example, along the path marked by black and white stakes, you come to the edge of a high cliff overlooking a vibrant blue sea flecked with white-tipped waves. Fork-tailed frigate birds soar and glide in the thermals, while the breakers crash on the rocks below. At one point the surf thrusts itself into the entrance of a lava tube blowhole and bursts out the other end in a 30-m (100-ft) fountain of white spray.

For most people, traveling to the Galápagos is a trip of a lifetime. Not just because it's an expensive enterprise, but because so few places on the planet remain where you can enjoy such close encounters with wild animals, and feel so near to Nature itself. For many, the Galápagos are as much about reinforcing a spiritual bond with the natural world so often lost in our urban lives, as they are about enjoying a wonderful vacation amid these "enchanted isles."

The islands are fragile and unique. Human intervention has already caused devastating repercussions; mainly the loss of unique species which once thrived upon only one island. "Lonesome George," the last giant saddleback tortoise of the Pinta breed, has become the island's icon. When George finally dies, so will his species. For this reason, it's essential to heed the warnings and advice of your guide regarding the dos and don'ts of the national park, but also to contribute in some positive way to the vital scientific research and environmental protection programs carried out in the Galápagos. The best way to do this is to become a friend of the Charles Darwin Foundation E-MAIL cdrs@fcdarwin.org.ec WEB SITE www.galapagos.org and thus a friend of the Galápagos itself.

Gold from ancient artifacts, like this mask ABOVE now in the Casa de la Cultura, was melted down and used in churches such as El Sagrario LEFT in Quito.

Go for Gold

When, in 1519, the conquistador Hernán Cortés arrived on the Mexican coast with his band of adventurers, he told the Aztec emperor Moctezuma's ambassadors: "We suffer from a disease which only gold can cure." The Spanish lust for gold defined the country's conquest of the Americas. Over the coming centuries, the conquistadors went to unimaginable lengths, committing unfathomable atrocities, in order to ease their disease.

The irony of Cortés's quote is that European diseases, more than steel, gunpowder or horses, delivered the New World to the Spanish. It is thought that maybe nine out of every ten people on the newly discovered continent perished in the first 100 years of the Conquest, representing some one-fifth of the entire human race at the time. Indeed, smallpox had spread to the Inca Empire long before the battle-scarred, ruthless but brilliant Governor Francisco Pizarro virtually stumbled upon it for the first time in the late 1520s. Fate could not have dealt him a better hand.

Historians believe smallpox killed the great Inca emperor Huayna Capac — and his most likely heir — just as Pizarro was first exploring Ecuador's Pacific coast. When the conquistador finally pushed deep into the empire in 1532, he found a land only recently recovering from the ravages of civil war. Huayna Capac's two sons, Atahualpa to the north and Huáscar to the south, had fought bloody campaigns in order to succeed their father's throne. Atahualpa, though victorious, was still anxiously awaiting news from his generals in the south. He was therefore little concerned by incoming

reports of "170 bearded white men" on his shores. Complacent in the extreme, he invited Pizarro to meet him at Cajamarca in northern Perú.

On that fateful day, in a bold and nigh-on suicidal move, Pizarro and the Spaniards captured the Inca. They also massacred some 7,000 of Atahualpa's troops, including his greatest lords. The captured Atahualpa soon realized what interested the Spaniards most: gold. He therefore offered a ransom in return for his life. He would fill a room to a height of two and a half meters (eight feet) with objects of gold and silver. The Spaniards walked away with over six metric tons (over 13,000 pounds) of gold and nearly 12 metric tons (nearly 26,000 pounds) of silver. Today such sums would be worth at least US$60 million. They then killed Atahualpa anyway.

And so began the conquest of the Incas. In Ecuador, virtually none of the original gold of the Incas remains. But pre-Columbian gold artifacts, jewelry and adornments rank among the country's most popular museum exhibits. In Quito, the Museo Nacional del Banco Central del Ecuador has the finest in the country. An extraordinary ceremonial gold mask from the Tolita culture, which the bank uses — controversially — as a logo, glows in its dark vitrine, alongside an entire salon of gold objects. Guided tours explain how the gold- and platinum-working techniques used by Ecuador's ancient coastal cultures were astoundingly advanced for

their times. The country's second greatest collection is housed in the Museo Arqueológico del Banco Central in Guayaquil, also highly recommended.

Although much of the captured gold was sent back to Spain to repay the debts of the Holy Roman Emperor Carlos V, much was also employed to gild the interiors of Ecuador's churches, elevating them to among the finest of the continent. Quito's Jesuit church, La Compañía de Jesús, considered to be the loveliest church in Ecuador, is a good example. It was only just completed before the order's expulsion from the New World in 1767. Behind its magnificent carved volcanic-stone façade, replete with bevies of bleeding hearts and choruses of angels, its massive altars, baroque columns and ceilings are laden, tip to toe, with gold leaf. Some seven tons of "saint-seducing" gold, it is said. The theatricality and extravagance of its interior are breathtaking. At the altar are the silver, platinum, emeralds, gold and pearls that the Spanish, at huge human cost, drove the Indians to unearth or smelt, now turned into exquisite crosses, or embroidered into the cloak of the Virgin.

Similarly, the altar, roof and choir of the colossal Iglesia de San Francisco, Quito's oldest church, are richly decorated with baroque carvings and gold leaf. Taking time to explore Quito and the country's — particularly Cuenca's — churches will leave you with little doubt that the Spanish went quite some way to cure their disease.

14

Live the Hacienda Life

The *patrón* of Hacienda Pinsaquí enjoys
riding about on his chestnut Arab stallion
inside his grand mansion. Don Pedro Freile,
the oldest of three Pedro Freiles, has a habit
of greeting guests in the living room, on
horseback, and riding down the stairway to
the *bodega* bar to join them for an *aperitivo*.
There he has a tot or two in the saddle, rather
in the style of a red-coated huntsman
gathered with his hounds before setting
off for the hunt.

One suspects there are many more stories
like this about the habits of the landed gentry
of Ecuador. The grand Ecuadorian haciendas
were built, after all, for good living. The word
hacienda conjures up images of grand country
estates, huge houses, cobbled courtyards,
horsemen with wide-brimmed sombreros,
masses of servants and old-fashioned luxury.
And that's exactly what haciendas are all
about, except that today many of the grand
Ecuadorian haciendas have become hotels
and some of the old families are learning
the tricks of the tourist trade.

There are several splendid haciendas
within easy reach of Quito that you can either
visit for a meal or where you can stay for a
night or more. Pinsaquí is an old mansion that
reminds me of an Indian maharajah's palace.
It boasts enormous guestrooms, old-fashioned
baths, beautiful furniture, fine gardens,
ambling llamas and horses, and excellent
food. Its walls are also thick with history: an
important nineteenth-century treaty between
Colombia and Ecuador was signed in the
house, and "The Liberator," General Simón
Bolívar, was a frequent guest.

In the same area north of Quito, the
exquisite Hacienda Cusín, originally
established in 1602, has been refurbished to a
standard fit to be photographed by glossy
New York lifestyle magazines. All rooms are
decorated with locally made furniture and
tapestries, the garden is particularly
enchanting and the food is first-class. Dinner
is served in a baronial-style hall under
chandeliers and candlelight. Services include
horses (which are well looked after), mountain
bikes, squash, Spanish lessons and nannies.
Aside from wallowing in residential luxury,
there are plenty of interesting walks and trips
to make in the surrounding area.

Around the Imbabura volcano from Cusín,
and reached by a stunning, bumpy old road,
you come to Hacienda Zuleta, a working dairy
farm tucked into a furiously cultivated, fertile

valley. The Plaza family, who own Zuleta, is
also deeply involved in local weaving, making
the hacienda a great place to learn more about
this highly praised Ecuadorian craft.

Eccentricity seems to be a characteristic of
many aristocratic hacienda owners, and I hope
Diego Bonifaz, a former government minister
and *patrón* of Hacienda Guachalá, won't be
offended if I include him on the fringes of
this group. A fine mind accompanies his
nonconformity, and Señor Bonifaz is a notable
historian and expert in rural affairs. He is
also the imaginative manager of the oldest
hacienda in Ecuador, which looks like a movie
set for a costume drama unfolding at the time
of the conquistadors. It is located northeast of
Quito near the town and volcano of Cayambe.
While accommodation is not as luxurious as
some other haciendas, the ancient messuage
does boast a large indoor swimming pool
heated by solar power. In mid-June, the
hacienda hosts a televised show-jumping
competition, and horses are available for
rental throughout the year.

My baptism in hacienda living came at
Hostería La Ciénega, about 20 km (13 miles)
north of Latacunga, just south of the looming
Cotopaxi volcano. La Ciénega is a huge and

OPPOSITE: Within a couple hours' drive of Quito,
Hostería La Ciénega is one of Ecuador's oldest and
finest haciendas. ABOVE: Gracious stately homes
such as Hacienda Cusín stimulate and soothe the
senses of visitors to Ecuador.

splendid Spanish-style stately home that is approached down a long avenue of towering eucalyptus trees, said to be the oldest eucalypti in the country. A beautifully kept inner garden with central fountain and bright, exotic plants and flowers adds to the sense of tranquility and grace, as if you had been transported back in time to an age of courtesy and gentle hospitality. The private chapel with its massive carved wooden door has heard the prayers of countless generations over four centuries. Only the rooms are slightly disappointing after so much grandeur. The best are rooms 8 and 9, which are huge and offer unparalleled views over the garden and, on the other side, down the never-ending avenue of trees.

If you want to throw a house party for a small group of friends and money is no object, the former monastery of Hacienda San Agustín de Callo should be on your list of possible locations. This extraordinary old colonial building's walls were made by Incas

for a temple that originally stood at this magical site, in the shadow of the world's tallest active volcano, Volcán Cotopaxi. Guests here live like the owners and, with the owners, share the big, comfortable living room with views of the great mountains. Meals are served in an elegant dining room, all four walls of which are made of the Inca blocks — you feel as if you're eating inside a pyramid. The Ecuadorian food at San Agustín is renowned, ranging from the simple but delicious *locro de papa* (potato soup) to more sophisticated dishes. San Agustín is also famous for its parties and festivals. Traditional dancing, music and bullfighting are part of the summer solstice celebration in June.

The above are just a few of Ecuador's fine haciendas. Others worth asking local travel agents or tour operators about include La Vega Ingenio San José and San Vicente, to the north, and Hualilagua, San José de Cabo, Puchalitola, Santa Ana del Pedregal and La Fontana to the south.

experiencing the biggest thrill of the ride. As the train wound its way around tight bends down the steep slopes, the vegetation became thicker and more tropical and the temperature rose. Eventually we clattered into hot and languid San Lorenzo 10 hours after our departure from Ibarra, only three hours late.

Of the country's once extensive rail network, only sections remain, and trains don't run as regularly as they used to. There are infrequent departures from Quito to Riobamba, from where the train no longer makes it to Guayaquil, but instead reaches Bucay and comes back again. Ecuador nevertheless boasts two train rides that must rank among the most thrilling in the world, both of which wind up and down the steep slopes of the Andes. Most travelers regard a train journey as one of the highlights of their trip.

The route from Quito to Riobamba (on Saturdays) takes about eight hours in antiquated equipment, passing Machachi, Lasso (for Cotopaxi), Latacunga and Ambato, and ending in the shadow of Volcán Chimborazo. You can board or disembark at any of these stops. The most dramatic section of track in the country lies between Alausí (south of Riobamba) and Sibambe, now run only for tourists at a steep US$15 a pop. It's known as the Devil's Nose, because of one particularly steep and perilous curve, but also perhaps because only the Devil knows how they managed to lay the track in the first place. From Bucay further south, the train heads back to Riobamba. This route runs on Wednesday, Friday and Sunday, leaving at 7 AM. Up until the damage wrought by the El Niño floods of 1997, the train from Ibarra ran all the way to the coast at San Lorenzo. However, only a shorter segment is currently used, mainly for tourists, though hopefully the entire route will one day be reinstated.

Train times, and whether they run at all, have been highly volatile over the last years, so it's best to check first. For the Ibarra train, call ((06) 950390, for Quito ((022) 513422, and Riobamba ((03) 961909. South American Explorers WEB SITE www.samexplo.org will also know the present state of affairs. Get to the station early, bring food and drink, and a cushion (or something, anything!) to sit on. For the Devil's Nose route, if you're going to sit on the roof, bring warm gear, especially for your head: it's biting cold in the morning.

Ride the Rails

On my last Andean train journey, from Ibarra to San Lorenzo, about 60 of us were squashed into a dim wagon about eight by three meters (26 by 9 ft) in size. We pulled out of the station at 7:30 AM, just a half hour behind schedule. Squinting through the slit windows I could see the early morning sun catching the green flanks of Volcán Cotacachi. Schoolchildren, Otavalan Indians, blacks from the coast and four backpackers shared floor space with sacks of fruit, kitchen pots, chickens, hi-fi equipment, straw mats and a dugout canoe. A man in a bright pink T-shirt pulled out a bottle of rum.

The sound of squealing brakes mixed discordantly with the shrieks of kids as if on a ghost train. Passengers rode on the top of the train, frequently ducking or even lying down flat to avoid being pushed over the edge by low-slung branches, yet certainly

Ecuador's old rail network is popular with locals and travelers alike.

Tick the "Volcano Land" List

At one point in my Ecuadorian travels, I became unhealthily obsessed with capturing on film the almost perfectly symmetrical cone of Volcán Cotopaxi, Ecuador's second tallest mountain and considered the tallest continuously active volcano in the world. I spent the best part of a day at the parking lot, just waiting for the weather to clear. It didn't. In fact, more often than not Ecuador's peaks skulk behind banks of cloud, most likely to reveal their full glory only to those who rise early and possess a certain amount of luck.

Ecuador harbors some of the tallest and most active volcanoes in the world. The country is bisected by two parallel mountain ranges, rather like a ladder, where barren *nudo* highland rungs separate fertile *hoya* valleys. Its volcanoes, and accompanying sizeable seismic activity, have defined its history in many ways. They loom like talismans above the fields of hard-working Indians who have inevitably personified them — the great Chimborazo, for example, is known as "Taita," or father. Towns such as Latacunga and Riobamba south of Quito have been founded and refounded over the centuries as a result of earthquakes and lava flows. More recently, scientists monitoring Volcán Tungurahua had the spa-town of Baños evacuated for fear of a major eruption, and in October 1999, Volcán Guagua Pichincha exploded, creating an 18-km-high (11-mile) mushroom cloud above Quito.

The indefatigable, nineteenth-century German explorer Alexander von Humboldt dubbed the road south of Quito the "Avenue of Volcanoes." And on clear days, the lofty, snowcapped peaks do indeed form an avenue as you travel south. Like keen birders, most travelers become avid volcano-spotters, ticking off a list of Ecuador's "Big Ten," the volcanoes that rise above 5,000 m (16,400 ft), as they travel the country.

Volcán Cotopaxi, at a height of 5,897 m (19,347 ft), is probably the country's most famous volcano. You can drive through the wild and beautiful Parque Nacional Cotopaxi up to the parking lot on the mountain itself at 4,600 m (15,092 ft). Climbers continue upwards to the *refugio* where they rest before attempting to climb the peak in the wee hours of the morning. For something more laid-back, check into the Hacienda San Agustín de Callo, where you can enjoy the view from a comfy armchair, *whiskicito* in hand.

Next on anyone's list is Chimborazo, the country's highest peak and at 6,310 m (20,702 ft) — trivia buffs get your pens out — the farthest point on the surface of the earth from the earth's center (due to the bulge at the equator). Until Mount Everest was discovered and measured, Chimborazo was thought to be the highest mountain in the world. In the nineteenth century, Humboldt climbed it, writing afterwards that the ascent ranked among one the most spiritual moments of his life. Even Simón Bolívar had a go. The first to reach the top though was the intrepid British climber, Edward Whymper, in 1880. As with Cotopaxi, you can drive up to its breath-inhibiting refuge at 4,800 m (15,748 ft), within a fauna reserve peopled by shy vicuña.

The central highlands around Chimborazo make excellent ticking country. Opposite the colossus, Carihauirazo (5,020 m or 16,470 ft) challenges even the most experienced mountaineers, while on the other side of Riobamba, the incisor peaks of El Altar (Cupac Urcu or "sublime mountain" in Quichua) bite into lapis skies. Within its amphitheater crater of jagged peaks, a stunning yellow-green lagoon can be reached on a three- or four-day hike from near Riobamba.

El Altar is just one of the three volcanoes that puncture the wilds of Parque Nacional Sangay. The most famous of these is Tungurahua, on its northwestern border. Although dare-devil climbers are returning to the peak since the eruption alerts of 1999, most visitors are content to visit a viewing station, spectacular at night, when the volcano lights up the sky with firework explosions. Competing with Cotopaxi for its photogenic, symmetrical cone, Volcán Sangay, the third volcano in the park, rises to 5,230 m (17,159 ft).

ABOVE: The snow-capped peak of Chimborazo. OPPOSITE: Broad valley in the Avenue of Volcanoes.

However, unlike Cotopaxi, Sangay is an angry mountain, considered to be one of the most active on the continent. Although climbing it is not discouraged per se, ash and rock explosions make the ascent very high-risk. Hikers wanting just to come within reach of the volcano, and to camp around its base, can arrange guides at the village of Alao, southeast of Riobamba. Arguably the best views of Sangay park's volcanoes is from Macas, or on the eastern skirts of the Andes in the Oriente. On a clear morning or evening, the snowcapped peaks seem to float above the tumbling forested hills.

For the country's third-highest volcano, head north of Quito. The mammoth Volcán Cayambe at 5,790-m (18,996-ft) peak is regarded as one of the hardest and most dangerous climbs in the country. The beautiful volcano glowers above the vast Reserva Ecológica Cayambe-Coca, which protects some 10 life zones as it descends from dizzying heights, through dense cloud forest and on down to the jungle of the Oriente. For the best views of the mountain, take the old road from Cayambe on the Panamericana towards Olmedo and Zuleta. Though not capped in snow, the famous Volcán Imbabura (4,609 m or 15,121 ft) lies further north still, looming over the weaving towns of Otavalo and Imbabura Province.

South of Quito, you can tick off the Ilinizas (two for the price of one!), the twin peaks 5,248 and 5,126 m (17,218 and 16,817 ft) high, often lacquered with fresh snow and usually pretty visible. The final volcano in the Big Ten is Volcán Antisana (5,758 m or 18,891 ft), southwest of the capital, one of the most frustrating to spot. Lucky individuals can admire its four great glacier-tipped peaks soaring into the sky from the road to Coca around the thermal baths of Papallacta.

Get Hatted

On a visit to the town of Jipijapa (pronounced delightfully as "hippy-happa"), I watched an old man sitting in the light of an open window, his long fingers flashing like knitting needles as he crossed and recrossed thin strands of white straw weaving the "wings" of a hat. For centuries, the long, uniform and supple fronds of the palm plant *carludovica palmate*, or *paja toquilla* in Spanish, have been used for weaving fine quality hats. Climatic conditions in the coastal area around the town of Jipijapa are among the best of the continent for its cultivation. And the very best so-called "panamas," known as *finos* or *ultra-finos*, are woven in or around the town of Montecristi, not far from Jipijapa in Ecuador's coastal Manabí Province. These hats can take one weaver a staggering three to four months to weave.

When the conquistadors arrived on the coast, they observed Indians wearing strange headdresses shaped like vampire wings. They were impressed by the durable hats, so tightly woven you could carry water in them. The Spanish named them *toquillas*, after the word for *toca*, headdress.

The hats' fame grew with time, and by the mid-nineteenth century Ecuador was exporting some 220,000. In 1855, they hit the big time: Ecuadorian panamas caused a sensation in Paris when a Montecristi *fino* was presented to Emperor Napoleon III, after which he was rarely seen without one. Thereafter the handy, portable panama replaced the straw boater, becoming a sophisticated fashion accessory. Many hats reached Panama, where vendors enjoyed a roaring trade from travelers passing through the canal on their way to the California gold rush. Such was their popularity, they became known as "panamas," when, strictly speaking, they should be called "Ecuadors."

Judging a hat requires experience. Tightness of weave, thickness and quality of fiber, color, smell, shape and touch all have to be considered. It's said the best hats are woven by moonlight, when there is no danger of the sun's heat damaging the straw before the hat has cured. They can be rolled up so tightly that they can pass through a napkin ring, and then spring back into perfect shape. Despite these wondrous properties, the days of these greatest of panama hats are probably numbered: there are only a dozen weavers left around Montecristi capable of making them, all of whom are over 70 years old.

Montecristi itself isn't an exciting town, but it's a good place to go if you're looking for the finest straw hat money can buy — and at a much better price than in London, Frankfurt or New York. I bought myself a fine Al Capone-style panama for US$32 that would cost well over US$80 elsewhere. It came rolled in a neat balsa box for easy packing. A *fino* costing about US$64 in Montecristi would sell for about US$200 in London, while the *fino-finos* and *ultrafinos* are even more expensive.

Today, 95 percent of Ecuador's panama hats are woven and finished in the Cuenca area, in the southern Sierra. Although *toquilla* straw still comes from the coast, *cuencano* buyers control the industry. In Cuenca, you can visit the

Hats woven by hand in Ecuador from *toquilla* straw, a centuries-old tradition, became known as panamas when they were exported to Panama in the nineteenth century.

factory of the Ortega family ((07) 809000 FAX (07) 876600 E-MAIL info@homeroortega.com WEB SITE www.homeroortega.com, Avenida Gil Ramírez Dávalos 3-86, which has been finishing hats for three generations now. It's best to phone in advance to ensure an English-language tour.

Run the Rivers

"Forward!" shouts Roberto the guide. Our paddles dig into the swirling water, projecting the raft into the whirling waves and eddies ahead. "Stop!" he cries again, deftly steering the craft around a menacing black boulder. "Back left, back left!" comes the command again, and we on the left side frantically pivot the paddles against our bodies, turning just in time to shoot down another frothing rapid.

"Go, go, go!" Roberto barks as we come flying down into a nasty whirlpool, the boat's prow buckling when we hit it, water cascading everywhere, bodies hurled left to right, front to back, shouts and whoops emerging from the foaming confusion, paddles all over the place, until we issue forth once again on a more tranquil section of the Río Toachi, a tributary of the Río Blanco which charges down from the Andes to the Pacific. After a break on a sandy beach, it's back in the boat for a further hour and a half of beautiful scenery, towering cliffs, bubbling rapids, screams of delight and yet another thorough drenching.

Running rivers, by raft and kayak, is Ecuador's fastest growing sport. The country, with its hundreds of waterways roaring down from the heights of the Andes, ranks as a whitewater paradise, among the world's top destinations for rapids-seekers. Regional rainy seasons differ, so opportunities run year-round.

Two operators cover the best rivers. Yacu Amu Rafting, based in Quito, is run by the friendly, highly experienced and safety-conscious Australian Steve Nomchong. With his experienced and multilingual guides, Steve arranges rafting trips from the relatively straightforward (grades III to IV) one-day along the Ríos Toachi and Blanco (beginning near Santo Domingo de los Colorados) to more demanding trips down the Río Quijos (Grades IV to V) and other tributaries (ending at the San Rafael waterfalls and with a bath at the Papallacta hot springs). He also offers a five-day, 120-km (74-mile) expedition from Macas in the Oriente down the Río Upano and the Namangosa Gorge (big Grade IVs!). The latter is as much about adrenaline as paddling through pristine rainforest and towering gorges embroidered with cascading falls.

The other, highly experienced and respected operator is Gynner Coronel's Ríos Ecuador, which operates mainly on the upper Río Napo (Grade III), and also on the Río Misahuallí (Grade IV) from October to March, which includes the beautiful Casanova Falls. Both these are in the Oriente. Adventour is another good operator, although it doesn't specialize in rafting any longer. These companies can also arrange trips (or rent equipment) for experienced kayakers who want to run Ecuador's truly white-knuckle rivers. These include the Mindo, Saloya, Topo, Pilaton and Upper Toachi. The companies also run beginners' kayaking courses.

The Río Patate, a highland tributary of the Pastaza, is also a popular run from the spa-town of Baños. Several operators organize this trip, but the only consistently recommended one is Río Loco ("Mad River"). Unfortunately, some other operators are inexperienced, their equipment substandard, and their guiding not up to scratch. You should be aware of this, and of the fatalities that have tragically occurred, before thinking you are saving a few dollars, when you are in fact playing with your life. For contact details of excellent operators see SPORTING SPREE, page 40 in YOUR CHOICE.

Get Twitching

Bird enthusiasts (nicknamed "twitchers") consider Ecuador, from its wild *páramo* (high moorland) and mountain forests to its coastal plains and dense Amazonian jungles, to be the hottest spot for birding in South America. Some 1,600 bird species have been recorded in Ecuador, about 18 percent of the world's total and twice the number found in Canada and the United States combined. And new bird species are still being discovered.

Such is the country's wealth of bird life, you don't have to be a dedicated birder to catch the twitching bug. The sight of trees full of vivid macaws and parrots in the Oriente, a cock-of-the-rock near the Cascada de San Rafael, or the comical boobies and swooping frigate birds of the Galápagos are enough to turn most people into bird enthusiasts overnight.

Birders arriving in Ecuador usually start with some of the lesser-used westerly roads down the slopes of the Andes from Quito to the coast. Close to Santo Domingo de los Colorados (on the road to Pedernales on the coast), the 40-year-old Tinalandia hotel has

High-wire crossing near Baños, a typical Andean footbridge.

long been a favorite with birders, while the old Nono road towards Mindo (northwest of the capital) becomes the Yes-Yes road when birders encounter a flock of a dozen or more species. The small town of Mindo is a mecca for cognoscenti bird-watchers, and a number of comfortable lodges have sprung up to cater to them (see MINDO AND RESERVA BIOLÓGICA MIQUIPUENA, page 100 for details). In the dense surrounding cloud forest some 400 species have been observed, including such trophies as the fabulous scarlet-crested, black-bottomed Andean cock-of-the-rock, along with golden headed and crested quetzals, plate-billed mountain toucans, grass-green tanagers and velvet-purple coronets. In the rich subtropical forest there are also howler monkeys, many brilliant butterflies and hundreds of species of orchids.

Another excellent area to spot the cock-of-the-rock is in the vicinity of the Cascada de San Rafael — also known as the Coca Falls — on the road from Quito east to Lago Agrio, close to the town of Baeza. Reports speak of dozens of the male birds coming together and making a raucous racket to attract females. The male with the loudest call and brightest colors generally wins the lady.

From Baeza, all roads lead to the Oriente, Ecuador's Amazon region. Here, the jungle lodges outdo each other with bird-species counts — some are as high as 550. Walks in the jungle are often rewarded with flocks of nose-heavy toucans, and early morning boat trips to *saladeros* (where parrots and macaws come to feed on clay to aid their digestion) provide wonderful opportunities to spot tens of species. Among the best lodges that organize specialist bird guides are La Selva Jungle Lodge, Sacha Lodge and Kapawi Ecolodge and Reserve.

After the Oriente, many birders head to the coast. Probably the most popular haunt is Parque Nacional Machalilla, because it encompasses several microclimates. The park includes the "poor person's Galápagos" — Isla de la Plata — home to all three types of booby, as well as frigate birds and waved albatrosses. Inland, the cloud forest up from the village of Agua Blanca also boasts good birding. Heading south of Machalilla, there are many rich salt ponds around Manglaralto and Salinas, the preserve of large numbers of seabirds.

Of the other highland areas, the most frequented are the Páramo El Ángel, close to Tulcán; the Pasochoa Reserve, about 40 minutes' drive southeast of Quito; and the Cajas and Podocarpus national parks in the southern Sierra, home to many stunning hummingbirds.

Explore the Rainforest World

"The big trees of the forest are very powerful," claims my Achuar guide Gilberto, standing in the shadow of a mammoth ceiba tree. "All plants and trees are people, but you can't see them normally. The tall ceiba earns great respect, but is also dangerous for newly born children. It whispers to them and makes them ill." He pauses and arches his neck back to look at the tree's top, some 40 m (130 ft) up in the canopy. Walking through the forest with Gilberto, the green and brown morass of decay and destruction comes alive. After an hour on a trail, his knowledge of plants, flowers, animals, myths and customs turns what seems like an impenetrable mass of life and death into a forest of revelation.

In common with many other Amazonian peoples, the Achuar, who are part of the Jívaro linguistic family, don't separate the waking world from the dream world, the "real" from the "spiritual." They use hallucinogens such as *naatam*, known more commonly as *ayahuasca*, or the "truth vine" *Banisteriopsis caapi*, under the guidance of a shaman for ritual trance purposes, a practice not recommended for the uninitiated. "When you take *naatam*, the forest comes alive," Gilberto explains. For most people though, the forest itself is hallucinogen enough. Although the missionaries have done their best to banish shamanism and prohibit the use of the forest's hallucinogens, both practices are still integral to the older generation of Achuar.

Further on, Gilberto points out an arrow-leafed plant carpeting the forest floor. "The *shishin* speaks kind words while you are in a

trance. It is very friendly. The shamans brush it over the body of a patient, chasing bad spirits." Another plant, *chirikiaspi*, gives the hunter strength and fortifies the lungs to be able to shoot monkeys high in the canopy with a blow pipe. "It also anesthetizes the body," explains Gilberto, "making you feel numb and able to walk for days without much food," which is exactly what the Achuar use it for: their territory is the size of Belgium or Maryland.

During the afternoon we sit on a little wooden bench drinking *nijiamanch*, a slightly acidic, yeasty, milky-white broth. It is made by one of the village women by chewing up manioc and spitting it into a big, earthenware pot where it ferments for a few days. It is said that this "beer," or *chicha* as it's known in most of the country after its Quichua name, tastes of the woman who makes it. As practiced beer drinkers, we had no trouble quaffing it down from bowls continually refilled by the a local shaman's first wife. Following Achuar custom, we carefully avoided looking her in the eye as she served us.

Drinking strange beer, taking herbal teas, eating new foods, and learning about the day-to-day lives of the Indians of Ecuador's rainforest is a worthwhile and humbling experience. It is worthwhile as an opportunity to glimpse a way of life different in almost every respect to that with which we are familiar, and because revenues from tourism undoubtedly play a part in protecting the fragile forests. Humbling because we are

confronted with a totally alien environment which most of us would be unable to cope with alone and unaided. Most people come away from meeting jungle peoples in awe of their self-reliance and their apparently simple, uncluttered lives. Most regard their jungle trips as among their most lasting memories.

One of the most positive developments in the last five years in Ecuador has been the indigenous peoples of the Amazon — whether Cofán, Siona, Shuar, Quichua or Achuar — taking control of tourism. Although many lodges and operators in the Oriente, as Ecuador's Amazon is known, enjoy good relationships with the Indians, many do not. For this reason, Indian organizations and federations, increasingly active on the national political stage, have begun their own autonomous operations. Joining a community-based and community-benefiting tour couldn't be easier in the age of the Internet: most of them are on e-mail. These tours are not for lovers of creature comforts. You will eat, drink, wash and sleep as the Indians do. That's part of the fun, and the experience.

Of the Oriente's comfortable jungle lodges, two stand out particularly for their work and relationship with the local Indians.

LEFT: The languid tranquillity of the jungle hides thousands of species of living creatures, such as this parakeet. ABOVE: Exploring the jungle can be a test of one's powers of adaptation, as well as a journey into mankind's past.

The nonprofit organization FUNEDESIN, behind the Yachana Lodge, between Misahuallí and Coca on the Río Napo, works closely and equitably with Indian groups. In a reciprocal arrangement, local people learn about things like bee-keeping, while tourists learn about medicinal plants. The lodge is run on strict ecological lines, with some of the best multilingual guides in the region. For more information, see MISAHUALLÍ, page 171 in EL ORIENTE. The other lodge which has attracted worldwide attention is Kapawi Ecolodge and Reserve (see page 176). In a unique arrangement with the local Achuar, the company that owns the lodge (but rents the land), Canodros, will hand the whole business over to the Achuar in 2011. In the meantime, outsiders are training the Achuar so that they can take over the operation. On trails from the environmentally low-impact lodge, visitors are always accompanied by both an excellent naturalist guide and an experienced Achuar, thus providing a doubly enriching experience.

Visit the Markets

"Eight? You want eight for it?"

"Sí, señor, precio muy bueno. Precio especial."

"Eight isn't 'especial'! How about two for ten, that's 'especial.'"

"Dos por diez? No, no, no, no…"

"Come on, ten for two. You're not going to sell anything at eight for one."

"Ay, bueno… Hecho. Dos por diez."

Hecho. Done.

And so another transaction is concluded at Otavalo's market, the country's most renowned. Although some people dislike haggling, others enjoy the interaction and joviality of it. Personally, I love nothing more than a good-natured haggle over a sweater, panpipe or fake pre-Columbian trinket. And such is the range and quality of the produce on sale at Otavalo, after a few hours of buying, you'll be forced to haggle: you'll have no money left!

Visiting Ecuador's markets provides the opportunity to be a part of the chaos, noise and hubbub, and to wonder at all the strange fruits, vegetables and unidentified pieces of meat floating in bubbling stews. It's to step into the lives of the highland Indians, and also back in time: markets have been held in the highland towns and villages since time immemorial. It is also to observe the dress-code of the villagers: does the black poncho on that man mean he's from Salasaca? Does the wide white felt hat on that woman come from

Saquisilí or Saraguro? The Indian names of these places are as elegant as the costumes of those that live there. You can watch them haggle over guinea pigs, laugh about misfortune, and gossip about the latest scandal or the price of milk.

Otavalo's main tourist market muffles a whole square, aptly named the Plaza de Ponchos. On Saturdays, hundreds of stands plug the avenues leading to the square. Those running east slowly become less touristy, dominated by pots and pans and Tupperware. Past the arcades of the produce market, they are jammed with piles of every variety of fruit, vegetable, fish and meat. Other stalls overflow with musical instruments (those infernal whirly drum things and the inevitable panpipes), intricately painted ceramic bowls, miniature paintings from the Indians of Tigua, wood carvings of jagged-jowled men, and jewelry of every size and description. The weavings range from rugs of symmetric red, brown and blue patterns to dark tightly-woven ponchos or bright woolly hats festooned with flowers, from the oranges, yellows and greens of hammocks through to quite Westernized sweaters and zip-up tops of just a few colors.

Although undeniably a tourist trap, the quality of the crafts on sale at Otavalo is so high most people don't mind feeling like another gringo. But in addition to visiting the markets, I would suggest you also tour the surrounding villages to meet the families of weavers and learn more about their craft. The most well known are José Cotacachi in Peguche, Miguel Andrango in Agato, and the Inti-Chumbi cooperative of Ilumán.

For tourist produce, Otavalo stands head and shoulders above any other highland town. But what the others lack in souvenirs they make up for in authenticity and local color. To the south of Quito, three markets take place on different days in the towns of Saquisilí (on Thursday), Zumbahua (on Saturday) and Pujilí (Sunday). By staying in the Latacunga area (perhaps at one of the haciendas), you can visit all three. In the central and southern Sierra, all the major towns spring to bustling, colorful life for their market days. South of Riobamba on Sundays, one of the most unique markets takes place at Cajabamba. Here, the highland Colta Indians dispense with any roofs or structures, and simply hold their age-old market by the side of the Panamericana highway.

Soak in a Spring

There's nothing quite like an early morning soak in a hot spring followed by a cold shower to set you up for the day. Wallowing in a hot tub, or being pummeled by jets of water, has to be one of the most relaxing pastimes known to man. Volcanic Ecuador overflows with hot springs, natural pools and spouting waterfalls. There is no better way to soothe aching muscles after a trek, horseback ride or rafting trip than to sit sublimely in a pool for an hour or two, or three. While researching this guide, I have to admit I found it hard to wrench myself from their pampering embraces.

The best hot springs within reach of Quito are the Baños de Papallacta, two hours by bus or car from the city, just off the road that descends over the rim of the Amazon Basin to Baeza. The springs here feeds five clean pools ranging from very hot to refreshingly cold.

The small town of Baños is another popular hot spring destination a few hour's ride by bus from Quito. Nestled in a valley surrounded by steep, verdant mountains, this attractive resort has become a favored stopover on the gringo trail in recent years. The town is now returning to normal following volcano alerts. The main baths are the Baños de la Virgen by the waterfall near the Palace Hotel at the southeast end of town. More pleasant though are the baths at El Salado, about a mile out of town off the Ambato road, which have more pools and are less crowded. Baños boasts plenty of great

places to stay, as well as numerous opportunities for horseback rides, treks and rafting trips.

If you're planning to spend a few days in the Imbabura region (Otavalo and Ibarra), then consider a soak in the appealing baths of Chachimbiro, northwest of Ibarra. The complex includes medicinal mineral baths, hydromassages, saunas and pools, as well as trails off into the surrounding hills and a decent restaurant. Accommodation inside the springs is basic but good value. Also in this area, 40 km (25 miles) west of Laguna de Cuicocha is the remote village of Apuela, set in the deep Andean cloud forest. Nearby, the Piscinas de Nangulví make for a welcome hot-spring soak. Basic accommodation is available there. Further north, close to Tulcán and the Colombian border, you'll find some lovely springs by the town of Tufiño.

Near Miazal in El Oriente, 50 km (31 miles) southeast of Macas over the Cutucu Mountain Range, a hot spring bubbles from the earth and flows from a rock in a naturally hot waterfall. Next to it, a cold waterfall of pure mountain water plunges down. Although particularly remote and inaccessible, where else can you find natural hot and cold waterfalls side by side in the middle of a tropical rainforest?

OPPOSITE: Colorful flowers and yarn on display at a Latacunga market. ABOVE: Bathing in hot sulfur springs at Baños.

The Great Outdoors

Ecuador is a gallery of stunning landscapes. From snowcapped, volcanic mountains and long stretches of unspoiled coastline to Amazon rainforests and the bleak splendor of the Galápagos Islands, the country offers the visitor a breathtaking spectrum of natural wonders. Of the world's 32 denominated "life zones," 26 are found here, in a country the size of Nevada, or slightly larger than the United Kingdom.

In geological time, Ecuador is a relatively young country formed by the collision of tectonic plates just a few million years ago. The clash of these subterranean titans threw up the great mountain system, the Andean *cordillera*, that forms the 6,500-km (4,000-mile) western fringe of South America. Like the Himalayas, these young, rugged and sharp-ridged mountains aren't yet time-hardened nor ground smooth and smaller by the relentless impact of wind and water.

Meanwhile, underground, the titanic plates continue to shift around, making Ecuador constantly vulnerable to sudden earthquakes and volcanic eruptions.

Lying 1,000 km (625 miles) off the Pacific coast, the Galápagos Islands were created from the solidified lava from erupting undersea volcanoes. It is thought that they are attached to a slowly moving tectonic plate, named Nazca after a pre-Incan coastal state. Below Nazca lies the stationary vent or "hot spot" in the earth's magma. As Nazca inches its way to the southeast, nudged by other titans to the north and west, the hot spot shoots torpedoes up from its hull, so to speak, creating new volcanoes and, possibly, new islands. This theory fits with the fact that the younger, more volcanically active islands such as Fernandina and Isabela are on the northwest side of the archipelago, while the older ones, such as Española, are to the southeast. It also supports the now current belief that the Galápagos Islands have never been physically attached to the mainland.

Including the Galápagos Islands, Ecuador consists of four contrasting regions, each one distinctly different from the others. The **Galápagos** are arid, volcanic outcrops patterned with moon-like lava flows and twisted rock formations. No soft Pacific palms fringe their rocky shores. Plants and creatures here that have adapted to these harsh conditions are tough and hardy — thick-skinned iguanas, giant armor-plated tortoises, blubber-bound sea lions, spiny acacia, spiky cacti, saltbush and scalesia.

OPPOSITE: Tracking through the Andes — what you lose in comfort by riding on top of a train you gain in experience and excitement. ABOVE: Rare and unique species of cactus are characteristic of the Galápagos Islands.

The coastline and the coastal plain, simply called **La Costa**, present a less fierce face — marshland, mangrove swamps (or what is left of them after the invasion of shrimp farms), creeks, estuaries and long stretches of empty beaches swathed with palm trees. The hot and humid coastal plains were thickly forested before man arrived with his machete to create banana, cacao, coffee, sugarcane and rice plantations. As these plantations encroached further upon the forest, Ecuador became a full-fledged banana republic and still ranks among the world's leading exporters.

Upwards and eastwards, the flanks of the Andes are clothed in mists and residual areas of thick cloud forests threaded with silvery waterfalls. In the highland valleys, the **Sierra**, the face of the landscape takes a more worn and hewn look. Tilled and re-tilled for centuries before the Incas and the Spanish came along, the ancient geometric fields, terraced on the steeper slopes, transform the valleys into tapestries woven in pastel shades of brown and green. Splashes of deep red on the ponchos of Indian women herding sheep provide a vivid color contrast, while llamas grazing by high mountain lakes embellish the pastoral scenes. Above the valleys tower snow-white peaks, stern and dangerous: the world's tallest active volcanoes.

Over the other side of the mountains, the eastern slopes of the Andes stretch towards the great Amazon Basin, the world's largest rainforest. The Ecuadorians call this vast area of their country **El Oriente**, The East. Rivers flowing down the Andes and through tribal lands eventually link up with the mighty Amazon on its 3,200-km (2,000-mile) journey across Brazil and into the Atlantic Ocean. The discovery of oil in the Oriente in the 1970s led to the building of new roads, to the destruction and contamination of huge tracts of virgin forest and to the arrival of increasing numbers of "colonists," as well as new diseases, cultural decimation and anger among the local indigenous populations.

Some 17 percent of Ecuador's land area is officially designated as national parkland, nature reserve or special recreation area. All of the country's ecosystems are protected in some form or another. The first national park created was the Galápagos Islands in 1959 and the first mainland park was Cotopaxi in 1975. Since then, many more national parks have been created: Machalilla, Yasuní, Sangay, Podocarpus and El Salado.

In addition there are huge areas of protected nature reserves, the largest being Cotacachi-Cayapas, Cayambe-Coca and Cuyabeno, all in the north of the country, as well as national recreation areas, natural monuments and private reserves. The largest of the last category are run by foundations, such as Ecuador's largest environmental NGO **Fundación Natura** ((02) 446081 E-MAIL natura@natura.org.ec WEB SITE www.natura.org.ec, Guayas 105 and Amazonas, Quito. International NGOs involved in some form in conservation efforts in Ecuador include **Conservation International** TOLL-FREE IN THE US ((800) 406-2306 WEB SITE www.conservation.org; **The Nature Conservancy** IN QUITO ((02) 248588 TOLL-FREE IN THE US (800) 628-6860 FAX (02) 462217 E-MAIL cprogram@q.tnc.org.ec WEB SITE www.tnc.org; and the **World Wildlife Fund** IN THE US ((202) 293-4800 FAX (202) 293-9211 WEB SITE www.wwf.org.

If you have the time it is well worth visiting four national parks representing the four major ecosystems of the country. The **Galápagos Islands**, with their extraordinary wildlife, are an experience of a lifetime. In the Andes, the most frequently visited national park is **Cotopaxi**, with its magnificent, cone-shaped volcano, the tallest active volcano in the world. The **Parque Nacional Machalilla** on the coast is stunningly beautiful, and the **Parque Nacional Yasuní** or **Reserva Faunística Cuyabeno** in Amazonia provide unique insight into rainforest wildlife.

Some of the parks and reserves are remote and difficult to reach and facilities aren't well developed. Visitors planning to stay a few days are advised to bring their own camping gear, water and adequate supplies. The entrance fees for national parks are generally US$10 for a highland park and US$20 for a lowland park, but some also vary according to tourist season. One payment allows multiple entry to the park for a week. Ecuadorian nationals pay considerably less. The entry fee to the Parque Nacional Galápagos is currently US$100 for foreigners.

Even though a portion of the comparatively high entrance fees goes towards administration and protection, sufficient manpower and equipment aren't available to prevent various kinds of destruction. Areas of some of the parks and reserves have been subject to illegal fishing, oil drilling, mining, ranching and colonization. The effects of the oil and logging industry on the Oriente have been particularly devastating. For more information on parks and reserves contact the **Ministerio del Ambiente** (Ministry of the Environment)

Numerous waterfalls, as this one in Baños, stimulate and soothe the senses of visitors to Ecuador.

((02) 548924 WEB SITE www.ambiente.gov.ec, whose main office is in the large building at the corner of Amazonas and Eloy Alfaro in Quito. Over the years, the parks system has come under various administrative agencies, including what used to be called INEFAN (the Ecuadorian Institute of Forestry, Natural Areas and Wildlife), and you might still find references to it as such. Contact details throughout the country should, hopefully, remain the same.

ECOTOURISM

Ecotourism has been defined as tourism that does no damage to the environment and wildlife and benefits the local people. One might add that it should educate and benefit the ecotourist as well. Because of increased concern about environmental issues and evidence of the damaging effects of tourism around the world, the concept is of vital importance and is likely to remain so as long as people travel.

' In Ecuador, the objectives of ecotourism are relevant throughout the country, and nowhere more so than in the Oriente, where cultural differences between tourists and Indian groups are most pronounced, and where corruption can easily occur because of disparities of wealth. It isn't surprising that some Indian groups want little or nothing to do with the "outside world" because they know that any contacts will ultimately be a threat to their way of life.

Visitors interested in the beneficial aspects of tourism and who are sensitive to the effect they have on the environment and people they encounter may wish to consider staying at places that support the principles of ecotourism. The following are examples of places that espouse ecotourist ideas by respecting the environment and working in harmony with local communities.

Kapawi Ecolodge and Reserve ((02) 256759 or (02) 445639 E-MAIL eco-tourism1@canodros.com WEB SITE www.kapawi.com lies in a remote area of rainforest in Pastaza Province near the border with Perú. Canodros, a Guayaquil-based company, initiated the project in 1996 with an isolated group of Achuar Indians. The goal was to start a trend in ecotourism by pooling resources and sharing benefits, while respecting the land and traditions of the people without damaging the environment. Under the terms of the agreement, Canodros has invested nearly US$3 million to build a state-of-the-art ecolodge on Kapawi lagoon, which they pledged to hand over to the local Achuar community in 2011. The company also pays a monthly rent to the local people and has promised that the majority of employees on the project will be Achuar. For their part, the Achuar offered wood, palm leaves and materials for the building, and to maintain the airstrip and restrict hunting within the area of the lodge. Apart from its enlightened relationship with the Achuar, the lodge is also extremely environmentally conscious. For more see KAPAWI ECOLODGE AND RESERVE, page 176.

The Ecuadorian-run **Hostería Alandaluz** (Winged City of Light) (/FAX (042) 780686 or (042) 780690 IN QUITO ((022) 505084 FAX (022) 543042 E-MAIL booking@alandaluz.com WEB SITE www.alandaluz.com, on the southern coast of Manabí Province, has achieved both national and international fame for its ecologically sound building and management. It represents the cutting edge of "green-building" ecotourism for a coastal resort, with filtering or composting toilets, organic gardens, recycled water, sustainable building materials such as *caña gradúa* bamboo, and community-based programs. In addition to all this praiseworthy stuff, its location and accommodation are stunning. For more information, see SOUTH OF MACHALILLA, page 199.

Also on the coast, but further north nearer Atacames, the secluded **Playa Escondida** (Hidden Beach) ((06) 733122 or (099) 733368 E-MAIL judithbarrett@hotmail.com WEB SITE www.ecuadorexplorer.com/playaescondida, ranks among the most magical eco-refuges on the coast. A handful of rustic cabins and a camping ground look out over big billowing trees and the sea. An observation platform, where you can sleep overnight, nestles in the semitropical forest which the Canadian owner, Judith Barrett, has been at pains to protect. She employs composting toilets in some cabins, and uninvited guests include turtles laying their eggs from July to September (see SOUTH TO MUISNE, page 189).

Describing itself as an "ecological inn and farm," **Casa Mojanda** (/FAX (099) 731737 E-MAIL mojanda@uio.telconet.net WEB SITE www.casamojanda.com includes nine guest cottages constructed from adobe, wood and other natural materials. The inn is on a hillside and dominates 10 hectares (25 acres) of Andean farmland overlooking the mountains of Imbabura and Cotacachi near Otavalo. Ecuadorian cuisine is cooked up from homegrown, organic produce. The owners also run the **Mojanda Foundation**, a not-for-profit organization dedicated to environmental protection in the Mojanda lakes region and to assisting community initiatives

in public health, education, organic agriculture and the arts (see also WHERE TO STAY, page 108 in OTAVALO).

South of Quito, on the loop around from Latacunga to Quilotoa and back (see AROUND LATACUNGA, page 122 of CENTRAL HIGHLANDS), the **Black Sheep Inn** ((03) 814587 E-MAIL blksheep@interactive.net.ec WEB SITE www.blacksheepinn.com is highly praised for its simple, homey atmosphere, good food and its stunning views. The "eco-lodgical" inn is run on strict environmental lines, and has also initiated laudable projects in the neighboring highland communities. If you want to hike around some of the most beautiful landscapes in Ecuador, or simply relax in high mountain climes, this is the place to base yourself.

There are many other praiseworthy ecolodges in the country. And no doubt more will appear in the coming years. Tourists can play a part in the "greening" of the industry by asking pertinent questions of hoteliers: do you recycle your waste? How do you heat your water? Do you have any water-management systems? The more tourists who ask these questions, the more establishments will adopt more ecologically friendly practices.

HIKING

As for how to enjoy the great outdoors, Ecuador offers endless possibilities for hiking and camping.

Most people's first ports of call are the national parks and reserves that ring Quito. Remember that even if you're not attempting to scale a peak, you should acclimatize before attempting long hikes at high altitude. Spend a few days in Quito before hitting the hills, and once in them, drink a lot of water. Sunburn and harsh conditions can also be a problem, so come well prepared. There are plenty of outdoor outfitters in Quito's Mariscal area if you've forgotten to bring anything. On anything but rocky terrain, I would recommend investing all of US$10 in a pair of rubber boots. Not the height of fashion next to your US$100-turbo-goretex-latest-purchase, but tried-and-tested by highland villagers throughout the country.

Although in some parks (Cotopaxi, for example) or on popular routes (up Imbabura, around Lagos Cuicocha or Mojanda) trails are well-marked, in other wilder areas trails are faint. You should bring a compass, have map-reading skills, and basic Spanish for asking directions (always ask at least three different people if possible!). For extra safety, bring a Geographical Positioning System (GPS), and plan your route carefully with a topographical map. Or else, hire a knowledgeable guide.

You should also be aware that the popular gringo hikes have suffered from robberies and worse in the last years. It's essential to inquire

Pacuya camp in the Reserva Faunística Cuyabeno, northern Oriente.

locally about the current situation. A last word of warning: be very wary of dogs. The second most important piece of equipment after good footwear is a strong stick. The Indian women who sell goods up and down Avenida Amazonas in Quito sell sticks with brass handles. Otherwise, always approach a highland house with rock or stone in hand, or if you encounter a dog, pretend to pick one up — that usually does the trick.

Independent hikers wanting to spend some time in the country's national parks or wilderness areas should obtain topographical maps (the best are 1:50,000 scale) from the **Instituto Geográfico Militar (IGM)** E-MAIL igm@mil.ec, at Venezuela 573 and Sucre (by the Casa Museo de Sucre, Old Town) or Senierges and Paz y Miño (above Parque El Ejido). They can also be ordered from abroad through WEB SITE www.bestdealecuador.com, or from the SAE, an organization you will find mentioned repeatedly in this book. **South American Explorers (SAE)** (/FAX (022) 225228 E-MAIL explorer@sae.org.ec, Jorge Washington 311 and Leonidas Plaza, Quito, can be an invaluable resource for advice, information and up-to-date travel news, as well as a place to meet fellow travelers. They often organize weekly group outings to various parks and peaks around the capital (for more, see GENERAL INFORMATION, page 82 under QUITO). Finally, excellent, how-to information for climbers and hikers is found in Rob Rachowiecki and Mark Thurber's *Climbing and Hiking in Ecuador*, Bradt: London, 2000. A helpful WEB SITE is www.cotopaxi.com.

King of the national parks near Quito is **Cotopaxi**. Access is pretty straightforward from the two entrances off the Panamericana, and every adventure tour operator worth its salt in Quito offers transportation and/or guides to the park. You can enjoy both short hikes around the refuge, or longer trails to Volcán Rumiñahui, for example. If you're lucky you might spot a condor or perhaps herds of wild bulls or horses, even a mountain lion. Parts of the park are so remote that you can camp there for a week and not see one other person.

Also popular close by is hiking in the shadow of the two **Ilinizas** volcanoes. Close to Quito itself, you can hike up both **Rucu** and **Guagua Pichincha**. The best access to the latter is from the pretty town of Lloa, reachable by bus from the capital.

North of Quito, possibilities abound. Around Otavalo, you can hike round the **Lagunas de Mojanda** or the **Laguna de San Pablo** in a day, passing through lots of villages

on the latter circuit. Also enjoyable is hiking around the **Laguna de Cuicocha**, further to the northwest, part of the enormous **Reserva Ecológica Cotacachi-Cayapas** (see AROUND OTAVALO, page 112, for more). Further west, the **Intag Cloud Forest Reserve**, in the vicinity of Apuela, has basic accommodation and great trails. Nearby is the **Bosque Nublado de Santo Tomás**. For more information on these, contact **Safari Tours** ((022) 552505 or (022) 223381 FAX (022) 220426 E-MAIL admin@safari.com.ec WEB SITE www.safari.com.ec, Calamá 380 and Juan León Mera, Quito. Heading up to Ibarra, the best access to **Volcán Imbabura** is from the small hamlet of La Esperanza, where you can base yourself at one of the friendly, family-run *hosterías* (see AROUND IBARRA, page 115 in NORTHERN HIGHLANDS).

Further north still, there are some great trails up to the haunting **Páramo El Ángel** (see page 116) close to Tulcán on the Colombian border. Fundación Golondrinas, an Ecuadorian NGO, is active in conservation work in the area and organizes treks from the village of El Ángel up to the *páramo*. For details contact Piet Sabbe, Cerro Golondrinas Project Coordinator ((022) 226602 FAX (022) 566076 E-MAIL manteca@uio.satnet.net.

One of the most popular, demanding treks south of the capital is the **Ruta del Condor**. It begins at the village of El Tambo, close to the Papallacta springs, crossing the Reserva Ecológica Antisana between the two peaks of Antisanilla and Antisana, before following various streams all the way down to Parque Nacional Cotopaxi. It takes three to four days to complete.

Further south of Quito, the owners of the Black Sheep Inn (see above) can point you in the right direction for many hikes in the stunning **Quilotoa/Tigua region**. The trek up to, and around if you wish, the lake of Quilotoa receives the most praise. Around the popular spa-town of **Baños** there are many trails to villages, day-hikes to great viewpoints, or longer four-day treks (see BAÑOS, page 127). Hikes up to Volcán Tungurahua, inside Parque Nacional Sangay, may or may not be off-limits when you read this. For excellent guides to Sangay, contact **Alta Montaña** IN RIOBAMBA ((03) 963694 FAX (03) 942215 IN QUITO (/FAX (022) 504773 E-MAIL aventurag@laserinter.net, Jorge Washington 425 and 6 de Diciembre, Quito.

Scientists believe the rainforest of the Amazon Basin could account for between 30 and 80 million species of plants and animals, perhaps as much as half of all the earth's life forms.

Riobamba is the natural springboard for hiking around both the mammoth **Chimborazo** (page 134) and the spiky **El Altar** volcanoes. For the former, contact the community-based project of **Pulingue San Pablo** (or "Waman Way") ((03) 949510 or (03) 949511 E-MAIL waman_way@hotmail.com (Spanish only) on the road up to the refuge. You can stay in simple cabins nearby. For more information contact Tom Walsh E-MAIL twalsh@ch.pro.ec.

Not to be outdone by Perú (it is in most other things), Ecuador has its own **Inca Trail**. The three-day trek begins at Achupallas, some 25 km (15 miles) from Alausí on the Panamericana south of Riobamba. The best day to start the trek is Saturday, when you can stock up on food at the market in Achupallas. The trek climbs to some 4,000 m (13,120 ft), passes various lakes great for camping, as well as parts of the old Inca cobbles, and finally reaches the Inca ruins of Ingapirca, and the town of the same name.

From the capital of the southern highlands, Cuenca, the most popular hikes explore the wild, cloudy and cold expanses of **Parque Nacional Cajas**. There are plenty of rivers, lakes and stunted forests, as well as stunning hummingbirds. Access to the park is straightforward by bus, and for guides you can contact various competent tour operators in the city (see GENERAL INFORMATION, page 139 under CUENCA).

In the very south of the country, both Loja (page 148) and Vilcabamba (page 150) offer good access to the much-lauded **Parque Nacional Podocarpus**. From Loja, the bus can drop you off close to the park entrance, from where you proceed to the first refuge. Good information in Loja is available from the **Ministerio del Ambiente** headquarters ((07) 563131 on Sucre between Imbabura and Quito, and from the **Fundación Ecológica Arcoiris** ((07) 577449 E-MAIL fai1@fai.org.ec, on Segundo Cueva Celi 03-15. Recommended tour operators include **Biotours** (/FAX (07) 578398 E-MAIL biotours@loja .telconet.net on Colón and Sucre, and **Aratinga Aventuras Birdwatchers** (/FAX (07) 582434 E-MAIL jatavent@cue.satnet.net, on Lourdes between Sucre and Bolívar. For guides from Vilcabamba, contact Orlando Falco of the **Rumi Wilco Ecolodge and Nature Reserve** (no phone) E-MAIL ofalcoecolodge @yahoo.com, or Charlie of **Cabañas Río Yambala** (no phone) E-MAIL rio_yambala@ yahoo.com or yambala@impsat.net.ec WEB SITE www.vilcabamba.cwc.net.

On the eastern side of the Andes, there are some great hikes to be enjoyed around **Baeza** and the **Cascada de San Rafael**, very popular with birdwatchers, and there are some tough treks back up into the Andes from Puyo, Tena and Macas that can be arranged with local tour operators (see the relevant GENERAL INFORMATION sections in these towns for details, pages 173, 168 and 176). In the Oriente itself, independent trekking is discouraged by the local Indians, and you should join a tour, preferably an indigenous-run one, for exciting hikes through the jungle, canoe trips down rivers and encounters with local communities (see EXPLORE THE RAINFOREST WORLD, page 24 in TOP SPOTS).

Heading down towards the coast, many people stop in the **Mindo** area for some great trails through dripping, epiphyte-clad cloud forests. The best way to enjoy these is to stay at one of the lodges (see GET TWITCHING, page 22 in TOP SPOTS, or HIKING AROUND QUITO, page 100 in ANDEAN HIGHLANDS).

On the coast itself, the most popular hikes are in and around **Parque Nacional Machalilla**, where you can find guides in the local villages to explore the dry and lower reaches of cloud forest. Operators in Puerto López (see SOUTHERN MANABÍ, page 197) can help with practicalities. Further north, in Bahía de Caráquez, contact **Guacamayo Bahíatours** ((05) 690597 FAX (05) 691412 E-MAIL ecopapel@ecuadorexplorer.com WEB SITE www.qni.com/mj/riomuchacho, Avenida Bolívar and Arenas, for information about the great **Río Muchacho** area. In the south, contact **Fundación Pro-Bosque** ((042) 416975 or (042) 417004, Edificio Promocentro, Cuenca and Eloy Alfaro in Guayaquil, for more information about the park and guided tours in the **Bosque Protector Cerro Blanco**, or other reserves close to the city.

BIRD-WATCHING

For detailed information on bird-watching, see GET TWITCHING, page 22 in TOP SPOTS. The identification bible for birders is *A Guide to the Birds of Colombia*, by Stephen Hilty and William Brown, Princeton University Press, 1986. An Ecuadorian edition is rumored to be in the pipeline. Not as good for identification, but with more practical information on 120 birding sites and maps, is Robert S. R. Williams et al's *Guide to Bird-watching in Ecuador and the Galápagos Islands*, Biosphere Publications (1996).

Among the recommended bird-watching operators employed by many agencies abroad is **Viajes Orion** ((022) 462004 FAX (022) 432891 E-MAIL vorion@uio.satnet.net WEB SITE www.vorion.com, Atahualpa 955 at Avenida de la República.

Sporting Spree

With extensive areas of wilderness and its varied terrain of mountains, rainforest, coast and islands, Ecuador is one of the great, and least expensive, destinations for adventure sports. The country's adrenaline-pumping outdoor activities include mountain climbing, mountain biking, caving, scuba diving, whitewater rafting, kayaking, paragliding, bungee jumping, surfing, four-wheel driving and horse riding.

MOUNTAIN CLIMBING
With 10 peaks over 5,000 m (16,404 ft), Ecuador has a reputation as a country for serious mountain climbing. Since the nineteenth century, European and American climbers have come to Ecuador in attempts to conquer both the mountain once thought to be the tallest in the world, Chimborazo, 6,310 m (20,702 ft), and the tallest continuously active volcano in the world, Cotopaxi, 5,897 m (19,347 ft). The German scientist and traveler Wilhelm Reiss conquered Cotopaxi in 1872, while the English climber, Edward Whymper, made the first successful ascent of Chimborazo in 1880. Accounts of his climbs in Ecuador can be found in his *Travels Amongst the Great Andes of the Equator* (it's out of print, but the SAE has a copy or two in its library).

Hundreds of people now climb these and other Ecuadorian peaks each year. Conditions vary from mountain to mountain, though climbing is usually best from June to September and December to February. There are *refugios* on the high slopes of most of the big mountains where climbers rest, preparing to begin the ascents around midnight — in order to reach the peak at dawn when visibility is at its best and before the sun softens the snow. Weather conditions also tend to be favorable during the full moon, aiding nighttime climbs. Experience and proper acclimatization is essential before climbing any of the higher peaks.

The Ecuadorian mountain guides association is called **ASEGUIM (Association Ecuatoriana de Guías de Montaña) (** (022) 568664, Calle Juan Larrea 657 and Rio de Janeiro, just off Parque El Ejido, Quito. They run a rigorous training program monitored by other experienced mountaineering associations. All guides carry two-way radios for contact with the nearest town or city. The ASEGUIM guides are also the only ones that have a mountain rescue service. This is costly (so come with adequate insurance!) but reassuring. Unfortunately, due to squabbles in Baños, not all the guides there are members of the association. Some who are not are still very good, while others are cowboys. Check carefully who you're dealing with.

Ecuador offers plentiful opportunities for mountain biking; speeding down Volcán Cotopaxi is one of the most thrilling trips.

For descriptions of the country's volcanoes, see TICK THE "VOLCANO LAND" LIST, page 18 in TOP SPOTS. Some of the most experienced and reputable climbing operators for the country include **Alta Montaña** (/FAX (02) 504773, Jorge Washington 425 and 6 de Diciembre, Quito, or ((03) 963694 FAX (03) 942215 E-MAIL aventurag@laserinter.net, León Borja 35-17, Riobamba; **Safari Tours** ((02) 552505 or (02) 223381 FAX (02) 220426 E-MAIL admin@safari.com.ec WEB SITE www.safari.com.ec, Calamá 380 and Juan León Mera, Quito; **Surtrek** ((02) 561129 FAX (02) 561132 E-MAIL surtrek@surtrek.com.ec WEB SITE www.surtrek.com.ec, Amazonas 897 and Wilson, Quito; **Andinismo** ((02) 223030, 9 de Octubre 479 and Roca, Quito; and **Sierra Nevada** ((02) 224717 FAX (02) 554936, Pinto 637 and Amazonas, Quito. In Riobamba, contact the **Asociación de Andinismo de Chimborazo** ((03) 960916, Chile at Francia, and **Andes Climbing and Trekking** (/FAX (03) 940964 E-MAIL ppurunca@ecu.net.ec, Colón 22-25. This list is by no means exhaustive. Most of these operators also sell or rent climbing equipment.

Contact the SAE for a list of the Quito-based **climbing clubs** that meet regularly and can be a great source of advice. There also some Ecuadorian **mountaineering journals**, such as *Montaña* and *Campo Abierto*, which are worth looking out for, as well as the great photographer-mountaineer **Jorge Anhalzer's** mountain guides to the five most-climbed mountains (Chimborazo, Cotopaxi, El Altar, Cayambe and Sangay).

MOUNTAIN BIKING

Blasting down mountains with only two wheels between you and the earth is becoming an increasingly popular way to spend a day or two in Ecuador. The country offers some awesome adrenaline rides, plunging down from mountains to the plains below. But Ecuador is also a great country just to enjoy from the seat of a bike, stopping at highland villages, coming across markets, and camping in the wilds or staying at humble *hosterías*.

On a practical level, as with climbing or hiking, you shouldn't overexert yourself too soon at high altitudes. Carry plenty of water, and lather yourself in sun-block. Bring a lock that passes through both wheels and the frame. Most buses will carry bikes on their roofs, but supervise the loading to avoid any damage. You can take your bike onto TAME domestic flights, but arrive early to ensure all goes smoothly. If you're renting bikes, then check them out carefully and go for a test ride before committing.

As a rule, it's best to avoid the congested and often dangerous Panamericana. So, for example, if heading north of Quito to Otavalo, head out to the Mitad del Mundo and continue on the old road through San José de Minas, and from Cayambe, take the old road to Zuleta and then cross over to Laguna de San Pablo and Otavalo. Heading south of Quito, ask for detailed directions for the quieter route through Machachi.

As for **routes**, one great ride is the thrilling, mostly downhill run from Baños to Puyo. In town, you'll find a plethora of places renting bikes (see BAÑOS, page 127). One of the most exciting rides is the "up hill by jeep, down hill by bike" Cotopaxi descent (see PARQUE NACIONAL COTOPAXI, page 124), but you can also do the "Latacunga/Quilotoa Loop" by bike (see AROUND LATACUNGA, page 122); or ride from Pichincha near Quito down to Nono near Mindo; down from the Papallacta hot springs to Baeza or beyond; and the long-distance Cotopaxi to Chimborazo expedition. These are just some ideas, and don't include the coastal rides which are also popular.

Many operators organize the above trips, providing support vehicles and all-inclusive deals. Among the most experienced are **Biking Dutchman** ((022) 542806 FAX (022) 567008 E-MAIL dutchman@ecuadorexploer.com WEB SITE www.ecuadorexploer.com/dutchman, Foch 714 and Juan León Mera, and **Arie's Bike Company** (/FAX (022) 906052 E-MAIL ariesbikecompany@latinmail.com WEB SITE www.ariesbikecompany.com Wilson 578 and Reina Victoria.

For the Cotopaxi area, **Hacienda San Agustín de Callo** (/FAX (03) 719160 IN QUITO (Mignon Plaza) (022) 242508 FAX (022) 269844 E-MAIL mplaza@access.net.ec WEB SITE www.incahacienda.com can arrange bikes with experienced guides. For the Otavalo area, both the **Hotel Ali-Shingu** and **Hacienda Cusín** rent bikes in excellent condition, but some operators in town do also (see OTAVALO, page 105). For Riobamba, contact Galo Brit of **Pro Bici** ((03) 942468 FAX (03) 961923, Primera Constituyente next to Banco Popular. In Cuenca, contact **Ciclismo Total** (/FAX (07) 451390, Solano 563 and Avenida del Estado. In Vilcabamba, horses are the preferred means of transport, but ask around for bikes. On the coast, **Hostería Alandaluz** can arrange bike tours too (see SOUTHERN MANABÍ, page 197).

HORSEBACK RIDING

An essential part of the old hacienda way of life, horseback riding is becoming an increasingly popular pastime with guests of

the new hacienda hotels. And since many guests are interested in visiting more than one hacienda, the owners and managers are developing a system whereby you can ride from one to another, while arrangements are made to transport your luggage. "Every day another horse, every day another hacienda" is this motto of this system. In the Otavalo area, Haciendas Cusín, Pinsaquí and Zuleta, as well as Casa Mojanda, can all coordinate tours for you (see OTAVALO, page 105). Highly recommended (but not cheap) trips throughout the country, ranging from short tours for inexperienced riders to nine-day expeditions, can be arranged with **Ride Ecuador** (/FAX (022) 437644 E-MAIL rideecuador@travelecuador.net WEB SITE www.travelecuador.net (a useful site).

More locally, **Hacienda San Agustín de Callo** (/FAX (03) 719160 IN QUITO (Mignon Plaza) (022) 242508 FAX (022) 269844 E-MAIL mplaza@access.net.ec WEB SITE www .incahacienda.com, offers rides around Cotopaxi, owns some wonderful horses and has experienced guides. Horse trails around Baños abound, but you should choose your nag carefully. Experienced guides and healthy horses can be found at **Hostal Isla de Baños** ((03) 740609, through Ivan at the **Pizzería Napolitano** near the Plantas y Blanco Hostal, or by asking around for **Caballos José** and **Angel Aldáz**.

For tours around Chimborazo, contact **Pulingue San Pablo** (or "Waman Way")

((03) 949510 or (03) 949511 E-MAIL waman_way @hotmail.com (Spanish only) or **Tom Walsh** E-MAIL twalsh@ch.pro.ec for local guides who know the trails like the back of their machetes. Riding horses through the wilds of Parque Nacional Cajas is a great way to explore the area. Contact **Monta Runa Tours** (/FAX (07) 846395 E-MAIL montarun@az.pro.ec at Gran Colombia 10-29 and General Torres, in Cuenca, for these.

Also very popular for horseback rides is Parque Nacional Podocarpus. The easiest way to arrange a tour there is through the operators in Vilcabamba. These include **Caballos Gavilan** ((07) 580281 E-MAIL gavilanhorse@yahoo.com, which has a long-standing reputation for fun trips; Martine and Bernard (who are French) of **Solomaco Lodge** (/FAX (07) 673186 E-MAIL solomaco@ hotmail.com; the community-based **Avetur** or **Centro Ecuestre** ((07) 673151; and Charlie and Sarah of **Cabañas Río Yambala** (no phone) E-MAIL rio_yambala@yahoo.com or yambala@impsat.net.ec WEB SITE www.vilcabamba.cwc.net.

On the coast, horsy tours can be arranged with **Hostería Alandaluz** (/FAX (042) 780686 or (042) 780690 IN QUITO (022) 505084 FAX (022) 543042 E-MAIL booking@alandaluz.com WEB SITE www.alandaluz.com, and also with **Guacamayo Bahíatours** ((05) 690597 FAX (05)

Equestrian events are highlights of Ecuadorian fiestas.

691412 E-MAIL ecopapel@ecuadorexplorer.com WEB SITE www.qni.com/mj/riomuchacho, Avenida Bolívar and Arenas, of Bahía de Caráquez.

WHITEWATER RAFTING

The many rivers gushing down the sides of the Andes offer great scope for exhilarating whitewater rafting and kayaking. See RUN THE RIVERS, page 22 in TOP SPOTS, for details of the best runs. Top operators include Steve Nomchong's **Yacu Amu Rafting** ((022) 236844 FAX (022) 226038 E-MAIL yacuamu@rafting.com.ec WEB SITE www.yacuamu.com.ec, Baquedano E5-27 and Juan León Mera, Quito, and **Ríos Ecuador** IN QUITO (/FAX (022) 558264, but based IN TENA (/FAX (06) 558264 E-MAIL info@riosecuador.com WEB SITE www .riosecuador.com, and **Adventour** ((022) 820848 FAX (022) 223720 E-MAIL info@ adventour.com.ec WEB SITE www.adventour .com.ec. The recommended company in Baños is **Río Loco** ("Mad River") (/FAX (03) 740929 E-MAIL riolocot@yahoo.com, Ambato and Alfaro.

SCUBA DIVING

Most keen divers head straight to the **Galápagos Islands** for encounters-of-a-lifetime with often huge schools of hammerhead sharks, sea lions, penguins, rays, turtles, and larger sharks such as the whopping whale shark. The islands are regarded as one of the world's best sites, mainly for the number of creatures you'll see, rather than corals. However, you should be aware that diving in the Galápagos is not for beginners, and that several tragic fatalities have occurred in recent years. The strong, often unpredictable currents can be a problem for even the most experienced divers, while water temperatures can drop quite dramatically and visibility can be severely reduced. To add to this, there is no decompression chamber on the islands, and none worthy of the name in the country. For more information, see SPORTS AND OUTDOOR ACTIVITIES, page 223 under THE GALÁPAGOS ISLANDS.

Two operators on the islands have received generally favorable comments from divers, though both have had their problems. The two, based in Puerto Ayora on Santa Cruz are: **Galápagos Sub-Aqua** (/FAX (05) 526350 IN QUITO (/FAX (022) 565294 E-MAIL sub_aqua@ga.pro.ec WEB SITE www.galapagos-sub-aqua.com, on Avenida Charles Darwin, where staff speak German and English, and **Scuba Iguana** (/FAX (05)

526497 E-MAIL info@scubaiguana.com WEB SITE www.scubaiguana.com, based at Hotel Galápagos. Both offer a full range of diving services, including introductory diving, full certificate courses, daily and live-aboard diving tours and full equipment rental. Prices from US$80 per day for introductory diving, with two boat dives, to first-class, seven nights, live-aboard diving tours for up to US$2,000.

The other, less challenging and not as spectacular place to dive in Ecuador is in the **Parque Nacional Machalilla** in Manabí Province. The recommended dive operator there is **Exploratur** ((05) 604128 E-MAIL explora1@uio.satnet.net, Malecón at General Córdova, but they'll require advance notice. You could also book through the **Hostería Alandaluz** (/FAX (042) 780686 or (042) 780690 IN QUITO (022) 505084 FAX (022) 543042 E-MAIL booking@alandaluz.com WEB SITE www.alandaluz.com, who employ trustworthy divers.

OTHER SPORTS

For another type of spill and thrill, Ecuador claims one of the world's highest **bungee jumps**. Many young Israelis traveling to South America after military service make a point of doing the 87-m (290-ft) "Andes bungee" from a bridge over the Río Chiche on the road from Quito to Puembo. Jumps are supervised by trained jumpmasters from **Andes Adrenaline Adventures**

((022) 226071 or (022) 227896 FAX (022)
508369, on Baron Von Humboldt 279,
Quito. Jumping takes place year round on
Saturdays and/or Sundays. Reservations
are required. You can also contact this
company for information about **paragliding**,
a sport which is only just taking off in
Ecuador. Another source of information for
gliders is the **Escuela Pichincha** ((022)
540347 or (022) 455076.

For more information about other
adventure travel opportunities contact the
SAE (see page 82 for details on membership).
Safari Tours ((022) 552505 or (022) 223381
FAX (022) 220426 E-MAIL admin@safari.com.ec
WEB SITE www.safari.com.ec, Calamá 380 and
Juan León Mera, Quito, is also an excellent
source of knowledge and ideas about
adventure travel in Ecuador.

The Open Road

Renting a car gives you the most freedom
and flexibility to explore the country. In the
course of a week or two you can experience
the lifestyles, culture and natural beauty of the
Andes, the Amazon jungle and the coast. But
if you decide to take this route, be aware of
some hazards and drawbacks. These include
confusing road signs or no signs at all,
inadequate road maps, dangerous roads and
dangerous driving (especially at night). You
must always be alert to the possibility of car
theft and never leave valuables in an
unattended vehicle. Also be aware that if you
have a serious accident in a remote country
area you could find yourself on the sharp end
of some on-the-spot punishment (see GETTING
AROUND, page 247 in TRAVELERS' TIPS, for more
information).

For these reasons self-drive vacations
in Ecuador are relatively uncommon. Most
people prefer to join a tour group, to contract
a chauffeur to drive them, or to travel
independently by public transportation.
The other main problem with car rental in
Ecuador is that the offices of the car agencies
are found only in Quito and Guayaquil.
If you're going to drive from one city to the
other, you should take at least a week to do
so. The companies then charge extra to return
the car. For this reason, I would recommend
doing a loop from Quito especially, and
generally from Guayaquil also. But the real
point of renting a car, apart from the
independence it confers, is to get to places
where public transportation is sporadic,
tough to coordinate, or just plain
uncomfortable.

IMBABURA LOOP

Beginning in Quito, head out along Avenida
Amazonas, following the signs for Ibarra,
which takes you on the Panamericana Norte.
Follow this road until it forks at **Guayllabamba**.
Take the right fork to visit the zoo (see
EXCURSIONS FROM QUITO, page 101). This road
continues to **Cayambe**, where it meets the
Panamericana. About two-thirds of the way
to Cayambe (around 24 km or 15 miles),
you pass the town of El Tingo. Take the right
turn up to **Cangahua** and the great Hacienda
Guachalá, nestled into the skirts of Volcán
Cayambe (see LIVE THE HACIENDA LIFE, page 15
in TOP SPOTS, for details of all haciendas
mentioned in this drive).

Just six kilometers (under four miles) north
of Cayambe, a right turn heads to **Olmedo**.
This is the old road to Quito, cobbled, bumpy
and spectacular. About 24 km (15 miles) from
the turn, you'll come to the area of Hacienda
Zuleta, known as **Angochagua**, and on to the
pretty mountain village of **La Esperanza**, a
good base for the hike up to Volcán Imbabura.

From La Esperanza, wind down to the
provincial capital of **Ibarra**. Here, you could
explore further north up to the **Páramo El
Ángel**, to the hot springs of **Chachimbiro**, or
head back round the volcano's west side to

OPPOSITE: Rackety buses known as *rancheros*
serve some of the most remote Andean villages.
ABOVE: Tree-lined road at Hacienda Cusín,
near Otavalo.

YOUR CHOICE

Otavalo. An old road loops around the **Laguna de San Pablo**, to the southeast of Otavalo. By taking it, you can visit the weavers of the villages of Ilumán, Peguche and Agato. On the far side of the lake, just after the town of San Pablo, stop for a wonderful lunch followed by a stroll in the gardens of **Hacienda Cusín**. From the lake, head back to Quito.

LATACUNGA LOOP

South of Quito, there's a drive that has become known as the "Latacunga Loop" (also "Quilotoa Loop"). It is fantastic, and you should allow at least four days to enjoy it properly. Driving out of Quito to the south isn't as obvious as to the north. In fact, it's quite stressful. My best advice is to keep looking for the signs for **Vilcarosa** as you drive south from the New Town along 9 de Octubre. You should come to a large traffic circle, which has a sign for the **Panamericana Sur** (the turn at 9 o'clock as you approach it). The earlier you begin this drive the better to catch Volcán Cotopaxi and the Ilinizas to the south in their full, brilliant glory.

About 25 km (over 15 miles) after the big junction at Alóag (where the road branches west to the coast via Santo Domingo) and over the pass, you come down to the entrance to **Parque Nacional Cotopaxi**. Although I wouldn't recommend driving all the way to the refuge in a city car, you can go quite a way and enjoy the views. With a high-

clearance vehicle, you can go all the way. Depending how you want to play it, you can visit all or some of the famous local markets: Saquisilí (Thursday), Zumbahua (Saturday) and Pujilí (Sunday). From Latacunga, take the right at the main junction as you enter town, by the bridge. This is the road for **Pujilí**, about 15 km (nine miles) away. From Pujilí, the in-parts-rough road winds over the *páramo* and coils its way through the lovely valleys of **Tigua**. Tigua is famous for its artists, who represent their world of mountains and fields and puffy clouds with great skill. Stop in the village by the church, about 40 km (25 miles) west of Pujilí, to visit the store there and talk to the locals.

The road from here deteriorates drastically. About half an hour on from Tigua, you come to the town of **Zumbahua**. Unless you're here on market day, there's not much to see and do except enjoy the highland atmosphere. Make sure you take the right turn (north) at the village. Roughly 14 km (nine miles) north, another dirt track branches up to **Laguna Quilotoa**, a popular hike for the healthy. The turn is badly signposted, so ask for directions.

Continuing north on the bumpy roads to close the loop, you'll pass the villages of **Chugchilán** and **Sigchos**. Now heading back eastwards, the road continues through **Toacazo** and then turns south back towards Latacunga. On the way you can make a side-trip to **Saquisilí**, the third town worth visiting for its market. From there it's a short drive back to the "Pana." You can obviously do this loop in reverse, by beginning at the turnoff from the Pana for Saquisilí.

COASTAL LOOP

The third route is a coastal one. Depending how long you want to drive for, you can elongate it by heading further south, perhaps coming all the way round to Guayaquil. To begin, you have two choices for leaving Quito and getting to the **Mindo/Nanegalito** area, where there are plenty of places to stay. I would suggest heading north to the **Mitad del Mundo** monument (watch for the signs pointing left as you leave the city on the Panamericana Norte, see above). The road is in good condition. From the monument, there are signs to **Nanegalito** due west. The other road to Mindo goes through **Nono**, but ask

ABOVE: Andean villagers walking back home along tree-lined roads. RIGHT: At 6,310 m (20,702 ft), Volcán Chimborazo, the tallest in Ecuador, towers over the former capital of Riobamba. Chimborazo was once thought to be the tallest mountain in the world.

your hotel or a tour operator to give you detailed instructions. The drive to Nanegalito is dramatic, plunging through a steep, forest-clad gorge with a rushing river below.

From Mindo, the road cuts west to **La Independencia**, where it forks. Take the right (northwest) for **Esmeraldas** on the coast, and begin to peel your highland gear off as you pass through increasingly humid climes, lined with vast palm-oil plantations. At Esmeraldas take the signposted coastal road towards **Atacames**. There are plenty of good places to stay around here. Driving on, you come to **Muisne**, 41 km (24 miles) south of Tonchigüe. Here, you could consider leaving your car with a local in order to take the boat round to the idyllic **Mompiche**. Or else, there's a very bad road (strictly four-wheel drive in the dry season) to Mompiche off the new highway which loops round from Muisne to **Pedernales** to the south. This new road doesn't appear on most maps, but it does exist, and is a joy after the ones that have come before, I can assure you. Pedernales is also accessible more directly from **Quito** via **Santo Domingo de los Colorados**, by taking the Alóag turn on the Panamericana south of the capital (see above).

From Pedernales, if you've rented a jeep, you can enjoy one of the most exciting drives in the country — what renting a jeep is all about — along the beach to **Cojimíes**. About halfway down this strip, hidden behind screen of coconut palms, you'll find the secluded **Hotel Coco Solo**. Make *absolutely sure* to check the time of the tides with the locals in Pedernales, or phone the Coco Solo for advice. You *do not* want to be caught out!

South of Pedernales, the road sweeps by more long semi-deserted beaches, where the only inhabitants are a few fishing families. After the uninspiring town of **Jama**, and shortly before wide beach-town of **Canoa**, you pass the turnoff for the **Río Muchacho** area, which you could visit for a day or two by arrangement with **Guacamayo Bahíatours** of Bahía de Caráquez.

The only way to continue further south is by catching the ferry from **San Vicente** over to attractive **Bahía de Caráquez**. San Vicente is 106 km (66 miles) from Pedernales. Alternatively, you can put an end to the Coast Loop here and trundle back to the highlands via Chone and Santo Domingo de los Colorados.

For those wanting to continue, the next major stop is the beach resort town of **Manta**, popular with Ecuadorians, but less so with international travelers. From here, you could, if you really wanted to, bump round the headland via small fishing villages and the town of **San Lorenzo**, to Puerto Cayo. More straightforward is the road south through the panama hat-making towns of **Montecristi** and **Jipijapa**, where you could stop to purchase a *fino*, before returning over the hills to the coast at **Puerto Cayo**.

A fantastic coastal drive south takes you into the wonders of **Parque Nacional Machalilla**, where there's a range of places to stay (such as the famed **Hostería Alandaluz**) and plenty to do close by. Moving on ever-southward, you pass the surf-dude hangout of **Montañita**, and then **Ballenita**. **Salinas** lies just south of here, where you could cruise up and down the Malecón with your music blasting and feel very Ecuadorian as a result. It's also worth stopping by in the town of **Santa Elena** to admire the intertwined ancient skeletons, Los Amantes de Sumpa, in the museum there. Heading west, there are a few more beach towns before arriving at the hustling and bustling **Guayaquil**.

LOOP THE LOOP

The roads that link the highlands to the lowlands of El Oriente are all in pretty terrible states of disrepair. The exception is the highway west of Quito, exiting via **Cumbayá**, which winds up to the **Papallacta Pass** and down to the famous hot springs. From there, however, it's dirt tracks or beaten-up asphalt all the way. If you've rented a jeep, enjoy rough roads and aren't in a hurry, then you might want to consider looping down from Papallacta via the **Cascada de San Rafael** and **Baeza**, and on south to **Tena**. From there you keep bumping along the skirts of the Andes south to **Puyo**, where you can head back up the mountains via the falls at **Río Verde**, and on to **Baños** and **Ambato**. At the jungle towns, you can take a brief trip into the jungle, or visit some of the local sights.

To elongate this loop, keep going south from Puyo all the way to **Macas**. From there, take the road (which should be completed by the time you read this) back to **Guamote** on the Panamericana (south of Riobamba) through the south of **Parque Nacional Sangay**. Taking the turn 71 km (44 miles) — but many hours! — after Macas, close to **Santiago de Méndez**, you can also climb back up to **Cuenca**. There are two routes for this, but I prefer the one that follows the Río Paute up to **Amaluza** (where there's a great dam) and back down to **Paute**. All three of these jungle-highland roads are as dramatic as they are rough. They are also prone to mudslides and delays, so ask for advice locally before setting off.

Backpacking

The greatest advantage of independent travel is that you meet up with all sorts of people on the road. You encounter fellow travelers on buses, trains, boats and planes, in jungle hostels and city cafés, waiting for a ferry to cross a river, standing in a check-in line at an airport. Inevitably, the same questions are asked: Where are you from? Where are you going? Where's a good place to stay in Baños? Which is the best beach on the coast? Where should I go in the jungle? In Ecuador, it's also quite likely you'll bump into the same people on the road, at least once. Part of the reason for this is that there are a number of regular routes and haunts that have become part of the well-worn "gringo trail." There's even a book by Mark Mann called *The Gringo Trail* (Summerdale, 1999) — it's pretty good.

It is easier than many people think to get around Ecuador using public transportation. People of all ages do it, some without speaking a word of Spanish, though the more of the language you know, the more you'll get from your trip.

For independent travelers in Ecuador, a few special considerations are worth bearing in mind. Though Ecuador is regarded one of the safest places for traveling in South America, it is always important to exercise caution while on the road, especially in areas

that are known to be dangerous (the Old Town in Quito, for example). Don't carry valuables (a watch, a camera) that you can do without; and avoid traveling with more than the minimum amount of money.

By "Western" standards, Ecuador is cheap. You can find *hosterías* and *hostales* up and down the country that charge as little as US$2 per person a night. You can eat a three-course lunchtime meal for as little as a dollar (if your stomach is up to Latin American bugs). Public transportation is cheap, with the rough rule of thumb being "a dollar for every hour traveled." Even domestic flights, allowing you to hop from one end of the country to the other, are not too expensive (Quito to Guayaquil for example is around US$50 one-way). Guided tours will probably be the backpackers' greatest expense. By forming a group with fellow travelers (check the notice boards at the SAE, or put your own one up) and bargaining hard, you can always bring the price down.

Some top spots on the gringo trail include the party town of **Atacames** on the coast, the beaches at **Canoa**, **Machalilla** and **Ayampe** in Manabí, and **Montañita** in Guayas.

In the Sierra, go to **La Esperanza** near Ibarra, the weaving villages around **Otavalo**,

The all-purpose *ranchero* provides transportation to country towns and villages, this one heading for the rough-and-tough mining town of Nambija, near Zamora in the southern Oriente.

camping in **Cotopaxi**, the **Black Sheep Inn** near Latacunga, the spa-town of **Baños**, camping or trekking around **Chimborazo**, sightseeing in **Cuenca** from a base at **El Cafecito**, and finally chillin' out in **Vilcabamba** at any one of the numerous places to stay.

In the Oriente, the most popular springboard towns for jungle trips are **Tena**, **Misahuallí** and **Puyo**, where, especially in the northern hemisphere summer high season, you can always find other travelers to make up a group.

Riding on the top of the train down or up the **Devil's Nose** is probably the biggie for most backpackers (it costs US$15), while **mountain biking** or **horseback riding** for a day around Baños, Otavalo, Cuenca or Latacunga or on the coast will cost about US$5 a day for bikes, and more for horses.

Living It Up

In Ecuador you can live it up in stylish surroundings and among luxury facilities of the highest standard.

Some of the historic **haciendas** in the Sierra, for example, are a treat, combining old-style comfort with modern conveniences. My ideal "hacienda loop" north of Quito would combine all the best haciendas while passing through stunning landscapes. Begin at Guachalá near Cayambe, famous for its cheeses and *bizcochos* (biscuits). From there, take the old, mainly cobbled road north to Zuleta to enjoy a wonderful old working hacienda and to meet local weavers — the trout at dinner is superb. Continue down to Ibarra and back up to Hacienda San Francisco. If you've done some horseback riding, massage your limbs back to life at the nearby, pleasant hot springs. Return south to Pinsaquí for a night or two among the historical walls, enjoy the market at Otavalo, and consider adding some more pampering at the luxurious Hostería La Mirage, a hacienda-style country hotel complete with a beautiful garden, palatial rooms, antiques, fine food, pool, spa and gymnasium. It's the only hotel in Ecuador to date to be part of the exclusive Relais & Châteaux group. Finish off amid the luxury and gardens of Cusín, or make up your own itinerary. Cusín can offer helicopter transfers from Quito for three to five people from

around US$800. For details and descriptions of these, see LIVE THE HACIENDA LIFE, page 15 in TOP SPOTS.

Though more confined in space, there is plenty of luxury aboard the many **cruise ships** that ply the waters around the Galápagos. Above all a wildlife destination, visitors can enjoy the highest standards of comfort and cuisine as they hop among the islands. The bigger cruise ships tend to be more luxurious, but some of the smaller boats have more flexible programs and their more manageable visitor groups lend themselves to better wildlife viewing. Medium-sized boats, such as *Coral I* and *Coral II*, operated by Kleintours ((022) 430345 or (022) 461235 FAX (022) 442389 or (022) 469285 E-MAIL kleintou@uio.satnet.net, Avenida Shyris 1000, Quito, offer a good compromise between comfort and wildlife experiences.

About 100 boats are licensed to operate in the Galápagos Islands. Ones that have been recommended in the luxury range include the *Ambassador, Freedom, Galápagos Explorer II, Encantada, Beluga, Suledae, Cachalote, Rembrandt van Rijn, Mondriaan, Santa Cruz, Isabela II, Reina Sylvia, The Delfín, Flamingo, Pulsar* and *Stella Maris*. It is important to note that others may be equally good, and that standards on each boat can vary from season to season, depending on the crew and guides. For details on how to book many of these, see GALÁPAGOS TOURS, page 224. Good web sites for browsing top-class boats include WEB SITES www.go2 galapagos.com and www.galapagosislands.com. Some people, Bill Gates among them, charter the entire yacht for themselves and their friends, although it's doubtful you'll leave your guide Mr. Gates' tip of US$3,000!

The **jungle lodges** in the Amazon Basin offer visitors another style of comfort. Conditions in the jungle are more basic and physically demanding than aboard a cruise ship or in the sybaritic city, but it can be equally satisfying and interesting. After a long, sweaty jungle trek, luxury can be as simple as a cold beer and a hot shower. The best way to get to these lodges is to catch a chartered flight from Quito to one of the jungle towns.

Jungle lodges known for the high standards of their amenities include the American-owned La Selva Jungle Lodge, about three hours by fast private launch from Coca; the luxurious, Swiss-owned Sacha Lodge and La Casa del Suizo where many of the amenities of a first-class hotel have been brought into the heart of the jungle; and the more remote Yuturi Lodge, a scenic five-hour journey by motorized canoe down the

Elegance and antiques characterize many old haciendas, such as Hacienda Hualigua de Jijon near Alóag, south of Quito. Some owners have opened their stately homes to tourists.

Río Napo from Coca. Also known for the high standards of its facilities and its commitment to ecotourism is Kapawi Ecolodge and Reserve.

The ultimate way to explore the jungles without getting your feet wet, as it were, is aboard the enormous, flat-bottomed riverboat, the *Flotel Orellana*, which cruises the Río Aguarico near the Peruvian border. Shore trips, guides, canoe rides, lectures and good food are included. Because of troubles on the Colombian border, its future is uncertain at the time of writing. Inquire with Metropolitan Touring ((022) 464780 FAX (022) 464702 E-MAIL info@metropolitan.com.ec WEB SITE www .ecuadorable.com, whose main office is at Avenida República de El Salvador N36-84, Quito.

To really live it up in Ecuador, go to the coast, where many Ecuadorians take their vacations. La Costa is the place to party. The **beach resorts** of Salinas, Manta and Bahía de Caráquez have some of the smartest and most luxurious hotels, but you will probably find the best party atmosphere at the lively but more down-market resorts of Atacames or Canoa. In other parts of the country, those wanting to live it up should head to the Luna Runtun resort above Baños, the Hotel Crespo or Oro Verde in Cuenca, and the best cabins and treatments at the Madre Tierra Ranch and Spa in Vilcabamba.

But if you're looking for bright lights and a variety of entertainment, head for the big cities. **Guayaquil** and **Quito** boast luxury hotels comparable to those anywhere else in the world, with first-class facilities ranging from swimming pools and business centers to fine restaurants, nightclubs and casinos. Top of the range in the commercial city of Guayaquil is the Oro Verde, where double rooms go for about US$200 per night, and the Hilton Colón, which is only slightly less expensive. The Swissôtel and the Hilton Colón International are the most expensive and glitziest hotels in the capital with every amenity that guests paying US$250 per night could reasonably expect. Also pretty luxurious are the Dann Carlton and the Marriott, and the over-the-top pomp of Mansión del Ángel.

Quito boasts some fantastic **restaurants** at prices that won't make your wallet groan. Only wine is comparatively expensive by North American or European standards, a good bottle of Chilean setting you back about US$20. Of the typical, upscale Ecuadorian restaurants, La Choza and Muckis (the latter a taxi ride out of town) are my favorites. For seafood, Mare Nostrum's beautifully restored mansion serves some wonderful dishes; superb Mediterranean food is La Viña's

specialty, and Avalon has a great range of international dishes in a stylish ambience. For French dishes at about half the price of a Parisian *brasserie*, Rincón de Francia commands the best reputation, while for some of the best sushi this side of Tokyo, check out the fashionable and excellent Sake or the more staid Tanoshi.

Away from Quito, the choice becomes more limited, but I can recommend the wonderful cuisine of Hacienda Cusín north of Quito (see LIVE THE HACIENDA LIFE, page 15 in TOP SPOTS), the excellent seafood and steaks of Luigi's in Riobamba, Villa Rosa and El Jardín in Cuenca, and the restaurants at the top hotels of Guayaquil, or else the Yacht Club's.

The two **tour operators** who have the most experience putting together luxury packages are Metropolitan Touring and Klein Tours (see above). They can arrange limousines, private jets, helicopters and stays in the best haciendas. For tailor-made tours through the Internet, WEB SITE www.bestdealecuador.com is very good.

Family Fun

Children can enjoy and benefit from a wealth of experiences while traveling in Ecuador. In the jungle, they can fish for snapping piranha, learn to identify colorful birds, or practice shooting darts through blowpipes with local kids. On a Galápagos cruise, I've seen children hugely delighted after swimming with sea lions, or experiencing close-up encounters with comical blue-footed boobies, penguins and frigate birds. They can meet exotic animals at the zoo (at Guayllabamba near Quito, or in Puyo in the Oriente, for instance), ride a horse in the Andes (around Otavalo, Latacunga, Riobamba, Baños or along the beach), paddle down a jungle river or buggy down the beach in a pickup truck. Many parents do take their children on just these sorts of adventures.

Although most Ecuadorian museums don't particularly cater to children's needs or attention spans, the Museo de la Ciudad in Quito, the Mitad del Mundo exhibits, and the ruins of Ingapirca are the exceptions to this rule.

It's possible to take your children along on group tours also, but some tour operators will not take children under the age of 12 on multi-destination itineraries and safari-style trips, either for reasons of insurance or because other adults in the group don't want the distraction of having kids about.

If a child is small enough to sit on your lap on a bus trip you won't have to pay a fare, but since some buses are uncomfortable, it might be prudent to pay for a seat. On domestic airlines children under 12 pay half fare, with or without their own seat. Infants under two pay 10 percent of the fare. Hotels usually give discounts for children and it's always worth bargaining. If two children are sharing a bed it should only be necessary to pay for one child. You may be able to find a hammock for the kids in smaller places and in lodges. Nights in a hammock are quite an experience.

Once along the Pacific coast or in Amazonia, the better hotels either have pools or access to places where kids can swim. Bringing children's snorkeling gear is a good idea, in case hotels or tour operators don't have any their size. In Quito all the luxury hotels we mention have pools, and most of them offer day passes for individuals or families, who may then also use the hotel's other health facilities.

Generally speaking, Ecuadorians are especially friendly to gringos traveling with children. And it has even been reported that travelers with children are less likely to be robbed!

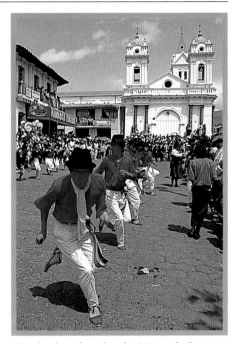

Cultural Kicks

Culture is all around you in Ecuador. In Quito it's in the naïf paintings made by the *indígenas* from Tigua that they sell to tourists — bright and detailed miniature scenes of village festivals, lamas and snowcapped volcanoes. It's in the weavings of the people of Otavalo, which they sell on street corners. It's in the baroque churches of the Old Town incorporating Inca motifs, built by artisans under the guidance of Spanish masters. It's in stark, roadside murals warning of the dangers of drug abuse, in modern public sculptures at intersections, in statues of past political and literary figures. Culture is in the cut of a poncho or a strain of Andean pipe music floating on the air.

It is said that the defining aspect of Ecuadorian culture is the fusion of ancient *indígena* artistic heritage with western thought and sensibilities imported by Spanish colonists in the sixteenth century. Certainly this curious amalgam led to the well-known **Escuela Quiteña**, or Quito School of Religious Art, which can be seen in churches and museums throughout the country, especially in Quito and Cuenca. Already skilled at carving, painting and working with gold leaf, local artisans executed, and interpreted in their own way, the religious themes of their Spanish masters. Among the best examples of

the school are found in the **Museo de San Francisco**, the **Museo Guayasamín**, the **Museo Nacional de Arte Colonial** and amid the colonial art section of the **Casa de la Cultura** museum, while the best religious art in situ is found in the **Iglesia de San Francisco** and the **Compañía de Jesús**. Another lovely church, as much for its setting as its atmosphere, is the **Santuario de Guápulo**, up on a hill in the east of the city.

But Ecuadorian culture dates back much earlier than the Spanish invasion of 400 years ago. To appreciate its depth and history, visit the extraordinary exhibits at the **Casa de la Cultura** museum complex, housed in the strikingly modern, circular glass building in the Parque El Ejido in Quito. Here you will find a well-displayed collection of artifacts that document Ecuador's ancient coastal cultures dating back nearly 6,000 years. You cannot fail to be impressed by the elegant gold and platinum ornaments, for example, that were made using sophisticated smelting techniques unknown in Europe until hundreds of years later.

Probably the most powerful modern expression of the combination of European and *indígena* sensibilities is in the paintings of the internationally known Indian artist, **Oswaldo Guayasamín**: harrowing images of suffering Indians, some of which are painted in a cubist style. A magnificent display of his

Street parades are highlights of Ecuadorian fiestas.

paintings can be seen in his private **Museo Guayasamín** in the exclusive inner Quito suburb of Bellavista. The next-best collection of contemporary art is found at Cuenca's **Museo de Arte Moderno**. The shows are temporary, but usually very good.

Ecuador may not be at the forefront of the continent's performing arts scene, but Quito's theaters — among them the **Teatro Charlot, El Patio de las Comedias** and **Humanizarte** — host all sorts of shows, mainly from Thursday to Sunday. Metropolitan Touring ((022) 464780 can give you details of various folk ballets or *música folklórica* which take place every week, and for other good venues, check the Friday supplement "Chévere" in *El Comercio*.

Outside the capital there is plenty more to satisfy the appetites of culture vultures, particularly if you combine your visit with a fiesta (see FESTIVE FLINGS, page 53). In **Cuenca**, some of the colonial and religious art and architecture is considered to be the finest in the country, and their Casa de la Cultura also hosts many arts-based events. The city is renowned for its churches, particularly the imposing **New Cathedral**, but also the teeny **Iglesia El Carmen de la Asunción** (one of my favorites in the country) or the gold-leaf altar of the **Iglesia de las Conceptas** and the **Iglesia de San Francisco** and **Iglesia de San Sebastián**. Its museums too are worthy of note: the **Museo de las Conceptas** houses many beautiful, but lurid, displays of crucifixes created by local artist Gaspar Sangurima; the **Museo del Banco Central** showcases local archeological finds and fine reconstructions of indigenous cultures, from Shuar huts to Sierran masked dancers; and the **Museo de Artes Populares** has a wonderful display of popular arts and crafts from across Latin America. Within a couple of hours' drive, the ruins at **Ingapirca** offer the finest example of Inca architecture in the country.

Even the much-berated **Guayaquil**, not usually known as a city of culture, boasts some great museums. In particular the **Museo del Banco del Pacífico** includes an excellent, well-presented and informative archaeological collection, while the **Casa de la Cultura** has a small collection of gold items to rival that of Quito. The city's best museum however has to be the **Museo Arqueológico del Banco Central**, which showcases a wonderful display of gold masks and jewelry, as well as notable anthropological and archaeological artifacts from the ancient coastal Valdivian culture.

You will also find culture in the **Amazon** rainforest and its indigenous people, in their

ingenious architecture, in the techniques of making blowpipes and dugout canoes, the ritual brewing of manioc beer, the use of hundreds of medicinal plants and the mystical role of the hallucinogenic vine, *ayahuasca*. Learning about the daily lives of inhabitants of the rainforests — whether their hunting and fishing, social structures, marriage or death ceremonies, or their relationship to nature — can be a hugely enriching experience (see RECOMMENDED READING, page 259 for background books).

On the **coast** there are many sites where archaeologists are researching long-forgotten civilizations. The most compelling is the **Amantes de Sumpa** museum in Santa Elena, close to Salinas. There you can wonder at the lovers (*amantes*) — skeletons who lay embraced for some 8,000 years before being unearthed only recently. Another import art archeological site is that at **Chirije**, close to Bahía de Caráquez on the coast. Contact Bahía Dolphin Tours ((05) 692097 or (05) 692086 FAX (05) 692088 E-MAIL archtour@telconet.net WEB SITE www.qni.com/~mj/bahia/bahia .html, for information about their ecolodge and small museum, and the archaeological site where many ceramic, gold and copper relics from the Bahía culture (BC 500–AD 500) have been found.

A world away on the northern coastline, in Esmeraldas Province, black culture with its **marimba music** and **voodoo**, brought by castaway slaves from Africa, is still thriving.

Shop till You Drop

The Spanish conquistadors were no doubt pleasantly surprised when they arrived four and a half centuries ago to find a land of weavers and craftsmen. Certainly today visitors become very excited about handwoven Ecuadorian clothes and handicrafts. Everywhere you go, it seems, there's something to buy. After a day or two in Ecuador your impression might be that the country is one big bustling bazaar selling handicrafts, bags, leather goods, ponchos, sweaters, wall hangings and woven waistcoats to tourists.

But as you travel further and see more of the country, away from the main tourist areas, you will see that most markets are geared towards local people, and that the merchandise on offer is of greatest interest to those who want to buy, say, plastic buckets or aluminum saucepans. You might be driving up through mountains on some remote dusty track and suddenly, spread out on the grass beside the road, will be a checkered carpet of handwoven items of woolen clothing minded by group of mountain *indígenas* in colorful, bulbous ponchos.

The first market most serious shoppers head for is **Otavalo**, about two hours by bus or car north of Quito. This is one of the world's great markets, where you can buy many Ecuadorian products — not only the well-known Otavalo-made items, but textiles and handicrafts from all over the country. What you might not find, however, are everyday items that local people wouldn't think about selling at big markets or to foreigners. The avid craft connoisseur has to look beyond Otavalo to the specialist craft villages and the smaller country markets.

Northern Ecuador is known for exquisitely embroidered skirts, blouses, tablecloths and napkins. Many of them are made in the west of **Imbabura Province** and can be bought in the markets of Otavalo and Ibarra. Excellent leather goods of all sorts, such as bags, purses, jackets, belts, trousers, even saddles, are made in **Cotacachi**, north of Otavalo, and are sold in shops and workshops in the village. For woodcarvings, go to **San Antonio de Ibarra** where the locals make everything from sculpture to furniture.

Ikat textiles, made with a sophisticated weaving technique in which the thread is tied and dyed in sections, are one of Ecuador's specialties. The process is used to make shawls, *macanas* (carrying cloths), ponchos and blankets. Good *ikats* are made in the **Cuenca** (Cañar) region, though the best *paños* (shawls with macramé figures) and scarves come from **Gualaceo**, and fine *macanas* are made in the **Salcedo** region.

Wool or cotton tapestries (*tapices*), often depicting images of *indígenas* and mountain scenes, are made around the village of **Salasaca** and in the Otavalo area. **Salasaca** and **Cañar** are known for their double-sided belts (*chumbis*), while knitted sweaters, hats, socks and gloves as well as woven ponchos, blankets and other woolen items are made throughout the Sierra. *Shigra* straw bags are made in the central Sierra, around **Riobamba** particularly.

Panama hats are woven in villages around Cuenca, although they originate from the **Montecristi** area on the coast, and some of the best ones are still made there. **Cuenca** is also known for its large, lidded reed baskets. Near Montecristi, the village of **La Pila** produces honest reproduction pre-Columbian figurines as well as (so it is said) fake antiques. Ceramics for everyday use are made in many places throughout the country, but some high-end work is produced in Cuenca. Quichua *indígenas* in central Oriente make coiled bowls and pots with hand-painted designs of Quichua life and mythology. **Chordeleg** near Cuenca specializes in filigree jewelry, while **Saraguro** is known for its decorative shawl pins (*tupus*).

In the **Oriente** too, a wealth of handicrafts is produced by the Amazon's indigenous people. Among these, wonderful woven palms take the form of baskets, handbags and more decorative flat bowls. The Indians fire fine ceramics, and are masterful carvers of local hard or soft woods. You could also buy blowpipes and darts (without the *curare* poison!) as an unusual souvenir.

Other markets worth visiting include the Monday market at **Ambato**; the Saturday market at **Riobamba** (note the tagua-nut carvings and the *shigra* bags); the Thursday market in **Cuenca** at Plaza Rotary (where you might be able to buy a cheap Panama hat); the **Gualaceo** Sunday market; the Calle Cuenca market on Wednesdays and Saturdays in **Quito**; and the daily Bahía black market in **Guayaquil**. Be aware that markets are ideal stalking grounds for pickpockets and sneak thieves, so hold tight to your bags and cameras at all times. For other markets, see VISIT THE MARKETS, page 26 in TOP SPOTS.

Religious icons and souvenirs on sale at Plaza de San Francisco in Quito's Old Town.

Short Breaks

Ecuador is an ideal country for a short break. Its size is its greatest asset in this respect. You can be in the jungle or on the beach in less than two hours from Quito. If you're flying in to Quito or Guayaquil for a few days on business it is worthwhile to spend an extra day or two outside the city. From Quito a good choice would be to visit a **hacienda** (see LIVE THE HACIENDA LIFE, page 15 in TOP SPOTS), most of which are around an hour's drive from the city. Any reputable travel agent in Quito will be able to make the arrangements.

If you also want to buy presents to take home, then head north to one of the haciendas near **Otavalo** (Cusín, Guachalá or Pinsaquí) so that you can visit the famous handicraft market on Friday or Saturday. For a close encounter with the world's tallest active volcano, head south to one of the haciendas near **Cotopaxi** (La Ciénega or San Agustín de Callo). For a touch of adrenaline, cycle down Cotopaxi the Biking Dutchman's "uphill by jeep, downhill by bike" one-day tour, or contact one of the rafting operators for a day-ride close to the capital.

If you are interested in bird life, then head for the small town of **Mindo** on the western slopes of the Andes, just 40 km (25 miles) northwest of Quito as the condor flies. In the cloud forest around the town some 450 species

have been observed. Nearby is the Bellavista Cloud Forest Reserve, a dome-shaped ecolodge on stilts with lots of windows and big balconies (see MINDO AND RESERVA BIOLÓGICA MAQUIPUCUNA, page 100, and GET TWITCHING, page 22 in TOP SPOTS).

Baños is another popular place for a few days' break from Quito. This small town surrounded by green hills on the flanks of the Andes has long been famous for its hot springs. There are also several good restaurants, hotels and a reasonably happening nightlife. There are plenty of good walks and bike rides outside the town. Frequent buses from Quito take about four hours, though you will probably have to change in Ambato.

For a short trip from **Guayaquil** your best bet is to head for the beach. The rather tacky resort of Playas is about two hours away by bus, while the upmarket resort of Salinas, 150 km (95 miles) west of Guayaquil, is popular with the rich and glitzy. In the high season, there are planes to Salinas. This is the place for *salsatecas*, *ceviche* and a bit of deep-sea fishing. If you're into the surfing scene, continue up the coast to catch the waves at Montañita, Ecuador's leading surfing beach, which attracts a young crowd from far and wide.

A short plane ride away from Guayaquil or Quito, consider visiting **Cuenca** to enjoy its wonderful churches and mountain air, adding a trek to the lakes of Parque Nacional Cajas, a visit to the craft-towns, and/or a hop up to the Inca ruins of Ingapirca. Alternatively, fly to **Loja** and catch a taxi down to the relaxing town of Vilcabamba, famous for the longevity of its residents. Check into the Madre Tierra Ranch and Spa for some recuperative pampering.

Festive Flings

Music, parades, dressing in costume, beauty contests, dancing in the streets, drinking, feasting, bull fighting, cock fighting, firecrackers — the Ecuadorians love a good party and there's nothing like a fiesta to generate the right mood. For gringos, fiestas are a great opportunities to join in and have fun. Villages and towns all have their own festival days, usually a local saint's day, while there are certain times of the year, notably **Carnaval** in the days before Lent, when the whole country celebrates.

The following are some of the main annual festivals, though don't be surprised if you happen upon a festival in the country about which nobody seems to know the significance. It could be some ancient ritual dating from pre-Hispanic times. But if the holiday falls in the middle of the week it is usually moved to a Friday or a Monday to make a long weekend (*un puente*, a bridge). And if it falls on a Saturday or Sunday it also moves to a Friday or Monday. Though it's fun to visit a town at festival time, accommodation fills quickly so it's advisable to make reservations.

Carnaval takes place in the week before Lent, usually in February. This is the biggest festival in Ecuador. Frenzied water fights in which nobody is spared are an Ecuadorian specialty. The people of Cuenca seem particularly fond of soaking each other. The only way to save yourself a drenching is to stay indoors or go to Ambato, where water throwing was banned because it became too rough. Instead, a festival of fruit and flowers takes place in Ambato in the last two weeks of February. On March 4, the annual **Peach Festival** is a wonderful sight to witness in Gualaceo, close to Cuenca. The peaches are, by the way, fantastic.

Following Carnaval, the next big celebration is for **Semana Santa** (Holy Week). This begins on Palm Sunday, a week before Easter Sunday, when people throughout Ecuador buy palm fronds in the market and weave them into ornaments. The processions of frond-wielding faithful emerging from churches at this time are particularly memorable. During Semana Santa religious

processions are held throughout the country. The colorful **Good Friday** procession in Quito is regarded as the most spectacular, with penitents and flagellants dragging crosses through the streets. Holy Thursday, Good Friday and Easter Saturday are all public holidays.

After Easter, Riobamba goes a bit *loco* on **April 21**, marking the Battle of Tapi with an agricultural fair and the usual street concerts and merriment at around the same time. In June, **Corpus Christi** is celebrated in many central highland towns usually on the ninth Thursday after Easter. Combined with pre-Christian harvest celebrations, it's a major festival in the **Cotopaxi** and **Tungurahua** provinces and elsewhere. Ornate masks and headdresses are sometimes worn and a dance procession takes place from **Salasaca** to **Pelileo** near Baños.

June also marks the revered **Festival of Saint John the Baptist (San Juan Bautista)** on the twenty-fourth. Otavalo and its surrounding villages shut down to enjoy the proceedings. There's dancing in the streets during the nights leading up to festival day, and on its eve people dress in the strangest of costumes, from blond gringos to cartoon characters. Ritual battles and stone-throwing take place outside the town, in which people have been known to be injured or even killed. The festival may have originated as a pre-Inca solstice celebration.

On the heels of San Juan come **San Pedro** and **San Pablo** (Saint Peter and Saint Paul) on June 28 and 29. These tend to merge with the Saint John the Baptist festival in parts of Imbabura Province. Bonfires are lit in the streets on the festival eve. Some areas associate themselves with Saint John, some with Saint Peter and others with Saint Paul. Saint Peter is the patron saint of Cayambe, where there are big parades and a ceremony for the "delivery of roosters," a throwback to feudal times. Similar fiestas, which probably originated as harvest celebrations, take place in other parts of the highlands such as southern Chimborazo Province.

On **July 25**, the boisterous city of Guayaquil marks its foundation with wild celebrations in the city, including beauty pageants, fireworks and parades that combine with the previous day's national holiday (the birthday of Simón Bolívar), while on a moveable date in early September, the **Fiesta del Yamor** takes place in the Otavalo area with plenty of razzle and dazzle and the election of a Fiesta Queen.

Like their former Spanish rulers, the Ecuadorians enjoy the thrill of bullfighting.

Galloping Gourmet

Because of its physical and cultural diversity, Ecuador is blessed with a wide range of fruits, vegetables and edible creatures. The Andes are the birthplace of the potato, for example, and several hundred species are grown here. The Incas knew ways of treating potatoes so that they could be stored for many years. They valued the potato not only as nourishment, but as a unit of time measure, the unit being the length of time it took to cook one.

As for tropical fruits, you will see and taste delicious varieties you never knew existed. The various forms of passion fruits, melons, mangoes, papayas, pomegranates, kiwis, kumquats, custard apples, bananas, guavas and tamarinds number in the thousands. My favorite is a berry-sized tomato known as *tomate del árbol* (tree tomato), which makes a delicious fresh fruit drink. Another unusual fruit is a *vavaco*, which looks something like a papaya but tastes more like a pineapple. *Naranjilla*, a greenish orange-type fruit, also makes wonderful juice (*jugo*), as do *maracuyá* (a delicious, deep-orange citrus), *taxo* (a small, plum-sized fruit), the white *guanábana* (custard apple) and *mora* (blackberries).

Before the Spanish introduced cattle, the favored meat in Ecuador was guinea pig, or *cuy*. It's still an Ecuadorian delicacy. Whole grilled guinea pigs (teeth bared, eyes closed and paws intact) are tasty and sweet — something like a cross between a chicken and a rabbit — but somewhat unprepossessing when presented on a plate. Ecuadorians enjoy discussing the best places to eat *cuy*. Some say Latacunga while others favor the *cuy* from Ambato or Baños.

More acceptable to European and American palates are some of the great soups of the highlands. *Locro de papas*, usually known simply as *locro*, a thick potato and cheese soup, is delicious and requires no culinary courage to consume. *Yaguar locro*, a potato soup made with blood sausage, avocados and onions, is equally tasty. *Fanesca*, a rich soup made with fish, eggs, beans and grains, is traditionally eaten during Holy Week festivities.

Another Sierra favorite among Ecuadorians and foreigners is *llapingachos*, potato pancakes or patties made with cheese and onions. And for a quick snack, *empanadas*, wheat flour pasties stuffed with cheese or meat, are filling and appetizing and can be bought inexpensively at a *panadería* (bakery).

Probably the country's most famous fiesta is held on September 23 and 24 for the **Fiesta de la Mamá Negra** in Latacunga, also known as the Fiesta de La Virgen de las Mercedes. Men dress up as women and blacken their faces and there's much dancing and drinking in the streets. Two weeks later there's yet another big parade in honor of Mamá Negra, which some people regard as the more authentic of the two.

All Souls' Day on November 2, is marked by laying flowers and gifts in cemeteries and lighting candles in honor of ancestors. Following this comes a slew of city-festivals, including **Cuenca Independence Day** on November 3, **Latacunga's** on November 11 with parades and a bullfight, **Loja's** on November 18, which extends for a week of festivities and cultural events, and finally **Quito's Foundation Day** — celebrated in the first week of the December. Bullfights take place at the Plaza de Toros — local *indígenas* aren't much interested in the historical implications of this festival. Following this, the lively annual **Baños Festival** takes place around December 16 (townspeople also pay homage to their local saint in October).

Christmas is obviously a good time for parties, though people tend to enjoy themselves with their families, and there aren't many particular festivals. Leading up to **New Year's Eve**, effigies are burned in the streets.

Empanadas de morocho are corn meal empanadas, usually filled with meat. The most typical mountain cooking is fried pork and roast pork — *fritada* and *hornado*. If you are really hungry, order a *chugchucaras*, a specialty of Latacunga, which is a big plate of fried pork with *mote* (corn), bananas, fried potato pancakes, popcorn and pork skin with a couple of eggs on top.

With its abundance of seafood, fresh fruits and vegetables, the best cuisine in Ecuador is found on the coast. The greatest glory of the coastal cuisine is *ceviche*, which is fresh fish or shellfish marinated using various recipes combining lime or lemon, chili, onions, coriander (*cilantro*) and perhaps other spices. Although the best *ceviche* comes from the coast, from Manabí Province in particular, the dish is popular throughout the country and indeed along the entire length of the Pacific coastline of South America. *Ceviche* can be made from fish, shrimp, lobster, clams, mussels, oysters or mixtures of all of these. If you like Japanese sushi and prawn cocktails you are sure to enjoy *ceviche*. It should be said that some people avoid *ceviche* because it is believed that it sometimes carries cholera bacteria. If you are concerned, avoid *ceviche de pescado* (fish) and *ceviche de concha* (clam) which are not even lightly cooked before marinating. Stick with *ceviche de camarón* (prawn) and clean-looking establishments.

Even if you avoid *ceviche* altogether there are still plenty of great seafood dishes to enjoy

on the coast. Try *viche*, for example, a soup of fish, crab, crawfish, conch and calamari with peanut and banana. Similarly, *cazuela* is a mixed seafood stew made with peanut sauce and green cooking bananas (*verdes*) served in a clay pot. A very thick *cazuela* can also be made into a flan-type pie, a real delicacy.

Esmeraldas Province is known for its *encocado* (made with coconut) dishes. You can have *encocado de pescado* (fish), *encocado de camarón* (prawn), *encocado de jaiba* (blue crab) and the supreme *encocado de cangrejo* (blue mangrove crab, found only in Esmeraldas). Another coastal specialty is *encebollado*, a hearty tuna soup eaten for breakfast; it's said to alleviate hangovers.

All Ecuadorian meals are served with a small side dish of hot sauce (*salsa picante*) made in various ways with chili peppers (*ají*). The spiciness of the sauce varies from place to place, so proceed with caution.

Typical alcoholic Ecuadorian drinks include various fruit concoctions made with a powerful sugarcane spirit (*trago*) as a base. A popular one is *canelazos*, which is a hot cocktail of *trago* mixed with cinnamon, sugar and lime. Pilsener and Club (both good) are the national beers, while the most popular bottled mineral water is Güitig.

OPPOSITE: Substantial fare at a Latacunga market. ABOVE: A multiplicity of fresh fruits LEFT and plenty of pork RIGHT are important ingredients of the varied Ecuadorian cuisine.

Unfortunately for a country that produces it, coffee is not well prepared in Ecuador, the most popular form being a concentrated liquid called *esencia*, to which hot water or milk is added. You can get proper coffee in some of the better hotels and in a few coffee shops in the cities.

Special Interests

NATURE AND CULTURE

For nature lovers, Ecuador offers almost every conceivable vacation option. There are many special-interest trips such as ornithology, wildlife, scuba diving or rainforest tours organized on a regular basis from Great Britain or the United States. A look at the small advertisements in the back pages of your favorite special-interests magazine will reveal a number of options. With the advent of the Internet and e-mail, it's pretty straightforward to book your tour through an Ecuadorian-based operator, or ask your hotel to organize travel arrangements. You will save yourself about 10 percent this way. The best companies are either mentioned in the previous sections, or are found in TAKING A TOUR, below.

A special mention is worth making of shaman and natural healing tours. These alternative trips to the jungle can be far more rewarding than your average rainforest trip. **Nuevo Mundo Expeditions (** (022) 564448 FAX (022) 565261 E-MAIL nmundo@interactive .net.ec WEB SITE www.nuevomundotravel.com, Coruña 1349 at Orellana, and **Viajes Orion (** (022) 462004 FAX (022) 432891 E-MAIL vorion @uio.satnet.net WEB SITE www.vorion.com, Atahualpa 955 at Avenida de la República, are both good choices for these.

LANGUAGE COURSES

Language courses are popular in Ecuador. The highland Spanish is pretty easy to come to grips with, and will immeasurably enrich your stay in the country. Lowland and coastal Ecuadorian is pretty fast and furious, and isn't recommended for beginners. Spanish courses are offered at a large number of language schools in the capital and also (at a slightly less expensive rate) in Otavalo, Baños and Cuenca (see those sections for details). Costs range between US$5 to US$10 per hour, depending on group size and the length of the course.

Recommended schools include the **British Council (** (022) 508282 or (022) 540225 FAX (022) 223396 E-MAIL helpdeask@britishcouncil.org.ec WEB SITE www.britishcouncil.org/ecuador, Amazonas N26-146 and La Niña; **Instituto Superior de Español (** (022) 223242 FAX (022) 221628 E-MAIL superior@ecnet.ec, Darquea

Terán and 10 de Agosto (they also have schools in Otavalo and Puerto Ayora, Galápagos); **Amazonas (**/FAX (022) 527509 E-MAIL amazonas @pi.pro.ec WEB SITE www.ecua.net.ec/amazonas, Amazonas and Jorge Washington (they organize dancing lessons, weekly excursions and jungle-based courses); and **Cristóbal Colón Spanish School (** (022) 506508 FAX (022) 222964 E-MAIL ccolon@southtravel.com WEB SITE www.southtravel.com, Avenida Colón 2088 and Versailles (they offer Internet facilities, cooking and dancing classes).

DANCING CLASSES

If you fancy learning some *un, dos, tres y…* salsa moves, or even some tango or cha-cha-cha, then Quito is a good place. Once you've learned your moves (or near enough) head to Seseribó for a test run. The cheapest way of joining a class is to combine it with a Spanish-language course. The schools have some of the best teachers, so call around for their advice. Otherwise, **Ritmo Tropical (** (022) 227051, 10 de Agosto 1792 and San Gregoria, Edificio Santa Rosa, is as good as any. Most charge about US$5 an hour. The South American Explorers has a members' recommended list that is useful for both language and dancing classes.

VOLUNTEERING

"Giving something back" by working on community or environmental projects is becoming increasingly popular the world over. Not only can you feel as if you're not just take-take-taking, but by spending time in a village or town, and working with or around local people, you can gain an insight into their ways that traditional "been there, done that" traveling obviates.

In Ecuador, the volunteer network is growing every year, and there are a number of projects up and running throughout the country. The best in-country resource for this is the SAE's list. People interested in their list of organizations should contact them; on Mondays they have a volunteer resource meeting at 1 PM in the Clubhouse. Other organizations include **EcoEcuador** E-MAIL ecoecuador@hotmail.com, for environmental projects, and the **EcoTrackers Network** WEB SITE www.ecotrackers.8m.com, Amazonas at Roca. On the Internet, the WEB SITE **www.workingabroad.com** is very useful in their "volunteering" section.

Many ecolodges or foundations associated with reserves around the country offer volunteering positions. These include, in the Oriente, **Jatun Sacha Foundation (** (022) 432240 or (022) 432173 FAX (022) 453583 E-MAIL jatsacha @jsacha.ecuanex.net.ec WEB SITE www .jatunsacha.org, and **Parque Pedagógico**

Etno-Botánico Omaere ((02) 226 315 or (03) 883001 E-MAIL admin@om.ecuanex.net.ec WEB SITE www.ecuanex.apc.org/omaere; around Mindo **Bellavista Cloud Forest Reserve** (/FAX (02) 232313 or (02) 901536 E-MAIL bellavista@ ecuadorexplorer.com or aecie3@ecnet.ec WEB SITE www.ecuadorexplorer.com/bellavista/ home, Jorge Washington E7-23 between 6 de Diciembre and Reina Victoria, Quito; on the coastal Río Muchacho area, arrange through **Guacamayo Bahíatours** ((05) 690597 FAX (05) 691412 E-MAIL ecopapel@ecuadorexplorer.com WEB SITE www.qni.com/mj/riomuchacho, Avenida Bolívar and Arenas, Bahía de Caráquez, and **Hostería Alandaluz** (/FAX (04) 780686 or (04) 780690 IN QUITO (02) 505084 FAX (02) 543042 E-MAIL booking@alandaluz.com WEB SITE www.alandaluz.com; and in the north, **Fundación Golondrinas** ((02) 226602 FAX (02) 566076 E-MAIL manteca@uio.satnet.net, Isabel La Católica 1559.

Taking a Tour

Dozens of overseas travel companies offer packages to Ecuador, while as many operators within the country offer a wide variety of tours. Very often the two categories are connected, with an overseas operator working with a tour company in Ecuador. Generally, it is more cost-effective to arrange a tour when you get to the country, but this might pose problems for those with limited time or those who don't speak Spanish. If this is the case, it will probably be better to shop around for a tour operator at home.

If you have three weeks available and want an overall experience of the country, I recommend that you start with a week on the Galápagos Islands. Follow this with a week in Quito and the Sierra, visiting Otavalo or Cuenca, including a couple of nights at a hacienda. Then spend three or four nights at a jungle lodge in the Oriente, and end your vacation relaxing on the coast, perhaps on the beaches of Manabí or northern Guayas. Although Ecuador is topographically extremely varied it is also compact, so it is easy to get around, either by plane or by road.

Below are some stand-out Ecuadorian tour operators:

Nuevo Mundo Expeditions ((02) 564448 FAX (02) 565261 E-MAIL nmundo@interactive .net.ec WEB SITE www.nuevomundotravel.com, Coruña 1349 at Orellana, is run by the English-speaking Oswaldo Muñoz who has been at the forefront of Ecuadorian ecotourism initiatives over the last decade. He was highly commended in Conservation International's 2001 Awards for Excellence. His company runs all sorts of high-end tours with excellent guides throughout the country, including adventure sports, Galápagos cruises, visits to the Solar Museum, as well as shaman and natural healing tours.

Another highly recommended and professional outfit is **Angermeyers' Enchanted Expeditions** ((02) 569960 FAX (02) 569956 WEB SITE www.angermeyer.com, Foch 769 and Amazonas, which is particularly good for birding, trekking and archeological tours, as well as running various Galápagos boats.

For travelers with a smaller budget, the competent **Sangay Touring** ((02) 550176 FAX (02) 560428 E-MAIL info@sangay.com WEB SITE www.sangay.com, Amazonas 1188 at Cordero, is run by English speakers. They too offer trips throughout the country, including climbing tours. Their prices are competitive and their guides recommended.

For trips into the Oriente, not all tour operators are ecologically or socially sensitive. Among those that are, **Native Life Travels** ((02) 550836 FAX (02) 569741, E-MAIL natlife1 @natlife.com.ec WEB SITE www.natlife.com.ec, Pinto 446 and Amazonas, is run by *indígenas* from Cuyabeno and has a good reputation; their prices are reasonable. The Canadian author of *Crisis Under the Canopy*, **Randy Smith** ((06) 880489 or (06) 881563 IN QUITO ((02) 540346 E-MAIL panacocha@hotmail.com WEB SITE www.amazon-green-magician.com

Courtship ritual of the waved albatross, the largest and one of the rarest birds of the Galápagos Islands.

has years of experience guiding in the Huaorani Reserve. **Emerald Forest Expeditions** ((06) 881155 IN QUITO (/FAX (022) 541543 E-MAIL emerald @ecuanex.net.ec, on Napo, is recommended for English-speaking guides and rustic four- to seven-day tours around Coca. **Tropic Ecological Adventures** ((022) 225907 FAX (022) 560756 E-MAIL tropic@ uio.satnet.sat WEB SITE www .tropiceco.com, Avenida República 307 and Almagro, Edificio "Taurus," Dpto. 1-A, Quito, runs a program with the Huaorani, where visitors spend a few nights in their territory and experience their way of life. In 1997, the company won a category in the prestigious ToDo Ecotourism awards. Also good for the Huaorani area is **Kem Pery Tours** ((022) 226583 FAX (022) 568664 E-MAIL kempery@ecuador explorer.com WEB SITE www.ecuadorexplorer .com/kemperry, Pinto 539, Quito. Finally, **Rainforestur** (/FAX (022) 239822 E-MAIL rainfor @interactive.net.ec, Amazonas near Roca (and also in Baños) has been recommended down the years by many a budget traveler. They have plenty of Oriente experience, but also run tours throughout the country.

The best tour operators for the Galápagos are detailed in GALÁPAGOS TOURS, page 224, the best climbing operators and the finest rafters in SPORTING SPREE, page 37.

Among the most well-known and reputable operators in the United States is **Eco Voyager** ((305) 665-9050 TOLL-FREE (800) 326-7088 E-MAIL ecotour@ecovoyager.com WEB SITE www.ecovoyager.com. They have years of experience and excel in trips to national parks with knowledgeable and often specialized guides. **Lost World Adventures** ((404) 971-8586 TOLL-FREE (800) 999-0558 FAX (404) 977-3095 WEB SITE www.lostworldadventures.com, 1189 Mountain Ridge Drive, Marietta, Georgia 30066, also comes highly recommended.

In the United Kingdom, I can recommend **Journey Latin America** ((0208) 747-8315 FAX (0208) 742-1312 E-MAIL tours@journey latinamerica.co.uk WEB SITE www.journey latinamerica.co.uk, 12-13 Heatherfield Terrace, London W4 4JE. They are excellent for the best flight prices, and also run group or tailor-made itineraries in Ecuador and throughout the continent. With plenty of experience and enthusiasm behind them, **Last Frontiers** ((01296) 658650 FAX (01296) 658651 E-MAIL info@lastfrontiers.co.uk WEB SITE www.last frontiers.co.uk, Fleet Marston Farm, Aylesbury, Bucks, HP18 0PZ, is another good choice. **Travel South America** ((01904) 704443, The White House, Chantry Lane, Bishopthorpe, York YO2 1QF, also has some great itineraries, while **Penelope Kellie Worldwide Yacht Charter and Tours** ((01962) 779317 FAX (01962) 779458, Steeple Cottage, Easton, Winchester SO21 1HE, can organize excellent Galápagos cruises. **Footprint Adventures** ((01522) 804929 FAX (01522) 804928 E-MAIL sales@footprint-adventures.co.uk WEB SITE www.footprint-adventures.co.uk has very knowledgeable birding, and other, guides on their books.

In Australasia, recommended companies include **South America Travel Centre** ((03) 9642 5353 TOLL FREE (1800) 655051 FAX (03) 9643 5454 E-MAIL satc@satc.com.au WEB SITE www .home.aone.net.au/satc/, 104 Hardware Street, Melbourne VIC 3000; **World Expeditions** ((02) 9264 3366 WEB SITE www.worldexpeditions .com.au, Level 3, 441 Kent Street, Sydney; and **The Adventure Travel Company** ((09) 379-9755, 164 Parnell Road, Parnell, Auckland.

For small-number birding tours, few guides in the United States surpass Richard Ryan of **Neo-Tropical Bird Tours** TOLL-FREE (800) 662-4852 FAX (973) 884-2211, 38 Brookside Avenue, Livingston, New Jersey 07039-4030. **Wilderness Travel** ((510) 558-2488 FAX (510) 558-2489 E-MAIL info@wildernesstravel.com, 1102 Ninth Street, Berkeley, California 94710, and **Adventure Discoveries International** (/FAX (615) 356-8731 E-MAIL trekfun@aol.com, Box 92188, Nashville, Tennessee 37209, have both been praised for their Ecuadorian programs.

For more information about choosing a responsible tour operator, which I would urge you to do, contact **The Ecotourism Society** ((802) 447-2121 FAX (802) 447-2122 E-MAIL ecomail@ecotourism.org WEB SITE www .ecotourism.org in the United States or for the United Kingdom, visit **Tourism Concern's** WEB SITE www.tourismconcern.org.

ABOVE: Tourism has not yet reached most of the beaches of Ecuador's Pacific coast. RIGHT: A flamingo on Isla Santa María in the Galápagos.

Welcome
to
Ecuador

Ecuador, in many ways, is an enigma. Ask the average person where or what it is, and most will draw a blank. For instance, most people don't know that the fabled Galápagos Islands make up part of its territory, or that its capital, Quito, boasts a World Heritage-listed Old Town, its dreaming spires glinting in the high Andean air.

Ecuador is one of the smallest countries in South America, semi-swallowed up by its larger neighbors: Colombia to the north, Perú to the south and southeast, and mammoth Brazil to the east. Bisected horizontally by the equator—from which its name derives — and vertically by the young volcanic Andes mountains, at only 270,670 sq km (104,208 square miles) Ecuador is only a smidgen larger than Great Britain, and no bigger than the state of Nevada. The loss of some half of its territory (in the Amazon) to Perú in 1942 and the pervasive influence of the United States over its economy and politics have resulted in Ecuadorians cultivating a deep inferiority complex. Yet, if Ecuador's mountainous, peak-and-trough topography were a crumpled handkerchief, smoothed flat the mere surface area of the country would by far surpass all expectations. Not unlike the country itself.

The density of its mountainous areas, its equatorial location and its position at the meeting point of two major Pacific currents all combine to create a diverse pattern of microclimates and a rich repository of plant and animal life. If the size of countries were measured by the variety of their bird population rather than by their physical dimensions, Ecuador — with some 1,600 recorded avian species — would be bigger than the United States and Canada combined. Measured in terms of the populations of some unique species of large turtles, pink dolphins, marine iguanas and other endemic creatures, Ecuador becomes the biggest country in the world — or even the only country in the world.

Ecuador is enormously wealthy in terms of biodiversity. Some areas of the country, particularly where the slopes of the Andes meet the rim of the Amazon Basin, are considered to be among the most biodiverse areas on earth. Hiking its parks, you descend from snowcapped peaks and bleak *páramo* moors, through dense cloud forest and on down to steamy rainforests. You traverse the land of the swooping condor to that of the harpy eagle, the redoubt of the shy spectacled bear to that of the revered jaguar.

In terms of people too, the country's size belies its wealth. Along with Perú and Bolivia, Ecuador's indigenous population ranks among the Andes' most visible, and more recently, vociferous. Traveling along the country's "Avenue of Volcanoes," brightly-clad Indians muster for their weekly markets, chattering in the highland language, Quichua. They gather for their festivals, where pre-Columbian animist beliefs have fused

with Catholicism over the centuries. Nearly every province or region in the country is inhabited by a different indigenous community, who distinguish themselves, above all, by their dress. Learning to recognize the often subtle differences and learning their histories and heritages, ranks among the most enriching experiences one can enjoy in the country.

Three distinct regions divide the country geographically and create diverse identities. On the coast, farmers known as *montuvios* are often mixed-blood Indians and the descendants of African slaves. In Esmeraldas Province, for example, marimba music and voodoo rites are still very much alive. On the coast too lies the country's largest city, Guayaquil, a hubbub of heat, commerce and fast-talkers, a million miles from the more sedate Sierra.

Across the highlands and down in the Amazon Basin, a tiny proportion of the population

lives in its expanses of rainforest. Pastaza, for instance, is the country's largest, yet least-populated province. Here the various Indian peoples have been dragged into the twenty-first century by the encroachment of oil companies, loggers and colonizers. The more remote groups, however, still live lives little-changed for millennia.

From the Amazon to the Andes is not only a huge change in altitude, which leaves one breathless when carrying bags, it's also a cultural jump from animist hunter-gatherers in some parts of the rainforest to baroque churches and slick city skyscrapers.

For the traveler, Ecuador offers a bottomless wealth of possibilities: from adrenaline sports such as whitewater rafting, mountain climbing and cross-country biking to less strenuous horseback rides among remote villages, visitors can try bird-watching in cloud forests, hiking the highlands or trekking rainforest trails. More sedate still,

wander its colonial churches and towns, observe the unique wildlife of the Galápagos, enjoy its cuisine or sink into the lap of luxury at one of its country haciendas. Beaches it has too, aplenty. Most of them are long, wide and empty, without a tourist or traveler, or even a local, to be seen. About the only thing that Ecuador doesn't have is a decent golf course.

As Charles Darwin wrote of the Galápagos Islands, which inspired his groundbreaking theory of evolution, Ecuador "seems to be a little world within itself." Little, certainly. But also, without doubt, a world within itself.

PREVIOUS PAGES: Known to local people as Taita (father), Volcán Chimborazo LEFT is the tallest peak in Ecuador's Avenue of Volcanoes. An indígena from Salasaca RIGHT, possibly of Bolivian descent. ABOVE: Poncho Plaza at Otavalo market, the biggest and best for hand-woven textiles, clothing and indigenous crafts. The busiest market day is Saturday, though Friday is also active.

The Country and Its People

In 1539, Gonzalo Pizarro left Quito at the head of a great expedition to find the city of El Dorado and the "Land of Cinnamon," which supposedly lay somewhere to the east. The expedition led his lieutenant, Francisco de Orellana, on an accidental odyssey which would eventually lead to the Atlantic shores of Brazil and the discovery of the mighty Amazon River. Ecuador's capital is duly proud of the fact. It has named its major artery Avenida Amazonas, and the wall of its cathedral in the Old Town reads "Quito's Glory is the discovery of the River Amazon."

Fed by humble springs up and down the high Sierra that slowly weave together, growing strong as they travel east, the Amazon River serves as a fine symbol for Ecuadorian ethnic diversity. And just as the river adds constantly to the South American landmass as it carries sediment down to its huge delta, in the same way immigrants have added to Ecuador's cultural landscape. Nowhere is this more apparent than on the streets of Quito. Sitting outside a café on busy Avenida Amazonas on a weekday lunchtime, the river of Ecuadorian life flows past.

Out on the sidewalk, indigenous peoples in traditional costumes and porkpie hats sell trinkets and paintings. Probably they are *indígenas* from Chimborazo Province in the highlands. Here they make colorful paintings on leather — brilliant miniatures of fiestas under snowcapped volcanoes; tourist art, to be sure, but charming in its own way, a glimpse into the dreamtime mind of the Quichua Indian.

There are estimated to be about two million highland Quichua-speaking Indians in Ecuador, mostly descended from the various tribes who lived in these parts of the Andes before the Inca invasion. Some are descendants of the Incas themselves, such as the black poncho-wearing, white-hatted folk from Saraguro, and others will have ancestors who were *mitmakuna*, peoples who were transferred by the Incas from other areas as educators, military personnel or administrators, or simply because they were considered to be trouble-makers.

Quechua, spelled with an "e," is the language of the Quechua peoples, the language imposed by the Incas. Part of the Andean-Equatorial family of languages, it is *lingua franca* among *indígenas* in Ecuador, Bolivia, Colombia, Argentina and Chile. There are several dialects, one of which is Quichua, which is commonly spoken in Ecuador. Quechua and Quichua are different transcriptions and are often used interchangeably, although Quichua is the most common usage in Ecuador. During the colonial days the Quichuas worked in feudal conditions on the estates of the big haciendas, and some still do. But with the land reforms of 1964, most of the estates were broken up and local Indians lost their jobs and security. Now they farm small holdings in the mountains or come to Quito to sell trinkets on the streets. Many of Quito's fast-growing population of about three million have come from the countryside in the last 30 years, and few of them have regular work. The last decades have witnessed a huge increase in the urban unemployed.

Back on the Avenida Amazonas, down the street, women from Otavalo, in their crisp, clean embroidered blouses, bright gold necklaces and long dark skirts, set up stands selling sweaters, shawls and ponchos. They feel themselves more *otavaleño* than Ecuadorian and are proud to wear their traditional costume. *Otavaleños* represent the success story of the highland Indians. Otavalo textiles are almost an international brand name, sold all over the world, though today *otavaleños* are just as likely to be archaeologists, accountants or doctors as weavers.

Blacks are a very small minority in Ecuador. They come mainly from the coast in Esmeraldas Province, which for centuries existed more or less as an independent state cut off from the rest of the country. Descended from slaves who escaped from a shipwreck off the coast in the sixteenth century, they have retained many aspects of their African culture, in particular the intricate rhythms of marimba music. Another community of blacks, heirs of local plantation workers, lives in the Chota Valley in the northwest of the country.

You won't see many people from the Oriente in central Quito either. The *indígenas* from the rainforest only come here when they have to: usually to protest the damage being done by oil companies to their traditional homelands, or to fight for their land rights. Organized by CONAIE (Confederation of Indian Nations of Ecuador), protests were held in 1992 against the 500th anniversary of Columbus's discovery of the Americas — which the *indígenas* consider to have led to a brutal conquest. In recent years, CONAIE has been at the forefront of national politics, heavily involved in the turmoil of 1999 and in negotiations with the government to the present.

There are several tribal groupings living in the Ecuadorian Amazon, ranging from the Cofán, the Siona and the Sequoia in the north, to the Huaorani in the central areas south of the Napo River, and the Shuar (also known as Jívaro) and Achuar in the Pastaza river area in the south. Each have their own customs and language, but many people speak Quichua and some Spanish. Other Quichua-speaking tribes, the Awa, the Cayapas and the Colorados, live in the coastal lowlands, but their numbers are dwindling.

PREVIOUS PAGES: Beaming seller of colored yarn LEFT at Latacunga market. Panama hat *supremo*, Homero Ortega RIGHT, from Cuenca. OPPOSITE: Ancient volcanic crater in the highlands of Isla Santa Cruz, Galápagos.

The Country and Its People

These ethnic minorities are only a small part of the crowds on Avenida Amazonas. Most are office workers and business people, smartly dressed in Western clothes, busy, walking fast to get things done on their lunch breaks or to grab a hamburger at a fast-food joint. These are mostly olive-skinned, mixed-race *mestizos*. Although they might have some Spanish blood, young *mestizos* are generally not much interested in the colonial past or the festivals that celebrate the founding of their city by the Spanish. They identify themselves as Ecuadorians and are less an ethnic category than a segment of the social spectrum. They make up about half of the population. You will meet mostly *mestizos* while in Ecuador.

You might see a few pure-blood *blancos* (whites) on Amazonas. Some perhaps are descended from the Spanish rulers, but in most of the old families there are traces of Indian blood. Most white faces you'll see have arrived in Ecuador in the recent past to work as English teachers, perhaps, or in the oil industry. Other groups include the Chinese, some of whose families arrived at the beginning of the century to help build railways, and Lebanese (known as "*turcos*"), most of whom live in Guayaquil. An economically powerful group, the former president, Abdalá Bucaram, is from a Lebanese family.

Roughly speaking, *blancos* make up 15 percent of Ecuador's racially mixed population of some 13 million, with *indígenas* accounting for 40 percent, *mestizos* 40 percent, and blacks five percent. But identity, like the different-hued tributaries of the Amazon itself, is fluid. A Quichua-speaking

Indian who moves to the city and finds work might regard himself as *mestizo*. But if he returns to his highland village, he might once again decide to call himself Indian. Often, distinctions are more social and economical than strictly racial.

PRE-COLUMBIAN TIMES

Who were the first South Americans, and when did they arrive on the continent? It is thought that the first humans to set foot here were descendants of Asian nomads who crossed from Siberia to Alaska over the Bering Strait. Over many generations these travelers moved down the American continent, through the Isthmus of Panama and into South America.

Some historians say the first evidence of man in South America comes from eastern Brazil and dates back 30,000 years, while others believe that humans have inhabited the continent for as long as 50,000 or even 80,000 years. It is further suggested that some of the first settlers may have been Polynesians who sailed across the Pacific many thousands of years ago and landed on the western coast.

The earliest firm evidence of human presence in Ecuador is thought to be Stone Age tools found in the Quito area dating from around 9000 BC. But the first signs of settled, pottery-making communities date from about 3000 BC, when the Valdivian tribes inhabited central areas of the coast. Artifacts and figurines made by the Valdivians can be seen in museums in Quito and Guayaquil.

Curiously, Valdivian pots are similar to Jomon pots made during a similar period on the Japanese island of Kyushu. Later coastal cultures made figurines that strongly resemble Asian Buddhas, and clay model houses that look like pagodas. But theories that there were long-distance travel connections between the respective cultures require further investigation.

What is certain is that many cultures, each with their own language, customs and style of artifacts, developed in coastal areas, sometimes trading with each other, sometimes fighting. The Machalilla culture, for example, extended along the coasts of southern Manabí and the Santa Elena Peninsula, lasting from about 1500 to 800 BC. An idiosyncrasy that the Machalilla people shared with some other coastal cultures was their practice of deforming their skulls as a beauty technique in order to increase the slope of the forehead and make the nose protrude.

In the same area, but at a later period, people of the Manta culture made balsa-wood boats and sailed as far as Chile and Mexico, trading pink spondylous shells from which they made jewelry. It is possible, even probable, that *manteños* also sailed to the Galápagos Islands. The people of the La Tolita culture (600 BC to AD 400), from northern

Esmeraldas, created beautiful gold and platinum jewelry using techniques that Europeans didn't develop until thousands of years later. Studies of these Ecuadorian coastal cultures indicate that they were the first of their kind to develop in South America, and helped shape the civilization of the continent.

In the Sierra, a similar mixture of tribal groupings developed, each with their own language, traditions, craft techniques and style of dress. In the south of the highlands, around present-day Cuenca, the Cañari Indians produced sophisticated textiles, such as *ikat* weaving, which is found nowhere else in the world except in Guatemala and Indonesia. The Cañaris also trained strong

superior weapons, armor and fearsome horses never before seen on the South American continent, gave them a powerful advantage.

Many local tribes joined the Spanish in their fight against their Incan masters. For their part, the Spanish used every means at their disposal to assert their power. When the conquistador Francisco Pizarro invited the leader of the northern part of the Inca empire, Atahualpa, to negotiations in Cajamarca in Perú, the Spanish promptly arrested him. Atahualpa arranged a huge ransom, enough gold to fill his prison cell and twice that amount in silver. Taking the treasure, the Spanish summarily put the Inca on trial, charging him with incest, polygamy, worshipping false gods and

military forces, which they deployed against the rising power of the Inca state towards the south in the fourteenth and fifteenth centuries. In time, however, the powerful, disciplined and highly organized Incan forces defeated the Cañaris and achieved their ambition of dominating the fertile valleys of the northern Andes.

THE SPANISH CONQUEST

For the first Spanish explorers, it was a lucky coincidence that they landed on the Pacific coast of South America in 1526 the year of the death of the great Inca chief, Huayna Capac, who left his empire divided between two sons, Atahualpa in Quito and Huáscar in Cuzco in the south. While two halves of the Incan empire were fighting each other, the Spanish stepped into a vacuum of power. Although Spanish forces were small, their

other counts that were crimes to the Spanish, but not to the Incas.

Atahualpa was found guilty and executed on August 29, 1533. In the last moments of his life the Inca chief converted to Christianity in order to qualify for the lesser sentence of execution by garroting instead of the more painful and prolonged death by burning. This duplicitous and tragic event was the blow that felled the once-mighty Inca Empire.

The Incas continued fighting the Spanish for two years after the death of their leader, but with ruthless efficiency the Spanish soon defeated Inca forces and destroyed their buildings, replacing

OPPOSITE: Pottery at a craft market in Cuenca. ABOVE: The Inca ruins at Ingapirca are the most important of their type in Ecuador. The original structure functioned as a fort, a temple or an observatory, or perhaps all three.

them quite rapidly with Spanish-style houses and Christian churches. When the Spanish leader, Sebastián de Belacázar, marched on the kingdom of Quito, he found the city in ruins. The Inca general, Rumiñahui, had ordered the destruction of the city rather than leave to the Spanish the sacred Inca temples dedicated to the worship of the sun and the moon. Quito was refounded by the Spanish as Villa de San Francisco de Quito in 1534, and the following year Rumiñahui was captured, tortured and executed.

In the early days, the province that is now the country of Ecuador was ruled by Spanish authorities in Lima, Perú, who themselves answered to the King of Spain. But in 1563 the colony was

granted the status of Audencia de Quito, a judicial and political body with considerably more autonomy, and more powers to deal directly with Madrid.

As the city grew in stature it developed its own school of art, the Escuela Quiteña, which combined Spanish religious traditions with local Indian inspiration. Paintings and sculptures produced at that time are still among Quito's greatest treasures. At the same time, the colonial masters expropriated large areas of land to form estates and used the Indians as a source of forced labor, while trying to convert them to Christianity. This system was called *huasipungo*. Observing the skill of the Indian weavers, the colonists established weaving workshops and imported new machinery and sheep to make wool.

Without much change, the colonial feudal system continued to operate for some 300 years.

In the eighteenth century there were several uprisings by oppressed Indians, but it took external changes to eventually disturb the equilibrium. The French Revolution, Napoleon's conquest of Spain, and the United States War of Independence fueled a nascent nationalism among liberal thinkers in South America, including Ecuador. People of Spanish origin who were born in Ecuador also resented the privileges of the Spanish-born elite who held the top positions of power in the country. With a growing demand for independence, the days of all-powerful, expatriate Spanish rulers were numbered.

INDEPENDENCE

Rumbling discontent turned to open violence. Supported by the "Great Liberator," Simón Bolívar, who had already fought for and won the liberation of his birthplace, Venezuela, Ecuador achieved freedom from colonial rule in 1822. In the final, decisive battle, Grand Marshal Antonio José de Sucre (after whom Ecuador's ex-currency was named), defeated Spanish colonial forces in the Battle of Pichincha and took Quito. Guayaquil, incidentally, had achieved independence two years earlier. Initially, Ecuador became part of the Bolívar's Federation of Gran Colombia, which included Colombia, Venezuela and present-day Panama, and managed to fight back the encroaching Peruvians in 1829 at the Battle of Tarqui. Following Venezuela's split from the Federation in 1830, the country also went its own way, becoming the República de Ecuador, ruled, ironically enough, by another Venezuelan, General Juan José Flores.

As in most post-colonial periods, things did not run smoothly in the early days of the Ecuadorian republic. Constitutions were written and rewritten, presidents came and went and power struggles that have characterized the country ever since soon emerged. Liberal-conservative polarization largely reflected traditional conflicts between the progressive and commercial values of the *guayaquileños* and *costeños*, and the more established, conformist beliefs of the *quiteños* and the *serranos* (highlanders).

Flores managed to stay in relative control until 1845, when he was ousted by a junta from the coast. Chaos ensued until the liberal general José María Urbina seized power in 1851, stamping his authority on the country for the next five years. Through these chaotic years however, slavery was abolished once and for all, and the tribute forced on *indígenas* finally ended. But by 1859, the country was once again pulling itself apart. In that year, "El Año Terrible," Guayaquil decided to become part of Perú, Cuenca declared its autonomy, Loja became a federal district and Quito created its own government.

A determined leader was required. It came in the form of Gabriel García Moreno, who came to power in 1861. He is remembered as the father of Ecuadorian conservatism. Although originally from Guayaquil, his early liberal ideas shifted to the right when he married into an aristocratic Quito family. He sought to unify the nation with ruthless efficiency through the Roman Catholic Church. Education and welfare were placed in the hands of the Church, ties to the Vatican were strengthened and Catholicism became a prerequisite for citizenship. At the same time Moreno embarked on some progressive projects, including the building of schools and hospitals and the construction of the railway between Guayaquil

industry, Alfaro's first move was to create a secular constitution and to eliminate the Church's power of censorship. He exiled clergy, seized church lands for the state, instituted civil marriages and divorce and broke the special links with the Vatican. He built ports and roads and oversaw the completion of Moreno's railway project, which provided an important link between the coast and the highlands.

Alfaro's first presidential term (1897–1901) was followed by more than a decade of political instability during which power was tossed back and forth between Alfaro and several opponents, chiefly General Leónidas Plaza (president from 1901–1905 and 1912–1916). At one point, nearly

and Quito. Moreno's political career and second presidential term came to an abrupt end in 1875 on the steps of the presidential palace, where a distraught farmer hacked him to death.

Following García Moreno's death, power remained in the hands of the conservatives. From 1884 to 1895, the conciliatory General Ignacio de Veintimilla attempted to find common ground between the liberals and conservatives. He initiated more large-scale public works programs and oversaw the country's booming export economy. But the export industry, concentrated in cacao, coffee, panama hats and tagua nuts, was in the hands of the coast, and the liberals.

Personifying the liberal side of Ecuadorian politics, the career of Eloy Alfaro Delgado, who was born in Montecristi on the coast, was similarly fated to that of his counterpart García Moreno. Elected president in 1897 with the backing of cacao

half of the national budget was spent on the military. In 1911, a full-scale civil war finally broke out, with Plaza managing to defeat Alfaro, murdering him and his supporters and burning them in the Parque Ejido.

CHAOS, CIVILIANS AND GENERALS

Most of Ecuador's twentieth century history is characterized by chaos. The country lurched from one economic or political crisis to the next. In the 1920s, the slump in cacao prices brought huge hardship to the common people, resulting in two uprisings, bloodily repressed in 1922 and 1923. The banking and, as a consequence, political

In Ecuador, you can usually tell where someone is from by their hat. OPPOSITE: At the animal market at Otavalo. ABOVE: A Cañari woman with child.

system, was controlled by the Banco Comercial y Agrícola de Guayaquil and the great cacao lords, known as "la argolla" (the "wedding ring"), whose loans led to huge inflation. By the Great Depression of the 1930s, Ecuador was once again descending into turbulence.

José María Velasco Ibarra emerged in these troubled times, and would come to play a decisive role in the nation's politics for the coming decades. However, his first term of office in 1934 lasted only months, followed by his exile in the 1940s. In 1941, Perú took advantage of Ecuador's internal fighting to invade the Oriente and the provinces of Loja and El Oro in the south of the country. Ecuador was forced to sue for peace,

with the Rio Protocol of 1942 ceding nearly half of its territory to Perú: a huge blow to a nation which believed it had given the Amazon to the world following Francisco de Orellana's voyage of discovery (and insanity?) some 400 years before.

Velasco Ibarra's second term in power, beginning in 1944, ended abruptly in 1947 following much hot-air and little concrete progress, except for his friends. Fortune, however, smiled on his successor, Galo Plaza Lasso. The son of the liberal Leónidas Plaza, but with strong links to the conservatives of the Sierra, Lasso was ideally placed to take advantage of the post-World War II banana boom. Within a few years of realizing the banana plantations' potential to save the country's economy, Ecuador had become the world's chief exporter, a claim it still holds today.

By the mid-1950s though, the price of bananas was slumping. In order to win his fourth term of office, Velasco Ibarra flirted with Cuban revolutionaries and ideas, thus winning the support of the left wing. His coalition of parties soon disintegrated however, following intense pressure from the United States and other Latin American countries to sever ties with the rebel Caribbean republic. Ibarra's term ended in a gun battle

in Congress and strikes throughout the country as he increased taxes on consumer prices. In 1961, the military brought his vice-president, Arosemena Monroy, to power, but replaced him with their own junta in 1962. Suppressing the left and civil rights, the junta feared a Cuban-style revolution would sweep the country. As a result, they passed the Agrarian Reform Law in 1964, which, though it failed to realize wide-scale redistribution of land, did do away forever with the *huasipungo* system.

In 1968, the military handed power back to the elected, and now sexagenarian, Velasco Ibarra. During his last term, amid more serious economic strife, he instigated the devaluation of the sucre and raised import tariffs. By 1970, he had assumed dictatorial powers, and the military, nervous at the candidature of populist Asaad Bucaram, and eager to control the nascent oil industry, deposed him in 1972.

The 1970s saw unprecedented economic growth in Ecuador. Per capita income grew some five times and employment by 10 percent, largely as a result of public works programs. The junta, led by General Guillermo Rodríguez Lara, sought to industrialize the economy as oil revenues flooded in from the fields of the Oriente. By 1976, the government had also accrued massive debts in its efforts to nationalize and industrialize. A bloodless coup led to a triumvirate of generals controlling the country until they finally called elections in 1979. Jaime Roldós Aguilera headed a center-left coalition, but his plans to restructure the economy foundered as the opposition led by Bucaram blocked his legislation in Congress.

Roldós Aguilera's term ended in conspiracy theories when he was killed in an airplane crash. His vice-president, Osvaldo Hurtado Larrea, attempted to continue his reforms, but was increasingly straitened by the slump in oil prices, high unemployment and soaring inflation. The country's foreign debt rose to US$7 billion. In 1984, León Febres Cordero Rivadeneira came to power at the head of a center-right coalition. A fan of neoliberal Reaganomics, Febres Cordero's policies became increasingly unpopular. In 1987, he was held hostage by supporters of the Air Force general, Frank Vargas, who had earlier attempted a coup, but negotiated his release after a half-day of captivity. The same year, an earthquake shook the Oriente, rupturing the vital oil pipeline and killing hundreds. Febres Cordero was forced to default on foreign debt repayments as the government coffers ran dry.

Faced with growing corruption scandals and accusations of human rights abuses, Febres

ABOVE: The river of Ecuadorian life flows along Quito's Avenida Amazonas. RIGHT: Plaza de la Independencia in the Old Town.

Cordero lost the 1988 election to Rodrigo Borja Cevallo, leader of the Izquierda Democrática (Democratic Left) Party. Despite Cevallo's policy of "gradualism" and his generally good record, inflation proved his undoing. In 1990, the Confederation of Indigenous Nations of Ecuador (CONAIE in its Spanish acronym) finally made its presence felt on the national stage. As waves of strikes paralyzed the country, CONAIE blocked roads and pressured the government to recognize indigenous rights and lands.

The government swung back to the right with the 1992 election of Sixto Durán Ballén. His modernization and austerity package

"mental incompetence" — a first, even in Latin American politics.

In a bizarre turn of events, three people claimed the presidency in February 1997: El Loco, his vice-president Rosalía Arteaga, and the leader of Congress, Fabián Alarcón. With crowds encamped at the presidential building, Bucaram finally resigned, fleeing to Panama. It is thought he personally pilfered several hundred million dollars during his term in office. Alarcón emerged from the crisis, but only just limped through amid more corruption scandals to the elections of 1998. Jamil Mahuad, the Harvard-educated mayor of Quito, won that election at the head of his centrist party.

proved hugely unpopular when fuel subsidies were abolished and consumer prices rocketed. Durán's administration also fell foul of various corruption scandals, culminating in his vice-president fleeing the country to avoid prosecution.

The hour of "El Loco" (The Madman), as Abdalá Bucaram (the nephew of Asaad) styled himself, had arrived. Bucaram was surprisingly swept to power in the 1996 elections, on a populist ticket in a campaign that included singing and gyrating on stage with scantily-clad women and promises to spend on the public sector. In office, however, he betrayed his leftist coalition. He pushed through harsh austerity measures, and lost most of his support with his bad-taste stunts. Corruption scandals involving his family also emerged, and Congress finally voted him out of office on grounds of

FROM THE SUCRE TO THE DOLLAR

Mahuad's economic woes were compounded by the disastrous impact of El Niño. The floods and storms not only killed hundreds of people and caused huge damage to the country's infrastructure, but also brought the vitally important banana industry to its knees. Economic growth slowed to zero. Amid rumors in early 1999 that Mahuad planned to peg the sucre to the dollar, the currency plummeted by 25 percent, as the President closed the banks to stem the withdrawing of deposits. Ugly scenes swept the country as general strikes and road blockades were put down by the military, often violently.

Mahuad pressed on, ending fuel subsidies and increasing utility prices overnight. In mid-1999, he froze US$8.6 billion of the country's bank deposits, sparking off another slew of strikes. CONAIE's supporters marched on the capital, while truckers and taxi drivers blockaded the highways, forcing Mahuad to delay the price hikes until December.

With the economy in tatters and the sucre devaluing daily, Mahuad made clear his plans to adopt the United States dollar as the national currency in January 2000. CONAIE took the news badly, quite rightly claiming that the move to the dollar would hit the country's indigenous, and by implication poorest, population hardest. By late January, thousands of *indígenas* had poured into the capital. The military eventually sided

various financial institutions has helped to offset the worst effects, but it is thought poverty is still on the increase.

Internally, one of the major issues concerns oil exploration in the Oriente and the rights of the local Indian populations. Others include the hike in sales tax, reforms of the public sector and transport subsidies. These are tough political issues that aren't likely to go away for some time. The effects of the United States-funded Plan Colombia ranks among the country's greatest worries. By 2001, refugees were ebbing over the Ecuador's northern border. Colombian guerillas and paramilitaries are active in the area, causing Ecuador to militarize further its borders. Left-

with the protesters, allowing them to storm the Congress on January 21. A "Junta of National Salvation" was announced, while Congress and the Supreme Court were suspended.

Congress, when back in session, controversially voted that Mahuad had abandoned his post. His vice-president, Gustavo Noboa, became Ecuador's sixth president in only four years. CONAIE agreed to Noboa's appointment but warned it would be back if he didn't improve the situation swiftly. In March, Noboa pushed through the dollarization legislation.

Since March 2000, the country has been rocked by various public-sector strikes demanding pay-raises, and by protesters calling for subsidies to offset the harsh effects of the dollarization process. Although there are signs of economic growth, prices have still risen while wages have stagnated. The US$2 billion aid package from

wing guerillas have held various oil workers hostage, and it's likely that tourism will decline in the northern provinces of Sucumbíos and Carchi, adversely affecting an already under-funded and remote part of the country. "Plan Condor," the hemispheric brother of Plan Colombia has also begun. The growth of United States' military base at Manta on the coast is increasingly controversial. The fear that Ecuador will become embroiled in its neighbor's troubles is very real — the last thing the country needs as it attempts to compete in the globalized economy of the twenty-first century.

OPPOSITE: Paintings by internationally known artist Oswaldo Guayasamín in his museum in Quito. ABOVE: Time out for a shoe shine in the backstreets of Quito's Old Town.

Andean Highlands

A twin chain of Andean mountains, the Avenue of Volcanoes, cuts through the center of Ecuador, from north to south, like the dislocated spine of some fossilized creature, each vertebra a volcanic peak. A series of wide, intensely cultivated, densely populated valleys lie between the parallel rows of mountains. These are the food baskets of Ecuador that for thousands of years have produced grain, fruit, vegetables and dairy products for the high Sierra. As you pass through the fertile highland basins you will see a panoramic patchwork of fields planted with all manner of crops. Stretching across some of these fields are huge plastic greenhouses used for one of the country's fastest-growing export businesses, the cultivation of flowers.

The Avenue of Volcanoes also cradles the main thoroughfare that runs up and down the spine of the country. For centuries local Quichua Indians and other *indígenas* have trudged this route, or ridden it on mules and donkeys, carrying crops from the fields and produce to market. So they do today, many still wearing traditional costumes of handwoven shawls and wide-brimmed hats and carrying huge loads on their backs. But more often these days they travel in cars, trucks or flashy, honking, dangerously speeding buses. Today this dusty, often pot-holed, sometimes smooth road that follows the ancient route is part of the rather grandly named Panamericana, or Pan-American Highway (theoretically it's possible to journey through North and Central American and down the South American continent without leaving the highway).

Traveling up and down the Panamericana (also known as "the Pana") through the Avenue of Volcanoes is a pleasure for any visitor who spends some time in Ecuador. To visit the famous tourist market at Otavalo, you pass north from Quito along the Panamericana by car or bus. To get to the popular spa resort of Baños you must go south through Ambato. If you want to stay at one of the fine haciendas of the Sierra you must take the road south or north. To go in another direction would mean hurtling down the steep slopes of the Andes, either towards the upper reaches of the Amazon Basin to the east, or to the coastal plain in the west. The Panamericana is indeed Ecuador's main transport artery.

For many foreign travelers the most dramatic and fascinating features of Ecuador are its mystical, majestic mountains. Some 30 peaks found in the vicinity of the Avenue of Volcanoes, some still smoldering, give the area one of the highest concentrations of volcanoes in the world. Much of the time these peaks are draped in swirling clouds and mists because, it is said, the mountains are shy and modest. But on a clear day the views over green fields to the snow-crowned peaks are spectacular.

At 6,310 m (20,702 ft), Chimborazo, Ecuador's tallest mountain, presides over the western chain of mountains, Cordillera Occidental. It was believed to be the tallest mountain in the world until Everest was surveyed in the mid-nineteenth century. Indeed, every Ecuadorian schoolchild knows that Chimborazo, which means "mountain of snow," is the world's tallest mountain if measured from the center of the earth — the earth bulges around the equator. The English climber, Edward Whymper was the first to climb Chimborazo, in 1880.

The tallest peak of the eastern, and geologically older, chain, Cordillera Central, is the stunning and almost perfectly symmetrical cone of Cotopaxi, which means "shining peak." At 5,897 m (19,347 ft), it is the world's tallest continuously active volcano. It has erupted some 50 times since 1738, and scars and lava flows from past volcanic activities can be seen in its vicinity. The 1877 eruption produced mudflows that traveled 100 km (62 miles). In 1997 people living near Cotopaxi reported that the snowcap was melting, fearing that the mountain would erupt again and destroy their homes and farms.

The upper part of Cotopaxi is permanently covered in snow and often hidden by clouds that at night are sometimes lit up by fires in the 360-m (1,180-ft) crater. The base of the volcano stands in open mountain grassland, the *páramo*, which is part of the bleak yet beautiful 34,000-ha (84,015-acre) Parque Nacional Cotopaxi. Only 50 km (31 miles) from Quito, this is Ecuador's most frequently visited national park. German scientist and traveler Wilhelm Reiss was first to climb Cotopaxi in 1872.

QUITO

Ecuador's capital, Quito is regarded as the most beautiful and stylish city in the Andes. Your first glance from the air, as you descend towards Aeropuerto Mariscal Sucre, reveals an urbanized, South American Shangri-La stretching along a high valley beneath a string of white-topped mountains. Taking a bus or taxi into town from the airport, you pass steel-and-glass office blocks, luxury hotels and shopping malls with supermarkets, fast food franchises and multiplex cinemas. At the same time you may experience the sickness of almost all major cities: traffic jams and pollution.

Further south, in the old part of the city, you come upon a world of cobbled streets, ornate baroque churches and colonial-style mansions with tiled roofs and quiet courtyards with tinkling fountains. You have now passed from the New

PREVIOUS PAGES: Fertile valley in the Andean highlands LEFT and local highland style RIGHT. OPPOSITE: Quito's Basílica del Voto Nacional towers above the streets of the Old Town.

Town to the Old. Together the old and new form a fast-growing, modern metropolis woven into the fabric of an old Spanish colonial town. On the sidewalks, office workers in smart suits talk on mobile phones, while local *indígenas* in colorful traditional costumes sell blankets, chewing gum ponchos, and lottery tickets. Million-dollar apartments owned by oil company executives and drug money launderers coexist with slums in impoverished barrios, where the poor and unemployed from the countryside live.

Aside from its high altitude, the most striking geographical feature of Quito is the length of the city and its bottleneck narrowness. From north to south it stretches some 30 km (19 miles), yet it is

only three to five kilometers (two to three miles) wide. To the north is the residential and business district of the New Town, to the south is an area of industry and low-cost housing, while at its heart is the historic center of the Old Town. This narrow strip of urbanized land is wedged between the steep slopes of Volcán Pichincha to the west and a deep canyon formed by the river Machángara to the east. In recent years the urban carpet has spread up the slopes of the mountain to the west and into the Los Chillos valley on the eastern side of the city.

Despite pollution in parts of the city at certain times of the day, Quito has an almost perfect climate best described as perpetual springtime. By midday the temperature usually reaches a pleasant high of about 22°C (72°F), while average nighttime temperatures are 11°C (52°F). Since the city is only a few miles south of the equator, there is little climatic variation through the year, though in the so-called winter months (October to May) it often rains in the afternoon. In spite of the agreeable climate, clouds often veil the surrounding mountain peaks. *Quiteños* say that they have two types of weather: either sunny with clouds, or cloudy with sunshine.

Old Town architecture.

In general, Quito's fine climate makes for good health and a feeling of well-being, but it takes most visitors a day or two to adjust to the altitude. At nearly 3,000 m (nearly 10,000 ft) above sea level, this is the third highest capital in the world, after La Paz in Bolivia and Lhasa in Tibet. You might find yourself out of breath carrying your luggage at the airport or walking up your first steep slope. Other symptoms of altitude sicknesses are headaches, nausea and lassitude. To deal with the problem, avoid alcohol and cigarettes, drink plenty of water, and lie down a lot. Almost everyone recovers quickly, but if you're not better within a day or two you're obviously not cut out for high altitudes, so cut your losses and head downhill.

Quito has all the attractions and amenities of most major cities. For tourists, the best-known and most useful area is Mariscal in the New Town, a series of streets running off and parallel to Avenida Río Amazonas, between the major cross-streets of Avenida Patria and Avenida Franciso de Orellana. Here you will find travel agencies, airlines, funky bars and restaurants, nightclubs, inexpensive hostels, the best and most expensive hotels, trendy galleries and exciting crafts and clothing shopping. Indeed, there is very little that Quito lacks. It even has its fair share of that common city blight, pickpockets, which means that visitors must take special care of themselves and their possessions at all times. In particular, it's advisable to avoid walking alone through the streets at night.

BACKGROUND

The takeover of the northern highlands around present-day Quito by the conquistadors was for the Spanish partly a matter of lucky timing. Only a few decades before the first Spaniards landed on the coast in 1526, many of the tribes of the area had been forced into the Inca Empire. At that time the far-flung empire itself was engaged in civil war as a result of rivalry between the two half-brothers, Atahualpa and Huáscar, respective leaders of the northern and southern territories. The Spanish exploited divisions among the Incas, murdered Atahualpa and won the support of the newly conquered tribes, who had no loyalty to their recently acquired Inca masters. In addition, Spanish firearms and cannons gave the "bearded white strangers" huge superiority in battle.

In 1534, Sebastián de Benalcázar, a lieutenant of the conquistador Francisco Pizarro, marched from the south up the spine of the Andes towards Quito. Near Riobamba, he and his cohorts met a huge Incan army, the largest Inca force ever gathered against the Spanish, which they managed to evade under the cover of night. Continuing north, the Spaniards gathered local tribespeople into their ranks and entered Quito in early December. They

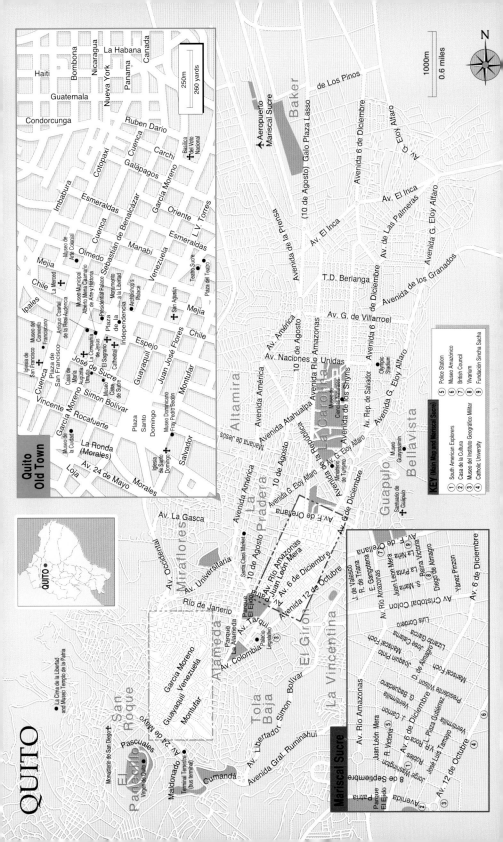

QUITO

Quito Old Town

KEY (Main Map and Mariscal Sucre)

① South American Explorers
② Casa de la Cultura
③ Museo del Instituto Geográfico Militar
④ Catholic University
⑤ Police Station
⑥ Museo Amazónico
⑦ British Council
⑧ Vivarium
⑨ Fundación Sincha Sacha

Mariscal Sucre

250m
260 yards

1000m
0.6 miles

N

skirmished with the Inca general, Rumiñahui (Face of Stone), who, realizing he was going to be defeated, burned down the Inca palace rather than leave it intact for the Spanish. On December 6, the Villa de San Francisco de Quito was officially founded on the ashes of the Inca town. Rumiñahui was captured, tortured and executed.

Though they retained the name Quito, which is derived from the Quitus, one of the tribes in the area, the Spanish lost no time in creating a new city in their own image. On the foundations of Inca houses they built their own churches and convents, monasteries and mansions, using Inca stones from the rubble for the floors and façades. Construction of the magnificent Iglesia de San Francisco began within weeks of the Spanish takeover, making it the oldest church in South America. In the traditional Spanish way, they built streets radiating from a main square in the center of the city, and they divided the city into 200 lots, one for each conquistador.

In order to embellish their grandiose buildings the Franciscans soon established the Quito School of Art (Escuela Quiteña), which was the first of its kind in South America. Local artists and craftsmen learned to make exquisite wooden polychrome sculptures and paintings, many of them characterized by savage Christian themes of martyrdom and mutilation. Quito's churches and museums contain a wealth of beautiful but gruesome renditions of Christ on the cross, and scenes of diabolical tortures that are part of a religious art movement that flourished throughout the Spanish colonial period. At the end of the sixteenth century, Quito became the seat of the royal Audencia, a governmental court, and was known as the "Cloister of America" because of the collection of religious edifices that occupied a quarter of the Old Town. In one square kilometer (a little over a third of a square mile) in the center of Old Quito there are 17 major Christian places of worship, while there are an estimated 86 churches in the whole city.

In 1978, UNESCO designated Old Quito as a World Heritage Site in recognition of the importance of its old colonial center. Development in the historic area became more strictly controlled, and a number of conservation projects were undertaken. There is still much to be done. Much of the Old Town suffers from deterioration, pollution, overcrowding, overuse and lack of sanitation and maintenance. From dawn to dusk, the city center is an overcrowded corridor for transporting people and goods between south and north. Leaded fuel turns the place into a veritable gas chamber, affecting everyone and everything.

Don't let such strong words put you off. Tourism is on the rise, and pickpockets seem to be on the decline. Although the Old Town has problems, its colonial architecture matches its splendid Andean setting like a jeweled pendant hanging from a magnificent mountain chain. The jewel might need some polishing, but tourists would do well to see Old Quito as more than a mere staging-post on the way to the Galápagos Islands.

GENERAL INFORMATION

There are three **Ministerio de Turismo** tourism offices in Quito E-MAIL ecuainfo@interactive.net (authorized) WEB SITE www.ecuaventura.com. The **main office** ((022) 224972 or (022) 507559, Avenida Eloy Alfaro 1214 and Carlos Tovar, is open between 8:30 AM and 5 PM, Monday to Friday, with a break for lunch. Similar hours apply for the office in the **Old Town** ((022) 514044, on the corner of Venezuela and Chile, but the **airport office** ((022) 246232, is open from 7 AM to 7 PM. Hotel reservations can be made from the offices in the Old Town and at the airport.

Independent travelers who want to get off the beaten track will find the nonprofit **South American Explorers (SAE)** (formerly known as the South American Explorers Club or SAEC) to be an excellent source of advice, information and up-to-date travel news, as well as a place to meet fellow travelers. Annual membership is US$50 for a single person and US$70 for a couple. For this outlay, members get a comfortable place to relax in a restored colonial building in central Quito, a good lending library and bookshop for maps and books about Ecuador, access to members' trip reports, knowledgeable and friendly staff, a mailing address and use of computers for e-mail, weekly talks and lectures, copies of the club's magazine, use of members' notice board, advice on where to stay, facilities for storing equipment, etc. They also organize weekly "walkabouts" of the Old Town, and trekking/climbing trips around the country.

The club's headquarters are in the United States ((607) 277-0488 TOLL-FREE (800) 274-0568 FAX (607) 277-6122 E-MAIL explorer@samexplo.org, 126 Indian Creek Road, Ithaca, New York 14850. (There are other clubhouses in Lima and Cuzco, Perú.) The SAE in Quito's New Town (/FAX (022) 225228 E-MAIL explorer@sae.org.ec is at Jorge Washington 311 and Plaza Leonidas, Mariscal Sucre (postal address: Apartado 21-431, Avenida Eloy Alfaro, Quito, Ecuador). The office is open from 9:30 AM to 5 PM, weekdays only. Nonmembers are allowed to visit once, but only members are allowed to use the facilities.

The **British Council** ((022) 508282 or (022) 540225 FAX (022) 223396 E-MAIL helpdesk@british council.org.ec WEB SITE www.britishcouncil.org/ecuador, at Amazonas N26-146 and La Niña, is

The Iglesia de San Francisco, dedicated to Quito's patron saint, is the city's largest colonial building and the oldest Christian structure in South America.

another well-known Quito institution. It includes book and video lending libraries, English-language newspapers, e-mail and Internet services, and a useful noticeboard. It also stages art events and has a good vegetarian café, La Galería. Non-members can use most of the facilities and the café, but there is an annual membership charge of about US$15 for each of the two libraries. The libraries and information services are open from 7 AM to noon and 3 PM to 8 PM, Monday to Friday. The Council can also organize Spanish courses. For more of these see SPECIAL INTERESTS, page 56 in YOUR CHOICE.

The **Ministerio del Ambiente** ((022) 548924 WEB SITE (for parks) www.ambiente.gov.ec is in the

monolithic building at the corner of Eloy Alfaro and Amazonas. It's pretty hard to get any sense from anyone there, but someone in the building will, eventually, be able to sell you books, leaflets and CD-ROMs about Ecuador's national parks and natural wonders. Good Spanish helps!

In an **emergency** dial (911 for the police, and (102 for the fire brigade. The best, English-speaking hospital is **Hospital Metropolitano** ((022) 265020, and among the best clinics is **Clinica Pichincha** ((022) 562408. English-speaking doctors include Wallace Swanson ((022) 449374 or (022) 470830, John Rosenberg ((022) 521104 and Renato León ((022) 238342 or (022) 552080.

For international and long distance domestic telephone calls, **Andinatel** has offices just west of the junction of Colón and Amazonas in the New Town (among others), Benalcázar and Mejía in the Old Town, at Terminal Terrestre and at the

airport. Cheaper "net-phones" are available in the Internet cafés listed below. See COMMUNICATION AND MEDIA, page 248 in TRAVELERS' TIPS for more information on calling from Ecuador.

Because Ecuador is such a great place for shopping, many travelers find themselves sending their new purchases home. If you're in this situation and are staying in the Mariscal area, go to the **post office** on the ground floor of the big, modern building at Reina Victoria and Colón. Don't seal your packages, and bring packing tape with you in case of inspection. The maximum weight is 20 kg (44 lb), and 70x30x30 cm (20x12x12 inches) is the maximum size. Another recommended Correo (post office) is Marítimo Aduana, on Ulloa 273 and Ramírez Dávalos, next to the Santa Clara market. Quito's two main post offices are on Espejo, between Guayaquil and Venezuela in the Old Town, and at Eloy Alfaro 354 and 9 de Octubre in the new. All poste restante mail for Quito goes to the Espejo branch unless marked "Correo Central, Eloy Alfaro." Post offices are open Monday to Friday 8 AM to 7 PM, and from 8 AM to noon weekends. But it's better to have mail sent to you care of SAE (see above) or care of American Express, Apartado 2605, Quito. A curious quirk of the Ecuadorian postal service, or an indictment of it, is that many *quiteños* use a private arrangement with Lufthansa, whereby mail with Ecuadorian postage can be dropped off at the airline office on 6 de Diciembre 955 and 18 de Septiembre to be sent on the next flight.

Mail and packages can also be sent by **FedEx** (Federal Express) ((022) 251356 or (022) 253552; **EMS** ((022) 543468 or (022) 569741, Eloy Alfaro and 9 de Octubre; **DHL** ((022) 556118, Colón 1333 and Foch, or ((022) 485100, Eloy Alfara and de los Juncos.

There is a plethora of **film and processing labs** on Amazonas. Among the best is Ecuacolor, near Roca. Also clustered around Amazonas are the most useful banks.

Topographical maps of Ecuador are available from the **Instituto Geográfico Militar** (IGM) E-MAIL igm@mil.ec, Venezuela 573 and Sucre (by the Casa Museo de Sucre, Old Town) or Senierges and Paz y Miño (above Parque El Ejido). They can also be ordered from abroad through WEB SITE www.bestdealecuador.com.

You won't find a shortage of computer terminals for **e-mail** in Quito. The greatest concentration is in what I have come to call "Gringolandia": the area around Juan León Mera and Calamá. Some are pretty basic no-frills affairs such as **Cybermania**, first floor, Amazonas 239 opposite Hotel HotHello, or the **Ecotrackers** headquarters further south. One of the best for speed and service is the popular **Papaya Net** at the corner of Juan León Mera and Calamá, or **Onda Cyber Café**, by the Maple II restaurant on Calamá. **Planeta Net** on Calamá, between Amazonas and Juan León

Mera, is also recommended for net phones. An hour of tapping shouldn't cost more than a dollar.

GETTING AROUND

Within Quito **bus** and **trolley** transportation is simple and inexpensive, but, as always, you must be careful with your bags and wallet. The relatively new trolley system, with its arched, glass-walled stops, runs along 10 de Agosto in the New Town and along Guayaquil and Montufar in the Old Town. A further route along 6 de Diciembre might be completed some time in the future. After running through the central corridor of the city, the trolleys branch off onto different routes to the suburbs. For the airport, take the trolley to Estación Norte and change to the Rumiñahui route heading north. At about US$0.20 per ride, the trolleys are inexpensive but still about twice the price of standard city buses. *Ejecutivo* bus services are a bit more expensive. Most buses run along the north–south city axis and have the name of their destination on a placard in the window: The No. 1 Aeropuerto bus goes to… well, where you would expect it to go.

Taxis are inexpensive compared to most other places in the world, but make sure that the driver uses his meter. If he claims it's broken, negotiate the fare beforehand or find another taxi. Don't be put off by horror stories of passengers being mugged by taxi drivers. Such rare incidents occur when the passenger is very drunk and/or it's an illegal cab. Only take the yellow cabs with a red taxi sign on top. Most taxi drivers are friendly, but if you don't like the look of one, don't get in the cab. If you want to be extra safe, only use cabs from lines outside major hotels. At night, taxi fares are up to 50 percent more than during the day, and fares are more prone to negotiation.

WHAT TO SEE AND DO

As the oldest and arguably the most beautiful city in the Andes, Quito has a wealth of attractions. The art and architecture of the Old Town is world renowned, the museums are a source of endless fascination, the shops and markets are a bargain-hunter's paradise, and Quito's nightlife is one of the world's best-kept secrets. A few days in Quito are enough to get a good taste of the city, but a lifetime isn't enough to decipher all its mysteries.

The first thing any visitor should do in Quito is to make a determined effort to take it easy. The excitement of a new place, limited time, high altitude dizziness and a desire to do everything at once may conspire to make you immediately want to rush out and explore the city. But altitude affects young and old, fit and unfit equally, so first let your body adjust to the thin air and subtle vibrations of this ancient mountain realm.

Walking the Old Town

Walking the streets, stopping where you fancy, and perhaps getting lost a few times is the best way to get the feel of a city. If you do this in Quito, however, don't bring anything of value with you, keep your camera hidden, and only bring a few dollars. Pickpocketing and bag slashing are special skills of the city. Generally speaking though, Quito isn't dangerous for tourists as long as you don't carry tempting targets for petty thieves. The less you have to lose, the safer and freer you will be. Don't walk about the Old Town alone at night, and take care wherever you are.

The best way to get a feel for the Old Town's geography is from on high. If coming from the New Town, consider making the neo-gothic **Basílica del Voto Nacional**, the highest church in the country, your first stop. Take the lift in the left tower up to the lookout terrace, where there's also a handy, if quirky, café, open 9:30 AM to 5 PM every day. From here, the Old Town with its dozens of spires and bell towers stretches across the valley, ending with the Panecillo Hill (topped by the Virgin). On clear mornings the views are simply breathtaking.

Looking across to the far left you'll see the small **Iglesia de San Blas**. It marks the northerly limit to the Old Town, and was one of the few churches open to Indians in colonial times. Slightly to the right of San Blas, downhill, you can make out the salmon-pink façade of one of the buildings on **Plaza del Teatro**. Coming out of the basilica, walk down Venezuela, past the wonderfully ornate carvings on the doors of the **El Carmen Bajo** church, and downhill and back one block to this restored square. It's dominated by the Corinthian columns of Quito's most ornate theater, **Teatro Sucre**, which hopefully should be up and running after restoration by the time you read this.

From the square, walk back along Guayaquil (once the street of wealthy commercial families) to the beautiful church of **San Agustín**, begun in the sixteenth century. Much of the church was rebuilt in the nineteenth century, but its dark interior and large canvases are still captivating. The adjoining convent boasts a lovely cloister, housing a museum of important paintings of the Escuela Quiteña on the second floor (open Monday to Friday 9 AM to noon, 3 PM to 5 PM, Saturday 8 AM to noon). In 1809, the first treaty of independence from Spain was signed here.

One block uphill on the crowded, pedestrian Chile, you come to **Plaza de la Independencia** (known locally as Plaza Grande). The square is overlooked by a number of distinguished civic buildings and is the setting for the Victorian-style **Monumento a la Libertad** (Liberty Monument) in the midst of palms and flowerbeds, old men and children, shoe-shiners and benches. The **Presidential Palace**, the **Archbishop's Palace**, the modern **City Administration Building** and the **cathedral** command the locus of the Old Town, yet much of the real power of the city has long since moved northwards to the New Town where most banks, big business and embassies are now located. Many of the big old mansions in the Old Town, once home to the rich and famous, are now tatty, rundown, divided up and rented to tenants. The cathedral, though grand and imposing from the outside, is a disappointment inside, despite guarding the tomb of Grand Marshal Sucre and being the site of the poisoning of the city's bishop in 1877.

You can poke your head inside the Presidential Palace, also known as the **Government Palace**, and glimpse a huge mural of Francisco de Orellana cruising down the Amazon. Echoing Quito's pride in this event, a sign on the cathedral's wall proclaims "Quito's Glory is the discovery of the Amazon River." Fittingly, since Orellana and Gonzalo Pizarro set off to find El Dorado, the lettering is in gold. It is not surprising that Ecuadorians resent the fact that a large chunk of the territory through which the great river flows, which once belonged to Ecuador, is now part of Perú.

Heading west along García Moreno you pass the cathedral's main chapel, the beautiful **El Sagrario**, which has recently been restored and is now an independent church. Further along you'll come to the magnificent volcanic-stone façade of **La Compañía de Jesús**, considered to be the loveliest church in Ecuador. Built by the Jesuits, it was only just completed before their expulsion in 1767. Its massive altars, baroque columns and ceilings are laden with tons of gold leaf, though some of its most precious treasures are kept in the vault of Banco Central and only displayed on festival days. It has been undergoing thorough restoration over the last years, but its exuberance and extravagance are still incomparable in Quito, and perhaps Latin America.

On the church's corner, walk up Sucre (once "Cotton Street") to the cobble-clad expanse of **Plaza de San Francisco**. On its far side stands the huge **Iglesia de San Francisco**, South America's oldest church, begun soon after the city was founded, in 1536. Though much of it has been extensively rebuilt after earthquake damage, the complex is still the largest of its type on the continent, reflecting the great powers enjoyed by the religious orders in colonial times. The church's interior rivals that of La Compañía, with more gold leaf than a conquistador could have dreamed of. Highlights include the unique carving of the winged Virgin by Bernardo de Legarda, and the altar and paintings of **La Capilla de Cantuña**, an adjoining chapel.

To the right of the church as you face its twin bell-tower is the **Museo del Convento Franciscano** ((022) 211124, open Monday to Saturday 9 AM to 6 PM, Sunday 9 AM to noon. Guided tours (ask for English) take you around the excellent collection of paintings, furniture and sculpture found in the beautiful cloisters, which once housed the city's Escuala de Artes e Oficios — you'll note the remnants of the pupil's paintings on the walls. The tour also includes a visit to the church's choir with its fantastic *mudéjar* (Moorish) ceiling, whose symmetrical patterns and gold leaf seem to float off up to heaven.

A good place to recharge your batteries or grab a light lunch is the café and *artesanía* shop at the foot of the church's steps, Tianguez (see WHERE TO EAT, page 95). Revived, you're now ready for the Old Town's best museums. Walk south on Cuenca or Benalcázar and turn downhill on Rocafuerte. Pass under the Arco de la Reina arch at the corner by the **Carmen Alto** church, and on García Moreno lies the **Museo de la Ciudad** ((022) 283882, which is open 9:30 AM to 5:30 PM Tuesday to Sunday. The Old Town's newest museum, it's aimed at foreigners and Ecuadorians alike, imparting a dynamic and occasionally interactive view of the city's social history, from its prehistoric inhabitants to the present day. The museum is housed within the beautiful Hospital San Juan de Dios, where the poor and sick were cared for until it closed 1974. It gives an excellent feel for the day-to-day lives of *quiteños*, from candle-makers and forgers through to artists and artisans. Also of note is the gruesome display of self-torturing implements owned by the city's saint, Mariana de Jesús, and the extraordinary series of three large canvases depicting the Conquest by contemporary artist Jaime Zapata. Guided tours are available in English.

For more of the city and its inhabitants' lives, the **Casa de María Augusta Urrutia** ((022) 580107 on García Moreno and the **Casa de Sucre** (022) 952860 both do a fine job. The former, open Tuesday to Sunday 9 AM to 5 PM, was donated to the Fundación Mariana de Jesús by its owner, Doña María after her death in 1987. Guided tours around the nineteenth-century house with its three patios offer a wonderful peek at the high-society world of Quito, with its European furniture, sewing rooms, drawing rooms and *salóns*. The house of the dashing liberator Grand Marshal Antonio José de Sucre (Calle Sucre at the corner of Venezuela; open Tuesday to Saturday 8:30 AM to 4:30 PM) is another fine late-colonial house. Though much of the exhibits pertain to military history, there are also many impressive examples of period furniture and paintings.

The **Plaza de Santo Domingo** lies to the south-east of Sucre's house. The square, enigmatically floodlit at night, is dominated by the **Iglesia de**

Santo Domingo, one of Quito's earliest. The interior and altar were redesigned in the nineteenth century, and pretty much ruined it, though the Chapel of the Rosary to the right of the altar is still a delight, and the adjoining **Museo Fray Pedro Bedón** showcases many beautiful Dominican treasures from the sixteenth to eighteenth centuries. It's open daily from 8 AM to 5 PM.

At the western corner of the square at Guayaquil, one of the town's most picturesque streets, **La Ronda**, loops down. The name comes from either the Spanish "rondar" (to patrol) (it once marked the city's southern limit) or was so named because it was once famous for its serenading musicians. Though rather rundown and unsafe

Escuela Quiteña (School of Quito), including a striking Virgen de los Dolores by Caspicara. At the time of writing, the museum was due to be restored and some of the collection rehoused, but usual hours are Tuesday to Friday 10 AM to 6 PM, and Saturday 10 AM to 2 PM. For more weeping Virgins and bleeding Christs, the nearby **Casa de Benalcázar** ((022) 288102 houses a worthy collection on Benalcázar and Olmedo, though the beautiful courtyard and restored house are arguably more appealing. Lunchtime concerts are sometimes held in the courtyard, and the museum opens Monday to Friday 9 AM to noon and 2 PM to 6 PM.

The last noteworthy museum in the Old Town is the **Antiguo Cuartel de la Real Audencia** ((022)

these days, there are some charming Spanish-style houses with balconies, reminiscent of Barrio Santa Cruz in Seville, with tile portraits of famous composers and musicians adorning some of the houses' walls.

The other delightful museums and streets of old Quito are found to the north of Plaza de San Francisco. At Cuenca and pedestrian Chile stands the **Iglesia La Merced**, built to commemorate the eruptions of Volcán Pichincha that threatened to destroy the city. Paintings amid the pink, white and gold-leaf extravaganza inside show scenes of erupting volcanoes. The cloisters of the adjoining convent are especially beautiful. One block across, at the corner Cuenca and Mejía, lies the **Museo Nacional de Arte Colonial** ((022) 212297. This stylish colonial mansion, once the home of the Marqués de Villacís, contains a good collection of work by some of the best artists of the

214018, which isn't well signposted and therefore is hard to find. It's on Espejo 1147 and Benalcázar, just off the Plaza de la Independencia, open Tuesday to Friday 8 AM to 4 PM, and 9 AM to 2 PM weekends. The house has undergone various incarnations: as a Jesuit mansion, barracks *(cuartel)* of the Spanish garrison, and then as municipal offices. The collection displays many fine paintings of the Escuela Quiteña. In what used to be prison cells in the basement, a gory waxworks made in France depicts the execution of nationalist martyrs in 1809, who were imprisoned here for nine months.

Walking the Old Town, you can't help but notice the large statue on its westerly hill, the **Panecillo** ("little loaf of bread"). Crossing the large Avenida 24 de Mayo, you come to the foot of the

Religious souvenirs are popular with Catholic visitors who come from all over the country to see Quito's magnificent churches.

Andean Highlands

hill, formerly a sacred Inca site for sun worship. Today the hill is dominated by the huge, winged statue of the **Virgen de Quito** trampling on a dragon, the city's most prominent landmark. It's a stiff, half-hour walk up to the statue; it's advisable to take a taxi up from the Old Town, not just to save your breath but because there have been a number of violent robberies on the path. Ask the driver to wait while you survey the white mosaic of the city below. Also highly recommended close by, the restored **Monasterio de San Diego** on Calicuchima 117 and Farfán, lies to the west of Panecillo hill. Visitors, who have to ring the doorbell to get attention, are given a guided tour of the monastery complex and the monks' quarters. The famous painting of Christ eating *cuy* (guinea pig) for his Last Supper is one of the highlights of the visit.

The other great spot to admire the town is where Gran Mariscal Sucre won the decisive battle for independence on the slopes of Volcán Pichincha on May 24, 1822. The **Museo Templo de la Patria** (open Tuesday to Friday 8 AM to 4 PM, Saturday 8 AM to 1 PM, Sunday 10 AM to 3 PM) now marks the victory spot. Along with military and historical artifacts, there is an impressive mural by Eduardo Kingman and an eternal flame in honor of those killed in the battle. From the adjoining monument, **La Cima de la Libertad** (Summit of Victory) there is a splendid view of Quito. As with the Panecillo, it's probably safest to take a taxi up and ask the driver to wait for you.

New Town Sights

Parque La Alameda marks the beginning of the New Town. At its southern end stands a dashing statue of Simón Bolívar. At the park's heart, the **Quito Observatory**, the oldest on the continent and still in use, can be visited on Saturday mornings. On Juan Montalvo, by the park, the **Palacio Legislativo** is where elected representatives debate national issues and in which outgoing president, Abdalá Bucaram, barricaded himself in an unsuccessful bid to hold on to power in 1997.

Just beyond the government building, **Parque El Ejido**, Quito's biggest downtown park, is a good spot to take a break, maybe have an ice-cream or a hot sweet potato, and watch a game of football or volleyball. This is a popular spot for *quiteños*, especially on weekends when an open-air art market descends on the northern end of the park. It's also a transition point from the Old to the New Town. From here traffic and pedestrians flow down the wide Avenida Río Amazonas, which is lined with sidewalk cafés, modern shopping malls, luxury hotels, tourist shops, restaurants, travel agents and trendy bars.

If there is any meaning to the concept of the one-unmissable-city-sight, I would say that in Quito it's the **Casa de la Cultura** museum complex, housed in its striking circular building, largely made of glass, in the Parque El Ejido on the corner of Avenida Patria and 12 de Octubre. As part of the complex, the **Museo Nacional del Banco Central del Ecuador** is a great place to start any exploration of Ecuador. It offers a wide cultural and artistic perspective on Ecuador's proud history — and some exhibits, such as an extraordinary ceremonial gold mask, will make your chin drop. Most impressive of the bank's museums is the **Sala de Arqueología**, with its dioramas and well-displayed artifacts from the pre-ceramic era (4000 BC) through the end of the Inca era (AD 1533). Techniques for working gold and platinum were astoundingly advanced for their times. Also fascinating is the uncanny similarity of some of the museum's objects to those found in Asia, and in Japan in particular, which leads to speculation that in ancient times there were links between the cultures across the Pacific Ocean. As for Incan gold itself, in the **Sala de Oro**, nobody can fail to be impressed by the beauty and sheer weight of the body adornments. Though not to be condoned, it is hardly surprising that the Spanish became carried away in their cruel quest for El Dorado. Further sections on colonial, Republican and contemporary art give a quite different perspective on Ecuadorian culture, as do the separate Casa de la Cultura museums of musical instruments, Ecuadorian art (particularly Eduardo Kingman's *indigenismo* canvases) and traditional dress from indigenous cultures. Hours at the **Banco Central museums** ((022) 223259 are Tuesday to Friday, 9 AM to 5 PM; Saturday to Sunday, 10 AM to 3 PM. Hours at **Casa de la Cultura museums** ((022) 565808 are Tuesday to Friday, 10 AM to 6 PM; Saturday and Sunday, 10 AM to 3 PM. The cultural complex also has a movie theater and a concert hall.

More masters of the Escuela Quiteña are exhibited at an excellent little museum attached to the Catholic University on 12 de Octubre, opposite Calle J. Carrión, a short walk northeast from the park. The main focus of **Museo de Jacinto Jijón y Caamaño** ((022) 529240 or (022) 529250, extension 128 or 242, is the archaeological collection bequeathed by the estate of the renowned eponymous Ecuadorian archaeologist. It is open weekdays 9 AM to 4 PM.

Back south of the Casa de la Cultura, you'll find the **Museo del Instituto Geográfico Militar**, which includes a geographical museum and a planetarium with shows several times a day. The Ecuadorian military make excellent and detailed country maps that are on sale at the institute, which is open Monday to Friday, 8 AM to 4:30 PM. The institute is on top of a hill at the end of Paz and Miño southeast of Parque El Ejido. Take a taxi or hike up the hill and don't forget to bring your passport, which you have to leave at the gate.

Entrance to the museum is free, but there is a small charge for the planetarium.

The other museum not to be missed in the New Town is the outstanding **Museo Guayasamín** ((022) 446455 or (022) 452938, José Bosmediano 543, Bellavista, a cultural multiplex covering pre-Columbian, colonial and contemporary art but on a smaller, more personal scale than the Banco Central or Casa de la Cultura. The best of the museum is the powerful, harrowing paintings of the internationally known artist, Oswaldo Guayasamín, while the pre-Columbian and colonial sections belonged to his private collection. The museum is housed in a private compound in the exclusive Bellavista area of the city, and the

the Amazon river and across the South American continent to the Atlantic, making him the first to complete such an odyssey. From here you get a sense of the scale of the "earthly paradise" of South America, as Christopher Columbus put it, "which no one can enter except by God's leave." A statue of Orellana stands far above the church, on Larrea at the end of González Suárez. Ask your taxi driver to drop you off here, and walk down the winding cobbled streets to the sanctuary. Walking clockwise round the church, past the university, you'll find a small, friendly café called El Patio, which gets lively on evenings at the end of the week, when Guápulo's bohemians and arty types come out to play.

pretty garden is embellished with Guayasamín's bronze sculptures. High-quality prints, posters and jewelry are for sale. The museum is open 9:30 AM to 1 PM and 3 PM to 6:30 PM, Monday to Friday, and 9:30 AM to 1 PM on Saturdays. To get there, either walk, take a taxi, or take the a Bellavista-bound bus from the junction of 6 de Diciembre and Eloy Alfaro.

While up in the hills, you could consider combining Guayasamín with one of my favorite Quito churches. It stands in the old village of Guápulo, right on the edge of the city looking down over Los Chillos valley. Peace and tranquility pervade the seventeenth-century **Santuario de Guápulo** with its beautiful paintings and sculpture and a superb carved pulpit (open 8 AM to 11 AM and 3 PM to 6 PM, or ask for the caretaker's house). From this church Francisco de Orellana set off on the expedition that eventually took him down

Another unusual institute in the New Town, which appeals to those who love reptiles, is the **Vivarium** ((022) 210863 or (022) 230988, on Reina Victoria 1576 and Santa María in the heart of the Mariscal tourist area, a living showcase of many of the species found in Ecuador. These include deadly fer-de-lances and anacondas, as well as iguanas, turtles and tortoises. The slinky beauties welcome visitors every day except Mondays, but take a rest at lunchtime. Call ahead to view them.

The best natural history museum in Ecuador, but sadly not equal to the splendor of the country's wildlife, is the **Museo de Ciencias Naturales** ((022) 449824 on the east side of Parque La Carolina on Rumipamba 341 and Los Shyris.

The colonial art section of the Museo Guayasamín in Quito, run by Oswaldo Guayasamín, Ecuador's best-known painter.

It is open Monday to Friday 8:30 AM to 4 PM, and weekend mornings.

Unfortunately, Indian tribes from the Amazon aren't well represented in Quito's museums. The **Museo Amazónico** ((022) 432915, located at 12 de Octubre 1430 and Wilson, has a small but interesting collection of weapons, costumes, artifacts, photographs, videos and books on Indian cultures. It is open mornings and afternoons from Monday to Friday, but closed at lunch time. The collection is housed within the Abya-Yala building, which includes an unsurpassed bookshop on indigenous issues (mainly in Spanish). The museum of the **Fundación Sincha Sacha** ((022) 230609, a nonprofit organization supporting Amazonian cultures on Reina Victoria 1780 and La Niña, has ethnographic artifacts, information on the peoples of the rainforest, as well as a gift shop. It is open all day from Monday to Friday, the gift shop from 10 AM to 6 PM Saturday.

SHOPPING

It won't take you long in the Mariscal district to realize you've come to the right place for souvenirs and handicrafts. The main area runs around Amazonas and Juan León Mera. **Galería Latina**, Juan León Mera 823 (next to Libri Mundi, see below), is one of the more expensive, but very high-quality stores, as is **Almacén Folklore Olga Fisch** in the Hilton Colón. Cheaper is **Hilana**, 6 de Diciembre and Luís Cordero, with wonderful woolen products. Other recommend stores along Juan León Mera include the **Centro Artesanal** and **La Bodega**.

The best bookstore from a tourist's perspective is **Libri Mundi** WEBSITE www.librimundi.com, with its main branch on Juan León Mera 851 and Veintimilla. The staff are extremely knowledgeable and helpful, and they stock a wide selection of English- and Spanish-language books (and magazines) on Ecuador that will supplement this guidebook. The other important bookstore is **Mr. Books** in the El Jardín mall at Amazonas and Avenida de la República (also good for general shopping). The **SAE** (see GENERAL INFORMATION, page 82), which also stocks new and old guidebooks to South America, runs a book exchange and a library.

WHERE TO STAY

Where to stay in Quito will be one of your most significant decisions on a trip to Ecuador. The capital is the tourist and transportation hub of the country, and the base from which to make various excursions to the highlands, the rainforest, the pacific coast or the Galápagos Islands. Visitors often find themselves coming in and out of Quito several times, so their hotel becomes a home

base. Obviously it's important that it's a comfortable establishment where you receive a friendly welcome, where messages are kept for you and where you can leave excess luggage you don't want to take on the road.

It's also important that your hotel is in a relatively safe area, which is why most of the establishments recommended here are in the New Town. The majority are in the Mariscal quarter because this is the most popular place for tourists, where the best shops, restaurants and hotels are located. There aren't many places to go in the Old Town after 9 PM and walking back at night, alone, is not my idea of fun. However, accommodation in the Old Town is far cheaper, and certainly more adventurous.

There are many hotels that offer excellent value for money. However prices tend to vary from published rates according to season and your personal negotiation skills. Whether or not the 10 percent tax and 10 percent service charge are included in the price of the room should be established before making reservations. Prices given here are for foreigners, as opposed to the cheaper rate for nationals.

The fact that a hotel isn't included in this listing is no indication that it is below standard. To the best of my knowledge all the hotels listed, except some of the less expensive hostels, have English-speaking staff, direct-dial phones and facilities for storing luggage. For price brackets, see ACCOMMODATION, page 248 in TRAVELERS' TIPS.

Very Expensive

By far the most expensive hotel in Quito, the **Hilton Colón International** ((022) 560666 FAX (022) 563903 E-MAIL reserv@hiltoncolon.com WEB SITE www.hilton.com dominates the corner of Avenida Río Amazonas and Patria in the New Town. Facilities of the swank 450-room hotel, popular with *le tout* Quito, include a pool, sauna and gymnasium, a business center and everything else you expect from a modern first-class hotel. The views from the luxurious rooms over the Alameda park are pretty unbeatable, not unlike the high prices.

Following in the Hilton's marble wake, up the hill from the Mariscal district is **Swissôtel** ((022) 566497 or (022) 567600 FAX (022) 568080 WEB SITE www.swissotel.com, 12 de Octubre 1820 and Cordero, New Town. A casino, swimming pool and excellent restaurants are part of the deal, popular with those who choose the most expensive on principle. Nonresidents can while away an evening at the plush casino, enjoying drinks on the house for minimum bets of a few dollars. The hotel often promotes special rates worth investigating.

The **Marriott** (/FAX (022) 972000 E-MAIL anamarriott@hotmail.com WEBSITE www.marriott.com is one of Quito's newest hotels, housed in a pretty horrific glass and concrete carbuncle at the traffic circle of Orellana and Amazonas, New Town. Once inside, it exudes luxury, and though catering mainly to the business traveler it provides all the services and facilities the upscale traveler might need, including an outdoor pool, saunas, cafés, shops and a travel agency. Reserve a room with a view of Pichincha. For something with more character but further away from Mariscal, the **Hotel Dann Carlton** ((022) 249008 FAX (022) 448807 E-MAIL hdanp@mail.waccom.net.ec, Avenida República de El Salvador and Irlanda, New Town, styles itself as an "English hotel" — whatever that is. Rooms are comfortable and appealing with all mod-cons, the staff are friendly, and prices include breakfast and use of the spa.

At the opposite end of the spectrum from these more business-focused hotels, and catering more to the romantic couple, the **Mansión del Ángel** ((022) 557721 FAX (022) 237819, Wilson E-29, New Town, is a Liberace symphony to brocade, four-posters, fluffy towels and gold leaf. Set in a centrally located refurbished mansion, bursting with antiques and covered in parquet floors, the Mansión prides itself on personalized attention and sofas to sink into. The price includes a full Continental breakfast served among the plants, flowers and statuary of their roof garden.

Expensive

At the top end of this category, the popular **Hotel Sebastián** ((022) 2232400 FAX (022) 222500 E-MAIL hsebast1@hsebastian.com.ec is neatly located on Almagro 822 and Cordero, New Town. With wooden balconies looking like apartments in an alpine resort, the 50 European-style rooms exude plenty of atmosphere, and the staff are very friendly. The fruit and vegetables served in their café and restaurant are all organically grown, and they employ biodegradable soaps in all laundry — unique in Quito. Also at the top end price-wise, the **Alameda Real** ((022) 562345 FAX (022) 565759 E-MAIL apartec@uio.satnet.net, Roca 653 and Amazonas, New Town, feels a bit stuck in the 1980s, but its suite-sized rooms with bar or kitchenettes, some with computer terminals, are popular with business people and upmarket tour groups. Its location is excellent.

Just creeping into this price range, but probably at the top of anyone's list, comes **Hotel Café Cultura** (/FAX (022) 224271 or (022) 558858 E-MAIL infocc@cafecultura.com WEB SITE www.cafecultura .com, Robles 513 and Reina Victoria, New Town. The 26-room hotel occupies a beautiful colonial mansion, replete with three open fires, colorful murals and comfy leather sofas. The building, which once housed the French Cultural Center, is seeped in atmosphere, comfort and style. Rooms range from singles to family suites, and

are all decorated individually, so take a tour to choose one that suits you (the best are on the two lower floors). The hotel also runs a useful travel service where they can make reservations with other unique establishments around the country, as well as help with the basics. They even serve an authentic English cream tea, complete with fresh cream, jam and scones, for the equivalent of about £1.50 — surely the world's best cream tea deal.

Café Cultura now enjoys some competition in the "converted old house" stakes, though among the following you swap tranquility for centricity. Among the best, **La Cartuja** ((022) 523577 FAX (022) 226391, Plaza Leonidas 180, New

Town, includes a dozen brightly decorated rooms ringing a garden patio within an old mansion, but there's also **Hostal Los Alpes** ((022) 561110 FAX (022) 561128 E-MAIL alpes@accessinter.net, Tamayo 23, New Town, which has warm and comfortable rooms inside a converted house, with a recommend restaurant attached. An equally well-run establishment, though lacking in the mansion-feel, is **Hostal Villa Nancy** ((022) 550839 FAX (022) 562483 E-MAIL npelaez@pi.pro.ec WEB SITE www.villa-nancy.com, Muros 146, east of the Mariscal district in New Town. The staff are bilingual and excellent. There is a garden and rates include magazines, breakfast and use of the sauna, adding to the attraction of the very comfortable rooms.

People from Tigua, near Latacunga, sell their paintings on the streets of Quito.

Moderate

On tree-lined Juan Rodríguez at the corner of Diego de Almagro in New Town, the **Apart-Hotel Antinéa** ((022) 506838 FAX (022) 504404 E-MAIL hotelant@access.net.ec WEB SITE www.hotelantinea .com bills itself as a piece of France in Quito, and although I failed to spot any tricolors or strands of garlic, it's certainly very comfortable with some charming decor, a good restaurant, and friendly staff. The price includes breakfast, and there are plenty of cozy social areas. In complete contrast style-wise, the recommended **Hot Hello** (/FAX (022) 565835 E-MAIL othello@cometoecuador.com WEB SITE www.cometoecuador.com/othello, on Amazonas N20-20 and 18 de Septiembre, New Town, is modern, clean and efficiently run. Some rooms give on to busy Amazonas, but don't suffer from too much noise pollution, and the price includes breakfast in their ground-floor café and a free shoe-cleaning service.

For the mansion feel without the empty-pocket feel, **Palm Garden** ((022) 523960 FAX (022) 568944, on 9 de Octubre 923 and Cordero, New Town, has a beautiful restaurant, bar and gardens, good service and well-appointed rooms. Although not housed within a mansion, **La Casa Sol** ((022) 230798 FAX (022) 223383 E-MAIL info@lacasasol .com WEB SITE www.lacasasol.com, Calamá 127 and 6 de Diciembre, New Town, does offer spotless rooms and a bright and breezy feel. It is consistently recommended. The high season rate just pushes it into this moderate bracket, but it does include breakfast.

The **Magic Bean** ((022) 566181 E-MAIL magic@ ecuadorexplorer.com WEB SITE www.ecuador explorer.com/magic/home, Foch 681 and Juan León Mera, New Town, is a well-known Quito hangout for the well-scrubbed backpacker prepared to pay a little extra for comfort and cleanliness. The accommodation is limited however, so reserve in advance. Spick and span doubles with attractive pine furniture and private bathrooms fall within the moderate bracket, whereas a bed in their dormitory room costs about US$8. Prices include breakfast at their recommended restaurant/café.

If you fancy waking up to the hustle and bustle of Quito, as opposed to another gringo face, the Old Town provides more character than the New Town, and can be fun for a night or two. The main problems are security and finding somewhere to eat at night. The only hotel with moderate prices here is the **Hotel Real Audencia** ((022) 950590 FAX (022) 580213 E-MAIL realaudi@hoy.net, at the northern corner of Plaza Santo Domingo at Bolívar 220, Old Town. Rooms are clean, comfortable and airy, but make sure you ask for one giving onto the square. The hotel includes a decent restaurant and bar, so you don't have to wander the streets at night.

Inexpensive

The good news is that there are a large number of inexpensive and excellent-value hostels in Quito — new ones keep popping up all the time. The bad news is that some of them are grubby, small-roomed, thin-walled and unsanitary. Those mentioned all have some positive attributes but aren't necessarily perfect in every way. Most of them have luggage storage and kitchen facilities and are good places to meet and exchange information with other travelers.

Among the best, and established since the late 1980s, is the **Posada del Maple** ((022) 544507 or (022) 237375 admin@posadadelmaple.com WEB SITE www.posadadelmaple.com (very useful), Juan Rodriguez E8-49 and 6 de Diciembre, New Town. Rooms vary in size, quality and price, so look around, but the general feel is friendly. It has a pleasant inner courtyard, terrace, an "Esmeraldeña" restaurant and an Internet café, and provides use of the kitchen. English is *not* spoken. Other consistently recommended places in this price range are **Hostal Camila's** (/FAX (022) 225412, 6 de Diciembre 1329 and Roca, New Town, run by a friendly couple, and the more modern **Hostal Charles Darwin** ((022) 234323 FAX (022) 529384 E-MAIL chdarwin@ecuanex.net.ec WEB SITE www.ecuanex.net.ec/hostal_darwin, in a quiet location on Colina 304 and Orellana, New Town, which includes breakfast in the rate. Both offer kitchen and storage facilities. Another quiet option, the **Casona de Mario** (/FAX (022) 230129 E-MAIL lacasona@punto.net.ec WEB SITE www.exploring ecuador.com/turismo/hoteles, at the corner of Andalucía 213 and Galicia, New Town, offers a range of good-value doubles and larger rooms in a house that has an attractive garden and amiable owners.

Before getting to the backpacker joints, some newer places offer excellent value. Among them is **Titisee Residence** ((022) 529063, Foch 535 and Reina Victoria, New Town, which feels very autochthonous in taste but is nevertheless absolutely spotless and perfectly comfortable. Similar, and popular with Israeli travelers, the **Gan Eden** ((022) 223480 E-MAIL ganeden163@hotmail.com, Pinto E8-24 and 6 de Diciembre, New Town, only offers five bedrooms (so reserve), with a mix of very clean and neat doubles with or without bath, as well as a modest restaurant and a lounge. Of the numerous other hotels of this ilk, the **Hostal Bask** ((022) 503456 E-MAIL hostalbask@latinmail.com WEB SITE www.hostalbask.ca.ec, Lizardo García E7-49 between Diego de Almagro and Reina Victoria, New Town, is pink, bright and breezy, offering singles, doubles and triples, kitchen facilities and a lounge area at very competitive prices.

At real budget level, **Hostal El Taxo** ((022) 225593 E-MAIL hostaleltaxo@yahoo.com located at Foch 909 and Cordero, New Town, is run by an enthusiastic Italian. It has plenty of artwork dotted about, a bamboo patio and a bohemian feel. The hostel offers either dormitory beds or double rooms with shared baths, and encourages long-term stays. **El Centro del Mundo** (/FAX (022) 229050, Lizardo García 569 and Reina Victoria, New Town, should perhaps be renamed "El Centro del Mochilero" ("backpacker"), providing the archetypal combination of good music, a party room, futons, a sun deck and stacks of information. Other haunts on the gringo trail are the acceptable-for-the-price **Hostal Tortuga Verde** ((022) 556829 FAX (022) 227882 E-MAIL tortuga_verde@lycos.de, at the corner of Juan León Mera and Pinto, New Town, above the El Bacalao bar-restaurant; **Dagui's**

((022) 228151 E-MAIL davidcando@hotmail.com, Calamá E6-05 and Juan León Mera, New Town, which also includes a café, bar and Internet service; and finally, the nearby **Crossroads** ((022) 234735 E-MAIL crossrds@uio.satnet.net, at the corner of Foch and Juan León Mera, New Town, which is overpriced for doubles, but good value for a bed in a dormitory room.

The best deal in the Old Town, with plenty of Old World charm, is the inexpensive **Hotel San Francisco de Quito** ((022) 951241 E-MAIL hsfquito @impsat.net.ec, Sucre 217 and Guayaquil, Old Town, with rooms (with baths) set around a lovely patio with a fountain. Another converted old building houses the **Viena Hotel Internacional** ((022) 954860 FAX (022) 954633 E-MAIL vienaint @uio.satnet.net, Flores 600, Old Town, which has seen better days, but is still acceptable with its neat, carpeted rooms (some with balconies) ringing a

flower-filled patio. Rates are inexpensive. In the same price category, without the charm, but with clean rooms with bath, **Huasi Continental** ((022) 957327, also on Flores at 332, Old Town, looks better on the inside than it does from the outside, and is very cheap. If you absolutely have to have a room with a view, few in Quito beat the **Hostal Residencial Sucre** ((022) 954025 on the corner of Plaza de San Francisco and Bolívar 615, Old Town. The hotel is really pretty beaten up but acceptable for the low price, if you get the view.

If you're arriving at the Terminal Terrestre de Cumandá and don't want to head into the New Town, there are a bevy of hotels in the surrounding streets. Among the best is **Hostal Cumandá** ((022) 516984, Morales 449, with clean and tidy rooms, though avoid the noisy ones on the terminal side. Cheaper still is **La Posada Colonial** ((022) 282859 FAX (022) 505240, Paredes 188, which isn't particularly colonial, but is friendly and clean.

Apartment Hotels

For long stays, you can chose between a room with shared facilities, or else fully furnished service apartments with television, laundry, etc. Many of them are very popular, so book well in advance. A good place to start looking for one is the Sunday (but also other days) edition of *El Comercio*, or else the notice boards at the SAE, the British Council, or the various cybercafés in Mariscal. For backpacker prices and feel, a recommended option is **Alberto's House** ((022) 224603 E-MAIL albertohouse@hotmail.com, García 648, which includes laundry facilities, a lounge and a pool table among shared bathrooms. The better fully furnished apartments include **Apart-Hotel Amaranta** ((022) 560585 FAX (022) 560586, Plaza Leonidas 194, and **Residencial Casa Oriente** ((022) 546157, Yaguachi 824 and Llona, close to Parque La Alameda. Rates run around US$100 to US$150 per month.

WHERE TO EAT

Quito might not be the gastro-capital of the world, but it does boast some excellent restaurants to suit all wallets. Best of all are the prices, which are extremely good value by North American or European standards. Note that reservations are rarely necessary, except in the more expensive establishments, for which numbers are listed. For pricing, see EATING OUT, page 248 in TRAVELERS' TIPS.

Expensive

If you want Ecuadorian food in style and comfort try **La Choza** ((022) 230839, Avenida 12 de Octubre 1821 and Cordero. Its name, which means "hut," belies its quality and swanky surroundings. It is

Where to stay in Quito will be one of your most significant decisions on a trip to Ecuador.

open from Monday to Friday for lunch and dinner (until 9:30 PM) and from Saturday to Sunday between 2 PM and 4 PM. The equally fancy **Mare Nostrum** ((022) 237236, Foch 172 and Tamayó, located in a beautifully restored mansion fitted out with coats of armor and a big log fire, serves excellent seafood. Try *mariscos* (seafood) with *encocado* (coconut). Other recommended restaurants serving Ecuadorian cuisine include **Rincón La Ronda** ((022) 540549, at Belo Horizonte and Almagro, which has live music most evenings and attentive service, and **Cocina de Kirsty** ((022) 501209, Whymper 184, which boasts great views from the balcony and excellent dishes, some of which are international.

Most of the luxury hotels have fine but expensive European-style restaurants. Best value are brunches with views at **Café Quito** in the Hotel Quito, or else the excellent Sunday buffet at the **Hotel Hilton Colón**. Top choice, however, for all around presentation, atmosphere and superb Mediterranean food is **La Viña** ((022) 566033, behind the Swissôtel on Isabela la Católica, coming close in style and standard to any restaurant in the "Old World." Other highly regarded restaurants for international dishes include **Avalon** ((022) 229993, Orellana 155, with wonderful oysters and a wide-ranging menu, and the out-of-town **Muckis** ((022) 861789 in El Tingo district, about a 30-minute cab ride from Mariscal. Muckis is an institution among well-healed *quiteños* on the weekend, and its indoor or outdoor dining is among the finest in the city.

For purely French dishes **Rincón de Francia** ((022) 225053, Roca 779, is long-established and very highly praised, as is the cheaper **Île de France** ((022) 5531747 on Reina Victoria. For some of the best sushi this side of the equator, check out the fashionable, stylish and excellent **Sake** ((022) 524818 at Rivet N30-166, and the more staid **Tanoshi** ((022) 567600 inside the Swissôtel on 12 de Octubre. For wonderful Thai dishes incorporating chilies, coconut, cinnamon and ginger, **Thai-an** ((022) 446639, Eloy Alfaro and Portugal (closed on Sunday evening), is regarded as the best Quito has to offer.

Moderate

In Quito, everyone has their favorite restaurant for *ceviche* (marinated seafood), an Ecuadorian specialty. Some people swear by **El Viejo José** (Old Joe), Reina Victoria and La Pinta; while others prefer **El Viejo Jorje** (Old George), which was opened in the same area by a disgruntled employee of Old Joe. Others say you should go to **Su Ceviche**, Juan León Mera and Calamá, where you can sit at an outside table. You might settle the argument by asking for *ceviche* at any of these restaurants. For a more varied menu, excellent-value Ecuadorian cooking can be found at **Las Redes**, on

Amazonas and Veintimilla, which is down to earth and intimate (closed Sunday evening and Monday). I recommend you plow straight in with a "gran mariscada" for two (cloth bibs provided). **Taberna Quiteña**, on Amazonas 1259 and Cordero, is also good for seafood, both of the above have live music most weekend evenings.

Typical Spanish food is popular in Quito and tends to be relatively expensive. For a great paella, head to **La Paella Valenciana**, Almagro 1727, and ask for the enormous seafood option, while for first-class Basque dishes, **Costa Vasca**, 18 de Septiembre 553, is friendly, busy and originally decorated. Another good choice is **El Mesón de la Pradera**, in a restored hacienda on Orellana and 6 de Diciembre.

For Italian, try **Il Grillo**, Cordero and Reina Victoria, which provides a good ambience amid its wood-paneled rooms and tasty pastas. **Il Risotto**, on Almagro and Pinto, enjoys a well-earned reputation for its pasta and risotto dishes set in a colonial house (try the excellent carpaccio followed by foie-gras risotto and finished with tiramisu), as do **Portofino**, on Calamá between Juan León Mera and Reina Victoria, and the more posh **Pavarotti**, on 12 de Octubre and Salazar, close to the Swissôtel. For pizzas, probably the best in town (for variety at least — it has some 50 on the menu!) is **El Arcate**, on Baquedano 358. It also serves good pasta and the service is particularly attentive. Other pizza places include **Ch' Farina** on Amazonas and Naciones Unidas, popular with local *quiteños*, or else **El Hornero** on Veintimilla 1149.

As in almost every city in the world, there's a host of Chinese restaurants (*chifas*) in Quito. Among the more moderately priced are **The Asia** on Amazonas near Plaza de Toros, **Hong Kong**, Wilson 246 and Tamayo, and **Casa China** on Cordero 613 and Tamayo. Also highly recommended for food, service and ambience is **Mágico Oriental**, 9 Octubre and Jorge Washington.

For meat-lovers, some of the best straight grills are served at **Texas Ranch** on Juan León Mera and Calamá, with good steaks amidst somewhat twee decor. The **Shorton Grill** on Almagro and Calamá and **El Toro Partido** on Veintimilla and 9 de Octubre also serve up decent-sized steaks. **La Terraza de Tártaro** ((022) 527987, on the top floor of the Edificio Amazonas on Veintimilla 1106 and Amazonas, boasts splendid views through wide picture windows, and the food is also recommended. For guaranteed indigestion, head to the Brazilian-run **Churrascaría Tropeiro** on Veintimilla 546, which at lunchtime offers an "all you can eat" option — salad bar also happily included.

At the ever-popular crossroads of Calamá and Juan León Mera you'll find a plethora of places to eat. For cheap French dishes, and great crêpes, try

La Crêperie on Calamá. At **Zocalo** you pay a bit more for their international dishes in a modern and trendy atmosphere, while the next-door Thai **Siam** is another good choice. Both of these have pleasant indoor and terrace seating.

Inexpensive

Cheap restaurants abound in the Mariscal area, popular with working *quiteños* on their lunch hour. You can get a three-course meal and drink for as little as a dollar here. Try the ones on Carrión at Juan León Mera, by the police station. For something a bit better, head to **Mama Clorindas** on Reina Victoria 1144 at Calamá, or else **Los Indios** at the arcade on Roca 750, where you can ask for the typical *llapingacho* (mashed potato patty with fried egg and chorizo sausage). A new, quite stylish place, serving Ecuadorian dishes with a modern twist, **Huaira**, on Calamá at Juan León Mera, is a good choice in the evenings. The friendly **Posada del Maple**, at the southern end of Calamá, specializes in seafood dishes from the Manabí region and is worth investigating for a cheap lunch.

For Chinese, **Chifa Mayflower** on Carrión and 6 de Diciembre enjoys a good reputation, while for Cuban, **Bodeguita de Cuba** ((022) 542476, Reina Victoria and La Pinta, is fun and feisty in the evenings, with live music on Thursday nights when you'll need to reserve. **Havana**, on Portugal and El Salvador, is also well recommended. Mexican food, though much hotter than Ecuadorian, is very popular. Among the best restaurants are the **Taco Factory**, on Whymper and Orellana, and **Tex-Mex**, on Reina Victoria 235, which is milder spice-wise.

Although it has delicious Indonesian and Indian items on the menu, the Dutch-run vegetarian restaurant **Double Dutch**, on Reina Victoria and Carrión, isn't exclusively Asian since it also does Greek and Italian dishes. But is the sort of restaurant that weary budget travelers pray for — inexpensive, tasty and safe. Other recommended vegetarian establishments include **El Marqués**, Calamá 443, **Windmill Vegetarian Restaurant** on Colón 2245, and **El Maple I,** inside the arcade at Roca 750, all good value for set lunches. For its breakfasts, baked potatoes, homemade pasta and vegetarian food, **Super Papa**, attached to the Alston Inn Hotel, Juan León Mera 741 and Baquedano, is rightly well known.

Magic Bean, at the corner of Foch and Juan León Mera, serves a tasty combination of light meals (sandwiches and kebabs) and excellent coffee. It's a friendly place to meet other travelers and pick up information. More down-market but with a similar formula is **El Cafecito**, on Luís Cordero 1124, which serves snacks, light meals and drinks. The bar section is a laid-back place for an early-evening drink.

Cafés

At **Café Cultura**, Robles at Reina Victoria, you can indulge yourself with homemade breads and scones and cream teas, and read or chat in the classy atmosphere of the café or library room. For Brits missing their tea, it's the only place in Quito to serve Earl Grey. In a similar sophisticated vein, **Art Forum**, on Juan León Mera and Wilson, combines a pleasant café with an art gallery, and **Grain de Café**, Baquedano and Reina Victoria, has homemade pies, the best cheesecake in town and a chilled-out feel (and service…). For great views of Parque La Carolina from the third floor of El Jardín mall, **Café Ceuce** caters for moneyed *quiteños* who come to enjoy its great national and international menu, but it's also a quieter café in the day. The airy **Gallery Café** at the British Council, Amazonas and Pinta, serves good vegetarian snacks, while **Lennon**, on Calamá and Juan León Mera, and the nearby cybercafé **Papaya Net** are both friendly places to chat and snack. Further up Calamá, **Café Sutra** serves delicious daytime snacks, converting into a popular meeting place in the evening, as does the art-exhibiting **El Pobre Diablo**, Santa María and Juan León Mera. For people watching, take a table on one of the four or five **outside cafés** between Nos. 400 and 500 on Amazonas.

In the Parque La Carolina area, for good cappuccino and a huge selection of delicious ice cream, as well as homemade chocolate truffles, go the **Corfú** on Portugal, which some claim is best place for ice cream in Quito. The best pastries in town are probably to be enjoyed at the **Swiss Corner**, Los Shyris 2137, and the best bagels at **Mister Bagel**, Portugal and Shyris. **Sató**, República de El Salvador N34-51, combines the original concept of a hairdresser-cum-art gallery-cum café/restaurant. Everything in the stylish place is for sale, from the plates to the glasses to the chairs, while the lunchtime salads or sandwiches are fresh and superb, if a tad pricey.

Old Town

The two moderately priced restaurants in the Old Town are **Hotel Real Audencia's** at the northern corner of Plaza Santo Domingo, and the elegant **La Cueva del Oso**, on Chile 1046, just off Plaza Grande. The Real Audencia's dishes are pretty uninspiring on the whole, though the views, especially at night, are unbeatable. The Cueva serves such Ecuadorian delicacies as *seco de chivo* (mutton stew), but also Italianate dishes, and is very good. The oldest café in Quito is the tiny **Café Modelo**, on Sucre 391, which has plenty of atmosphere and cheap snacks such as *empanadas*. At **Tianguez**, a first-rate café on Plaza de San Francisco, you can relax and buy souvenirs after a neck-bending church tour, though the lunchtime meals are a bit pricey.

NIGHTLIFE

Quito's nightlife is one of its best-kept secrets. Some Ecuadorians are surprised to learn how much goes on after hours in their own capital. Places are qualified by "rowdiness rating."

In the two-star category for **cafés, pubs, bars and clubs** (the cafés listed above being in the one-star range), the upmarket and arty **Café Libro**, Almagro and La Pradera, has literary posters and cool music, with live jazz on Thursdays and folkloric events on Fridays. **El Pobre Diablo**, Santa María and Juan León Mera, also with a somewhat arty atmosphere, is as friendly as a Dublin pub. Try the top-class Irish coffees. The young crowd at **Aladdin**, Almagro and Cordero, enjoy smoking hookahs outside on the terrace, while they're very young and oh-so-beautiful at **La Boca del Lobo** (also a good café/restaurant) on Reina Victoria at Calamá. **La Reina Victoria**, Reina Victoria and Roca, is an English-style, English-owned pub with darts, draught beer and sandwiches, but without the mad cows.

Turning up the volume into the three-star rowdiness category, **Lacienda**, Rafael León 1030, is stylish with great views of the Guápulo church plus a dance floor, good atmosphere, good service and good music, and caters to over 25-year-olds. **Varadero** bar and restaurant, next to the La Bodeguita de Cuba on Reina Victoria and Pinta, appeals to a similar crowd and has plenty of exotic South American cocktails from Cuba Libres (rum and Coke) to Canelazos (cane alcohol flavored with lime and cinnamon). The live music is also excellent. **Arribar**, Juan León Mera and Lizardo García, is a fairly rough joint with pretty loud music and a pool table, popular with backpacking gringos and gringuettes.

In the four-star action and rowdiness range, where you have to shout in people's ears to make yourself understood, there are many lively clubs in the Mariscal area. On Friday and Saturday nights **Tequila Rock**, Reina Victoria and Santa María, is bursting, as is the nearby **Papillon**, Santa María and Almagro. Other currently "in" spots among the clubbing crowd are: **Gasoline**, Salazar and Tamayo; **Final**, Gonzalez Suarez and Camino Guápulo; **No Bar**, Calamá and Amazonas; and **Joy**, República and America.

On the salsa scene, the best beats break out at **Seseribó**, Veintimilla and 12 de Octubre. "El Sese" is considered to be the hottest *salsateca* in town. Don't bother coming until at least 11 PM. Screaming on its heals is **Cali Salsateca**, Almagro and Orellana, where those Latin rhythms pulse through the night into the early hours. For a genuine *peña* show with folkloric music and dancing, the reasonably priced **Nuncanchi**

Peña, opposite the Universidad Central, Avenida Universitaria and Armero, is a popular choice. There are performances most days except Sunday and Monday.

Entry to many clubs requires an ID or credit card and there is often a cover charge of up to US$4. In most clubs entry is entirely at the discretion of the doorman. Popularity ebbs and flows in the club and pub world so many of those that are hot today may be gone tomorrow.

CINEMAS AND THE ARTS

The two main cinemas in Quito, which are up to Western standards, are **Multicines** ((022) 265061, in the CCI complex at Naciones Unidas and Amazonas, and **Cinemark** ((022) 260303, at Plaza de las Américas at the corner of Avenidas República and América. Both have about seven screens and good sound. For listings, refer to Section D of the

El Comercio. Multicines is a lot closer to Mariscal, but doesn't have many appealing restaurants close-by, apart from Ch'Farina across the road. Get to them early for popular releases, or else book by phone (MasterCard only). The only other cinema of note is the art-house **Casa de la Cultura** ((022) 220966, at Patria and 6 de Diciembre. The Casa is also the city's best venue for classical music, theater and dance.

For other good venues for the arts, check the Friday supplement "Chévere" in *El Comercio.* Among the best theaters are **Teatro Charlot**, at Cordero and Reina Victoria, and **El Patio de las Comedias**, at 18 de Septiembre and 9 de Octubre. **Metropolitan Touring** ((022) 464780 can also give you details of various folk ballets or *música folklórica* shows happening in the city. Also, watch out for shows at **Humanizarte**, a small, often quite experimental, theater on an alley off Lizardo García, by Plaza Leonidas.

HOW TO GET THERE

By Air

Most intercontinental visitors to Ecuador arrive at Quito's Aeropuerto Mariscal Sucre. International carriers who fly into the city regularly include American Airlines, Continental, Iberia, KLM, Lufthansa, Air France, and the South American airlines Copa (Panama), Avensa (Venezuela), Avianca (Colombia) Lacsa (Costa Rica), Viasa (Venezuela), LAB (Bolivia), AeroPerú and Cubana. Ecuadorian airlines flying internationally in and out of Quito are TAME and Ecuatoriana.

Facilities in the airport terminal include a cafeteria, gift shops, an Andinatel telephone office and a tourist information office, where reservations for hotels can, theoretically, be made. If it's your first visit to Ecuador and you're not

Quito's nightlife is one of the city's best-kept secrets.

AROUND QUITO

on an organized tour you might feel more secure making reservations before you arrive, although even in peak season there are always rooms available in Quito. Some travelers just hop in a cab and ask the driver to take them to a suitable hotel or hostel.

A taxi from the airport to the center of town, a distance of about 10 km (six miles), should be about US$4. Some drivers try to charge more for journeys from the international terminal so bargain hard, or just walk down to the domestic terminal where fares tend to be less expensive. Alternatively, stroll over to the avenue in front of the terminal and flag down a metered taxi or take a southbound bus.

If you're leaving Quito by air on an international flight, don't forget there is a **departure tax** of US$25, payable in cash. There is no departure tax on domestic flights, nor if you are leaving the country overland.

By Bus

Most travelers in Ecuador rely heavily on the extensive, inexpensive network of buses for trips throughout the country. With Quito as the main transportation hub, the starting point for most long-distance journeys is the bus terminal,

Terminal Terrestre, at Maldonado and Cumandá, a few hundred meters south of Plaza Santo Domingo in the Old Town. Finding the terminal might be the most difficult part of your journey since it isn't clearly marked on some maps. When using the terminal for the first time it's probably best to take a taxi, which from most parts of Quito won't cost more than three or four dollars. Once you're familiar with the terminal, you can take the trolley bus along 10 de Agosto to the Cumandá stop and walk down the steps.

The most reliable information about buses can be obtained at the terminal, where each bus company has an office. There are frequent buses to all the main towns and cities, making it unnecessary to buy tickets in advance except on major holidays and festivals. Just show up with a destination in mind (or not, if you want to be truly adventurous) and you'll find a bus going there shortly. Because there are usually thick crowds at the bus terminal, keep an especially sharp eye on your belongings.

By Train

The old, decrepit but charming **Quito Railway Station** is on Maldonado south of the Old Town. Take a taxi or buses No. 1 or 2 heading south.

For more information on train rides, see RIDE THE RAILS, page 17 in TOP SPOTS.

EXCURSIONS FROM QUITO

From Quito there are many fascinating places you can visit on a day-trip, or if you prefer, you might stay a night or two.

LA MITAD DEL MUNDO

In 1736 a team of scientists sponsored by the French Academy of Sciences arrived in Ecuador with the most up-to-date astrolabes, compasses, telescopes and other scientific instruments. Part of their mission was to calculate the precise position of the notional equatorial line as it passed through the country. They also wanted to take readings to resolve contemporary disputes about the shape of the earth. The work of the eight-year Geodetic Mission in Ecuador showed that the earth did indeed bulge in the middle, as English scientist Isaac Newton had predicted. At the same time the scientists helped lay the foundations for the metric system that eventually became the global standard.

Busts of these 12 learned scientists (nine members of the Academy of Science in Paris, two Spanish mathematicians and one Ecuadorian scientist) can be seen be seen at La Mitad del Mundo (The Center of the Earth), some 15 km (nine miles) north of Quito. More prominent than the busts, though, is the massive 30-m (100-ft) high obelisk of volcanic rock capped with a brass globe four meters (13 ft) in diameter. This tapered tower was built in 1986 to replace a smaller one erected in 1936 to mark the 200th anniversary of the Geodetic Mission. The massive monument straddles the equatorial line as delineated by the scientists.

The most popular activities for visitors to La Mitad del Mundo are walking the equatorial line, being photographed on both sides of the world at the same time, or just jumping from one side of the earth to the other. There is also a deep fascination among visitors about whether water turns in opposite directions in the southern and northern hemispheres as it drains from a basin or flushes from a toilet. Efforts to resolve this riddle — and to achieve a straight flush exactly on the equatorial line — keep children occupied for hours.

The complex of facilities surrounding the monument at La Mitad del Mundo has developed a theme park atmosphere. Partially built as a typical colonial town, there are gift shops, restaurants, a tourist office, a **planetarium**, a very good model of Old Quito and even a bullring, which is used occasionally. But the main attraction is the monument itself that houses an excellent **ethnographic museum**. After buying a ticket, visitors take the elevator to the ninth floor to an observation deck for a panoramic view of the surrounding hills. Walking down the stairs, you pass through the museum with dioramas and displays of ethnic costumes and artifacts that give a vivid and informative picture of Ecuador's great diversity of peoples and cultures.

The best restaurant in the complex is **Equinoccio**, which is near the entrance. Here you can get typical, well-prepared Ecuadorian food, accompanied by live Andean music. This is a good place to sink your teeth into the national delicacy, *cuy* (roasted guinea pig, a favorite of the Incas), as you will not find it on the menu at many Quito restaurants. Equinoccio is in the moderate price range. If you want to pay less there are snacks available in the complex and some inexpensive *comedores* (eating rooms) in the nearby village of San Antonio.

On the other side of the village is a small **solar museum**, open only by appointment, containing an intriguing solar chronometer and other astronomical gadgets. Those interested in seeing the museum should contact its curator, Oswaldo Muñoz of **Nuevo Mundo Expeditions (** (022) 552839 in Quito. Incan and pre-Incan artifacts indicate that the early inhabitants studied the path of the sun and were aware of the significance of the equator, as well as the special magic of this location. They were also able to predict eclipses as far ahead as this present century.

Interestingly, it has been suggested that the equator has shifted in the last 2,000 years due to a wobble of the earth on its axis. According to this theory, a pair of peaks known as **La Marca**, just five kilometers (three miles) north of La Mitad, were on the previous line, as was the nearby pre-Columbian solar observatory of **Rumicucho**, the ruins of which are currently being excavated by the Banco Central. Possibly connected to this cosmic pattern is another site further to the east, **Cochasquí**, where there are tombs that look like truncated pyramids and where, even these days, dance festivals are held on solstices and equinoxes.

Further east on the same path is the 5,790-m (18,996-ft) peak of **Volcán Cayambe**, the third-tallest mountain in Ecuador and the highest point in the world on the equator. There is an enormous cylinder cut into the flanks of the mountain, where at noon on solar equinox the sun makes no shadow in the circle. Whatever the significance of these ancient sites, the ghosts of inhabitants past still cast their magic. As you look up to the sky, you can imagine the heavens stretching equally and infinitely from pole to pole while the earth spins beneath your feet.

Buses from Quito to La Mitad del Mundo leave from the El Tejar bus stop in the Old Town. You can also get on them as they pass along Avenida América in the New Town. But they tend to be very crowded, especially on weekends, so you are better off sharing a taxi or contacting a travel agency in Quito to join a guided tour. Tours often include some of the sites mentioned above as well as the nearby crater of the extinct **Volcán Pululahua**, an impressive spectacle, some 300 m (nearly 1,000 ft) deep and four kilometers (just over two miles) in diameter, at the bottom of which is a village and a beautiful old hacienda.

HIKING AROUND QUITO

For the fit and energetic there is no shortage of good hiking and climbing trails near the capital. The closest crater is **Rucu Pichincha** (4,627 m or 15,180 ft), which is a hard day's hike if you want to return to Quito by nightfall. To climb the crater summit of the active volcano **Guagua Pichincha** (4,794 m or 15,728 ft) takes longer and requires an overnight stay in the hut below the summit. It is important to be aware that there have been a number of robberies, muggings and rapes on the roads leading out of the city suburbs, as well as attacks by dogs, so it is advisable to go with a large group and to take a taxi or a jeep for the first stretch up into the hills. If you are thinking of taking either of these hikes, check first for the latest information on the best routes and current conditions at one of the agencies specializing in climbing or with the SAE.

For easier hiking in the nearby countryside, **Reserva de Vida Silvestre Pasochoa** is a subtropical forest area less than an hour's drive southeast from Quito. Popular for school outings, the reserve attracts some 20,000 visitors per year. Several mapped trails crisscross an extinct volcanic crater rich with plants and wildlife. There are camping and hostel facilities in the park, but no shops or restaurants. For maps and more detailed information contact the **Fundación Natura** ((022) 446081 E-MAIL natura@natura.org.ec WEB SITE www.natura.org.ec, Guayas 105 and Amazonas, Quito, which runs the reserve.

MINDO AND RESERVA BIOLÓGICA MAQUIPUCUNA

The small town of Mindo on the western slopes of the Andes, just 40 km (25 miles) northwest of Quito as the condor flies, is a mecca for cognoscenti bird-watchers. In the dense surrounding cloud forest some 450 species have been observed, including such trophies as the fabulous scarlet-crested Andean cock-of-the-rock, the toucan barbet, the plate-billed mountain toucan and the velvet-purple coronet.

But you don't have to be a dedicated "twitcher" to appreciate Mindo's charm. If you prefer, you can simply enjoy the novelty and privacy of staying in a luxury tree-house *cabaña* 10 m (33 ft) above

the ground, in the cloud forest canopy. Here in your bamboo aerie you can lie under your mosquito net while listening to a chorus of toucans sounding like the screeching of rusty nails being clawed from old lumber. Or you can just wander forest paths observing the unique ecosystem of the western slopes of the Andes, enjoying nature at its most abundant. **Río Mindo** gushes down the steep mountainside, blazing a foaming path for hair-raising whitewater rafting.

But if it's birds you're after, your man is Vinicio Pérez, birdman extraordinaire, who usually can be found by asking around at the few bars in town, or you can leave a message with Vinicio's sister in Quito ((022) 612955, who should know the top twitcher's whereabouts. If he takes you birding, be prepared to get up at 5 AM and walk for two hours up steep slopes and through thick undergrowth. Your reward should be a magnificent arboreal show starring the incredible crimson-coated Andean cock-of-the-rock chorus line.

If you want to stay in a treehouse in Mindo, contact **Hostería El Carmelo de Mindo** ((022) 538756 FAX (022) 408355 in Quito. Their best *cabañas* are in the moderate range, but they also have less expensive ones and camping facilities and dormitories for US$5 to US$8. Horseback riding is available. More upmarket and expensive is the delightful **Mindo Gardens Lodge** ((022) 230463 FAX (022) 564235. There are also several less expensive, more basic places where you have to bring your own sleeping gear. Mindo shows all the signs of becoming increasingly popular with travelers and nature lovers in the years to come.

About 32 km (20 miles) north of Mindo, on the same western slopes of the Andes, is the **Reserva Biológica Maquipucuna**, most of which is primary cloud forest. In this wildlife-rich area, species of close to 2,000 plants, of some 322 birds, more than 200 butterflies and 45 mammals have been recorded. It's no wonder that Maquipucuna attracts naturalists like moths to a flame. For information about lodgings, prices and transportation to the area contact **Fundación Maquipucuna** ((022) 507200 or 507202 FAX (022) 507201 E-MAIL abi@maqui.ecx.ec, in Quito at Baquerizo 238 and Tamayo, Box 17-12-167.

Some gringos fall in love with the wild jungle landscapes and decide to make the place their home. In 1991, British backpacker, Richard Parsons, bought a 120-ha (about 300-acre) abandoned farm in the Maquipucuna area for a song. Using eucalyptus logs and bamboo, and with the help of local labor and his wife Gloria, Parsons constructed an ecolodge shaped like a geodesic dome on stilts, with lots of windows and big balconies. Built on three levels and roofed with thatch, there are five triple rooms on the first floor and dormitory rooms above. Perched on the edge of a steep hill, the futuristic cupola looks out over the thick jungle carpet of the **Bellavista Cloud Forest Reserve** ((09) 490891 where tanagers, toucans and other birds of this paradise flash brightly among deep shades of green. Prices range from moderate with three meals, but cheaper accommodation is also available in nearby houses. For more information and reservations (/FAX (022) 232313 or 901536 E-MAIL bellavista@ecuadorexplorer.com or aecie3@ecnet.ec WEB SITE www.ecuadorexplorer .com/bellavista/home, Jorge Washington E7-23 between 6 de Diciembre and Reina Victoria, Quito.

RESERVA ECOLÓGICA ANTISANA

Although little known and difficult to get to, the Reserva Ecológica Antisana, 57 km (36 miles) southeast of Quito, offers breathtaking scenery of the *páramo* and views of the eponymous, snowcapped mountain, where wild horses roam and condors cross the sky. This dramatic wilderness is a great place for riding, hiking, camping and living in the wild. Visitors must bring their own supplies, though there's a lodge owned by a water company where it's possible to stay. Access is by car only (four-wheel drive recommended) and a permit is required. For more information contact **Fundación Antisana** ((022) 433851 in Quito, Mariana de Jesús and Carvajal. You can also get special permission to enter the territory of Hacienda Pinatura, owned by Carlos Delgado, who can be contacted at Avenida 6 de Diciembre 1024 in Quito. Or make inquiries on the way to the reserve at Pintag, where you can find a guide.

HOT SPRINGS

Volcanic Ecuador has many hot springs, natural pools and spouting waterfalls hidden deep in the jungle, some being rather hard to get to. Near Miazal in Morona-Santiago Province there are twin waterfalls, one hot and one cold, like hot and cold showers. Indian tribes consider waterfalls to be sacred. Waterfall aficionados should contact Jean Brown of **Safari Tours** ((022) 552505 FAX (022) 223381 E-MAIL admin@safari.com.ec WEB SITE www .safari.com.ec, Calamá 380 and Jean León Mera. Brown knows Ecuador's waterfalls and hot springs like few others.

The best hot springs within reach of Quito are the **Baños de Papallacta**, two hours by bus or car from the city, just off the road that descends over the rim of the Amazon Basin to Baeza (see PAPALLACTA, page 158 in EL ORIENTE).

About an hour by road from Quito are the thermal pools of **La Merced** and **El Tingo**, but they tend to be overcrowded on weekends. Far better are some private pools at **Ilaló**, just a few kilometers from La Merced, where US$2 gives access to cleaner and less-crowded facilities. Buses run from Quito to the above places. If possible, avoid weekends.

ZOOLÓGICO GUAYLLABAMBA AND CAYAMBE

Just off the Panamericana 32 km (20 miles) north of Otavalo lies about the best zoo in the country. The facilities are open Tuesday to Sunday 10 AM to 5 PM, and you can have an English-speaking guide take you round the primarily native fauna. There are several species of monkeys, pumas and ocelots, and some bright parrots and birds. Unfortunately, the condor enclosure is far too small, but otherwise, the zoo is excellent by Latin

American standards. The zoo is about one kilometer (a quarter of a mile) north of the town of Guayllabamba, and bus drivers can drop you off at the entrance, from where it's about a half-hour's walk. On the weekends there's a free bus service.

By staying right at the split in the Panamericana (not going via Tabacundo), about two-thirds of the way to **Cayambe** (around 24 km or 15 miles) you pass the town of El Tingo. Here take the right turn up to **Cangahua** and the great **Hacienda Guachalá** ((022) 363042 TOLL-FREE IN THE US AND CANADA ((800) 451-6034 FAX (022) 362426, nestled into the skirts of Volcán Cayambe (see LIVE THE HACIENDA LIFE, page 15 in TOP SPOTS, for details of the hacienda). The hacienda makes a wonderful base from which to admire the glowering Volcán Cayambe and to explore the wonders of the **Reserva Ecológica Cayambe-Coca**, as well as the pre-Columbian ruins of Cochasquí or Quitoloma nearby. By continuing on the road south of Cangahua, you'll come to the pretty hot springs of **Oyacachi**.

The sitting room of a hacienda, a glorious spot to end a day traipsing around the outskirts of Quito.

Northern Highlands

The two northern Sierra provinces, Imbabura and Carchi, contain some of the most stunning scenery in Ecuador. Majestic volcanoes, wild *páramo*, deep green valleys and mystical lakes form a panoramic background to diverse Andean cultures. Colorful markets, traditional costumes, haunting music and ancient handicrafts are surviving facets of a lifestyle that predates the Spanish conquistadors and even the Incas.

OTAVALO

This unremarkable small town, about two hours north of Quito on the Panamericana highway, is nonetheless one of the most popular destinations for visitors to Ecuador. Its world-famous market of indigenous crafts, textiles and clothing ranks among the best in Latin America. The population of the town is around 50,000, most of whom are *mestizos*, but about twice as many Quichua-speaking *otavaleños* live in the surrounding areas and flood into town on market days.

BACKGROUND

Indígenas in the Otavalo area have been spinning and weaving for longer than anyone knows. Following the Inca conquest 500 years ago, despite a long and fierce resistance by the Otavalans, the victors from the south extracted a textile tribute. Though the Incas were only in control for about 40 years, this was long enough for them to leave their mark. The Quichua language spoken by the Otavalan Indians comes from the Incas and the elegant women's costume, which is still universally worn, is said to be closer to Inca dress than any in the Andes today. After the Spanish defeated the Incas in the middle of the sixteenth century, they set about exploiting the weaving skills of the Otavalans by setting up textile workshops (*obrajes*) where hundreds of *indígenas* were forced to work unbearably long hours. Some of the workers were less than 10 years old. Many committed suicide to avoid the intolerable conditions.

The Spanish introduced modern machinery, including treadle looms, as well as sheep, wool and techniques of production weaving. From the early eighteenth century many haciendas operated weaving workshops, and at the beginning of the twentieth century Otavalan weavers began making imitation British tweeds. Land reforms in 1964 gave weavers more independence, tourism began to develop in the area and the weaving industry started to take off. Today the Otavalo *indígenas* are considered to be the most prosperous indigenous group in Latin America. They own many businesses in Otavalo, including crafts shops, restaurants, bars and travel agencies, and they have developed an international network to sell their products to neighboring countries as well as to North America, Europe and Japan.

More than three-quarters of Otavalan *indígenas* are thought to be involved in the textile industry in some way, whether weaving and spinning at home or working with one of the larger production houses or retail outlets. The Otavalan weaving phenomenon is a fascinating story of how a small indigenous community has pulled itself out of the trap of poverty and developed its own successful, worldwide business operation.

While achieving commercial success, the Otavalan *indígenas* have also managed to maintain their cultural identity and traditions. Most visibly, they still wear their unique traditional costumes. Otavalan men favor calf-length white trousers, gray or blue ponchos, rope sandals and dark felt hats, while women display embroidered white blouses, dark skirts and shawls, masses of golden glass beads around their neck, red bead bracelets and cloth headgear which is folded in various significant ways. Most distinctively, both women and men wear their hair in a long single pigtail that is often tied back with a colorful woven band. The traditional costumes are worn daily at home and in the villages, not to impress tourists in the market.

GENERAL INFORMATION

Though there is no tourist office in Otavalo, there are several useful travel agents who can arrange visits to weavers' homes in the town and to craft villages in the surrounding countryside, as well as horseback riding, hiking and visits to ecological reserves or the hot springs of Chachimbiro. Recommended is the anthropology-slanted **Zulaytur** ((06) 921176, Sucre and Colon, where Señor Rodrigo Mora speaks English and is very helpful. Also recommended is nearby the indigenous-run **Zulay Diceny Viajes** ((06) 921217, and **Inti Express** ((06) 921436.

For international telephone calls, the **Andinatel office** is on Calderón and Sucre, and if you want to mail a poncho home, the **Post Office** is at the corner of Salinas and Sucre (for shipping size matters, see GENERAL INFORMATION, page 82 under QUITO). The **Policía Municipal** is up Avenida Norte. For medical emergencies, **Hospital San Luís de Otavalo** is on Sucre, on the northern edge of town. WEB SITE **www.otavalo-web.com** is useful, and there are plenty of Internet cafés dotted about town.

Some gringo travelers who want to learn Spanish while in Ecuador choose to study in Otavalo because it's slightly less expensive and slower paced than Quito. The **Instituto Superior de Español** on Sucre 11-10 and Morales is worth

PREVIOUS PAGES: Countryside LEFT near Otavalo. Weaver RIGHT from Agato near Otavalo. OPPOSITE: Tahuantinsuyo workshop in Agato.

checking out, but asking around will produce results too. Some of these travelers make some money exporting sweaters and other textile products they buy in Otavalo, but most end up keeping the goodies for themselves.

WHAT TO SEE AND DO

Otavalo's main attraction is its vibrant *artesanía* market. On Saturdays one of the squares in the center of town, **Plaza de Ponchos**, as is it is aptly called, is covered with a labyrinth of small shops and stands selling almost every textile and craft item made in Ecuador — ponchos, gloves, hats, woolen blankets, hand-knitted sweaters, woven wall hangings, scarves, shirts, shawls, ceramics, embroidered blouses, table cloths, string bags, baskets, sandals, leather goods, carvings, beads, buttons, bric-a-brac and more.

Tourists arrive here by the busload from Quito. Prices are probably a bit lower than in Quito, but you have to bargain. The stallholders will reduce their prices considerably but prefer to haggle with good humor. Use a lot of smiles and laughter. Walk away if the price is too high, by all means; it just might be lower when you return.

Some visitors are surprised that some of the goods are so touristy, with bright, garish colors. In fact the Otavalan weavers and textile makers are quite aware of the taste of the majority of their customers, so if you're looking for unusual or antique pieces you will probably be better off going to Quito or to some of the other markets around the country.

There are in fact three markets in Otavalo on Saturdays: the noisiest, the **animal market** on the western side of town off the Panamericana, starts at dawn with squeals of piglets, bartering Indians, flocks of chickens, lowing cows, textile and breakfast and necklace hawkers, and is over by about 10 AM; the *artesanía* **market** in Plaza de Ponchos bustles from 7 AM until about 6 PM; and the **produce market**, which is divided between the new covered market at Plaza Copacabana near the railway station and the area around Plaza 24 de Mayo. The *artesanía* market has become so popular that not only has it spread physically into the narrow side streets off Plaza de Ponchos, but it has also stretched in time so that there are market stands in the plaza throughout the week. Many people prefer the quieter market days on Wednesdays and Fridays when prices are often lower.

In addition to being a great place for shopping, Otavalo is a photographer's dream. The bold colors and striking designs of the Andean textiles and wall hangings combined with the elegant costumes and strong faces of the *otavaleños* make for powerful images. But it's important to be sensitive to your subjects. If possible, ask permission before you photograph somebody. The concept

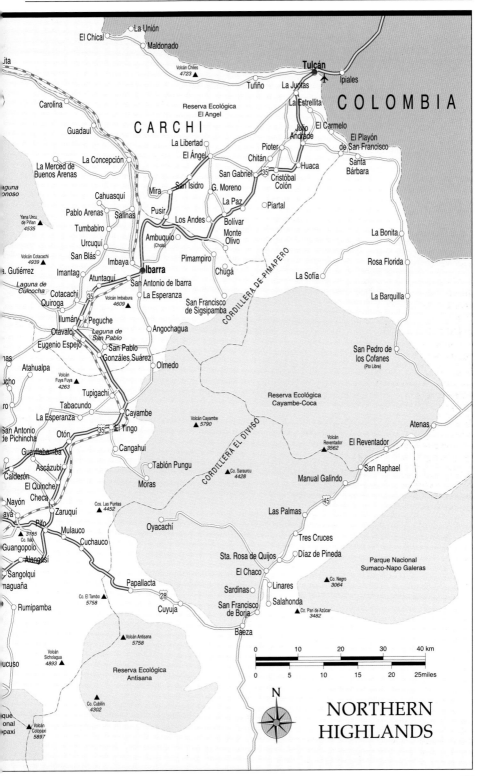

NORTHERN
HIGHLANDS

of *minga*, or reciprocity, is important in *indígena* society. If you want to photograph a stallholder, buy something before you ask permission—some give and take is always appreciated. The markets are also good hunting grounds for pickpockets and sneak thieves. Be aware of your bags and cameras at all times.

The best way to photograph weavers at work is to take a **guided tour of** *indígenas'* **homes**. You can buy products straight off the loom and, with permission, photograph the weaving process. Tours of nearby weaving villages are also popular (see below by village names).

If you're in Otavalo for any length of time, and you've shopped until you've dropped, there are

a few small, reviving museums. The **Museo Arqueológico** is attached to Pensión Los Andes on Roca and Montalvo and is free to guests. It's run by a dapper, eccentric and slightly deaf *señor*. The **Instituto Otavaleño de Antropología** is just beyond the Panamericana, on the northern edge of town. It includes information in both English and Spanish and is a good introduction to the culture and traditions of the Otavalan *indígenas*. To see weaving in situ without having to go to a nearby village, visit the Maldonado family on Sucre 6-08 who give **demonstrations** of backstrap loom techniques and sell their products. A different, "interesting" insight into the local way of life can be seen at the cockpit on 31 de Octubre and Montalvo, where **cockfights** take place on late Saturday afternoons or evenings.

WHERE TO STAY

For descriptions of the most luxurious and exclusive accommodation in the area, at **Hacienda Cusín** ((06) 918013 or (06) 918317 FAX (06) 918003 E-MAIL hacienda@cusin.com.ec WEB SITE www .haciendacusin.com, or **Hacienda Pinsaquí** (/FAX (06) 946116 or (06) 946117 IN QUITO (/FAX (022) 546253 WEB SITE www.haciendapinsaqui.com, see LIVE THE HACIENDA LIFE, page 15 in TOP SPOTS.

For such a small town Otavalo has a lot of hotels. Most of the week they are relatively empty but on Friday nights, before the big market day on Saturday, they tend to fill up, so it is recommended to make reservations.

Moderate

One hotel in Otavalo has an almost legendary reputation. The **Ali Shungu** ((06) 920750 E-MAIL alishngu@uio.telconet.net WEB SITE www.ali shungu.com, Quito and Quiroga, means "good heart" in Quichua, and the welcome is warm, the gardens pretty and the food first-class. Ali Shungu is run and owned by two Americans who fell love with Ecuador over 20 years ago and decided to settle and build their own hotel. Warm, sunny, secure and well-maintained, with 16 rooms two spacious apartments and a reputation for excellent cuisine, the hotel is in a quiet residential area, just a few blocks from the handicrafts market. It has a lovely garden with views of Volcán Imbabura, folk music on weekends and can help with most travel arrangements. The hotel runs a shuttle bus service for guests between Quito and Otavalo, and includes an apartment for five.

Out of town, equally highly praised by guests, and at about the same price, the ecologically oriented **Casa Mojanda** (/FAX (099) 731737 E-MAIL mojanda@uio.telconet.net WEB SITE www.casa mojanda.com nestles into 10 ha (25 acres) of farmland and a forested gorge overlooking the sacred mountains of Imbabura and Cotacachi. About six kilometers (nearly four miles) or 15 minutes by car from Otavalo, the inn has nine guest cottages constructed from adobe, wood and other natural materials. Prices include two excellent meals, with cozy doubles, dormitory accommodation and a cheaper rate for a separate adobe house up the hill. Betty and Diego Falconi, who own the inn, arrange excellent village tours, horse-riding trips, hikes to the lakes, etc. They are also involved in health and other projects with the local community; see their web site for more details.

Inexpensive

In town there are several good value, more conventional hotels. Of the modern ones, popular with the many Colombian tourists, **Hotel El Indio Inn** ((06) 922922 FAX (06) 920325, Calle Bolívar 904, is smart, clean and conveniently located, with terrace and restaurant. At about the same price, **Hotel Coraza** ((06) 9212256 E-MAIL h.corraza@uio .satnet.net, Calle Calderón and Sucre, also feels new and clean, with fluffy towels and good furnishings. **Hotel Otavalo** ((06) 920416, between Moreno and Montalvo, has large rooms (ask for the ones with external windows), big beds but erratic water supplies (often a problem in Otavalo). For something cheerier, **Doña Esther** ((06) 920739 E-MAIL ilderoma@yahoo.com WEB SITE www.dona

esther.otavalo-web.com, Juan Montalvo and Roca, is French-Ecuadorian run, with bright rooms with private baths ringing a flowery patio. There's also a good bar and pizzeria. Not to be confused with Hotel El Indio Inn, the also recommended **Hotel El Indio (** (022) 920060, Sucre 12–14, has carpeted rooms, modern fittings and a decent restaurant.

There are many choices in the budget range. The most popular backpacker option is **Hostal Valle del Almanecer (** (06) 920990 FAX (06) 921159, Roca and Quiroga, with shared rooms and baths in a beach-style, terracotta-tiled building. It has a pleasant courtyard, hammock slings, and a restaurant. It's a good place to meet fellow travelers for making up cheaper tours, and also rents mountain bikes. **Hotel Riviera Sucre (** (06) 920241, on the corner of García Moreno and Sucre, represents very good value, with a range of colorfully painted rooms, a small garden and very helpful staff. On the square, you exchange views from a window or balcony for noise levels, but the **Hostal Los Andes (** (06) 921057 is utilitarian, clean and tidy. Another popular, slightly less expensive hostel is **Pensión Los Andes** (no phone), on Montalvo, where rooms are tatty and beds are cheap. Although it lacks hot water, the hostel does have its own private archaeological museum.

WHERE TO EAT

With so many gringos coming into town for the market, there are several laid-back restaurants where you can hang out, meet people and read the experiences of fellow travelers in what are known as "the good, the bad and the ugly" comment books. Oh, and you can also have something to eat and drink. One of the best-known such places used to be an unpretentious little pie shop overlooking Plaza de Poncho called **Shenandoah**. It is still there and you can still get good pies, ice creams and milkshakes, but as Otavalo becomes increasingly popular the competition is growing. The town's best bakery, **Rico Donut**, is on Modesto Jaramillo and Colón. **Plaza Café**, across the street, is another a friendly hangout and it serves good dinners for about US$5. Also on Plaza de Poncho **Café Mundi** (Quiroga and Modesto Jaramillo), has atmosphere, music and vegetarian food. **Quino**, on Roca and García Moreno, is recommended for seafood, **Ali Micuy** on Modesto Jaramillo and Quiroga for good vegetarian dishes, while **Pizza Siciliana**, on Sucre and Calderón, is known for tasty, generous pizzas and vegetarian dishes. Pizza Siciliana also has an outlet in the Hotel El Indio Inn. And don't forget the mid-priced restaurant at **Ali Shungu**, open to nonresidents of the hotel (last order at 8:30 PM), or the **SISA** arts center, on Abdón Calerón between Bolívar and Sucre, with its restaurant upstairs, both with live music on weekends.

NIGHTLIFE

It might be said that Otavalo doesn't have much nightlife, but if you like live Andean music, salsa dancing, cane alcohol and a raucous atmosphere, what more do you need? There are a few *peña* (folkloric music club) bars, of which the best known are **Peña Amauta**, at Jaramillo and Salinas, with good local bands; **Peña Tucano**, Morales and Sucre; and **Peña Tuparina**, Morales and 31 de Octubre. *Peña* bars come and go all over Ecuador so ask around to find out about the latest hot spots.

HOW TO GET THERE

There is no main bus terminal in Otavalo, though one is about to be constructed. Buses north to Ibarra and south to Quito leave from Calderón between Bolívar and Roca regularly. Ask at the local travel agents for information about buses to the smaller villages. There are buses about every 15 minutes to Otavalo from Quito up until about 6 PM. The journey takes about two hours. Make sure you catch a bus that goes into the center of town rather than continuing on to Ibarra, in which case you will be dropped off on the Panamericana highway and will have to walk a kilometer (about half a mile) into town. Transportes Otavalo and Transportes Los Lagos are recommended. Buses from these companies drop you off near Plaza Copacabana where there is a taxi stand. Buses leave from here for some of the outlying villages. Taxis from Quito to Otavalo should cost about US$40 and take about an hour. The train service between Quito, Otavalo and Ibarra has not been running for several years.

AROUND OTAVALO

PEGUCHE

The small Andean village of Peguche, less than an hour's walk northeast from Otavalo, is best known for **tapestry weaving**, lovely **waterfalls** and **music**. You can get to the falls by following the railway tracks east of town and heading northwards. Follow the tracks and the cobblestone road until they split. Continue on the road up the hill and to the right into the forest park. If you get lost, ask for *las cascadas* and you'll be directed to the mist-shrouded falls. To get to the village, follow the railway tracks all the way. Near the center of the village you can't easily miss the two galleries of master tapestry weaver and designer, **José Cotacachi**. José may take you to see some home weaving, but it helps if you speak Spanish. If not, it might be better to join a tour to Peguche in

Children at Peguche.

Otavalo. Several groups of well-known Indian musicians come from this village.

Just outside Peguche lies the much-loved and friendly **Hostal Aya Huma** ((06) 922663 FAX (06) 922664 E-MAIL ayahuma@uio.satnet.net, run by a Dutch-Ecuadorian couple, which has a good restaurant, live folk music on Saturdays, locally woven blankets to keep you warm, a garden and quiet surroundings. The hostel also includes Spanish lessons among its offerings. Rooms are inexpensive. At about the same price, **Peguche Tio Hostería** (/FAX (06) 922619, near the police station, promotes local handicrafts and culture with enthusiasm and is well recommended.

ILUMÁN

About three kilometers (almost two miles) north of Peguche is the weaving community of Ilumán, makers of tapestries, felt hats and ponchos. The village is also famous for its **traditional healers**, who chase away sickness using ancient rituals and a vast knowledge of local herbs and plants, some of which are now used in Western medicine. People from all over the Sierra come to see the healers of Ilumán. One Spanish speaking *gringa* I know came away from a healing session with her clothes covered in spittle and the colored juices of herbs, but cured of her ailment. In the northeast corner of the village plaza, demonstrations of pre-Inca backstrap loom weaving take place at the **Inti Chumbi Co-op**, on the second floor of Conterón family's house. Weavings are on sale.

AGATO

Special demonstrations of traditional weaving also take place in Agato, three kilometers (two miles) east of Peguche. At the **Tahuantinsuyo weaving workshop**, Ecuador's most famous weaver, **Miguel Andrango**, demonstrates backstrap loom techniques using handspun wool and natural dyes. This is of particular interest to those with a special curiosity about weaving. His products, more expensive than those made on the upright loom and colored with chemical dyes, aren't usually for sale at the Otavalo market but can be bought at his workshop and at Hacienda Cusín (see page 108) on weekends. There are buses to Agato from Otavalo and a taxi costs only about US$2.

LAGUNA DE SAN PABLO

From Otavalo there are a number of paths leading down to Laguna de San Pablo, just a couple of kilometers southeast of town, which is a popular spot for water sports. If you walk via **El Lechero** (don't ask me why this hill is named "The Milkman"), you get fabulous views of the lake and **Volcán Imbabura**. You can walk or take a bus all the way

around the lake, stopping off at one of the hosterías. And you can rent a canoe at **Club de Tiro** on the shore. **Hostería Puerto Lago** offers evening cruises on the lake with music and cocktails.

LAGUNAS DE MOJANDA

For a more solitary lakeside experience, make your way to Lagunas de Mojanda, a series of six mountain lakes 18 km (11 miles) south, and 1,200 m (3,937 ft) higher than Otavalo. The largest of these is Laguna Grande de Mojanda, also known as **Caricocha**. The best way to get there is by taxi from town, costing about US$10, and to hike back. If you want to stay overnight, bring a sleeping bag and tent because the *refugios* up there aren't usually fit for habitation. If you are interested in riding up to the lakes or trout fishing when you get there, contact a local travel agent or inquire at **Hacienda Cusín** or **Casa Mojanda Inn** (see WHERE TO STAY, page 108 under OTAVALO). There's a cheap and friendly place to stay, close to Casa Mojanda: **Hostería La Luna** (/FAX (09) 737415 or 816145, which has various cabins, some with kitchens, and can provide meals on request. They also rent mountain bikes.

COTACACHI

Just 15 km (nine miles) north of Otavalo (take the turn six kilometers or nearly four miles north), the small town of Cotacachi is the **leather capital** of Ecuador. There are few places in the world where you can get a better deal on a genuine leather jacket, skirt or handsome travel bag. Market day is Saturday, though dozens of stores are open throughout the week. Curiously, leather goods from Cotacachi are one Ecuadorian product that is not sold in the big market in Otavalo. Another local product is *alpargatas* (sandals) popular with people of the region. There's also a modest **Museo de las Culturas** set in a pretty cloistered building by the Iglesia La Matriz, on García Moreno.

In town, the best inexpensive hotel is **El Mesón de las Flores** ((06) 915009, within an old colonial house with an attractive central courtyard, while just west of town is the very upmarket **Hostería La Mirage** ((06) 915237 FAX (06) 915065 E-MAIL mirage1@mirage.com.ec WEBSITE www.larc1.com, a hacienda-style country hotel with a beautiful garden, palatial rooms, antiques, fine food, spa, swimming pool and gymnasium. It's the only hotel in Ecuador to date to be part of the exclusive Relais & Châteaux group. Rooms with half board are well over the expensive bracket. **Hacienda Pinsaquí** (see LIVE THE HACIENDA LIFE, page 15 in TOP SPOTS) is also nearby; rates run about US$90 for a double with no meals.

On the road near Peguche, a weaving village near Otavalo.

LAGUNA DE CUICOCHA

Another spectacular mountain lake is Laguna de Cuicocha, about 16 km (10 miles) west of Cotacachi town. This deep, blue crater lake with two islands in the middle is a popular recreation area on weekends. Motor boats can be rented to explore the lake, though the islands are off limits because of research projects. A walk around the lake takes about five hours. Be warned: those berries that look like blueberries are actually something else — and they are poisonous. A round-trip by taxi from Cotacachi costs about US$10, and there are two decent restaurants nearby, as well as a modest place to stay on the hill.

The lake is part of the enormous **Reserva Ecológica Cotacachi-Cayapas** that stretches down the western highlands to the tropical lowlands of Esmeraldas Province. Just south of the reserve and about 40 km (25 miles) to the west of Laguna de Cuicocha is the remote village of **Apuela**, set in the deep Andean cloud forest. Nearby are the **Piscinas de Nangulví** thermal baths. Basic accommodation is available. There are a few buses each day along the scenic but jolting road between Otavalo and Apuela.

FOREST RESERVES

The rich and humid cloud forests, populated by a huge diversity of plants, birds and mammals, are disappearing even faster than the better-known rainforests. Deforestation on the western slopes of the Andes is threatening the survival of mammals such as mountain tapirs, spectacled bears, spider monkeys and pumas. In an attempt to counter this destruction, several adventurous and dedicated individuals have established protected reserves. Their objective is to safeguard the forest from logging, conserve the natural environment and protect endangered species.

Two such ecoactivists are Carlos Zorilla and Sandy Statz, whose **Intag Cloud Forest Reserve**, in the vicinity of Apuela, is a model of environmental friendliness. Rustic wooden cabins, solar-generated electricity and homegrown vegetables are indicators of their philosophy. Visitors can see their operation and explore the jungle for themselves for US$45 per person per day, including all meals and guides. For **reservations** FAX (06) 923392 E-MAIL intagcz@uio.satnet.net, or write to Intag at Casilla 18, Otavalo, Imbabura, Ecuador, giving at least two months notice. For information on more of these sorts of ecological enterprises, contact **Safari Tours** ((022) 552505 or (022) 223381 FAX (022) 220426 E-MAIL admin@safari.com.ec WEB SITE www.safari.com.ec, Calamá 380 and Juan León Mera, Quito.

IBARRA

For most visitors to Ecuador, Ibarra, the provincial capital of Imbabura, is a stopover en route to somewhere else. Notably, it used to be the starting point of the antiquated, single-track railway that plunged down the slopes of the Andes to the coastal town of San Lorenzo. The town is also a transit stop on the Panamericana highway on the way to or from Colombia. But Ibarra is more than a transportation hub. Known as the White City, it's a handsome, old-fashioned town of white-walled colonial buildings and peaceful squares filled with flowering trees. The odd horse-drawn cart still clomps along cobbled streets. Its altitude of 2,210 m (7,251 ft) gives the city a refreshingly comfortable climate and its population of nearly 100,000 creates enough activity without making it too busy. It might not be a great cultural or entertainment center, but Ibarra is a pleasant place to enjoy the slow-paced, everyday pleasures of Ecuadorian life, with several sights nearby to keep one busy.

BACKGROUND

San Antonio de Ibarra, the city's full name, was founded in 1606 and was named after Miguel de Ibarra, then-President of Quito's Royal Audencia. In its early days it became the administrative center of the exploitative textile industry. In spite of a massive earthquake in 1868, which killed most of its 6,000 inhabitants and destroyed many of its buildings, Ibarra has retained or rebuilt many of its fine colonial houses. The growing town gradually became, and still is, the main market for the region's agricultural products, such as cotton, sugarcane, coffee, cereals and livestock. It remains a center for textiles and silverware and has a large sugar refinery. Ibarra's population is a mixture of *indígenas*, blacks and *mestizos*.

GENERAL INFORMATION

The helpful **Tourist Information** office ((06) 958547 is on Olmedo 956 and Velasco, open Monday to Friday 9 AM to 1 PM and 2 PM to 5 PM. For travel and other information, also check with the tour companies **Nevitur** ((06) 958701, Bolívar and Oviedo, or **Turismo Inti Pungo** ((06) 255270, Rocafuerte and García Moreno. **Bike House** on Grijalva 7-22 and Olmedo rents mountain bikes.

Banco del Pacífico (Pedro Moncayo and Olmedo) and **Banco Pichincha** (Mosquera and Bolívar) both change travelers' checks, and **Banco del Austro** (Colón and Bolívar) has a Visa ATM. For international **phone calls**, the Andinatel office is on Sucre, a block north of the main square, Parque Pedro Moncayo (open 8 AM to 10 PM),

while the **Post Office** is on Salinas 6-64, between Oviedo and Moncayo. A recommended **doctor** is Dr. Eduardo Benítez ((06) 955592, Oviedo 8-40. The **Immigration Office** is on Olmedo and Villamar. Two centrally located Internet places are **Sí del Ecuador** on Parque Pedro Moncayo and **World Computers**, Pedro Moncayo between Bolívar and Sucre.

WHAT TO SEE AND DO

You can see most of the main city sights of Ibarra in a day. To get your bearings, look for the huge **obelisk** near the railway station, dedicated to the man who gave the city its name, Miguel de Ibarra. Walk a couple blocks eastwards along Velasco and then three blocks north along Bolívar to the **Parque Pedro Moncayo**, named after a famous journalist and diplomat of the nineteenth century. Some fine buildings surround the clipped-grass, tree-

lined square, including the city cathedral, whose main interest is its magnificent golden altar and powerful portraits of the 12 apostles. To its south, **Plaza Francisco Calderón**'s attraction lies in the new **Plaza de la Ibarreñidad** development where well-healed *ibarreños* come to enjoy the restaurant, bar and shops.

Two blocks west of Pedro Moncayo square, you come to **Parque de la Merced**, as it's usually called, or Parque Dr. Victor Manuel Peñaherra, its official name. A bust of this eminent son of Ibarra, a lawyer and academic, stands in the park. Nearby is the **Basílica La Merced**, crowned with a statue of the Virgin. The opposite side of the plaza is dominated by the imposing Mediterranean-style **Ministerio de Agricultura y Ganadería**. Under its arches, bright stalls vend wonderful *nogadas* (a bit like nougat) and also *helados de paila*, a type of

The cloud forests on the slopes of the Andes are rapidly disappearing.

sorbet. Head to the nearby Heladería Rosalía Suárez for a greater selection.

For some local culture, the **Museo Banco Central**, Sucre and Oviedo, displays both general Ecuadorian archeology and more local history, including gold funeral masks. You can ask for a guided tour, and printed information is available in English. The museum also houses a small café, and is open Monday to Friday, 8:30 AM to 1:30 PM and 2:30 PM to 4:30 PM. Ibarra's other museums of interest are the quirky **Museo y Zoológico Dominicano** at the northern end of Bolívar by the Dominican church, which combines a modest religious art collection with cages of iguanas, sloths and birds, and the **Museo Atahualpa de Caranqui**,

In town, the best top-end inexpensive place is the **Hotel Royal Ruiz** (/FAX (06) 641999, Olmedo 9-40 and Pedro Moncayo, with carpeted rooms that have private bath and phone. There is also a sauna and a steam room. The best and most frequented budget accommodation is found at the friendly **Hostal Imbabura** (06) 950155 FAX (06) 958521, Oviedo 9-33 and Narváez. Tall rooms share baths, with a good café for breakfasts in the flowery patio. There are also several inexpensive hostels and hotels near the station.

Ibarreños enjoy the best cafés north of the capital: great places to sip a drink and people-watch. Among the best are the **Café Arte**, Salinas 5-43 and Oviedo, which doubles as an art gallery,

set on the site of an excavation of what is thought to be the birthplace of Atahualpa, the last Inca king.

WHERE TO STAY AND EAT

Few visitors stay overnight in Ibarra unless they prefer its peace and quiet to weekend Otavalo. If you do take a room, one of the moderately priced options is **Hotel Ajaví** (06) 920941 or (06) 955555 FAX (06) 955640 or (06) 952485, about a kilometer (just over a half mile) from the town center on the main road from the south. The comfortable, modern hotel has a restaurant, bar, pool and sauna. A bit further out of town, the **Hostería Chorlaví** (06) 932222 FAX (06) 932224 is about the same price, but blends an appealing colonial hacienda with antique furniture and comfortable rooms, as well as an excellent restaurant. Book ahead on weekends.

Coffee Café ΚΑΦΕ, at the corner of García Moreno and Rocafuerte, with great original cocktails, or **Café Floralp**, slightly further out and run by Swiss people who make fantastic yogurts and milkshakes from their own dairy. **El Barbudo** on Plaza de la Ibarreñidad is a good place to chill out in the day, and converts into a buzzing bar at night. From there, most partiers go on to **Tequila Rock** on Oviedo and Sucre, open until about 2 AM.

The best place to eat in the Ibarra area is probably at Hostería Chorlaví, a short taxi ride south of town; but in town, the **Fantasías Gourmet** on Bolívar 10-90 and Avenida Pérez Guerrero has sophisticated seafood dishes, and **El Manchego** at the corner of Oviedo and Narváez serves good Ecuadorian favorites amid cowboy decor. Otherwise, **La Estancia**, Garcia Moreno 7-66, is recommended for its rather expensive grills and **Antojitos de mi Tierra** on Plaza de la Ibarreñidad, with its outdoor seating, is one of the best places for a good lunch. For an inexpensive evening pizza, try **La Trattoria Rusticana** on Parque Pedro Moncayo. My own favorite is the least expensive of the lot: the **open market** held near the station. Stand-up stalls and sit-down snack shops cover the complete range of tasty local dishes. The *empanadas* (cheese-filled pastries) are as good as any I've had in Ecuador.

How to Get There

There are frequent buses between Ibarra, Otavalo, Quito, Tulcán and other major towns. Bus companies use their own terminals, clustering close to the obelisk area. This will change when the new bus terminal is finally finished. **Transportes Otavalo**, Avenida Galindo and Ávila Mariano Acosta (west of the obelisk), is probably the best line for Otavalo, while **Aerotaxi**, at Luís Borja and Avenida Mariano Acosta, is about the fastest and most comfortable to Quito. If arriving at night, take a taxi to your hotel, since the area around the train station and south of the obelisk is unsafe.

The Train to San Lorenzo

The train journey down the Andes from Ibarra to San Lorenzo is one of Ecuador's great adventures. It can also be one of its worst nightmares. First, you have to find out if the train is running, and if so, when. In recent years it has been out of action for months at a time because of landslides and breakdowns, and the El Niño floods of 1997 and 1998, which also caused extensive damage. At present, the train only runs a part of the way, and is used mainly for tourists. See also RIDE THE RAILS, page 17 in TOP SPOTS.

For information, call the station ((06) 950390, or check with the SAE in Quito for the latest developments. Locals now take the far cheaper, but less romantic, buses.

AROUND IBARRA

There are several pretty towns and villages in the vicinity of Ibarra. Of special interest is **San Antonio de Ibarra**, which bears the full name of the city itself and is only six kilometers (four miles) away. San Antonio's reputation for **woodcarving** is known throughout Ecuador and increasingly in other countries. Particularly famous are the realistic carvings of religious figures, elderly people, and nudes, some of which are almost life size. Craftsmen also carve chess sets, furniture, mirror frames, animals and some modernist pieces. The main square and main street of the village are lined with galleries and workshops, the best known being **Galería de Arte Luís Potosí**. Buses leave the obelisk in Ibarra every 20 minutes

or so for the short journey, though you can also ask for directions for the two-hour walk.

La Esperanza and Around

Seven kilometers (five miles) south of Ibarra is the dinky, stretched-out village of La Esperanza, the best starting point for climbing the daunting **Volcán Imbabura** (4,609 m or 15,121 ft) and the slightly less demanding **Loma Cubilche** (3,836 m or 12,585 ft). From La Esperanza, Bolívar gathered his troops before routing the Spanish under General Agualongo in Ibarra, and today, travelers occasionally gather magic mushrooms from the same slopes. In La Esperanza, there's a choice of rustic accommodation at either **Casa Aida** ((06) 642020, with a range of cheap and cheerful rooms with shared baths, or the cheaper **Casa María** ((06) 641973. The owner of Casa María, Patricio, is an excellent guide for walking and mountain-biking in the area. Ask around for the local leather, wood and embroidery artisans.

The area from here to Cayambe (north of Quito) is one of my favorites in the whole country. South of La Esperanza, the village of Zuleta lies 14 km (nearly nine miles) up the bumpy old road to Quito. There are many embroidering families in the area, as well as a trout and dairy farm at the beautiful, expensively priced **Hacienda Zuleta** ((022) 262580 WEB SITE www.zuleta.com (see LIVE THE HACIENDA LIFE, page 15 in TOP SPOTS), honey on sale, and stunning countryside.

North of Ibarra

Just four kilometers (two and a half miles) north of Ibarra is the well-known lake, **Laguna de Yahuarcocha** (Lake of Blood), so-called because of a great battle between the Incas and local Cara Indians, whose bleeding bodies were thrown into the lake, turning the water red. A motor racetrack now circles the lake spoiling its natural setting.

The great hot springs of **Chachimbiro** lie northwest of Ibarra, past the little village of Urcuquí, about 38 km (23 miles) of winding, partly-cobbled road through beautiful countryside. The site of the springs has been developed over the years, and the result is supremely relaxing, except on weekends when it gets pretty crowded. The complex includes medicinal mineral baths, hydromassages, saunas and swimming pools, as well as walks in the surrounding hills and a decent restaurant. Accommodation (no phone) inside the springs is basic but good value, and includes the entrance fee that visitors pay. For something more comfortable and private, the Freile family of Hacienda Pinsaquí own another old, moderately priced mansion close by called **San Francisco**

Ibarra, the capital of Imbabura Province is a handsome, old-fashioned town.

(/FAX (06) 946116 or (06) 946117 IN QUITO (/FAX (022) 546253 WEB SITE www.haciendapinsaqui.com.

To get to the springs, either share a taxi, or catch the only bus up, leaving at 7 AM from the stop on Pedro Moncayo and Flores (though ones to Urcuquí leave every 30 minutes). The bus returns to Ibarra at around noon.

Heading north on the Panamericana, the road down to San Lorenzo forks off at **Salinas**, about 25 km (15 miles) from Ibarra. Following the highway, you enter the dry and dusty **Chota Valley**, inhabited by descendants of slaves who still retain many of their tribal traditions. At **Mascarilla**, about 33 km (20 miles) out of Ibarra, the road forks again. The Panamericana continues to the right,

town. Rooms are spick and span and comfortable, meals decent, and tours (on foot, horse or bike) excellent. **Fundación Golondrinas** also is also active in conservation work in the area and organizes treks from El Ángel. For details contact (((022) 226602 FAX (022) 566076 E-MAIL manteca@uio .satnet.net, Isabel La Católica 1559.

TULCÁN

The capital of Carchi Province, Tulcán, just six kilometers (four miles) from the Colombian border, is a transit point for travelers going to and from Colombia. The town was a thriving smuggling center until a free-trade agreement in 1992.

while to the left, the old road to Colombia bumps up to **La Mira**, 15 km (nine miles) away, famous for its firework fiestas (particularly on February 2 for the Virgen de la Caridad).

RESERVA ECOLÓGICA EL ÁNGEL

The route up from La Mira leads to the friendly highland village of El Ángel (a further 25 km or 15 miles from La Mira), and the access point to the **Páramo El Ángel**, an area of mystical lakes, windswept grasslands and the curious, hairy-leafed, treelike **frailejón** plant, said to be the biggest plant in the world. If you want to explore this little-visited ecological reserve, ask for the offices of the **Fundación El Ángel**, or take a tour with the best hotel in town, the **Hostería El Ángel** (/FAX (06) 977584 E-MAIL rsommer@ecuanex.net.ec, which is by the traffic circle to the south of the

Now it has become a shopping center for Colombians whose stronger currency make goods here less expensive than in their own country. Some drug smuggling goes through the town, giving it a higher-than-average crime rate and making the streets unsafe at night. It isn't a great town for hotels and restaurants so there's not much point in staying overnight unless you get stuck in transit.

GENERAL INFORMATION

The **tourist information office** ((06) 983892 is on the second floor at Pichincha 467 between Bolívar and Sucre. It should be open each morning and afternoon except Saturday. **Eccotur** ((06) 980386, a travel agency, is on Sucre at the Plaza can sell flights to Quito or Cali. There are **Andinatel** offices for international calls on Olmedo and Ayacucho, and at the Terminal Terrestre bus terminal about two kilometers (just over a mile) southwest of the center of town. All the useful banks for ATMs, travelers' checks and changing money to Colombia pesos are found around the Plaza de la Independencia. About the best place to change money is the **Casa de Cambio** at the corner of Bolívar and Ayacucho. The **Colombian Consulate** is at Bolívar and Junín. Tulcán's two big fiestas are on April 11, and November 19.

WHAT TO SEE AND DO

Though Tulcán isn't renowned for its tourist sights, there is one unique and unlikely attraction that is consistently recommended. This is the **topiary**

The smartest, most modern hotel is town is the **Hotel Sara Espindola (**/FAX (06) 986209 or 985925, at Sucre and Ayacucho. Light rooms come with hot water (essential at 3,000 m/9,840 ft), cable televisions and telephones. In the budget range, **Hotel Alejandra (** (06) 981784, on Sucre and Quito, is recommended for clean rooms. **Hotel Machado (** (06) 984221 FAX (06) 980009, Ayacucho and Bolívar, is also very good value, with large cable televisions, towels, soaps and phones.

Tulcán boasts some good Colombia restaurants, where you can try *pollo sudado*, a great chicken dish. The two best are **El Patio** on Bolívar and Pichincha, and **Los Arrieros** on Bolívar and 10 de Agosto. **La Fogata** is a popular place

garden in the cemetery two blocks north of the **Parque Ayora**. Fantastic figures carved from cypress bushes create one of the greatest masterpieces of the hedge-clipper's art. The epitaph of Sr. José Franco, the cultivator of the gardens, reads: "In Tulcán, a cemetery so beautiful that it invites one to die."

Also near Tulcán, you can gain easier access to the *páramos* than at El Ángel. Head west to the little village of **Tufiño**, where there are some lovely thermal springs nearby, and continue climbing to the highlands around Volcán Chiles. Ask the tourist office for transportation practicalities.

WHERE TO STAY AND EAT

Hotels in Tulcán tend to fill up quick with Colombian shoppers. It's a good idea to call ahead, especially on weekends. All of them are inexpensive.

for pizzas and Ecuadorian food, and **Bar Era** a decent place for a beer.

HOW TO GET THERE AND AWAY

Crossing the border from Ecuador into Colombia or vice versa is a simple matter as long as your passport is valid. Both countries give a 90-day tourist visa to almost all nationalities. There are regular buses and minibuses between **Parque Ayora** to the border at **Rumichaca**. The border is open from 6 AM to 9 PM. Money changing facilities are available but carefully check your transactions. Note that there are occasional customs and immigration checks on the road between Ibarra and Tulcán.

OPPOSITE: Highland landscape near Otavalo. ABOVE: Some of the most beautiful mountain landscapes in Ecuador can be seen around Ibarra.

Central
Highlands

The intrepid German explorer and naturalist, Alexander von Humboldt (1769–1859), climber of many of Ecuador's tallest mountains and holder of the world climbing record for 30 years, named the twin range of mountains running from Quito to Cuenca the "Avenue of Volcanoes." The description is apt and the name stuck. Travelers going south from Quito by road or rail eagerly strain their eyes and stretch their necks for views of these fabulous mountains. On very clear days, one can see nine of Ecuador's 10 highest peaks, though most people will be happy to spot looming Chimborazo in the distance. Many people are disappointed, as I have been frequently, because the peaks have a habit of cloaking themselves in drifting white clouds. Nevertheless, you will see much stunning scenery in the central highlands, along with picturesque colonial towns, feisty festivals and multifarious markets.

LATACUNGA

An unfortunate claim to fame of this highland town, the capital of Cotopaxi Province, is its propensity for catastrophe. In 400 years it has been devastated or destroyed by earthquakes and volcanic eruptions of nearby Volcán Cotopaxi about 10 times, and subsequently rebuilt. The most recent disaster, an earthquake in 1996, left several dead and thousands homeless. Not surprisingly, light-gray pumice stone is a favored building material.

The name Latacunga means "God of the Waters" in Quichua, though it has also been suggested that it is derived from words meaning "land of my choice" in another Indian language. If the latter is true, perhaps this is why *latacungaños* are so obstinate about living in their disaster-prone town. It is usually said that the danger of another eruption is very small, yet an old man who lives nearby told me he had four healthy children, no debts, but one major nightmare — that one day Cotopaxi would erupt again and destroy his farm.

Latacunga has some pretty gardens and squares. Otherwise it doesn't offer a great deal to the visitor except for its proximity to natural wonders, remote Andean villages, and the nearby market of Saquisilí, which many consider to be the best Indian market in Ecuador (see page 124, under AROUND LATACUNGA).

GENERAL INFORMATION

There is no tourist information office in town but you can pick up a tourist map from **Metropolitan Touring** on Quito and Guayaquil. Banks cluster close to the main square, Parque Vicente León. **Banco Popular** has a MasterCard ATM, and

Filanbanco a Visa one. **Banco del Austro** and **Banco de Pichincha** change travelers' checks. The Andinatel and post offices are on Quevedo and Maldonado, and there's an Internet café on Salcedo, close to the northeastern corner of Parque Vicente León.

WHAT TO SEE AND DO

Most visitors use Latacunga as a base from which to explore the region, and most spend little time in the town. Those who do tend to congregate around **Parque Vicente León**, the tourist area of the city. The main municipal buildings are here also, as is the city's **cathedral**, restored in 1973.

A lively, sprawling **market** spreads over several blocks east of **Río Cutuchi**, the big day being Saturday. If you suffer from cultural withdrawal while in Latacunga your best bet is to visit the **Molinos de Monserrat Museum** of ethnography and art, on Vela near Maldonado, open Tuesday to Saturday on an erratic basis.

FESTIVALS

An unusual characteristic of the usually macho *latacungaños* is their love of dressing up as black women. This they do at the **Fiesta de la Mamá Negra**, a raucous celebration of street dancing, heavy drinking, Andean music and fireworks, held each year on September 23 and 24. Another **parade** in honor of the Black Mama takes place two weeks later. And on November 11 Latacunga celebrates its **anniversary of independence** with bullfighting and yet more exuberance.

WHERE TO STAY AND EAT

Many people stay in Latacunga for Saquisilí's Thursday market (see below), so booking is advised for Wednesday nights. Reservations are also necessary during the town's fiestas. On other days, the town is very quiet. Accommodation is pretty functional; those looking for more comfort or character should consider the hosterías in the local area.

Expensive

If your budget can stand it, the best places to stay are at the hacienda **Hostería La Ciénega** ((03) 719052 FAX (03) 719182 IN QUITO ((022) 541337 or (022) 549126 FAX (022) 549126 E-MAIL

la_cienega@andinanet.net WEBSITE www.geocities
.com/haciendaec, Cordero 1442, about 20 km
(13 miles) north of town, or the **Hacienda San
Agustín de Callo** (/FAX (03) 719160 IN QUITO
(Mignon Plaza) (022) 242508 FAX (022) 269844
E-MAIL mplaza@access.net.ec WEB SITE www
.incahacienda.com, close to the entrance to Parque
Nacional Cotopaxi (see LIVE THE HACIENDA LIFE,
page 15 in TOP SPOTS).

Inexpensive

In town, the best hotel is probably **Hotel Rodelú**
((03) 800956 FAX (03) 812341, on Quito, near the
Parque Vicente. Rooms are fairly comfortable, with
private bathrooms and televisions, and there is
an Italian restaurant as well. Cheaper, and very
friendly, the **Hotel Tilipulo** ((03) 803130, at
Guayaquil and Quevedo, includes balconies in
some rooms, private bathrooms, televisions and
phones. The owner is very knowledgeable and
helpful with travel information. On the budget
end of the scale, **Hotel Estambul** ((03) 800354,
on Quevedo and Salcedo, is friendly and safe
and helps with travel arrangements. Rooms are
spacious and bathrooms shared.

Food-wise, there are many inexpensive and
good-value restaurants in town, but none to rave
about. Look out for **Pollos Gus** on the Panamericana, **La Borgoña** and **El Mashca** on
Valencia, and **Parrilladas Los Copihues** on Quito
for the best steaks and meat dishes. The best rec-
ommendation is **Pizzería Rodelú** in Hotel Rodelú.
Pingüino on Quito has the best ice creams. Most
restaurants close early.

HOW TO GET THERE

There is no central bus station in Latacunga. Buses
to Quito leave from Plaza Chile (also called Plaza
El Salto) by the market, and buses going south on
the Panamericana leave from the other side of the
river, at Avenida 5 de Junio, close to the train
station. The buses to Pujilí, Zumbahua and western villages are also nearby. For other villages, such
as Saquisilí, there's a stop on Benavídez, north of
the market. The train station for the Quito–
Riobamba route lies on the west side of the
Panamericana.

AROUND LATACUNGA

Several remote Andean villages are hidden in the
mountains above Latacunga. The circuit known
as the **Latacunga Loop** takes in several of these
villages and the emerald-blue crater lake of
Quilotoa. It's one of the most beautiful trips in
Ecuador. It's an adventurous journey: roads are
rough, directions confusing, and there are reports
of many beggars in the lake area. It's probably best
to go by car with a guide, but you can also take a

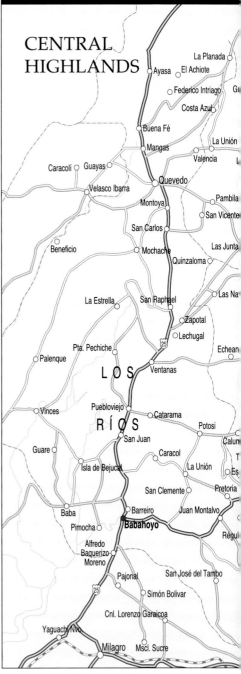

CENTRAL HIGHLANDS

bus, as many of the villages have services from
Latacunga. Check return times carefully before
you leave, and seek advice from hoteliers in
Latacunga.

About 10 km (six miles) west of Latacunga is
the village of **Pujilí**, where the Sunday market is
the main attraction. There is the odd modest hotel

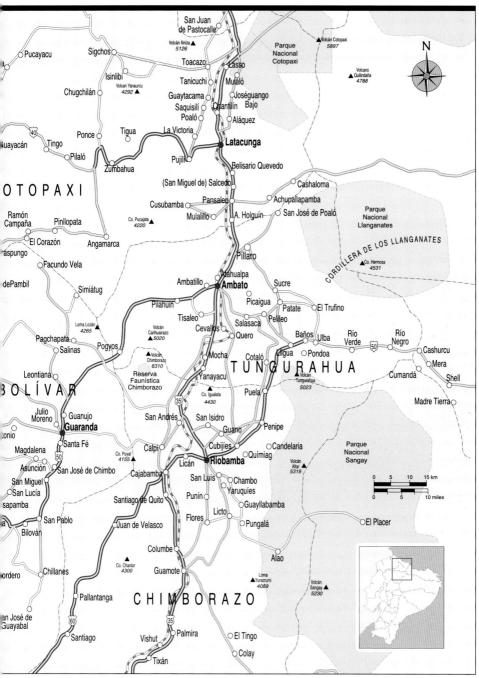

and restaurant. The town is renowned for its Corpus Christi celebrations in June. Continuing for another 60 km (37 miles) through grandiose mountain scenery brings you to the small settlement of **Zumbahua**, known for its market, held on Saturday, and attendant festivities that include bullfighting and prodigious imbibing of alcohol.

Llamas transport goods to market, and horses carry home *vaqueros* (cowboys). There is some basic accommodation in Zumbahua if you want to join in the pre-market revelries on Friday night.

Before Zumbahua, about 40 km (25 miles) west of Pujilí, lies the valley of **Tigua**, known as the center of production of detailed and charming

Indian paintings on sheep's hide or canvass, of the sort that are sold on the streets of Quito. This naïve Andean art depicts village life, rural scenes, volcanoes, lamas, festivals, and the myths and dreams of the local *indígenas*. A young Indian girl hardly more than 12 years old tried to sell me such paintings, claiming she had done them herself. Skeptically, I asked her to sketch one of the scenes in my notebook. She did so perfectly. I bought the painting. In the village of Tigua, stop by at the artists' cooperative above the church. An *hostería* was under construction when I last visited, contact E-MAIL jeancolvin@hotmail.com for further information.

About 14 km (nine miles) north of Zumbahua you come to **Laguna Quilotoa**. The road is badly signposted, so if you are driving you will need to ask for directions. The lake isn't visible from the road and you have to climb up to the crater rim before you can look down onto the emerald waters surrounded by steep volcanic slopes. A precipitous path goes down to the water's edge and it takes five or six hours to walk around the lake. Near the crater rim is the small community of **Ponce-Quilotoa**, where travelers can stay at **Cabañas Quilotoa** (no phone), which is run by an artist named Humberto, or at **El Refugio de la Laguna**. Tigua paintings, carved masks and other artifacts are on sale. Warm clothes are needed because it gets chilly at night here. The daily bus from Latacunga to Chugchilán passes through the community.

The best place to stay in the area is the **Black Sheep Inn** ((03) 814587 E-MAIL blksheep@ interactive.net.ec WEB SITE www.blacksheepinn .com, about 20 km (12 miles) further north along the road from the lake, near the village of **Chugchilán**. Owned by a couple from Seattle, the Black Sheep Inn is highly praised for its simple, homey atmosphere and its stunning views. Facilities include a book exchange, horseback riding, good information about the area and local Inca ruins, and good food. Rates are inexpensive in the bunkhouse, which sleeps eight, and moderate for rooms with shared bathrooms and hot showers. All include breakfast and dinner, with discounts available. If you want to hike around some of the most beautiful landscapes in Ecuador, or simply relax in high mountain climes, this is the place to base yourself.

Continuing north around the Latacunga Loop, you come to the village **Sigchos**. Don't bother to stay unless you plan to hike in the **Toachi Valley**. Going westwards, the road continues through **Toacazo** and then turns south back towards Latacunga. On the way you can make a side-trip to **Saquisilí**, a small town with a big reputation for its Thursday market, one of the best known and most commercially important in Ecuador. Though interesting textiles are on sale, the mar-

ket is more a living, working Andean emporium and a central hub for the web of communities of *indígenas* in the surrounding mountains who come to town to do their trade and meet friends. Visitors are attracted by the colorful costumes of the local people, the main theme being red ponchos and felt porkpie hats.

South of Latacunga, 14 km (nearly nine miles) on the road to Ambato, you pass through the town of **San Miguel de Salcedo**. It's an unremarkable place, except for fans of ice cream, who say the town produces some of the best in the country.

PARQUE NATIONAL COTOPAXI

At a height of 5,897 m (19,347 ft), the awesome and beautiful **Volcán Cotopaxi** is the tallest continuously active volcano in the world and the second tallest peak in Ecuador, after Chimborazo. With its cone of almost perfect proportions, often veiled in swirling mists, it is a mountain of might and mystery, and an object of worship that local *indígenas* believe to be inhabited by powerful spirits.

Seldom quiescent for more than about 15 years, Cotopaxi has erupted many times, devastating the surrounding terrain. Fumaroles smoke in its crater, which is 360 m (1,180 ft) deep and 700 m (2,297 ft) in diameter at its widest. At night, fires sometimes light up the clouds that cover the cone, reminding the onlooker of the mountain's potential for destruction.

The upper part of Cotopaxi is permanently covered with snow, its flank gray with lava and volcanic ash, while the base stands in the open grassland of the *páramo*. The wild and desolate area surrounding the mountain, which includes pine forests and several lakes and streams, encompasses the 33,393-ha (82,515-acre) Parque Nacional Cotopaxi. The park also contains several other high peaks, of which 4,712-m (15,459-ft) Rumiñahui is the most important.

The most frequently visited park in the country, Parque Nacional Cotopaxi contains campsites, rustic *cabañas*, a small museum, footpaths and a basic tourist infrastructure. But because of its size, the park invariably seems deserted, except on some weekends during the dry season, which runs from June to August.

The park is one of the last refuges of the endangered Andean condor (the name is derived from the Quichua word *cuntur*). With a wingspan up to three meters (10 ft) and weighing up to 13 kg (28 lb), and up to 120 cm long (almost four feet), *vultur gryphus* is the world's biggest bird of prey. Visitors lucky enough to spot this rare black raptor will note the flashes of white on its wings and the white frill at the base of its neck. Several other rare birds can be seen in the park, including various highland hummingbirds and the orange-faced caracara falcon.

As for mammals, the rare Andean spectacled bear makes its home in remote parts of the park, out of sight of visitors. Pumas (mountain lions) and Andean foxes are sometimes glimpsed, while llamas are easy to spot because a captive herd is kept near one of the park entrances. You might also spot white-tailed deer, rabbits and the teeny red brocket deer. Wild bulls munch green grasses and wild horses gallop across wide plateaus.

Parque Nacional Cotopaxi is an excellent place for hiking, cycling and camping. One of the best camping spots is by the shore of **Laguna Limpio Pungo**, at about 3,880 m (12,730 ft), but you can also stay in the *refugio* at 4,800 m (15,748 ft), which has bunk beds and cooking facilities, but gets extremely cold at night.

The entrance fee to the national park is about US$10, with a further US$10 for a night in the refuge, and about US$1 per night to camp. The main entrance from the east side of the Pan-americana is open 7 AM to 3 PM, though you can leave the park until about sunset. Acclimatization is very much necessary before visiting the refuge, with altitude sickness a real threat.

Buses from Latacunga and Quito drop you on the Panamericana, by one of the two roads that run up into the park, but then it is a long hike or hitchhike to get into the park itself. Alternatively, take a taxi from Latacunga. Many tour companies in Quito run tours to the park.

Some companies in Quito organize tours in which mountain bikes are carried to the park on the top of jeeps. After cycling around the *páramo*, exploring some Inca ruins and picnicking, the jeep grinds up the mountain as far as the rough road goes, which is to the parking lot at 4,600 m (15,092 ft), just below the *refugio*. Wearing helmets, pads and warm clothes, the mad bikers take off down the mountain. It's not as easy as it might sound because your wheels get trapped in ruts and some of the surface is loose, but it's fantastic fun. You need a good bike with good brakes. **Biking Dutchman Tours** pioneered these "uphill by jeep, downhill by bike" adventures and offers very professional service. In Quito, the biking Dutchman (Jan Lescrauwaet) can be contacted at ((022) 568323 FAX (022) 567008 E-MAIL dutchman@ ecuadorexplorer.com WEB SITE www.ecuador explorer.com/dutchman, Foch 714 and Juan León Mera, Quito. Another recommended operator is **Arie's Bike Company** (/FAX (022) 906052 E-MAIL ariesbikecompany@latinmail.com WEB SITE www.ariesbikecompany.com, Wilson 578 and Reina Victoria, Quito.

Another way of literally getting a grip on Cotopaxi is to actually climb the mountain. To achieve this you need to be fit and acclimatized to the altitude, and have some climbing experience,

a professional guide, climbing equipment and gritty determination. It isn't a technically difficult climb, but professional advice is advised. Numerous agencies in Quito offer two-day Cotopaxi climbing packages, for details see SPORTING SPREE, page 37 in YOUR CHOICE. Ensure the Ecuadorian Association of Mountain Guides (**ASEGUIM — Asociacíon Ecuatoriana de Guías de Montaña**) has approved the guides (see SPORTING SPREE for more on this issue).

AMBATO

The city of Ambato, destroyed by earthquake in 1949 and subsequently rebuilt, is the fourth-biggest city in Ecuador and the capital of Tungurahua Province. But this rather ugly metropolis with a population well over 100,000, known for its production of shoes and cement, and for food processing and distilling alcohol, doesn't have too much to offer tourists. Travelers from Quito usually pass through on their way to the popular resort of Baños, or they continue southwards along the Panamericana towards Riobamba and Cuenca.

GENERAL INFORMATION

The **Tourist Office** ((03) 821800 is on Guayaquil and Rocafuerte, close to the Hotel Ambato. It's open 8:30 AM to noon and 2 PM to 5 PM weekdays only. **Filanbanco** for Visa ATM and **Banco del Pacífico** for MasterCard ATM are close together on Parque Cevallos. **Metropolitan Touring** has a branch at Rocafuerte and Montalvo. **Andinatel** and the **post office** are both on Castillo, by the Parque Juan Montalvo. **Ciudad Andina**, Castillo 528, has the fastest Internet connection.

WHAT TO SEE AND DO

The **Museo de Ciencias Naturales** in the Colegio Nacional Bolívar is filled with stuffed birds and animals, some of them looking a bit forlorn and ragged. There's also a memorable collection of old photographs of Ambato, as well an interesting geological collection. The museum is open 8:30 AM to 12:30 PM and 2:30 PM to 6:30 PM weekdays only. Visiting the homes of Ambato's most illustrious citizens is also possible. Ask the tourist office for details of the houses of well-known Ecuadorian writers Juan Montalvo (1833–1889) and Juan León Mera (1832–1894), which is known as **La Quinta de Liria**. They are in the suburbs, a walk or taxi ride away.

The city is also famous for its exuberant **Fiesta de Frutas y Flores** during carnival time in February, when water throwing, so popular in the rest of the country, is banned — in Ambato they use foam instead! The **Monday market** is the country's largest, though it isn't known for its *artesanía*.

WHERE TO STAY

Ambato's accommodation is pretty limited, but there's a choice of in-town hotels, or the ones in the quieter suburbs.

Moderate

For an extremely good-value bed for the night, **Hotel Ambato (** (03) 847020 FAX (03) 827197 hambato@hotmail.com, Guayaquil at Rocafuerte, fits the bill. Rooms are comfortable and modern, with private bathrooms, cable televisions and telephones. The hotel also includes a casino, a bar and a recommended restaurant. Of the options

outside the center, the most pleasant is **Hotel Villa Hilda (** (03) 845014 FAX (03) 845571, Avenida Miraflores. The hotel is located in the quiet suburb of Miraflores, and though the rooms vary in size and quality, the gardens are very attractive and there's also a small swimming pool.

Inexpensive

There are quite a few bland but good-value hotels downtown. The two best are the **Gran Hotel (** (03) 824199 FAX (03) 824235, Lalama and Rocafuerte, with hot water, telephones, televisions and a restaurant, and the **Hotel Pirámida Inn (** (03) 824092 FAX (03) 854358, Cevallos at Egüez, with similar facilities but no restaurant. There are a number of cheapies around Parque 12 de Noviembre. About the best for the price, with reliable hot water, is **Residencial La Unión (** (03) 824215, Espejo and 12 de Noviembre, but check out the others too.

WHERE TO EAT

In the moderate price category, the French **La Buena Mesa**, on Quito near Rocafuerte, competes with the good international dishes at the **Hotel Ambato** for the city's best restaurant. La Buena Mesa's great atmosphere and friendly service gives it the edge, in my opinion. The other slick place worth trying is the **Restaurant El Gran Alamo**, Montalvo near Sucre, which is Swiss-run and tasty.

A good choice for atmosphere and inexpensive food is the Cuban **Cuba Son** on Guayaquil near Bolívar, which doubles as a lively bar. The **Restaurant El Alamo** is the poorer cousin of the "Gran Alamo" above, but is still good value and welcoming. The best pizza is found at **Pizzería Fornace** on Cevallos near Montalvo, which also serves a range of Italian dishes. For a steak, try **Parrilladas El Gaucho** on Bolívar near Quito. **El Patio Café Cultural**, on the corner of Parque Juan Montalvo, is a good café that also hosts many cultural events. The best place for a beer and a dance is **Cervecería Bufalo** on Olmedo and Mera, or else the posher **Restaurant Coyote Disco Club** on Bolívar near Quito.

HOW TO GET THERE

Ambato's airport isn't used for public transportation. The bus station lies two kilometers (under a mile) northeast of downtown, on Avenida las Américas. Buses to there leave from Parque Cevallos and taxis are inexpensive. There are plenty of buses to all destinations north and south on the Panamericana, as well as Guayaquil, or down to the Oriente. The train station is close to the Terminal Terrestre, with expensive trains to Quito on Friday and Riobamba on Saturday.

AROUND AMBATO

All the highland villages around Ambato are good places to catch local fiestas. May and June are probably the best months, with big Corpus Christi celebrations in Salasaca and Pelileo, and in Santo Vintio on June 15.

The road from Ambato to Baños (with great views of Volcán Tungurahua on clear days) passes through the small, nondescript village of **Salasaca**, which is known for the weaving of *tapices* (tapestries). It is said that the Salasaca Indians were originally *mitmakuna*: people who had been forced to move to Ecuador from Bolivia by the Incas as punishment for revolt. Certainly they have their unique style of dress, with black woven ponchos and wide-brimmed, white felt hats. Some of the words they use for describing the weaving process are said to be similar to those once used in the ancient Inca capital of Cuzco. It is well worth stopping for a while in Salasaca to check out the weavings. Ask for the house of **Alonsa Pilla**, who gives demonstrations of traditional techniques and sells great tapestries.

Just five kilometers (three miles) further down the road is the little town of **Pelileo**, denim capital of Ecuador, just the place to buy a pair of jeans on Saturday market day. A few kilometers north of Pelileo, off the main Ambato–Baños road, is the attractive village of **Patate**, reminiscent of the Douro Valley in Portugal, with its grapevines and views over Río Patate. The **Hotel Turístico Patate** ((03) 870177 IN QUITO (022) 590657, is a pleasant, inexpensive place to stay, where tours into the little-known **Parque Nacional Llanganates** can be arranged. A cobbled road, with wonderful views down to the patchwork of fields in the valley, leads from Patate to **Hacienda Manteles** (/FAX (03) 870123 IN QUITO (/FAX (022) 505230, also a good base for exploring, horseback riding, bird watching, hiking and fishing. The moderately priced hacienda encompasses 1,600 ha (3,960 acres) of cloud forest, and there are magnificent views of Volcán Tungurahua. The homemade food is first-class, served in a homelike, weaving-adorned restaurant with a roaring fire. The treasure of the Inca leader Atahualpa is said to be buried in the vicinity of nearby village of El Triunfo on the river Muyo.

BAÑOS

Baños is one of the most popular destinations for tourists and travelers in Ecuador. This small town, nestled in a valley surrounded by steep, green mountains has long been a well-regarded hot spring resort, and in recent years has grown to become a favored stop on the gringo trail. This popularity was dramatically cut short in 1999 however, when the nearby Volcán Tungurahua decided to vent its lava spleen. The local authorities placed the town on orange alert, with a high likelihood of a major eruption. In October, they ordered the evacuation of the town's 20,000 inhabitants and closed the roads in and out of the town. Months later, the feared major disaster hadn't happened, and while tour operators offered tours to view the erupting mountain, desperate local residents literally fought their way back to their homes and jobs. By early 2001, the town had resumed its "normal" slow-paced life, though the threat of eruption and evacuation is ever present.

International restaurants, reasonably priced hostels and hotels, several adventure travel agencies, access to both the jungle and the mountains, plenty of nearby attractions and activities, an agreeable climate and some fine shops — all of these make Baños a good spot to hang out for a few days or more in a relaxed atmosphere. Beneath its touristy surface Baños has its own small-town character and charm, but, when all is said

and done, "it's one of those places that everyone visits simply because everyone *else* goes there" as the author of *The Gringo Trail*, Mark Mann, put it. One curious local specialty is toffee made from sugarcane, which you can see being pulled in sticky strings from hooks in shop doorways.

BACKGROUND

Extraordinary paintings of what appear to be death and disaster in the Basílica, dedicated to Nuestra Señora de Agua Santa (the Virgin of the Holy Water), are a clue to the popularity of Baños with local Catholics. Images of people falling from breaking bridges as they cross ravines, cars toppling from cliffs or villagers fleeing erupting volcanoes are as violent and lurid as Japanese comic books. But there is an important difference. In the Baños paintings nobody gets hurt, because at the last moment they are saved by the miraculous intervention of the Virgin of the Holy Water. Like Saint Christopher, the Virgin has the power to prevent accidents, which is why many people believe it to be a wise precaution to make offerings and prayers to her image before embarking on a long journey. Also of interest at the basilica is the adjoining museum with the usual display of ecclesiastical costumes, stuffed animals and freak fetuses. One calf's head preserved in formaldehyde has three eyes, two noses and a triple palate, reminiscent of some modern art.

Also believed to have special powers is the holy water itself that is generated in the bowels of Volcán Tungurahua and emerges in the Baños de la Virgen and other outlets. Bathing in and drinking these waters is said to cure various ills and is a major attraction for visitors. The town's location also makes it a gateway between the jungle and the Sierra. According to rumor, Baños has long been a transit point for illegal and contraband goods, including drugs.

GENERAL INFORMATION

Although it doesn't have a tourist office, Baños is a vibrant center of information because of the proliferation of travel agencies and the number of passing travelers. **Café Hood** (see below) keeps comment books containing advice about good places to go, agencies to use and guides to avoid. Staff and owners of cafés, restaurants, hostels and hotels can also be good sources of information. For the latest information on Volcán Tungurahua and Baños' status, see the newspaper *El Comercio*'s WEB SITE www.elcomercio.com or contact the SAE WEB SITE www.samexplo.org. You should ask your hotel for details of emergency evacuation procedures.

Weaver from Salasaca.

On the town's main square, Parque Central, you'll find the **Post Office** and the **Andinatel** office. **Banco del Pacífico**, at Ambato and Halflants, has a MasterCard ATM. **Internet cafés** are plentiful (this is the gringo trail after all), with one at Reyes near Ambato, or another on 12 de Noviembre at Oriente.

TOURS

It's not easy to choose between tour operators if you want to do a jungle or climbing trip. Most of them are good but there are occasional reports of bad guides, poor food and inferior equipment. Guides should have a license issued by Ministerio

Tsantsa ((03) 740416 or (09) 668012 E-MAIL shuar@ gmx.de, in a small office on Ambato and Halflants. They specialize in trips to the Río Aguas Negras in the Cuyabeno.

Other agencies might be less expensive or even better—it very much depends on who your guide is on your trip. Jungle trips cost about US$45 per day per person and climbing trips about between US$55 and US$80 depending on the size of your group and not including the national park entrance fee. It's a good idea to withhold half the tour fee until completion of the trip.

Baños is a small enough town to get anywhere within a few minutes on foot. People are generally helpful, and even without speaking Spanish,

de Tourismo while natural history guides should have a "Naturalista" credential issued by the Ministerio del Ambiente. Whitewater rafting guides should be able to produce AGAR certification, and climbing guides are certified by ASEGUIM (see SPORTING SPREE, page 37 in YOUR CHOICE for more on this issue).

Rainforestur (/FAX (03) 740743 E-MAIL rainfor @interactive.net.ec, Ambato near Maldonado, or IN QUITO (/FAX (022) 239822, Amazonas 420 near Roca, enjoys a good reputation, particularly for jungle tours to the Cuyabeno region, and climbing tours in the highlands. Some of their guides speak German and French, as well as English and Spanish. **Julio Verne Expeditions** (/FAX (03) 740253 E-MAIL julver@interactive.net.ec, Oriente near Halflants, also has good guides and equipment for both the jungle and climbing. One of few Shuar Indian-run companies, also recommended, is

gesticulated sign language directions will usually suffice. This is a good place to learn Spanish, since tuition and living costs are lower than in the capital and it's such a pleasant place. Several schools and private teachers are available. **Pepe Eras** ((03) 740232, **International Spanish School** ((03) 740612, and **Baños Spanish Center** ((03) 740632 are all recommended. Check with Café Hood for names of other schools and teachers.

WHAT TO SEE AND DO

It would be a missed opportunity to go to Baños and not experience a hot spring bath. The main baths are the **Baños de la Virgen** by the waterfall near the Palace Hotel at the southeastern end of town. There are showers, changing rooms, three pools of varying temperatures, and the cost is minimal. Dress code: a bathing suit. The baths open at 4:30 AM and the earlier you get there the better. A dawn immersion in a hot spring sets you up for the day. Even more pleasant are the baths at **El Salado**, about a mile out of town off the Ambato road. These are less crowded and there are more pools. There's also a cold waterfall to cool off your steamed-up body.

Some people complain that the baths are dirty; it's true that they aren't as immaculate and modern as their counterparts in, say, Japan. But don't be concerned by the slight coloration in the water; it is caused by the water's mineral content. The other complaint from some *gringas* is that the locals stare at them, which is all the more reason to go early, when fewer people are around.

Outside of town, heading to Puyo, about 20 km (12 miles) down the rough but dramatic old road, you come to the village of Río Verde. From here, walk down a trail to the right which takes you down into the canyon of the Río Pastaza, where there's a mighty waterfall, aptly named **El Pailón del Diablo**, the Devil's Cauldron. Below the canyon is a wooden suspension bridge and a path that leads to **El Otro Lado**, (the Other Side), an exquisite house with three separate *cabañas* that is totally isolated and surrounded by dense jungle and views of the canyon. The hostería unfortunately closed in 2000, and its future is uncertain. You can ask Quito or Baños travel agents for any news.

There are many good walks and horse rides around Baños. A popular excursion is up to the **Bella Vista cross** that overlooks the town, about an hour's steep walking up a path leading off Calle Maldonado. Bring a stick in case of dogs, and it's best to go in a group because robberies have been reported in the area. Other walks include a two-hour climb to **Illuchi** village, which gives you great views over the Baños valley and to Volcán Tungurahua, or else the longer hike to the village of **Lligua**, via the falls of Cascada Inés María.

Just 20 minutes' walk from the town along the Ambato road is the **San Martín Zoo**, a surprisingly large and well-maintained *ecozoológico* with a variety of native animals and birds including jaguars, tapirs, spectacled bears, harpy eagles and condors. Many died in the trauma of evacuation, but the zoo was up and running again in 2001. Also recommended are the **Basílica** dedicated to Nuestra Señora de Agua Santa (the Virgin of the Holy Water) and the adjoining museum.

SPORTS AND OUTDOOR ACTIVITIES

Mountain Biking

Want to feel like a kid again, with the warm wind blowing on your face as you speed down a long hill on a bike? Here's the place to do it: from Baños down the road to Puyo, a classic bike ride of about 70 km (44 miles), descending from 1,800 m

(5,905 ft) to just under 1,000 m (3,280 ft). Though the road is rough in parts and it's not all downhill, the effort and aching muscles are rewarded by stunning views of the green flanks of the Andes, threaded with silvery waterfalls and dotted with orchids and bromeliads. The road is often under repair, so ask around before committing to renting a bike. The entire journey through the canyon of the Río Pastaza to Puyo takes about six to eight hours, but you can do a shorter version just to Río Verde, about 20 km (12 miles) down from Baños. From Puyo, or Río Verde, you can get back up to Baños on one of the regular buses with your bike strapped to the roof. There are many places to rent bikes but check them carefully, especially the brakes, tires and gears, before deciding on one. Prices for a day's rental start at US$4.

Horseback Riding

Similar precautions have to be taken with renting horses. A couple of old nags that a friend and I stupidly committed ourselves to before inspecting had open sores on their backs and were clearly unfit for riding, so we lost our deposit. We would have been better off trying the horses at the German-run **Hostal Isla de Baños (** (03) 740609, which are well looked after. You can also rent good horses by contacting **Ivan** at the **Pizzería Napolitano** near the Plantas y Blanco Hostal. **Caballos José** and **Angel Aldáz'** horses also have a good reputations. They charge about US$10 per half day, more if accompanied by a guide.

Whitewater Rafting

Río Loco ("Mad River") **(**/FAX (03) 740929 E-MAIL riolocot@yahoo.com, Ambato and Alfaro, is the operator with the best and longest reputation for rafting trips on the Pastaza and Patate rivers. But there are others. With masses of water and thundering rapids, followed by sudden stillness and silence, river trips are a great way of exploring the tropical rainforest.

WHERE TO STAY

With the large number of hostels and hotels in Baños, visitors usually have the luxury of choice, and prices are not generally high. I have not included addresses here because it's easy to get directions at the bus station to where you want to go in this small town.

Expensive

If money were no object I would be tempted to stay at the **Luna Runtun Resort (** (03) 740882 or (03) 740883 FAX (03) 740376 E-MAIL info@luna runtun.com WEB SITE www.lunaruntun.com, in the foothills of Volcán Tungurahua overlooking

The El Salado baths at Baños are the best at this popular hot spring resort.

the town. According to the brochure for this swish, new Swiss-managed resort of chalet-style bungalows, this was the favorite spot of the Inca emperor, Huayna Capac, where he "enjoyed lavish dances and voluptuous orgies with his most beautiful and desirable wives before the discovery of America." No voluptuous orgies were on offer when I visited the resort, but it does have almost every other facility you can think of, including rooms with fireplaces and private flower-filled terraces, along with child daycare, conference facilities, special programs and excellent food. The views of the valley are fantastic. Prices include breakfast and dinner, and horseback trips can be arranged.

Moderate

Baños boasts two mid-priced hotels, both next to each other by the Virgin Falls. The older is the **Palace Hotel ℄** (03) 740740 FAX (03) 740291 E-MAIL mastalir@tu.pro.ec, a well-known, old-style establishment. Though some of its many rooms are rather dark, they are quite comfortable, and the newer ones are far more attractive. The hotel has its own hot-spring baths, saunas, Jacuzzis, a pleasant garden, a pool, a restaurant and other facilities. **Hotel Sangay ℄** (03) 740490 FAX (03) 740056 E-MAIL sangaysp@ecuanex.net.ec WEB SITE www.sangayspa.com has seen better days and could do with an overhaul. The older "colonial" rooms are decidedly overpriced, but the newer "executive" ones are better value. The Sangay has similar facilities to the Palace, though not as appealing. Both hotels charge a small fee for the use of their facilities by non-guests.

Inexpensive

There is a range of higher-priced inexpensive hotels, all with plus points which make them hard to rank. With a homey atmosphere, the German-run **Isla de Baños ℄**/FAX (03) 740609 E-MAIL islaba @interactive.net.ec WEB SITE www.ecuaworld .com/flash/isla includes lovely gardens, big but simple rooms and a good bar and restaurant. Similar in feel, but more colorful, is the well-established **Hostal Cultural ℄**/FAX (03) 740083 E-MAIL hostal cultural@yupimail.com. Flowers fill the hotel and rooms, while all rooms have private bath, two of them (more expensive) with fireplaces. Their restaurant serves delicious vegetarian, Indian and Swedish dishes—quite a combination. For about the same price, the French-run **La Petite Auberge ℄** (03) 740936 is pretty and colorful, and also has fireplaces in every room and a nice garden. Slightly more expensive, **Hostería Monte Selva ℄** (03) 740566 or (03) 820068 FAX (03) 854685 enjoys a great location nestled into the hills at the south end of Halflants. The rooms are comfortable and airy, and the complex includes a small pool, a sauna and exuberant gardens.

This being the gringo trail, there is a glut of budget-priced hotels in town. My own favorite is the aptly and charmingly named **Plantas y Blanco** (Plants and White) ℄/FAX (03) 740044. Outstanding features of this popular hostel are its central location, its rooftop terrace with panoramic views, 24-hour serve-yourself drinks, a constant supply of free bananas, clean rooms, Internet service, videos and morning steam baths. It's not surprising it is often full. About the same price, but not as new, the **Hostal El Pedron ℄** (03) 740701 is friendly, with a pleasant terrace for meals, clean rooms (either shared or private bath). Of the numerous other options, I thought **Residencial Lucy ℄** (03) 740466 was about the best value considering most rooms have private bathrooms with hot showers for under US$3 per person.

WHERE TO EAT

Although many of the restaurants in Baños are of vacation-resort mediocrity, there are plenty of good ones. Much favored by the smarter end of the backpacking brigade is the celebrated **Café Hood**, on Martínez near Halflants, a vegetarian hangout with good coffee, pancakes, omelets, tacos and a Hindu Plate. Along with an alternative atmosphere, a book exchange and scrapbooks of useful information for travelers, the café shows films at around 8 PM. Other places frequently recommended include the **Marianne**, **Le Petit Restaurant** and **Closerie des Lilas**, all of them French. La Closerie is the best value, to my palate. **La Bella Italia** is popular for Italian and local food, as is the Italian-run **Scaligeri**. El Marqués and **La Casa Mía** both usually have live Andean music and serve tasty Ecuadorian dishes, while **Restaurant El Artesano** (next to Plantas y Blanco) serves Middle Eastern food. **Regine Café Alemán**, whose name reveals its culinary roots, **Café Higuerón** and **Café Cultura**, with a focus on homemade breads and pastries, are all recommended for tasty breakfasts and lighter meals. **El Jardín** has a pleasant patio and good service: a place in which to linger a while. Since Baños is a small town, your hotel or hostel can tell you how to get to these places.

NIGHTLIFE

Baños might not have a reputation for rip-roaring nightlife like Guayaquil or even Quito, but it is a town that likes to party. As you walk around in the day you're sure to be offered flyers for a *peña* (folk music event) that evening. And they are worth checking out, as Baños attracts some very good Andean music groups. Locations change frequently but the small *peña* bar **Ananitay**, 16 de Diciembre and Espejo, has been around forever. On weekends live music starts about

10 PM and goes on until 2 AM. There's a very cheery atmosphere and plenty of dancing with the drink of choice being big jugs of warm *canelazos*, a mixture of *aguardiente* (cane spirit), sugar and *naranjilla* (bittersweet orange), spiced with cinnamon. The vibrant music and joyful spirit of the evening creates a friendly sociability among locals and gringos.

Near Ananitay is a big, cavernous music bar in the theme of an old sugarcane factory, with ancient machinery as part of the decor. The place can be as dead as an abandoned church, but on other occasions it rocks and shakes like dried beans in a maraca. It's called the **Bamboo Bar**, which is confusing because there's another Bamboo Bar, sometimes known as the **Bambooze Bar**, a friendly, popular place with pool tables and good music. On Ambato near 16 de Diciembre, a busy bar is **Donde Marcelo** which has a teeny balcony from which to people-watch, and some pool tables. Baños may be the smallest town in the world to boast its own (no doubt counterfeit) **Hard Rock Café**, on Alfaro, another popular spot with gringos. Ask around town for other places.

HOW TO GET THERE

Due to mudslides from Tungurahua and repairs on the Baños–Puyo road, don't be surprised by delays getting to and from the town. The Terminal Terrestre bus terminal is on the main highway, on the north side of town, within walking distance of all cheaper hotels. Regular bus services to Ambato, Quito and Riobamba abound. Transportation eastwards and downwards to Puyo and the Amazon Basin is less frequent. Baños is a popular getaway for a weekend break from Quito, and buses are pretty full at these times. It's sometimes best to change in Ambato for a connecting bus as opposed to waiting.

PARQUE NACIONAL SANGAY

The vast and inaccessible Parque Nacional Sangay stretches like a huge blanket of dense vegetation over the eastern flanks of the Andes, from just south of Baños to almost as far as Macas in the south. The park's terrain and wildlife exemplify the diversity, wildness and impenetrability of huge areas of the relatively small country of Ecuador. Most of the steep, thickly vegetated slopes span altitudes of more than 4,000 m (13,123 ft) over a horizontal distance of just a few kilometers as the condor flies. If the park were ironed flat its surface area would be far greater than its 517,715 ha (1,279,288 acres).

Its mountain forests are too thick and inhospitable for human habitation, but they are home to many strange and rare creatures — spectacled bears, ocelots, mountain tapirs, porcupines,

jaguarundis (wild cats) — some of which are unknown anywhere else on earth. Few humans penetrate this wilderness because the slopes are too steep and the jungle is too thick. Roads that traverse the park are recent. The highly controversial Guamote–Macas road is due to be finished in 2001, and there are plans for further road-building within the park. As a result of the damage caused by road-building, UNESCO placed the park on its "National Parks in Peril" list.

The park, too gentle a word for such a hostile patch of land, is also the footplate for three of the ten tallest mountains in Ecuador: **Tungurahua** (5,023 m or 16,479 ft), **El Altar** (5,319 m or 17,451 ft), and the still active **Volcán Sangay** (5,230 m or 17,159 ft). None of them are easy to climb: Tungurahua is presently off-limits; El Altar the most technically challenging; and Sangay, because of constant volcanic activity, is probably the most dangerous (see RECOMMENDED READING, page 259 in TRAVELERS' TIPS for mountain climbing guidebooks with information about these and other Ecuadorian mountains).

Exploration of Parque Nacional Sangay is beyond the scope of this book, but for those who want to do so the **Ministerio del Ambiente** office is very helpful. They can be contacted in Riobamba (see GENERAL INFORMATION, below under RIOBAMBA) or at the main office ((022) 548924 WEB SITE www.ambiente.gov.ec, Amazonas and Eloy Alfaro, Quito. The organization provides information about the park, advice about guides, and even free transportation to the three entrances to the park: Alao, Pondoa and Candelaria.

One of the most experienced and professional companies organizing hikes in the park is **Alta Montaña** IN RIOBAMBA ((03) 963694 FAX (03) 942215 IN QUITO (/FAX (022) 504773 E-MAIL aventurag@laserinter.net, Jorge Washington 425 and 6 de Diciembre (see GENERAL INFORMATION, below under RIOBAMBA).

RIOBAMBA

The capital of Chimborazo Province, Riobamba likes to call itself the "Sultan of the Andes," which is perhaps pushing travel brochure hyperbole a bit far. Forming the agricultural center of the region, with a population of more than 100,000, the town is, however, blessed with one of the most dramatic geographical settings in the country: on clear days, the volcanoes of Chimborazo and El Altar provide the most captivating backdrop imaginable. At an elevation of 2,700 m (8,858 ft), it is a pleasant country town with some eye-catching colonial architecture, and comes alive during market day on Saturday. The small-scale cement, ceramics, textiles, shoe manufacturing, food processing and native artifact industries make it the hub of local commerce. Although not a popular tourist destination, Riobamba makes a fine base for exploring the region, and a departure point for the thrilling train ride down to Guayaquil.

BACKGROUND

In pre-Inca days the Peruhá tribes settled the Chimbo region. After the Inca conquest, in typical Inca manner, many of these tribes were forced south, while people from the south were moved north to replace them. As a result there is a great mixture of *indígenas* in the region who wear a variety of traditional costumes and hats.

In 1534 the Spanish took over an Inca site where the modern town of Cajabamba is located, 19 km (12 miles) south of present-day Riobamba. Eleven years later a Spaniard, Pedro de Cieza de León, on an epic 17-year horseback journey from Colombia to Bolivia, praised the lodgings at Riobamba and wrote of "beautiful fair fields, whose climate, vegetation, flowers and other features resemble those of Spain."

In 1797 a huge landslide devastated the town, killing hundreds of inhabitants. The survivors moved the city to its present location, bringing their cathedral with them, which they rebuilt brick by brick. In 1830 the first Ecuadorian constitutional congress met at Riobamba and proclaimed the republic. Several surviving buildings, including the old cathedral, many in need of restoration and repair, are sad memorials to the city's previous capital status.

GENERAL INFORMATION

The helpful **tourist office** ((03) 941213, 10 de Agosto (the town's main thoroughfare, called Avenida León Borja further north) at 5 de Junio, three blocks from the main plaza, Parque Sucre, is open most weekdays from 8:30 AM to 5 PM with a break for lunch. For information about Parque Nacional Sangay and Volcán Chimborazo, contact the **Ministerio del Ambiente** ((03) 963779 on Avenida 9 de Octubre near Duchicela. To telephone or to send or receive faxes, **Andinatel** is on Tarqui between Veloz and Primera Constituyente, and the **Post Office** is on Avenida 10 de Agosto at Espejo. **Filanbanco** is at Colón and Primera Constituyente, and **Banco del Pacífico** at Ángel León and Veloz. There's a decent **Internet café** on Rocafuerte off 10 de Agosto.

Several tour operators and guides in town are helpful with expeditions and climbing. A good starting point for advice and guiding is Enrique Veloz of the **Asociación de Andinismo de Chimborazo** ((03) 960916, Chile at Francia. All guides should be members of the association. **Alta Montaña** ((03) 963694 FAX (03) 942215 E-MAIL aventurag@laserinter.net, León Borja 35-17, run by Rodrigo Donoso, has been summiting

Chimborazo for years. In addition to organizing good equipment and first-class guides, they can arrange treks along the Inca trail to Ingapirca, or horseback riding and mountain biking trips. **Andes Climbing and Trekking** (/FAX (03) 940964 E-MAIL ppurunca@ecu.net.ec, Colón 22-25, are also very experienced. For mountain bikes in good condition and excellent guides, contact Galo Brit of **Pro Bici** ((03) 942468 FAX (03) 961923, Primera Constituyente next to Banco Popular. There's also a branch of **Metropolitan Touring** ((03) 969600 FAX (03) 969601 WEB SITE www.ecuadorable.com on León Borja just north of Brasil.

Note that most restaurants and sights are closed on Sundays. The town's big day celebrates the independence battle of Tapi on April 21, 1822, when an agricultural fair is held, with the attendant parades, bands and dancing.

WHAT TO SEE AND DO

A gold "monstrance" encrusted with pearls and diamonds is the greatest and best-known treasure to be seen in Riobamba. A monstrance? My dictionary defines it as an "ornamental receptacle in which the consecrated Host is exposed in Roman Catholic churches for the adoration of the people." The beauty of the object itself defies the ugliness of its appellation and it is well worth seeing if you have time to visit the religious art museum, **Convento de la Concepción** on Argentinos and Larrea, which has been well-restored by the Banco Central and contains a fine collection of gold artifacts, jewelry and religious art. Ask for a guided tour since signs are pretty poor. The museum is open 9 AM to noon and 2 PM to 5 PM Tuesdays to Saturdays.

But the main attraction of Riobamba, as in so many of other Sierra towns, is its **market**. Each Saturday the streets and squares of the city fill up with stallholders and hawkers selling a wide range of household goods and food products, as well as local crafts and artifacts. Souvenirs such as shawls, ponchos and woven belts can be found around Parque de la Concepción, at the intersection of Orozco and Colón. Woven bags made from *cabuya* fiber, known as *shigra*, are local specialties, as are baskets and mats woven from reeds from the shores of nearby Lake Colta.

Riobamba is also an important center for the **tagua nut** trade. This is a palm nut, about the size of a small hen's egg, which is relatively soft when taken from the fruit and easily carved. After being exposed to air and light for a while it becomes as hard as ivory. The tagua, which comes from the lowland rainforest, is used to make buttons, carved ornaments and even chess sets. Tagua products make great souvenirs because they are so small and easy to carry. Chess sets cost about US$20. Since the commercial use of tagua nuts is seen as an alternative to cutting down the rainforest, any purchase you make will be an act of environmental friendliness. To see craftsmen carving the nuts, visit the **Tagua Shop** on León Borja 35-17 and Uruguay, which also has a good selection of tagua products.

To enjoy the "Sultan of the Andes" at its best, head to the observation platform at **Parque 21 de Abril**. The panoramic views of the city and its surrounding peaks are magnificent on a fine day.

WHERE TO STAY

Riobamba has more than its share of large, inexpensive, rundown hotels with antiquated plumb-

The **Albergue Abraspungo** ((03) 940820 FAX (03) 940819, about three kilometers (almost two miles) out of town on the road to Guano, combines new, large rooms around an old hacienda, with a bar and restaurant and horseback riding. Similarly priced and also out of town, **Hostería El Troje** (/FAX (03) 964572, four kilometers (two and a half miles) down the road to Chambo, is pretty similar, though has the plus of a swimming pool and a tennis court.

Inexpensive

In town, no hotel has established an undisputed reputation for quality and style. In the center, **Hostal Montecarlo** ((03) 960557 FAX (03) 961577,

ing, bare light bulbs and holes in the sheets. But don't despair: there's also a quota of clean, bright, modern hostelries that meet the expectations of today's tourists.

Moderate

The best hotels in the province are found out of town. About 15 km (nine miles) north of the city, the restored hacienda **Hostería La Andaluza** ((022) 904223 FAX (03) 904234 E-MAIL francarenas@ yahoo.com has come to be regarded one of the best south of Quito. Although not as old as its counterparts around Latacunga, the Andaluza is still extremely comfortable and peaceful. Rooms are furnished with attractive antiques and come with log fires, cable televisions and telephones. The excellent restaurant compliments an exercise room, sauna and cozy bar. The other two bucolic alternatives are slightly cheaper.

10 de Agosto 25-41, is housed within an old mansion and is about the most appealing. Rooms are clean and comfortable, but quite dark. At the opposite end of the spectrum, the **Hotel Zeus** ((03) 968036 FAX (03) 962292 E-MAIL hotelzeus@laserinter .net, León Borja 41-29, is very much a modern hotel, though it lacks an elevator — don't take a room on the fourth floor. Rooms are all commodious, with private bathrooms, hot water and televisions. It also has an acceptable restaurant.

Getting cheaper, the **Hotel Whymper** ((03) 964575, Miguel Angel León and Primera Constituyente, has big rooms, some of them with views, but make sure you ask to see yours before committing, since some of them are pretty poky. Friendly and clean, the **Hotel Tren Dorado** (/FAX (03) 964890, Carabobo 22-35, is convenient for the

Riobamba's old colonial cathedral overlooks Parque Maldonado.

early morning train and the owner can organize local tours. For about the same price and equally welcoming is the **Hotel Los Shyris** ((03) 960323, Rocafuerte at 10 de Agosto. **Hotel Imperial** ((03) 960429, Rocafuerte and 10 de Agosto, right in the center of town, is clean, friendly, popular, sometimes noisy, and budget priced. Luggage can be stored and the hotel arranges good value tours to Chimborazo.

WHERE TO EAT

Only one restaurant stands out in Riobamba, but the others are not so bad that you'll starve.

Moderate

Although this restaurant is unbecoming from the outside, and pretty tacky on the inside, the food is another matter. Run by the best chef this side of Quito, Luís Shugulí, **Luigi's**, on León Borja, is a great find. I suggest you wade straight in with a giant *gran mariscada* for two and a bottle of Chilean white. The seafood is absolutely first-class, and Luís's accompanying sauces are nothing short of perfect. Service is very attentive, though the *bolero* music can be pretty infernal unless you like that sort of thing. Back closer to the center, the most atmospheric restaurant-bar in town is **El Delirio**, situated in the house once occupied by the Great Liberator, Simón Bolívar, on Primera Constituyente near Rocafuerte. Bolívar wrote a famous epic poem in this house about the failure of his dream, his personal delirium. If this powerful historical association isn't enough, the food is very good and garden enchanting.

Inexpensive

Recommended for tasty Ecuadorian dishes are **El Mesón de Inéz**, Orozco and Morales; **Cabaña Montecarlo** (quite romantic at night), 10 de Agosto 25-45; and the charmingly named **Chifa Joy Sing**, on Guayaquil near the station, which serves an inexpensive but satisfying Chinese meal. **Restaurant Candilejas**, 10 de Agosto 27-33, serves tasty Ecuadorian food in a warm atmosphere, while **Pizzería Il Paladino**, García Moreno 24-42, ranks among the best pizza joints in town. The other is **Pizzería San Valentín** on León Borja at Torres, which is popular with flirting teenagers; it also serves Mexican food and American staples.

NIGHTLIFE

Not many travelers come to Riobamba for its nightlife. But if you happen to be in town and that's what you want, there's a reasonable amount of action around the eastern end of León Borja, especially on weekends. On the *peña* beat, names to look out for are **El Faraón**, and **Media Luna**. For *discotecas*, try **Casablanca** and **Gems Shop**.

For salsa on weekends check out the **Unicornio** on Pichincha and Villarroel.

HOW TO GET THERE

There are two main bus stations. Buses for Baños and the Oriente leave from the **Terminal Oriental** on Avenida Espejo and Luz Elisa Borja, while all other long-distance buses depart from **Terminal Terrestre**, just over a kilometer (half a mile) northwest of the town center on León Borja. A few blocks south of Terminal Terrestre there is an area from where buses depart for many local towns, while buses to Guano leave from the north of town on Rocafuerte and New York.

The **train station** lies on Avenida 10 de Agosto and Carabobo. There is only one line, which goes north to Ambato and Quito and south to Alausí, Bucay and Guayaquil. There are very few trains. In fact there were no trains at all for 10 years after the El Niño storms of 1982 and 1983 while repairs were made to the tracks. This less-than-hectic timetable is nevertheless subject to change and you should call ((03) 961909 for the latest times. The latest information is that trains leave Riobamba at 6 AM every day of the week except Tuesdays and Thursdays. The Quito train runs twice a week, on Saturdays and Sundays, departing at 9 AM. The most exciting and scenic section of this remarkable mountain railway is between Alausí and Bucay, known as the **Devil's Nose** because of its steep gradient. Some people take the train only between these two towns, and complete the rest of their journey by bus. Riding on the roof of the train and ducking overhanging branches is a travel experience not to be forgotten (see RIDE THE RAILS, page 17 in TOP SPOTS for more).

AROUND RIOBAMBA

The major trip from Riobamba is to **Chimborazo**, 6,310 m (20,702 ft), known to the local *indígenas* as Taita (father) Chimborazo, which is paired with Mama Tungurahua. First climbed by the English mountaineer Edward Whymper in 1880, the "Big Ice Cube" attracts numerous mountaineers during peak climbing season in December and from June to September. Only serious and experienced mountaineers should attempt this peak. Full ice- and snow-climbing equipment, and a good guide, are required. It is easy enough, however, to reach the first *refugio* at 4,800 m (15,748 ft) by car or jeep from Riobamba, though acclimatization is necessary. The agencies in Riobamba have various places to stay close by. Then it's about an hour's slow climb to the second refuge at 5,000 m (16,404 ft), from where the views are stunning. Here you can stay the night for about US$10 if you have a warm sleeping bag. Climbs to the summit begin around midnight and take about 10 hours, with four hours for the return trip. Many hotels arrange reasonably priced day trips to the *refugios* for small groups (about US$20 per person) while a serious climb can be arranged with agencies listed under GENERAL INFORMATION, above.

Alternatively, you can contact the community of **Pulingue San Pablo** (or "Waman Way") ((03) 949510 or (03) 949511 E-MAIL waman_way@ hotmail.com (Spanish only) on the road up to the refuge. The community, with funding from the Canadian government, has set up a grassroots ecotourism and sustainable agriculture project just on the border of the Reserva de Producción Faunística Chimborazo, which is run by the Ministerio del Ambiente. The locals have organized themselves into a guiding cooperative, offering trekking, climbing and horseback riding tours around the area. They have also reintroduced environmentally friendly alpaca to the area (the reintroduced vicuña are already thriving), as well as setting up trout farms. You can stay in simple cabins nearby. For more information contact the dedicated Canadian, Tom Walsh E-MAIL twalsh @ch.pro.ec. Entrance to the reserve (i.e. to the *refugio*) costs US$10 per person. If you have your own vehicle, you can make a great day-trip by looping round to the town of Guaranda and back (see THE OPEN ROAD, page 41 in YOUR CHOICE).

For the less energetic, there are plenty of other attractions around Chimborazo. Journeys to **neighboring villages** on local buses provide an insight into the traditional Andean way of life, and a backdrop of superb scenery. A few kilometers north of Riobamba, rug-making is a specialty of the village of **Guano**, with various handicrafts for sale in its numerous craft shops. **Santa Teresita**, a bit more to the north, boasts its own thermal baths a short walk from the bus stop.

SOUTH OF RIOBAMBA

South of Riobamba, the Panamericana splits close to Cajabamba. The southwesterly route ploughs down the mountains towards the coast and Guayaquil or Machala. This is the "Panamericana Internacional" and the fastest route south to Perú. The southeasterly road, the "Panamericana Ecuatoriana," winds south towards Guamote, Alausí, Ingapirca and eventually, Cuenca (references to the Panamericana in this chapter and the Southern Highlands chapter apply to the Ecuadorian one).

There's not much to see in **Cajabamba**, but if you come on Sunday, the fields close to the road junction are turned into an outdoor market by the local Indians—one of the most unique sights in the highlands. About four kilometers (two and a half miles) beyond Cajabamba lies the **Laguna de Colta**. The road passes the little chapel of **La Balbanera**, on the site of one of the

country's oldest churches. The lake is stunning on a clear day, and sometimes you can see local Colta *indígenas* gliding through the reeds on rafts. You can walk around it in around two hours. Heading south on Panamericana, on the beautiful road that hugs the railway tracks, you come to **Guamote** after 47 km (30 miles), a pretty town with a busy Thursday market — one of the biggest and most unspoiled in the country. From Guamote, the new dirt road to Macas in the Oriente strikes east, while the Panamericana coils its way south.

About 50 km (31 miles) south of Guamote lies **Alausí**, the starting-point for the most dramatic part of Ecuador's rail network: the plunge down

La Nariz del Diablo (The Devil's Nose) (see RIDE THE RAILS, PAGE 17 in TOP SPOTS). The small town, with its church, plaza and cobbled streets, comes alive for its Sunday (and smaller Thursday) market. The best hotel in town is the **Hotel Americano** ((03) 930159, García Moreno 159, with clean, comfortable rooms with hot water. Book ahead for Saturday night. Buses to Riobamba and Cuenca are regular, though they leave you on the Panamericana, about a kilometer (half a mile) from the town.

In Riobamba's Parque Maldanado stands this statue of Pedro Maldanado, an Ecuadorian geographer who was a member of the French team that surveyed Ecuador in the eighteenth century.

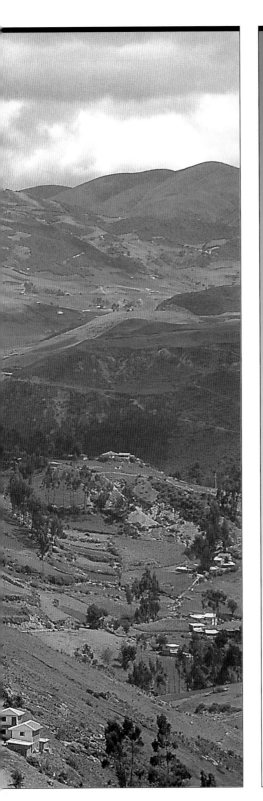

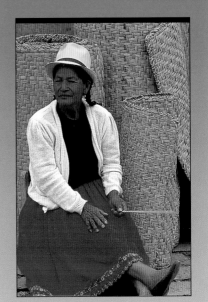

Southern Highlands

Traveling south down the spiky, mountainous spine of Ecuador, a slow change takes place. After the climax of Chimborazo, the peaks become lower and the mountain ranges flatten and spread. You feel you are leaving Quito far, far behind you and the pace of life becomes increasingly *tranquilo*. Until the early 1960s there were no paved roads linking Cuenca, the third-largest city in Ecuador and the central hub of the region, to Quito and the coast. Many communities are still isolated for lack of proper roads, creating a sense that some of the beautiful hills and valleys are in a deep sleep. Vilcabamba, known as the Valley of Eternal Youth because of the longevity of its inhabitants, was cut off from the rest of the country until only a few years ago. Now this beautiful valley is slowly becoming a destination of choice for cognoscenti travelers. More than in the rest of the country, there is a strong sense here of the Inca past. At Ingapirca, once a major stronghold and now the most important Inca ruin in Ecuador, the spirit of the Incas still hangs in the air.

CUENCA

Considered the most beautiful city in the country, Cuenca likes to call itself the Athens of Ecuador. But its narrow, cobbled streets, houses with wrought-iron balconies, flower-filled patios and many fine old churches are more reminiscent, to my mind, of ancient Andalusian hill towns like Ronda in southern Spain. "Of all the earth, as far as I know it," wrote the early twentieth-century traveler Harry A. Franck, "Cuenca has the most perfect climate." Most visitors wholeheartedly concur.

The city is proud of its colonial-style architecture, its many churches and its artistic and intellectual heritage. The University of Cuenca is rated as one of the best in Ecuador and Latin America, and at the same time the city is something of a colony of artists and artisans. The city ranks among the most Roman Catholic of the continent; its motto is "Primero Dios, Después Vos" (First God, Then You). Cuenca is also the biggest production center of the misnamed "panama" hat. If you enjoy exploring back-street markets, delving into old churches, museums and craft shops, sitting around in patio cafés and watching the world go by, then Cuenca is for you.

BACKGROUND

The Cuenca area was inhabited by Cañari Indians who put up a long and fierce fight against the Incas moving up from the south in the fifteenth century. Under the command of the Tupac Inca Yupanqui, the Incas eventually prevailed and built themselves a splendid city called Tomebamba in an area the Cañaris called "Guapondelig," which

means "plain as vast as the sky." The city was designed as a northern version of the magnificent Inca city of Cuzco. Reports spoke of buildings set with precious stones and emeralds, and sun temples covered with sheets of the finest gold. Sadly, Tomebamba was a short-lived accomplishment. Before the Spanish conquistadors' invasion the Incas destroyed their own creation. Today, not much remains of the Inca city aside from a few excavated walls by the Río Tomebamba.

In April 1557, the Spanish founded the city of Cuenca to the northeast of the ruins of the Inca city, in an area known as Paucarbamba, which in the Quichua language means "plain of flowers." It was a well-chosen site with fertile soil watered by four rivers and a pleasant, spring-like climate. In typical fashion, the Spanish at once began building the cathedral on the west side of the main plaza, Parque Calderón. As the city grew, and more buildings were constructed workers sometimes unearthed Inca artifacts. In 1980, excavations by the river, undertaken by the Banco Central, uncovered Inca tombs and skeletons, and silver and gold relics.

GENERAL INFORMATION

The CETUR **tourist office**, at Hermano Miguel and Presidente Córdova, supplies maps of the city, and a useful small brochure called *Estar en Cuenca*. Other useful information about Cuenca and the environs is available from some of the tour companies. The small **Expediciones Apullacta** ((07) 837815, Gran Colombia 11-02 and General Torres, is particularly helpful and can arrange reasonably priced individual or group tours to El Cajas, or good "craft tours" in the easterly villages. **Ecotrek** ((07) 642531 FAX (07) 835387, at Larga 7-108 and Luís Cordero, run by the friendly and experienced Juan Gabriel Carrasco, enjoys a good reputation for more adventurous climbing and jungle trips, and arranges encounters with shamans. Similar tours can also be arranged by the very amiable and professional Juan Diego Dominguez of **Nomada's Adventures** ((07) 838695 or (07) 830995 E-MAIL pdelsol@impsat.net.ec, Gran Colombia 21-157. Both are good English speakers. **Monta Runa Tours** (/FAX (07) 846395 E-MAIL montarun@ az.pro.ec, at Gran Colombia 10-29 and General Torres, arrange horseback tours of El Cajas, while **Ciclismo Total** (/FAX (07) 451390, Solano 563 and Avenida del Estado, do the same but on mountain bikes. **Metropolitan Touring** ((022) 831185, Sucre 6-62 and Borrero, also acts as a helpful travel

PREVIOUS PAGES: Wide fertile valley LEFT in the Southern Highlands; the surrounding mountains are slightly less high than in the north. A lady selling reed mats RIGHT in Cuenca. OPPOSITE: The Museo de las Conceptas in Cuenca has an impressive display of religious art and artifacts

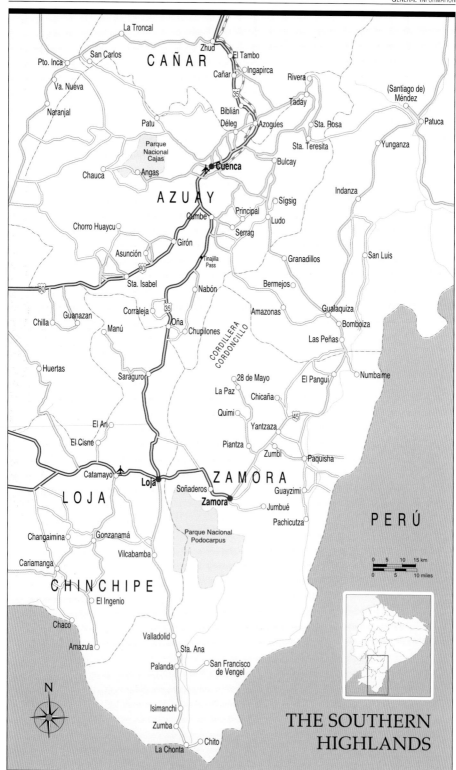

THE SOUTHERN
HIGHLANDS

agent. **TAME** airlines has its office on Benigno Malo off Calle Larga.

For international phone calls, fax services and some Internet terminals, **Pacifictel** is on Benigno Malo between Córdova and Sucre, and there's also a regional phone office across the street, called **Etapa**. Other Internet cafés include **CuencaNet** at the corner of Calle Larga and Benigno Malo, and **Alfnet**, Borrero and Honorato Vásquez. The **Post Office** is on Gran Colombia (the main shopping street) and Borrero. For MasterCard ATMs, head to **Banco del Pacífico** at the corner of Tarqui and Gran Colombia; for Visa, **Filanbanco** is on the corner of Sucre and General Torres.

WHAT TO SEE AND DO

With its historical interest and good shopping, there's plenty to do in Cuenca, except perhaps at night, if bars and discos aren't your cup of tea. The city is a big mouthful of culture, and if you don't want to suffer from intellectual indigestion by trying to see too many things in too short a time, your best bet is to be ruthlessly selective.

Start in the central plaza of the Old Town, **Parque Calderón**, a good place to sit on a park bench and absorb the atmosphere of the city. The *cholas cuencanas* (local *indígenas*) saunter by in their wide skirts and white or colored panama hats, neatly dressed old Cuencan gentlemen sit reading newspapers, and shoeshine boys proffer their services. The pink marble façades and magnificent sky-blue domes of the **Catedral de la Inmaculada Concepción** (New Cathedral) overlook the square's elegant houses. The domes are the finest features of the cathedral, but because of design miscalculations when construction began in the 1880s, they were too heavy for the building, so the bells still haven't been hung. Take a look inside the cathedral with its fine stained glass and the marvelous play of light in its vast interior. The New Cathedral was built because the Old Cathedral, **Iglesia del Sagrario** (on the other side of the square but rarely open to the public) had become too small for the burgeoning congregation of Cuencan Catholics.

Just round to the left of the Old Cathedral as you face it, the small Plazoleta del Carmen is more commonly known as the **Plaza de las Flores**. Here, *chola* women sell their multifarious bright flowers in front of the little whitewashed eighteenth-century **Iglesia El Carmen de la Asunción**.

Visiting Cuenca's 30-odd fine churches could keep you occupied for weeks, but if you only have time to see one other religious wonder it should be the **Museo de las Conceptas**, housed in the infirmary of the Convento de las Conceptas on Hermano Miguel 6-33. The chapel contains a beautiful, but lurid, display of crucifixes created by local artist Gaspar Sangurima, considered to be the

Father of Arts and Crafts in Cuenca. Among the religious art from the seventeenth to nineteenth centuries, the poignant toys of the nuns-to-be are also displayed. The museum is open Monday to Friday 9 AM to 3:30 PM, and it's worth popping into the adjoining **Iglesia de las Conceptas** to admire its fine gold-leaf altar and impressive carved wooden doors. Also close to the church, on Presidente Córdova 6-26, is the small, privately run but enlightening **Museo de Identidad Cañari**, on the first floor of an antiques shop.

It might be said that arts, crafts, and religion, in reverse order, are what Cuenca is all about. Certainly there are enough churches and museums to back up such a theory. The other two admired

for their beauty are the rebuilt **Iglesia de San Francisco**, by the square of the same name, which is famed for its beautiful carved high altar and gold-leaf pulpit, and the **Iglesia de San Sebastián**, about six blocks west of Parque Calderón and marking the Old Town's limit. The seventeenth-century church is among the city's oldest, fronting a peaceful little square that belies its fame as the city's most headline-grabbing crime. It was in this square that the surgeon of the French Geodetic Mission was murdered over his love affair with a Creole woman.

The **Museo del Banco Central**, just out of the center of town at the Pumapungo archaeological site on Larga and Huayna Capac, does a fine job of displaying artifacts (with some beautiful jewelry) relating to regional Inca and pre-Inca

Cuenca's main plaza, Parque Calderón, is dominated by the "new" cathedral begun in the 1880s.

civilizations, as well as great reconstructions of indigenous cultures, from Shuar huts to Sierran masked dancers. The archeological site isn't particularly inspiring, but was where most of the artifacts displayed originated. More interesting is the nearby **Ruinas de Todos los Santos** (open Monday to Friday 8 AM to 4 PM) which features old Incan walls and trapezoidal niches.

Unfortunately the **Museo Remigio Crespo Toral** was closed for renovation work at the time of writing. The personal collection of the illustrious Doctor Crespo ranges from pre-Hispanic artifacts through religious art and on to his *salón* as it was in the early twentieth century, and is worth catching when it reopens. Close by, at the bottom of the steps leading from Calle Larga to the *barranco* (riverside), the enjoyable **Museo de Artes Populares** is housed within the beautiful old mansion of the Centro Interamericano de Artesanías y Artes Populares (CIDAP). Colorful arts and crafts from across the Americas fill the display rooms, including musical instruments, ceramics, woodcarvings

and papier-mâché, with some works for sale. CIDAP is open Monday to Friday 9:30 AM to 1 PM, and 2:30 PM to 6 PM, Saturdays 10 AM to 1 PM. From here, you can walk along the grassy banks of the Río Tomebamba.

If you want to enjoy some more contemporary art, head to the **Museo de Arte Moderno**, close to Plaza San Sebastián. The museum, open Monday to Friday 8:30 AM to 1 PM and 3 PM to 6:30 PM, hosts temporary exhibitions of both national and Latin American artists, generally of high quality. The other place for some modern art is the **Casa de la Cultura**, near the Old Cathedral. On the second floor, exhibitions of local artists are held, and paintings sold.

For the best views of the city, take a taxi across the river and up to the **Mirador de Turi**, south of the center. The location is safe, and the panorama of the city, when illuminated on Friday and Saturday nights, stunning to say the least.

SHOPPING

Some say Cuenca is the best place in Ecuador for shopping. And it's true that prices seem as good, if not better, than elsewhere in the country and there's plenty of choice. Around **Gran Colombia** and roads leading off it, shops sell *ikat* weavings, woolen sweaters, leather goods, carvings, gold and silver items, basketwork, antiques, filigree work, jewelry, precious stones, paintings, sculpture, candelabra, pottery, ceramic tiles, cameras, camping equipment,

panama hats, and more. The area around the Iglesia and **Convento de Las Conceptas** is also packed with some great antiquarians and souvenir shops. The two **main markets** are around the **Plaza de San Francisco** and **Plaza Rotary**, which are best for craft items. Stands are open most days of the week, but the main market days are Thursdays and Saturdays.

You can also visit a **panama hat factory** where the finishing stages are carried out, the main work on the hats having been done in the weavers' homes. One of the largest is **Homero Ortega y Hijos (** (07) 809000 FAX (07) 876600 E-MAIL info@homeroortega.com WEB SITE www.homeroortega.com, Avenida Gil Ramírez Dávalos 3-86, close to the Terminal Terrestre. It's best to phone in advance to ensure an English-language tour. You could also ask the tourism office or one of the tour companies for other possibilities.

WHERE TO STAY

Cuenca has a good reputation for its hotels and hostels, from the top to bottom of the range. But it is a good idea to ask for discount because hotels are often prepared to charge less than the printed rates, depending on the season, of course.

Very Expensive

Swishest of all Cuenca's hotels, the Swiss-run **Hotel Oro Verde (** (07) 831200 FAX (07) 832849, on Ordóñez Lazo on the northwest outskirts, boasts all the facilities of a swank hotel. Service is generally excellent, and the restaurant first-class. It's a taxi-ride from the busy center of town, but is therefore very peaceful.

Expensive

Always highly praised for character and friendliness is the **Hotel Crespo (** (07) 842571 FAX (07) 839473 E-MAIL hcrespo@az.pro.ec WEB SITE www .hotel-crespo.com, Larga 7-93 and Cordero. Rooms with high ceilings and fantastic views of the Río Tomebamba combine Old World charm and modern conveniences. For about the same price, the **Hotel El Dorado (** (07) 831390 FAX (07) 831663 E-MAIL eldorado@cue.satnet.net, Gran Colombia 7-87, is as smart as the Crespo but without the charm. However it does include a gym, sauna and steam-baths to make up for this. Both hotels include airport or bus terminal transfers in their prices.

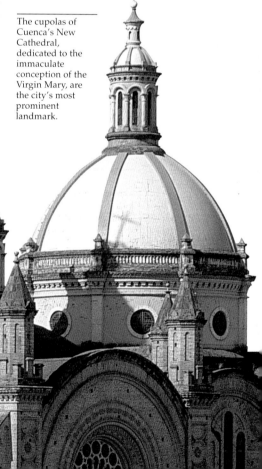

The cupolas of Cuenca's New Cathedral, dedicated to the immaculate conception of the Virgin Mary, are the city's most prominent landmark.

Moderate

Set within a lovely old mansion, the **Hotel Inca Real** ((07) 823636 FAX (07) 840699 E-MAIL incareal @cue.satnet.net, General Torres 8-40 between Sucre and Bolívar, has plenty of well-appointed and comfortable rooms set around their flower-filled patio. The feel is bright and breezy, and rates include breakfast. The best choice for the price.

Inexpensive

Cuenca has a number of good value *hostales*. Those with an Old World atmosphere and at the top end of the price bracket include the **Hostal Chordeleg** ((07) 824611 FAX (07) 822536, on Gran Colombia and Torres, whose old-house setting and glass-

with shared or private baths, and the ones by the garden extremely peaceful. Book ahead if possible. The Swiss-owned **El Cafecito** ((07) 827341, sister to its namesake in Quito, on Honorato Vásquez and Luís Cordero, is a popular backpacker stop. Rooms come with either a shared bathroom, or else there are slightly more expensive ones with private bathrooms overlooking the garden. The feel is friendly and relaxed, reggae wafting over the clients in the patio-bar-restaurant (recommended) covered with its glass and canvas ceiling.

One *hostería*, about an hour by road from Cuenca, that has been highly recommended is **Hostería Uzhupud** ((07) 250339 FAX (07) 806521,

covered patio are more inviting than the rooms themselves, though they are still a very good value; and the **Hostal Colonial** ((07) 823793 FAX (07) 841644 E-MAIL hcolonia@cue.satnet.net, Gran Colombia 10-13 and Padre Aguirre, with one of the town's prettiest patios, decent-sized rooms, Internet facilities and a popular restaurant. For about the same price, in a restored and modernized mansion, **Hostal La Orquidea** ((07) 824511 FAX (07) 835844 E-MAIL orquihos@etapa.com.ec, Borrero 9-31 and Bolívar, includes some rooms with balconies and other pokier ones, so ask to see them first. All the rooms have telephones, refrigerators and televisions, and are spotless.

For about half the price of the above, the **Macondo Hostal** ((07) 840697 E-MAIL macondo @cedei.org, Tarqui 11-64 and Lamar, is set within a beautiful old colonial-style house with a garden at the rear. The rooms are pretty and very clean,

a Spanish-style complex of several buildings with nice terraces, gardens, views and a large pool. Although reasonably expensive, they also have less-expensive accommodation for students and children.

WHERE TO EAT

Cuenca enjoys a wide range of good establishments, ranging from regional meals to international fare, the best south of Quito.

Moderate

On Gran Colombia 12-22, **Villa Rosa**'s tables fill an attractive, low-lit patio, and is worth experiencing even if just for a bowl of soup and a basket of bread. Service is excellent, but I would stick to the *sugerencias del chef* for the best food of the day. Similar in style and price, **El Jardín** on Presidente

Córdova is a romantic location with a good range of international and French dishes.

The restaurant at the Hotel Alli Tiana (at the corner of Presidente Córdova and Padre Aguirre), **El Mirador** ((07) 821955, lives up to its name with fantastic views, especially on floodlit weekends. The food however is pretty bland and disappointing, but worth it if you phone for a window seat. The other restaurant serving great *comida típica* within its appealing courtyard and dining room is **Los Capulies**, Borrero 7-31. They have live music Thursday, Friday and Saturday. The restaurants at the Hotel Crespo and El Dorado are also recommended.

Inexpensive

For Mexican food, Cuenca has the fine **El Pedregal Azteco**, Gran Colombia 10-29, where meals are served within a lovely old mansion, with live mariachi bands playing on the weekend and attentive service. **La Cantina Bar and Restaurant**, on Córdova and Borrero, has a beautiful restaurant with excellent food, often accompanied by live music. Peaceful in the day, but quite trendy in the evenings, **WunderBar**, on Calle Larga at Hermano Miguel, serves good set lunches in its appealing garden.

Good standard budget fare is served in the patio of **El Cafecito**. For local food at reasonable prices, **El Refugio** on Gran Colombia is safe and tasty, while there are several Italian restaurants to choose from. Among the best is the popular **La Napoletana Pizzería**, Avenida Fray Vicente Solano 3-04, and the two on Gran Colombia close to Luís Cordero: **Los Pibes** and **La Tuna**. If you have a taste for ice cream and cakes, **Heladería Holandesa**, on Benigno Malo 9-45 off the main square, is the popular, organic, choice; its counterpart across the street, **Tutto Freddo**, is also excellent.

NIGHTLIFE

Despite its sedate image and the impression that everyone in Cuenca is in bed by 10 PM, there are a number of hot nightspots in the city if you can dig them out. For a night on the town you could do worse than head to the **Piccadilly Pub**, on Borrero and Córdova, where pictures of red London buses on the wall and pints of beer give visiting Brits a dose of nostalgia. The pub has a pool table in the back and lively music. Ask the barman or fellow customers about clubs and discos. Chances are you'll be told of bars on Ordóñez Lazo near the Hotel Oro Verde. **Saxon** might be mentioned and **La Morada del Cantor** will be recommended for good *peñas*. If you don't have any luck at the Piccadilly, try **La Cantina** across the road. **WunderBar** (see above) gets busy and more boisterous at night, with **Kaos**,

Honorato Vásquez 6-11, is also a cool place for a beer with pool tables. **Ubu**, also on Honorato Vásquez, serves food in the day, but gets lively at night. **La Mesa** on Gran Colombia, is regarded as the best salsa joint, while **ETC** under the Hotel Conquistador on the same street, plays a wider range of loud music.

HOW TO GET THERE

The Terminal Terrestre **bus terminal** is one kilometer (just over a half mile) northeast of the town center, and five minutes' walk from the **airport**. Regular buses go to all major cities, and planes go to Quito and Guayaquil. Buses for the Gualaceo Sunday market leave from the corner of Avenidas Benalcázar and España, just southwest of the main terminal.

AROUND CUENCA

The attractions of Cañar Province should keep you in the area for a few days, using the city as a base. The region boasts beautiful natural scenery in the Parque Nacional Cajas, Ecuador's most important Inca ruins, and small market and craft towns tucked up in the hills.

NORTH OF CUENCA

Driving north from Cuenca on the Panamericana highway you soon arrive in Cañar Province. You'll notice that the hats of the local *indígenas* here are no longer the straw panamas favored by the *cholas cuencanas*. Instead, the Cañari Indians wear white felt hats with a wide, turned-up brim, or plain old felt trilbies with a narrow brim and an indented crown.

Nothing to do with hats, of course, but on the whole the Cañaris are a proud but rather sad community. In spite of fierce resistance they were subjugated by the Incas, many of them being forced to move south as *mitmakuna*. Then, after they fought on the side of the Spanish, they were sent to work in gold and silver mines by their colonial masters. Six hundred years ago the Cañaris dominated what is now southern Ecuador. Today they are reduced to some 40,000 people scratching a subsistence herding cattle in the highlands of Cañar Province.

Continuing north, one of the best highways in the country passes through the old colonial town of **Azogues**, the provincial capital, named after the Spanish word for mercury, which was mined in the area. A few kilometers further is the mountain village of **Biblián**, with a vertiginous church, **La Madona del Rocío**, built high into the cliffs above the village.

Small shops line the back streets of Cuenca.

Ingapirca

Coming by car it's a further 20 km (12 miles) or more along the road, which here hardly merits the designation of highway, before you turn off to the right into a patchwork quilt of pastel greens, browns and yellows spread over wide, sweeping valleys and smooth round hills. This is the approach to the ruins of Ingapirca, an Inca fort, temple, or observatory, or perhaps all three. In spite of extensive archaeological research, nobody has figured out the function of this massive stone complex that commands the brow of a hill and dominates the valleys for miles around.

Ingapirca might not be as impressive as some Inca sites in Perú, but it is the best Ecuador has. Some find the ruins boring while others, like myself, find it a moving experience to see and touch the beautifully cut stones, fitted together so accurately and without mortar by craftsmen of a vanished civilization. There are good walks in the area around the ruins and you can visit a rock formation, known as the **Face of the Inca**. If possible, combine a trip to the ruins with a visit to the **Friday market** at the nearby village of Ingapirca, where Cañari cowboys in sheepskin chaps loll drunkenly on their horses while the women, all of them hatted and wearing traditional costume, quietly shop for potatoes, *cuy* (guinea pig) and shining aluminum pots and pans.

Any travel agent in Cuenca can arrange guided tours of Ingapirca. There's also a direct bus that leaves the Terminal Terrestre at 9 AM and 10 AM and returns at 1 PM and 3 PM. Check the times as they may well change. Entrance to the ruins complex is about US$5 and includes the well-presented and enlightening adjoining museum.

EAST OF CUENCA

Many of the villages around Cuenca excel in crafts and have interesting markets. The small village of **Chordeleg**, which can be reached in about two hours by bus from Cuenca, changing at **Gualaceo** (a good stop for lunch and a stroll along the river), is a center for filigree jewelry. As well as jewelry stores and a busy Sunday market, the village boasts a small ethnographic museum with information about local handicrafts, including explanations of how the *ikat* process works. Not far away are the villages of **Bulcay** and **Bulzhun**, known for backstrap weaving of *macanas* (*ikat* shawls). A further 18 km (11 miles) along from Chordeleg, **Sigsig** is another lovely mountain village, known for its panama-hat weavers.

PARQUE NACIONAL CAJAS

About 30 km (19 miles) west of Cuenca, the Parque Nacional Cajas embraces a striking landscape of more than 200 lakes, wild *páramos* and countless ponds lying placidly under barren cliffs, protecting some 28,800 ha (71,165 acres). This under-explored, high-altitude natural marvel, where temperatures drop below freezing at night and which can be cold and rainy in the afternoon, is for the adventurous, well-prepared and well-insulated hiker. On a clear morning the views are spectacular. The park is home to the highest-growing tree in the world, the diminutive quinua tree, as well as many rare species of plants, birds and animals. Spotting the fantastically named high-altitude hummingbirds — sapphire-vented puffleg and the purple-throated sunangel, for example — is reason enough to brave the wintry conditions. Fishing is also good on Laguna Toreadora, on the north side of the park, where you'll find a ranger station. The driest time to visit is between August and January, but it'll probably rain anyway. For more information contact one of the tour agencies in CUENCA listed under GENERAL INFORMATION above. Ecotrek is connected with the Huagrahuma Páramo ecolodge on the edge of the park. There are buses from Cuenca to the entrance to El Cajas every day except Thursday, leaving from San Sebastián church at about 6 AM, which return at 3 PM (check the return time with the driver). Entrance to the park costs US$10, but is rarely enforced.

SOUTH FROM CUENCA

The Panamericana highway splits once again about 20 km (just under thirteen miles) south of Cuenca. The junction wasn't even signposted last time I drove this way. The southwesterly route coils down the mountain to the tropical coast, banana plantations and black faces multiplying as you pass through the towns of Girón, Santa Isabel, Pasaje and eventually Machala on the coast. The southern route passes through spectacular scenery as it climbs to the Tinajilla Pass at 3,527 m (11,571 ft), and through the *páramo* of Gañadel. There are no trees, nor houses — just scrub, grassland and barren, desolate, empty mountains. With virtually no other vehicles on this bumpy, potholed highway the driver swings the bus around bends at hair-raising speeds, with cliffs to one side and steep precipices to the other. At one point, I looked down on a valley filled with a white lake of clouds. The state of the Panamericana from Cuenca to Loja leaves plenty to be desired.

After more than three hours we stopped in the pretty main square of the small town of **Saraguro**, 165 km (102 miles) south of Cuenca, where an attractive, smartly dressed young woman wearing a black bowler hat, snow-white blouse, wide

The *indígenas* of the small town of Saraguro are thought to be descended from Inca tribes who settled the area.

black skirt and black woolen shawl closed with a
large silver pin, holding a small child, climbed
down from the bus. She was one of the Saraguro
indígenas, said to be descended from the Inca tribes
who settled this area. The shawl pin, or ***tupu***, is a
characteristic Saraguro accessory, as are filigree
earrings, both of which are family treasures passed
down from generation to generation. This traditional jewelry can be bought in some of the small
shops in town.

The Inca ruins in the area are overgrown and
hard to find, definitely off the gringo trail. The
best place to stay is the **Pensión Saraguro** close to
the church. Try **Mama Cuchara** on the square for
a simple meal.

LOJA

For most travelers Loja is a place to change buses
on their way down on the scenic-but-slow route
to Perú, or else continue to Vilcabamba further
south. But should you get stuck, or choose to stay
a while, Loja is a pleasant old colonial town with
two universities, a law school and a conservatory.
Although one of the oldest towns in Ecuador,
founded in 1548, little remains of its colonial architecture. Most of it, and very pretty it is too, dates
from the eighteenth and nineteenth centuries.
When Alexander von Humboldt passed through
Loja in 1802, he was so impressed by the variety
and richness of the flora, he dubbed the town the
"Garden of Ecuador."

GENERAL INFORMATION

The **tourist office** (/FAX (07) 572964 is at Valdivieso,
on the block south of Parque Central. The **Pacifictel**
office is on Eguiguren, a block east of Parque
Central. The **post office** is on the corner of Sucre
and Colón. For the Internet, try **Cybercafé** on
Plaza Santo Domingo. **Filanbanco**, with a Visa
ATM and facilities to change travelers' checks,
is at Valdivieso and 10 de Agosto, and **Banco de
Guayaquil**, for MasterCard, is at Eguiguren, off
the Parque Central. For travel services, such as
flights to Quito or Guayaquil, try **Hidaltur** ((07)
571031 FAX (07) 562554 E-MAIL fhidalgo@loja
.telconet.net, on Bolívar 10-33. If you're heading
for Perú, the **Peruvian Consulate** ((07) 571668, is
on Sucre 10-64, open 8:30 AM to 5 PM weekdays
only. Loja's big celebrations take place on September 8 for the crowd-pulling Virgen del Cisne processions. Its independence day is November 18,
and the town's founding is celebrated on December 8. For information on nearby Parque Nacional
Podocarpus, see page 153.

Loja Province in the south is one of the least-visited
region of Ecuador.

What to See and Do

Loja has a wealth of pleasant plazas: the main square, **Parque Central**, is hemmed by the cathedral with its eye-catching statues, and by the **Museo del Banco Central**, home to a small archeological collection (open Monday to Friday 9 AM to 4 PM); **Plaza San Francisco**, at Bolívar and Colón, and **Plaza San Sebastián** (or de la Independencia) are also colorful pockets of Lojan life. Loja's independence from Spain was declared here amid the colonial buildings in 1820. Near the pretty church of **Santo Domingo**, on Bolívar and Rocafuerte, look for the **Almacén Turístico Artesanal**, which sells a good range of locally made ceramics. Also of interest could be the **Jardín Botánico** housed within the national university at the south end of town, open 9 AM to 4 PM weekdays and 1 PM to 5 PM on weekends. For a great view of the city, and an enjoyable amble, head to the **Virgen de Loja** statue by following Rocafuerte east across the Río Zamora.

Where to Stay and Eat

Due to the popularity of the Virgen del Cisne processions, Loja has plenty of hotels. But since not that many tourists come through the town, at other times of year some of the cheaper establishments shut up shop altogether. Book well ahead at festival times.

Moderate
Loja's most upscale hotel is the **Hotel Libertador** ((07) 560779 or (07) 570344 FAX (07) 572119, Colón 14-30. Rooms are modern, spacious and comfortable, with telephones, good hot showers and cable televisions. The hotel's Spanish-inclined restaurant, **La Castellana**, is probably the best eating establishment in town.

Inexpensive
Slightly cheaper than the Libertador, **Hotel Ramses** ((07) 571402 FAX (07) 581832, also on Colón 14-31, has similar facilities and large, welcoming rooms, as well as breakfast thrown in at their decent restaurant: very good value. Cheaper still, if not so comfortable, is **Hotel Podocarpus** (/FAX (07) 581428 E-MAIL hotelpod@hotmail.com, Eguiguren 16-50. Breakfast is also included here, and there's a restaurant. **Hotel Los Ejecutivos** ((07) 560004, Universitaria 10-96, is rightly popular, with clean, decent rooms with hot showers for about US$6 a double. There are plenty of other cheapies south of Parque Simón Bolívar.

In addition to the hotels with restaurants mentioned above, one of Loja's best is **Rincón de Francia** on Valdivieso north of Parque Central. Although the food isn't particularly French, it is

very good (and cheap), served in an inviting courtyard dotted with artworks. For tasty seafood, **Cevichería Las Redes**, 18 de Noviembre past Riofrío, is a good choice, with the next-door **Restaurant Safari** acceptable for a stopgap.

Nightlife

If you're passing through on a Sunday, head to Parque Central, where a military band plays in the evenings and Lojanos come to enjoy a *paseo*. For indoor entertainment, try **Millenium Bar** on the square at the weekends, or **El Viejo Minero**, Sucre at Azuay, which is a nice place for a drink and a chat, with the next-door **Cabañitas Peña Bar** good for dancing.

How to Get There and Away

La Tola airport is 30 km (19 miles) west of Loja, in the town of Catamayo. It takes under an hour to get there over a stunning, winding road. This road continues through wild hills all the way down to Machala, although parts of it are truly tortuous. **TAME** ((07) 585224 has early morning flights to both Quito and Guayaquil most days of the week. There are also flights to Piura in Perú. Buses to Vilcabamba leave from the **Terminal Terrestre**, where the bus from Cuenca gets in, but there are also faster minibuses run by Vilcabambaturis. Even faster are shared taxis from the southern end of Aguirre. Other destinations served include Guayaquil, Macará or Huaquillas on the Peruvian border and Zamora.

VILCABAMBA

Nestled into a fertile green valley in Ecuador's "Deep South," Vilcabamba is famous for the longevity of its inhabitants: its main thoroughfare is called the Avenue of Eternal Youth. Vilcabamba is also one of those places that has achieved a reputation almost entirely by word of mouth. Young backpackers and aging hippies talk about the hallucinogenic juice of the San Pedro cactus, which once grew abundantly in the area. Following various incidents however (including one gringo walking naked across the main square), the local people and government have since all but eradicated the plant. Certainly, you'll no longer find it for sale in the local shops. To the average traveler, the reason for the town's enduring popularity resides in its beauty, relaxed and friendly feel, and inexpensive, welcoming establishments.

A popular *tambo* (the Inca word for a roadside inn or storehouse) on the gringo trail, the town gets more touristy every year, but it only takes a bit of imagination to strike out into the lovely countryside. Similar to Baños, though smaller and without the hot springs, Vilcabamba makes a great base from which to explore the surrounding hills, valleys and rivers by foot or on horseback, to meet local people and fellow travelers, or simply to pamper yourself after some hard days on the road.

BACKGROUND

One morning I sat down for breakfast on the open terrace overlooking the valley with Jaime Mendoza, co-owner of Madre Tierra. He spoke in glowing terms of the charms and healthfulness of Vilcabamba and the longevity of its inhabitants. The altitude of about 1,500 m (4,921 ft) creates the perfect pressure for your health, in particular your heart, he explained, and the year-round

temperature of between 17°C (63°F) minimum and 26°C (79°F) maximum is ideal. Furthermore, the water, which comes from the watershed in ancient forests in the nearby Parque Nacional Podocarpus, is laced with gelatins that destroy toxins in your body.

On average only one person in 1,470,000 lives to be a hundred, Jaime explained, but a study in Vilcabamba showed that of a population of 3,000, as many as 64 people were proved to be over 100 years old. When I pointed out that some studies disputed such figures, he dismissed them with a wave of his hand. Hard evidence is lacking, but there certainly seems to be many a sprightly sexagenarian or octogenarian around town. Whatever the truth about the longevity of the inhabitants of Vilcabamba, it is certainly a very pleasant place to be. Many are the stories of people who come here for a few days and stay for years.

The town's name stems from the *wilca* or *vilca* tree, similar to the acacia. It was regarded as sacred by the Incas and other pre-Columbian peoples, and though now increasingly rare, it's the reason the town is known as the "sacred valley."

GENERAL INFORMATION

The modest **tourist office** lies on the square (closed Tuesday and Friday; open 8 AM to noon and 2 PM to 6 PM) and provides maps and information leaflets. Two **Internet cafés** have popped up close-by, and there's also a **Pacifitel** phone office. A useful web site for Vilcabamba is at WEB SITE **www.vilcabamba.org**.

WHAT TO SEE AND DO

There's little to see or do in Vilcabamba apart from enjoy the balmy climate. The leafy square, dominated by the neoclassical church, is the town's main focus, alive with chirping, flitting birds at dawn or dusk, and the odd oldie. Walking for about 15 minutes down the Calle Diego de la Vaca will bring you to the **Area de Recreación Yamburara**, which includes a small zoo and orchid garden. For a more strenuous hike, ask the tourist office for directions to the **Cerro Mandango**, or there are great hikes up towards Podocarpus from Cabañas Río Yambala (see below). One of the best guides in the area is Orlando Falco of Rumi Wilco

LEFT: These woven bands are a specialty of the Cuenca region. RIGHT: An elderly woman from Vilcabamba, a town known for the longevity of its inhabitants.

Ecolodge (see below), who speaks perfect English as well as being a zoologist with 20 years guiding experience. Many hotels offer massage and beauty treatments, as do some locals in town. Madre Tierra has the most extensive list of treatments.

For horseback riding tours, you can either arrange one with your hotel, or else talk to the operators around the square. New Zealander Gavin Moore runs **Caballos Gavilan (** (07) 580281 E-MAIL gavilanhorse@yahoo.com, which has a long-standing reputation for fun trips. Martine and Bernard (who are French) are newer, and run **Solomaco Lodge (**/FAX (07) 673186 E-MAIL solomaco@hotmail.com, taking riders up to their lodge in the hills, with noteworthy French

SITE www.ecuadorexplorer.com/madretierra, a friendly ecolodge that has expanded over the years in the hills just to the north of town. Starting as the private home of a Canadian-Ecuadorian couple who used to put up friends and friends of friends, it has grown in the past years into a complex of *cabañas* among landscaped gardens, complete with restaurant, small swimming pool, bar and health spa.

Accommodation ranges from slightly damp, older cabins through to more comfortable doubles with private baths, and on to the highest quality cabins in Vilcabamba (in the moderate price-bracket), some of them quite a walk from the main house. Prices include healthy breakfasts and ex-

cuisine included. The community-based **Avetur** or **Centro Ecuestre (** (07) 673151 employs horses from various owners around the town and local guides. Competition is pretty fierce among them, so hunt around for the best prices and horses.

WHERE TO STAY

Vilcabamba has come quite a long way from its hippy hangout days, and you'll find a surprisingly extensive, and good, selection of hotels and lodges, though none of them attain luxurious standards. All are good value, with the choice of ones in town or more bucolic options.

Moderate to Inexpensive

Many who travel to Vilcabamba have heard of **Madre Tierra Ranch and Spa (** (07) 580269 or (07) 580687 E-MAIL hmtierra@ecua.net.ec WEB

cellent dinners, much of the produce coming from the ranch's organic farm, with vegetarian options available. Guests enjoy discounts at the health and beauty center, which offers treatments from reiki and massages, clay baths and sea salt rubs to hair and scalp treatments. They can also arrange horseback rides, hiking and bird-watching tours.

For something less sophisticated but equally charming, **Cabañas Río Yambala** (no phone) E-MAIL rio_yambala@yahoo.com or yambala@impsat.net.ec WEB SITE www.vilcabamba.cwc.net, or Charlie's Cabins as it is sometimes called, is situated about four kilometers (two and a half miles) southeast of the town, down a rough dirt track. The main house, where meals are served, sits just above the rushing Río Yambala, while the simple, peaceful wooden cabins hide up in the hillside, among the woods, flowers and fruit trees. Some have catering facilities, and all enjoy great views from hammock-slung porches or balconies. Owners Charlie and Sarah own a piece of land and a refuge on the border of Parque Nacional Podocarpus, and organize highly recommended horseback tours up in the hills. Prices are very reasonable and include delicious breakfasts and dinners, and transfers from town.

Closer to town, on the approach road, the most sophisticated option is **Hostería de Vilcabamba** ((07) 580271 FAX (07) 580273, an attractive and well-appointed hotel with swimming pool, sauna and hydro-massage included in prices at the top of the inexpensive range.

Inexpensive

Not far to the south of town, a new place called **Izhcayluma** (no phone) E-MAIL izhcayluma@ yahoo.de, boasts tranquility and great views from its hilltop. The cabins, all with private bathrooms and hot water, are spotless and neat, if a bit charmless. The complex includes a restaurant and bar, and a swimming pool. Also out of town, but tucked under the hill to the north, the **Rumi Wilco Eco-lodge and Nature Reserve** (no phone) E-MAIL ofalcoecolodge@yahoo.com will bring a smile to the face of many a simple traveler. Run by a friendly, knowledgeable and dedicated couple, accommodation consists of an attractive house lifted on stilts just by the river, a set of simple adobe-block cabins up the hill, and another house boasting magnificent views on a bluff overlooking the town. All are self-catering with hot water. The nature reserve, slowly being reforested, extends over 40 ha (99 acres), and the owners Orlando and Alicia put a third of their profits into various environmental-management programs.

Cabañas El Paraíso ((07) 580266 FAX (07) 575429, on the approach road to town, are clean, comfortable and, curiously, have their own pyramid for energizing sessions, as well as a swimming pool. The best budget place in town is **Olivia Toledo's rooms**, a block from the main square and costing only US$3 to US$4 per night. Also in the center of town, the **Hidden Garden** (/FAX (07) 580281 E-MAIL hiddengarden@latinmail.com does indeed include a flower-filled garden (and a small pool), with backpacker-friendly prices that include breakfast and kitchen privileges.

WHERE TO EAT

Most hotels provide their own restaurants, which have good reputations, and there are a number of cheap Ecuadorian or pizza places around the square. The nicest place in town, the Madre Tierra-run **La Terraza** on the square, serves good international fare from burritos to Thai. A healthy walk out of town (follow the signs), the French meals at **La Tasca** (also an hostería) include great trout in white wine sauce.

HOW TO GET THERE

The town's bus stop is two blocks from the main square. Buses, vans and shared taxis regularly run the hour-to-hour-and-a-half journey to Loja and back. If you're heading for an out-of-town lodge, take a taxi for about a dollar.

PARQUE NACIONAL PODOCARPUS

Wild, remote and in many parts unexplored, Parque Nacional Podocarpus's 146,300 ha (361,511 acres) of diverse natural habitats, ranging from upper tropical rainforest in the east through cloud forest and up to alpine *páramo* (moorland), makes it of supreme importance to science. The meeting of Amazonian and Andean weather patterns creates ecosystems that make endemism common (two species of tanager, for example, are found nowhere else). More than 550 species of birds have been recorded, among the highest counts in the world, with some estimated 3,000 to 4,000 plant species. Several threatened species of birds, as well as large mammals such as mountain tapir, pudu deer, giant armadillo, spectacled bear and jaguar, depend on Podocarpus for their survival. The park (named after the country's only native species of conifer) is also the original source of quinine — from the cinchona tree (called *cascarilla*) and used in the treatment of malaria — and ranks among Ecuador's richest cloud forests.

GENERAL INFORMATION

You can get information and basic maps about the park from the **Ministerio del Ambiente** headquarters in Loja ((07) 563131, on Sucre between Imbabura and Quito. Probably a better source of information (particularly for birding field guides) is the **Fundación Ecológica Arcoiris** ((07) 577449 E-MAIL fai1@fai.org.ec, on Segundo Cueva Celi 03-15 in Loja. The entrance fee to the park is US$5, and visits can be made from Loja, Zamora or Vilcabamba. The *refugio* at the northern Cajanuma station (ten kilometers/six miles south of Loja and about eight kilometers/five miles from the entrance on the highway) has good facilities, but if you want to go up to the highland lakes, a one-day hike, you'll need camping equipment.

In Loja, a recommended tour operator is **Biotours** (/FAX (07) 578398 E-MAIL biotours@ loja.telconet.net on Colón and Sucre. For more specialized bird-watching tours, contact **Aratinga Aventuras Birdwatchers** (/FAX (07) 582434 E-MAIL jatavent@cue.satnet.net, on Lourdes between Sucre and Bolívar.

Vilcabamba's climate, altitude and pure water are said to account for the health and longevity of its residents.

El Oriente

Nobody knows how many species of plants and animals live in the tropical rainforests. Conservative estimates suggest a figure of about 30 million species. But as scientists continue to probe this mysterious and largely unexplored realm, some believe that the figure could be as high as 80 million or more, and that rainforests could account for more than half of life forms on earth.

Roughly speaking, species already accounted for in the rainforest include 80,000 trees, 3,000 land vertebrates, 2,000 freshwater fish, almost half the world's 8,500 species of birds, and 1,200 different kinds of butterflies. Among these diverse life forms, many of them endemic to the Amazon rainforest region, and some of them endangered, there are all sorts of weird and wonderful creatures: a monkey small enough to sit in the palm of your hand (pigmy marmoset), the world's largest rodent (capybara), the world's biggest snake (anaconda), and the world's noisiest animal (the howler monkey, whose voice can carry as far as 16 km or 10 miles).

In addition to many food plants, several medicinal plants have been found in the rainforest, such as quinine for malaria and *curare* — used by Amazonian hunters to paralyze prey, and in Western medicine as a muscle relaxant during surgery, and for Parkinson's disease. Hallucinogenic plants, such as *ayahuasca*, used by shamans in religious and curing rituals, are being studied in the west for possible medical and psychiatric use. Many more such herbs from the rainforest medicine chest may be discovered in the future, as long as the oil industry, miners, loggers and farmers don't destroy it.

In the Amazon Basin, some 200 tribal groups guard a priceless biological heritage contained in an area of about five million square kilometers (almost two million square miles) of tropical forest. Over a period of about 10,000 years, generations of these peoples have lived on the wettest place on earth, where rainfall averages 25 cm (100 inches) a year.

In the Ecuadorian part of the Amazon Basin, known as El Oriente, there are many such indigenous peoples, totaling an estimated 100,000 souls. The biggest groups are the Siona-Sequoia, Cofán, Huaorani, Quichua, Shuar and Achuar. Some of them have only recently been in contact with people outside their forest environment, and it is thought that there are still small groups that continue to be totally isolated. Others, however, have either been in touch with the world outside for years and have adapted to it, or have been destroyed by its alien diseases. One of the country's most pressing problems is the future of the Oriente: balancing the nation's need for economic growth with human rights and environmental sustainability. To date, the battle has been won by the oil and the logging industries. Ecuador enjoys the grim fame of having the Amazon Basin's highest rate of deforestation.

Tourism can play a part in the protection of these precious forests, and ensure greater autonomy for their people. Revenues from visitors undoubtedly bolster the argument for the rainforest's protection. With their wages as guides or "hoteliers," rainforest people are better placed to fight for their land rights, acquire decent medical care and educate their children in the ways of the Western world. But the tourism industry has only recently truly begun to improve its sometimes quite negative environmental impact, and to establish more equitable relationships with the Oriente's Indians. Although Ecuador ranks among the leaders of the continent in ecotourism, visitors can still play a positive role in challenging the tourism industry's tendency to "green wash" and "window dress." They can force it to effect actual, substantial changes, whether environmental or social. Even better, they can contact one of the indigenous-run tour operators that have begun to organize their companies in recent years.

Ecuador's northern share of the Amazon Basin is probably the most visited by travelers. Thanks to the infrastructure built by oil companies since the 1960s, the region is one of the most accessible in the entire basin. The country's most luxurious and comfortable lodges are based here, and one of the country's largest wildlife reserves, the Reserva Faunística Cuyabeno. Although pockets of primary forest remain, much of the northern Oriente has been irredeemably damaged by the oil industry and colonization. Roads have been built, airstrips cleared, rivers polluted and indigenous people virtually wiped out. Taking time to visit the more remote areas and lodges will therefore prove more rewarding. As the effects of the Plan Colombia antidrug efforts increase, with guerrillas and refugees coming over the border and military escalation, it's likely many jungle tours will move their operations further south.

The central part of the Oriente is less explored from a tourist perspective and favored by more adventurous or budget travelers. Infrastructure in its main towns of Tena and Puyo has improved greatly over the last years, with Misahuallí west of Tena also becoming an important springboard. In all three, you'll find competent, often indigenous-run operators who can take you for jungle treks, caving or birding, and on river trips along the Napo, the Pastaza or one of their tributaries, or even whitewater rafting. As a rule, the farther away from the settlements and the highway you travel, the more pristine the forest.

PREVIOUS PAGES: The dugout canoe LEFT is the traditional form of transport in the rainforest. A Cofán Indian RIGHT from the Reserva Faunística Cuyabeno. OPPOSITE: All rivers in Ecuador's Oriente eventually flow into the Amazon.

From Puyo, the southern Oriente highway bumps and rattles along the eastern foothills of the Andes. Inca gold came from some areas in the Southern Oriente, and gold is still mined in technologically primitive open-sky operations and by ever-hopeful individuals and families. The southern part of the Oriente isn't as popular with tourists as the areas to the north. But for those who like to travel way off the beaten track there is the advantage of visiting places where the rare gringo is greeted with more than usual friendliness. The town of Sucúa, south of Macas, is the headquarters of the Shuar Indian federation, from where tours can be arranged to Shuar territory near the Peruvian border.

GENERAL INFORMATION

If your time is limited and it is within your budget, the easiest way to see something of the Oriente is to buy a package tour from a reputable operator, either in your own country or in Quito. This way all arrangements will be made for you. You will be flown from Quito to Lago Agrio, Coca, Tena, Shell (near Puyo) or Macas, from where it will probably be a rough road ride and then a motor-driven dugout canoe to the lodge where you are staying. In this way you will experience the rainforest but won't suffer too much hardship.

Alternatively, you can fly in independently and book a tour when you get to one of the gateway towns, all of which have hotels, tourist facilities and agents who can arrange jungle trips that are less expensive than they would be if you organized them from home or in Quito. In this way you will probably save some money but it will take more time. The least expensive way is to go by bus. Of the four main land routes into the Oriente, the shortest is from Quito over the Papallacta Pass down to Baeza. From this old, colonial, but somewhat bypassed, town you can head on to Lago Agrio or Tena. But the bus ride is long, bumpy and uncomfortable, and many people who go out by bus under their own steam decide to fly back.

One of the key factors in choosing a tour is the guide. If possible, meet the guide who will be taking you through the jungle to see if you get along with each other, whether he or she is knowledgeable about the things that interest you and, most importantly, how well you share a common language. Also ask to see the **guide's license**, as there are many stories of people being cheated by unlicensed guides. And check the terms of the agreement carefully to see what you have and have not paid for. Rubber boots, for instance, an essential item, might not be included in the deal. The usual rates for guides (*not* tours) is between US$25 and US$50 per day, half of which you should pay at the end of the trip.

Before leaving downriver you must show your passport and register its number at the port captain's office on the waterfront.

Operators might seem charming and plausible when you talk to them in their offices, but when it comes to equipment, food, routes and other facilities they might be a bit shaky. One trick is for guides to say they'll take you to their home village, but once there they have nothing to do with you. They've simply used your tour as a way to visit their family. Untrustworthy operators, it seems, will go to any lengths to win your confidence, even falsely using the name of a well-known guide. The best way to find a guide is by word of mouth. Talk to other travelers and read the comment books kept in some of hotels and cafés. The South American Explorers in Quito is also a very useful source of recommendations.

PAPALLACTA

About 70 km (43 miles) over the Eastern Cordillera from Quito, in a pleasant setting on the rim of the Amazon Basin, the cloud-forest town of Papallacta makes a convenient stopping point on the way to or from the Oriente. The town is also a destination in itself, particularly for week-ending *quiteños*, its chief attraction being its very hot springs. The drive up from Quito is as spectacular as it is winding, cresting at a pass over 4,000 m high (13,123 ft) and sometimes sprinkled with snow.

The main baths are the Termas de Papallacta, a one-kilometer (half-mile) uphill hike from the main Quito-Baeza road, where about half a dozen pools range from ridiculously hot to brass-monkey cold. Though the water isn't clear, because of the mineral content, the complex has recently been refurbished and the pools are clean. Changing facilities are available and the cost is about US$2. On a clear day there are beautiful views from the baths of Volcán Antisana at 5,758 m (18,891 ft).

If you're stopping off at Papallacta on your way down to the Oriente by bus, it's best to do so on a weekday to avoid crowds. The springs are even more alluring on your way back up from the rainforest, when you can relax and soak away your aches, pains and stings from your jungle-weary, bus-jolted body. Buses between Baeza and Quito can drop you off at the beginning of the path up to the *baños*.

WHERE TO STAY AND EAT

There are some new, attractive but rather expensive *cabañas* and rooms at the pools themselves, the **Termas de Papallacta** (/FAX IN QUITO (022) 557850 E-MAIL papallac@ecnet.ec WEB SITE www .papallacta.com.ec, Foch E6-12 and Reina Victoria. The Termas offers a range of accommodation, from

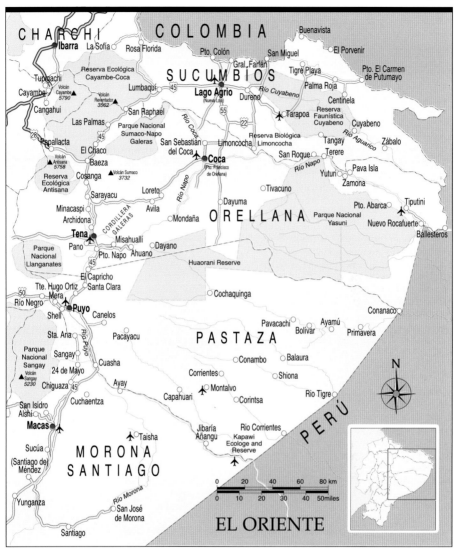

EL ORIENTE

cheap camping, moderately priced rooms with shared bathrooms, and expensive cabins that sleep up to six and have private bathrooms. The restaurant at the pools, **Café Canela**, is good, serving some excellent trout. Less expensive accommodation can be found in the village down the hill at **Hotel Quito** (no phone), the backpacker's choice, or at **Residencial El Viajero** (no phone).

THE ROAD TO LAGO AGRIO

The road from Papallacta to Lago Agrio passes the main town of Baeza before continuing northeast along the Río Quijos. For most of the way it follows the trans-Ecuadorian oil pipeline, along which oil is pumped from the oil fields deep in the Oriente, up, over the Andes, and down to the

Pacific coast. The pipeline and the road itself were cut through the jungle after oil was discovered north of Lago Agrio in the late 1960s. Settlements of colonists and small coffee farms are now strung along the twin thoroughfare, and much of the primary rainforest has been cut down, though higher up, great tracts of cloud forest remain.

Baeza lies at the junction of the Tena and Lago Agrio roads. Founded in 1548, but refounded a further three times, the town is a pleasant, sleepy place, with some great walks to enjoy in the surrounding hills. The main town lies about two kilometers (a mile and a quarter) from the road junction. The best, cleanest and friendliest place to stay is the **Hostal San Rafael ₵** (06) 320114. Seventeen kilometers (10 miles) along the rutted road to Tena, birders flock to the **Cabañas San Isidro Labrador**

(IN QUITO (022) 465578 FAX (022) 228902, Carrión 555, which is an expensive but very beautiful ranch with tasty cooking (meals included in the price) and friendly staff.

Back on the road to Lago Agrio, about two hours out of Baeza on the right, a path leads down to the 145-m (483-ft) Cascada de San Rafael, the highest falls in Ecuador. Bus drivers will know where to stop if you ask for "Las Cascadas." After about half an hour's walk, passing the **San Rafael Lodge** (no phone), where you can stay the night or camp, you come to a ridge with a great view of the misty falls. The bird-watching here is almost as impressive as the mighty falls themselves: there's a good chance of spotting the brilliant Andean cock-of-the-rock. Look out for a cross in memory of a Canadian photographer who fell to his death in the area in 1988. It might deter you from a risky climb to the foot of the falls, which is steep, slippery and treacherous.

A bit further east on the other side of the main road is the hard-to-find head of the trail to Volcán Reventador, a relatively small mountain by Ecuadorian standards (3,562 m or 11,686 ft), but nevertheless a two to four day hike to the peak. Take a guide if you plan to climb this recently active volcano, as it's easy to get lost.

LAGO AGRIO (NUEVO LOJA)

Continuing the bus route west for another four hours, you come to the oil town of Nueva Loja, better known as Lago Agrio, a nickname coined by American oil men, from the Spanish words for the oil town of Sour Lake in Texas. The town is the capital of Sucumbíos Province and has a population of about 20,000 to 25,000. Though many of the roads are now paved, rubber boots and muddy streets, and bars and brothels, are the defining characteristics of Ecuador's biggest oil town. Jungle trips can be arranged here, but if you want to see pristine primary forest this probably isn't the best place for it. Lago Agrio is a place to observe the interaction between multinational oil operations and ancient lifestyles of indigenous Amazon peoples, as prospecting and drilling destroys lives, traditions, habitats and homelands.

GENERAL INFORMATION

The **Ministerio del Ambiente** office ((06) 830129, on Eloy Alfaro and Avenida Colombia, is open mornings and afternoons from Monday to Friday. If you want to explore the area this is a good place to start. Among other things they should be able to tell you which agencies are licensed to operate in the nearby Reserva Faunística Cuyabeno, so you can avoid those cowboy outfits that sometimes get turned out of the reserve. Recommended tour operators (see also the Quito-based ones,

below) in Lago include the indigenous-run **Sionatours** ((06) 830232, 12 de Febrero 267, which takes visitors to various Siona communities in the area with Spanish-speaking native guides. Other good sources of local information are the **Frente de Defensa de la Amazonía** (/FAX (06) 831930 E-MAIL admin@fda.ecuanex.net.ec WEB SITE www.ecuanex.net.ec/fda, Eloy Alfaro 352, and **Manuel Silva** at the Casa de Cultura library ((06) 830624, Manabí and Quito.

There is an **Andinatel** office on Avenida 18 de Noviembre, just off the main plaza. The **TAME** ((06) 830113 office is on 9 de Octubre and Orellana.

WHERE TO STAY AND EAT

Lago Agrio's shortage of good hotels is evidence it is not a tourist town. Most people come here to work and aren't too fussy where they rest their weary heads.

The better hotels are pretty overpriced (moderate) for what you get, but are nonetheless comfortable. The newest place to stay is **Araza Hotel** ((06) 830223 FAX (06) 831287, Avenida Quito near Guayaquil, with a range of spick and span rooms, all with air conditioning, hot water, telephones, televisions and 'fridges. Prices include an American breakfast. Similar, but slightly cheaper, the **Hotel El Cofán** ((06) 830527 FAX (06) 830526, on Avenida Quito at 12 de Febrero, has pretty much the same feel, and identical facilities.

The inexpensive **Hotel D'Mario** ((06) 830172 FAX (06) 830456, Río Amazonas, is justifiably popular, with rooms ranging from clean doubles with private bath, hot water and fans, to more expensive ones with air conditioning, telephones and televisions. The best budget bed is probably at **Hostal Secoya** ((06) 830451, Avenida Quito, with cold water and basic rooms, some with private bath. There are many other cheapies along Río Amazonas close to the junction with Avenida Quito, so search around.

The downstairs restaurant at the Hotel D'Mario serves generous pizzas, fried chicken and other popular gringo food. For a more upmarket experience try the restaurant at the El Cofán or at the Araza. Cafetería Jackeline on Río Amazonas serves good breakfasts.

HOW TO GET THERE

Lago Agrio's airport is just five kilometers (three miles) east of the city center, an inexpensive yellow-truck taxi ride away. They operate a morning flight to and from Quito Monday to Saturday and an afternoon one Monday to Friday. The bus

OPPOSITE: The Amazonian rainforest TOP is one of the wettest places on earth with an annual rainfall of 25 cm (100 inches). An Indian woman BOTTOM shows off the products of her vegetable garden.

terminal is a short ride to the north of town. It takes between eight and ten hours to reach Quito, depending on the bus and whether it breaks down or not. Long-distance buses leave from here, while buses to Coca leave from Avenida Quito. If you're heading to Tena, go back to Baeza and change buses there. Transportes Putumayo buses, at Alfaro and Colombia, go to the Colombian border, as well as east towards the Cuyabeno.

RESERVA FAUNÍSTICA CUYABENO

Just 20 km (12 miles) east of Lago Agrio lies the western tip of the 606,000-ha (1.5-million-acre) Reserva Faunística Cuyabeno, founded in 1979 to protect the rainforest from encroachment by oil companies and settlers. The area is considered to be one of the most important areas of natural beauty and ecological diversity in the Amazon Basin. Its dense primary jungle forest is home to various Indian groups, including the Cofán, Siona, Sequoia and Shuar. There is also abundant birdlife and myriad rare and exotic plants and creatures, from pink dolphins, caiman, electric eels, manatees and anacondas to jaguars, tapirs, agoutis, peccaries, armadillos and tortoises.

Unfortunately, despite its protected status, oil and logging companies have ravaged much of the region. Wells have been drilled, roads built, forests cut down and millions of gallons of raw crude oil spilled into its rivers, creeks, swamps and lagoons. During the last 20 years or so, spills from the trans-Ecuadorian pipeline, which Texaco built in 1972, totaled 72 million liters (16 million gallons), more than half again what was spilled in the *Exxon Valdez* accident. Spills such as these contribute to high rates of malnutrition and health problems among the local *indígenas*, including birth defects and neurological disorders. In recent years, following the enlargement of the reserve in 1991, Indian organizations and conservation groups have fought hard to save the rainforest from more destruction (see THE GRINGO CHIEF, below). The NGO Conservation International TOLL-FREE IN THE US (800) 406-2306 WEB SITE www.conservation.org has been at the forefront of many projects to improve park infrastructure and protection.

Despite massive damage, vast areas of the Cuyabeno and its surroundings are untouched and unspoiled, so that visitors to the park may see no evidence of the environmental spoilage and contamination. Local people play an increasingly active part in tourism, and there are a number of lodges and camps where visitors can experience the rainforest in all its pristine beauty. To an extent, ecotourism is seen as a viable and less-destructive alternative to the petrodollar, and has played an important role in saving parts of

this precious rainforest. The entrance fee to the park is currently US$20 per person from July to September, and US$15 the rest of the year. The rainiest months run from March to September.

TOURS OF THE CUYABENO

Many Quito-based companies organize tours in the area. **Native Life Travels ℓ** (022) 550836 FAX (022) 569741, J Pinto 446 and Amazonas, run by *indígenas* from Cuyabeno, have a good reputation and their prices are reasonable. **Nuevo Mundo Expeditions ℓ** (022) 564448 FAX (022) 565261 E-MAIL nmundo@interactive.net.ec WEB SITE www.nuevomundotravel.com, Coruña N26-207, has a reputation of

being ecologically sensitive and organizes tours to the Cuyabeno River Lodge. Its owner, Oswaldo Muñoz, has been an inspirational leader of the Ecuadorian Ecotourism Association since its inception. **Metropolitan Touring ℓ** (022) 464680 or (022) 464470 FAX (022) 464702 E-MAIL info@metropolitan.com.ec WEB SITE www.ecuadorable.com, República de El Salvador N36-84, Quito, runs excellent camps on the shores of Lakes Iripari and Imuya outside the reserve. The same company also operates an enormous, flat-bottomed riverboat, the *Flotel Orellana*, which cruises Río Aguarico near the Peruvian border. This is the ultimate way of exploring the jungle in style and comfort. Shore trips, guides, canoe rides, lectures and good food are all included in the price. Several tour companies in Lago Agrio (see above) organize less expensive tours to Cuyabeno and the surrounding area.

THE GRINGO CHIEF

It's been used in more than a few headlines in the past, and there's no other nickname for him: "The Gringo Chief." His name is Randy

OPPOSITE: Cofán house in the jungle. ABOVE: Colonization has proceded apace in Ecuador's rainforest. Politics come soon after.

Borman, American-born, son of missionaries working in the Oriente, and brought up with a blowpipe in his mouth. When his parents left Ecuador, Randy stayed on in the jungle. He is a missionary himself, but not in the conventional sense. Randy's mission is to slow the destruction of the rainforest and protect its wildlife and the cultural identity of the people among whom he was raised, the Cofán Indians. He speaks Cofán, his wife is Cofán and he lives with a community of Cofáns who have elected him as their chief.

When life became impossible in the Cofán village of Dureno near Lago Agrio—hunting lands cut to pieces because of deforestation — Randy

companies in Ecuador are being forced to admit that the rainforest isn't a vacant land, where they can do whatever they like. Oil companies are now required by the Ecuadorian government to take out "cleanup insurance" to cover spills and other contamination. The destructive, but profitable, oil boom is destined to end when Ecuador's oil reserves run out in a couple decades—by which time, environmentalists warn, most of the country's primary rainforest will have been destroyed.

For information about visiting the Cofán community in Zabalo contact Randy directly at ℂ (022) 470946 E-MAIL cofan@attglobal.net. Check out the Cofán WEB SITE www.cofan.org.

and a group of Cofáns moved deeper into the jungle. They settled miles down the Río Aguarico at a spot called Zabalo near the Peruvian border. Randy still spends most of his time there, living in traditional Cofán style. He takes adventure tour groups into the jungle. He hunts wild pigs with a lance. He cuts his own dugout canoes from forest trees. And he defends the Cofáns against cultural extinction. Like David against Goliath, he fights the good fight against slayers of the rainforest and its wildlife.

Among other events in the course of his skirmishes in the jungle, Randy and his "braves" have destroyed an unmanned drilling platform built illegally on Cofán land and kidnapped a 23-man seismic testing crew for trespassing. He has also helped with lawsuits in the United States against oil companies. Thanks to people like Randy, the Cofáns and other Indian groups, oil

COCA

The jungle town of Coca is no place for sightseeing, nor a destination of choice for most travelers. The river port's *raison d'être* is as a transportation hub where you hop off a plane and jump into a boat going downriver, or stay no longer than it takes to arrange an expedition into the interior. Like Lago Agrio, it is a field base for oil workers. The town has no aesthetic merits, unless unpaved streets, muddy in rain and dusty when dry, and dilapidated, shanty-style buildings are your idea of civic beauty. One unimpressed writer described Coca as a "gritty, dirty, riverside pit."

The town owes its importance to its strategic location at the confluence of Río Coca and Río Napo. If you were able to continue on far enough downriver, across the border into Perú (which isn't legal), you would come to where the Río Napo joins Río Marañon and turns into the Amazon. From there the world's mightiest river flows for some 3,200 km (2,000 miles) across South America to the Atlantic Ocean. Such was the incredible journey of Francisco de Orellana, who in 1542 made the first documented voyage down the Amazon. For this reason Coca's official, but seldom-used, name is Puerto Francisco de Orellana, it is capital of the Orellana Province.

GENERAL INFORMATION

Foreigners arriving in or leaving Coca by river are required to show their passports at the *capitanía* by the landing dock. For those on group tours this will most likely be taken care of by the agency, as will downriver transportation by motorized canoe. For independent travelers, boats usually leave around 8 AM Mondays (and sometimes Thursdays) and return on Sundays (and sometimes Wednesdays).

Other useful facilities in Coca include an **Andinatel** office, a **post office** and a **Ministerio del Ambiente** office ((06) 880171 (Amazonas and Bolívar) for rainforest information. Entrance fees are paid here for protected nature reserves. Forget using travelers' checks or credit cards.

There is no tourist office worthy of the name, but there are a number of private agencies. Although there are many operators offering cheap trips, bear in mind that the likelihood of non-English speaking or inexperienced guides, bad food, basic accommodation and engine troubles increases with every dollar you think you're saving. The Hotel El Auca is a good hub to meet guides and fellow travelers. **Emerald Forest Expeditions** ((06) 881155 IN QUITO (/FAX (022) 541543 E-MAIL emerald@ecuanex.net.ec, on Napo, is recommended for English-speaking guides and rustic four-to seven-day tours. **Selva Tours** ((06) 880336 has also received favorable reports. The Canadian author of *Crisis Under the Canopy*, **Randy Smith** ((06) 880489 or (06) 881563 IN QUITO ((022) 540346 E-MAIL panacocha@hotmail.com WEB SITE www .amazon-green-magician.com has years of experience guiding in the area, particularly within the Huaorani Reserve. Reserve well ahead. See THE HUAORANI RESERVE, page 167 for more information.

WHERE TO STAY AND EAT

It's worth booking as far ahead as possible for accommodation in Coca. Not that it's brilliant, but more that it's limited. The best hotel in Coca is **Hostería La Misión** ((06) 880260 FAX (06) 880263, on the riverfront. Facilities include a restaurant and bar and a swimming pool with river views, as well as a number of rooms with air conditioning, hot-water private showers and cable television, others with fan only. In the center of town,

Hotel El Auca ((06) 880127 or (06) 880600 is a popular choice. With a restaurant and big garden, and rooms with fans and hot water, it's good value. A little less expensive and quieter is **Hotel Oasis** ((06) 880206, on the waterfront. The amenable staff can book rooms and trips to both the Yuturi and Yarina lodges (see below). The restaurants at La Misión and El Auca are probably the best in town. For a beer and a burger go to the American-run **Bar** (aka Papa Dan's) on the riverfront; for jungle food, such as capybara, the world's largest rodent, try **El Buho**. After your meal, head to the **Krakatoa Bar** on the riverside, west of the docks.

HOW TO GET THERE

The airport is just outside town on the Lago Agrio road. There are two **Aerogal** ((06) 881452/3 flights most days to Quito, taking about 45 minutes, one in the morning and the other in the afternoon. Flights are regularly full, so confirm your reservation. There are also irregular Air Force flights to Oriente airstrips. The best way to try your luck with these is to ask around at the air bases. Most buses leave from the new Terminal Terrestre on the north side of town, but some leave from the center. Check carefully. There are buses to Quito (10 to 12 hours), Ambato (12 hours), Santo Domingo (11 hours), Tena (six hours) and Lago Agrio (three hours).

JUNGLE LODGES BEYOND COCA

Downstream from Coca on the Río Napo there are a number of well equipped lodges tastefully constructed in native style, while incorporating modern features. Most visitors staying at these places pay for their tours in advance in their country or in Quito.

Best known of these resorts is the American-owned **La Selva Jungle Lodge** ((022) 554686 or (022) 550995 FAX (022) 563814 or (022) 567297 WEB SITE www.laselvajunglelodge.com, 6 de Diciembre 2816, Quito, winner of an ecotourism award in 1992, about three hours by fast private launch from Coca. In a wonderful spot overlooking Laguna Garzacocha, the lodge is considered one of the best of its kind in Ecuador. Facilities include comfortable rooms, good food, a butterfly farm, a small research station and two bird-watching towers. Kerosene lighting ensures that the magical jungle sounds at night aren't drowned out by an electric generator. Canoe trips and jungle treks with both indigenous and English-speaking knowledgeable guides are part of the package, and camping in the rainforest can be arranged. Bird life abounds

The *Flotel Orellana* carries tourists in luxury accommodation deep into the rainforest — the most comfortable way of exploring the Amazon without getting bitten.

around La Selva, with more than 500 species, including the rare zigzag heron. A four-day package currently costs under US$700, excluding the Quito–Coca airfare.

About 10 km (six miles) upriver from La Selva is the equally comfortable and well-run native-style *cabaña* complex, the Swiss-owned **Sacha Lodge (** IN QUITO (022) 566090 or (022) 509504 FAX (022) 236521 E-MAIL sachalod@pi.pro.ec WEB SITE www.sachalodge.com, Zaldumbide 375, Quito, where comforts of a first-class hotel have been brought into the heart of the jungle to the shores of a blackwater lagoon. Facilities and activities are much the same as La Selva, one small difference being that Sacha has electric lights and hot-water baths. The large difference is the impressive 300-m (984-ft) canopy walkway, slung through the forest about 30 m (98 ft) above the ground. Local people work at both La Selva and Sacha, but visits to *indígena* communities are not part of the program at these lodges, to avoid what could be artificial, perhaps even embarrassing encounters. Sacha's rates are slightly more expensive than La Selva's.

A scenic five-hour journey by motorized canoe down the Río Napo from Coca and along one of its tributaries, **Yuturi Lodge**, is the most remote of the upmarket *cabaña* complexes. Facilities aren't as luxurious as the two upriver lodges (no hot water and no English-speaking guides), but activities include exciting nighttime caiman watching and visits to a local *indígena* community. At around US$450 for a five-day, high-season package from Quito, prices are lower than La Selva and Sacha. For more information contact **Yuturi Jungle Adventure (**/FAX (022) 504037 E-MAIL yuturi @yuturi.com.ec WEB SITE www.yuturi.com.ec, Amazonas 1324 and Colón, Quito. Or check with Hotel Oasis in Coca (see above).

There are a number of less expensive, more basic facilities along the tributaries of the Río Napo offering good jungle experiences. About an hour downriver from Coca, **Yarina Lodge** includes 20 rustic cabins with private baths, trails through the forest and canoe paddles. English-speaking guides can be arranged, and stays of a few days are discounted. Contact the Hotel Oasis in Coca. About an hour further from Yarina, you come to the Catholic mission of Pompeya. Here, you can ask around for somewhere basic to stay and eat. Visits can be arranged to **Isla de Los Monos** (Monkey Island) and the **Pompeya museum** of indigenous artifacts and ceramics.

At the lowest end of the price scale, but right near the top in terms of ecotourism, **Cabañas Limoncocha**, in a beautiful setting only an hour by boat from Coca, is run by AIL (the Indigenous Association of Limoncocha). The complex belonged to the upmarket Metropolitan Touring group before they moved their operations to the

Río Aguarico because of mining activities. But now that those activities have abated, wildlife is returning and the local Quichua community is running the show. For more information contact AIL, at **CONFENIAE (** (022) 220326 FAX (022) 543973, Avenida 6 de Diciembre 159, Quito. Or ask travel agents in Coca for the ecotourism coordinator of the project.

On the Napo beyond La Selva (but before Yuturi), lies Lago Pañacocha. Protected by a forest reserve, it joins the Yasuní and Cuyabeno reserves together. The lake is fed by various coiling tributaries, which have been largely untouched, making for excellent wildlife-spotting adventures. A group of conservation organizations recently bought up the lodge on the lake and there are plans to expand facilities. For bookings and more information, contact **Centro de Investigaciones de los Bosques Tropicales (CIBT) (**/FAX (022) 540346 E-MAIL cibt@ecuanex.net.ec, Alemania 339 and Eloy Alfaro, Quito.

The last village in Ecuador before the Río Napo enters Perú is **Nuevo Rocafuerte**, about 12 hours downriver from Coca. From here you can cross into Perú or find a guide for the Parque Nacional Yasuní. There is a basic hostal, but no restaurant in town. The boat leaves Coca on Monday mornings, and returns Thursday mornings.

THE HUAORANI RESERVE

The traditional home and hunting grounds of the Huaorani rainforest people has been in the Napo area for millennia. In the past few years, however, their land and lifestyle have been damaged and mightily disturbed by the petrochemical and tourist industries. The Huaorani reacted by imposing tolls for the use of their rivers, and entrance fees to their communities, most of which are now part of the Huaorani Reserve south of Coca. Sometimes they demand gifts, which oil companies usually pay because it helps them to obtain concessions.

In his book on the impact of tourism on the Huaorani people, *Crisis Under the Canopy,* Canadian writer Randy Smith says tourist guides have complained that "the Huaorani are becoming less interesting to the tourists as they become more 'civilized,' leaving nudity and other traditional ways behind." This assertion crystallizes the dilemma of tourism for *indígena* peoples. The implication is that *indígenas* can benefit from tourism only if they retain traditional ways so they can be viewed like creatures in a zoo. No wonder Huaorani are skeptical about tourist visits.

Yet in the same book, Smith goes on to say that in a survey of 18 Huaorani communities that he conducted in 1992, 14 reacted favorably to the idea of being involved in ecotourism projects.

Quoting this survey in his book, *The Ecotourist's Guide to the Ecuadorian Amazon*, Rolf Wesche points out that the tendency is for each Huaorani community to establish separate arrangements with individual guides. Smith advises visitors to use a guide who has good relations with the communities, or a tour company that is partially Huaorani owned. Coca-based guides that the author recommends are Juan Enomenga, author Randy Smith, Julio Jarrín and Tseremp Ernesto Juanka. Travelers with a particular interest in entering the reserve are advised to ask around for these guides in Coca.

Travelers who want to visit the Huaorani and are sensitive to their situation should read the

people and works with Moi Enomenga. The company recently won a category in the prestigious ToDo! Ecotourism awards. Other tour operators with good relationships with the Huaorani are **Kem Pery Tours** and **Safari Tours** (see SPORTING SPREE and TAKING A TOUR, page 37 and 57 respectively in YOUR CHOICE).

PARQUE NACIONAL YASUNÍ

Ecuador's largest mainland park, Yasuní extends over a whopping 962,000 ha (2,377,128 acres). It protects a range of rainforest habitat, from forested hills to periodically flooded lowlands. Although it was first established in 1979, the boundaries of

excellent and highly recommended book, *Savages* by Joe Kane. One quote from the Huaorani Moi Enomenga sums up their position: "We do not want to be civilized by your missionaries or killed by your oil companies. Must the jaguar die so that you can have more contamination and television?"

A good place to locate guides to Huaorani territory, or for general travel information, is Papa Dan's Bar by the river in Coca. **Tropic Ecological Adventures (** (022) 225907 FAX (022) 560756 E-MAIL tropic@uio.satnet.sat WEB SITE www.tropiceco.com, Avenida República 307 and Almagro, Edificio "Taurus," Dpto. 1-A, Quito, runs a program with the Huaorani, where visitors spend a few nights in Huaorani territory and experience their way of life. Andy Drumm, the founder of Tropic, is a Fellow of Britain's Royal Geographical Society, an advisor to the Huaorani

the park were extended eastwards following the creation of the Huaorani Reserve in 1991. The park is renowned for its huge biodiversity, although to date little of it has been studied. Recognizing its importance, UNESCO declared it a Biosphere Reserve and many conservationist groups have been involved in its protection. The park faces serious threats from the oil industry: the Maxus consortium enjoys exploration rights in the park for instance. Thankfully, the road Maxus and its predecessor Conoco built has been maintained off-limits for colonizers, and environmental damage from exploration kept to a comparative minimum. The park is extremely remote, and seldom visited. However lengthy tours can be arranged with guides from Coca agencies, as well as the Quito-based ones listed previously.

The rainforest is a cornucopia of medicinal plants, many of them yet to be discovered.

TENA

The small town of Tena (population around 20,000) is the capital of Napo Province, the biggest but most sparsely populated of Ecuador's provinces. The town is situated among low-lying hills, green valleys and fast-flowing rivers where agriculture spreads along road corridors, but tracts of thick forest still carpet riverbanks and hillsides. Founded by the Spanish in 1560 at the strategic junction of Río Tena and Río Pano, the town was an important colonial center in the Ecuadorian Amazon for trade and Christian proselytizing. Only about six hours by bus from Quito, Tena is one of the most

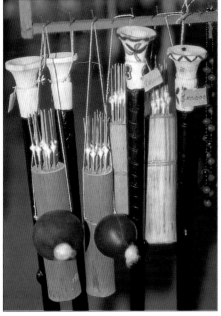

accessible destinations in the Oriente and increasingly a base for many types of jungle adventures.

While missionaries go into the jungle to convert the natives, young backpackers go in search of spiritual knowledge and simple life in natural surroundings. When they return from jungle trips and Quichua villages, they enthuse about rafting down rivers, showering under waterfalls, exploring caves, tracking down ancient rock inscriptions, sleeping in jungle huts, spotting rare species of wildlife and medicinal plants, panning for gold, entering blowpipe shooting competitions, sampling exotic foods and participating in shamanic ceremonies. Above all they speak about the friend-

ABOVE: Blowpipe darts in quiver; the traditional hunting weapon of the rainforest is still used by local tribes, and played with by tourists. OPPOSITE: Panning for gold is an ancient practice in this gold-rich land.

liness and amazing knowledge of plants and animals of their Quichua hosts. One friend of mine was shown how to roll a wound-up vine leaf over his legs and arms to pull out the hairs, as the people in the *campamento* (camp) where he was staying thought he would look more attractive without body hair.

GENERAL INFORMATION

Tena is divided in two by the Río Tena, linked by a footbridge and a vehicle bridge, with the bus terminal, some hotels and agencies on the south side and the main square along with more hotels and the airport on the north. There's a **Tourist Office** by the market, near the airport north of town, which tends to be open Monday to Fridays in the mornings and afternoons. As usual in Ecuador, you get better information by chatting with travel agents and fellow travelers. There are **Andinatel** and **post offices** on Olmedo. The best Internet café is **Piraña.net** on 9 de Octubre, though the connection could be better. Useful banks include **Banco del Pichincha** on Mera (north side) and on 15 de Noviembre the main avenue on the south side; and **Banco del Austro** also on 15 de Noviembre near the footbridge.

WHAT TO SEE AND DO

Though a pleasant town, Tena isn't an architectural gem, nor is there much to do aside from socializing with locals and fellow travelers. The most interesting attraction is the **Parque Amazónico**, situated on an island on the Río Pano. The park encompasses 27 ha (67 acres) with self-guided trails through some forest and animal pens. There is also a nice spot for swimming and picnicking. It's open 9 AM to 5 PM. Most people come to Tena to explore the jungle or to pan for gold in the rivers, and prefer to stay in *cabaña* complexes outside of town. Several agencies in town can help with these activities, though don't expect to get rich quick with gold; a few grains is all you're likely to find.

TOURS FROM TENA

A good starting point for organizing a budget jungle trip is FOIN (Federación de Organizaciones Indígenas), who represent many Quichua communities in the upper Napo area. They have their own tour operator called RICANCIE (the acronym for their ecotourism and cultural network), established in reaction to the exploitation of outside tourist operators coming into their villages. A number of programs have been developed, from camping in the jungle to taking part in spiritual ceremonies with a shaman. Accommodation is usually in traditional Quichua *cabañas*, and it is possible to visit several Indian communities.

Sharing your culture by dancing or singing with your hosts, and helping with communal work may be part of the program. Inquiries should be made care of Tarquino Tapuy, **RICANCIE (** (06) 887072 E-MAIL ricancie@ecuanex.net.ec WEB SITE http://ricancie.nativeweb.org, 15 de Noviembre 774. Prices are between US$35 and US$60 per day, depending on the size of the group and the guide. It helps if you speak Spanish, but there are some English-speaking guides.

"Jungle Trip in Tena — Highly Recommended!" This is the headline of an account of a jungle trip made by an experienced traveler. "I can't think of anyone I would rather be in the jungle with than Olmedo and Oswaldo. As guides they are the best — extremely knowledgeable about the flora and fauna, giving fascinating insights into the secrets of the jungle…" Travelers in Ecuador were passing this account from hand to hand like a treasure map. Those who did go exploring with Olmedo and Oswaldo (his son) Cerda were extremely satisfied. To find these all-star guides, contact **Sacharicsina (** (06) 886962 on Tarqui 246.

Another highly recommended agency for jungle tours is **Amarongachi Tours**, operating out of their hotel, **Traveler's Lodging Amarongachi (**/FAX (06) 886372, 15 de Noviembre 432. The company arranges jungle stays or accommodation at their own **Shangri-La Cabañas**, on a cliff overlooking the Río Anzu. It has established joint ventures with Quichua communities, most of which are along the Río Jatunyacu, southwest of Talag.

Local Quichua *cabaña* complexes are popular with budget travelers, not only because prices are reasonable, but also because the visitor will have a more intimate contact with people in villages.

Another stop on the Tena adventure trail is the 3,732-m (12,244-ft) **Volcán Sumaco**. The climb is a five- to six-day round trip involving hacking your way with a machete through the jungle wilderness of **Parque Nacional Sumaco-Napo Galeras**, one of the newest and least-known national parks. Contact one of the climbing agencies in Quito for more information.

Ancient and curious rock inscriptions, known as **petroglyphs**, are a unique attraction in the Tena region. In spite of years of research their origin or significance has not been explained. It is believed they were carved for traditional rites. There's a good guide to these mysterious markings in *The Ecotourist's Guide to the Ecuadorian Amazon*, available in Quito bookstores. Though the book gives their locations, most of the petroglyphs are buried under vegetation and you will need a guide to find them. It also gives tentative interpretations of the ideographs, such as "looks like a spider, or a frog, but is in fact a jaguar," or, "spirit that blends itself with a light ray."

The Tena area is also known for its numerous and magnificent limestone caves, many of which haven't been explored, or even discovered yet. The most famous are the gigantic Cuevas de Jumandi, about four kilometers (two and a half miles) north of the village of Archidona. To get around the caves you need a reliable, strong flashlight, rubber boots and a hat. The hat not only protects you from low-slung stalactites, but also from the resident vampire bats whose radar navigation systems don't detect human hair. Contact guides at RICANCIE or Tena agencies for more information (see above).

SPORTS AND OUTDOOR ACTIVITIES

At the other end of the tranquility scale from a jungle jaunt or river paddle, for whitewater rafting and kayaking through spectacular jungle scenery, great things are said about Ríos Ecuador. Highly experienced guides run trips for all levels of skill and experience, some of them through giant rapids and rollercoaster waves. Based on global experience, the company believes that the Upper Napo and Río Misahuallí offer some of the best and most exciting kayaking and rafting in the world. Chief instructor Gynner Coronel is one of the country's top kayakers and has competed all over the world. Rates run from about US$50 per day to US$300 and up for a full, five-day kayaking course. For more information, contact **Ríos Ecuador** IN QUITO (/FAX (022) 558264 E-MAIL info@riosecuador.com WEB SITE www.riosecuador.com, or go to their headquarters in Tena inside the Hostal Camba Huasi building, across the street from the south side of the bus terminal, (/FAX (06) 887438.

WHERE TO STAY AND EAT

Most of the accommodation in Tena is basic and inexpensive, but two places offer more comfort. Moderately priced **Hostal Los Yutzos (**(06) 886717 or (06) 886458, Augusto Rueda 190, is a friendly, family-run place right on the banks of the Río Pano, opposite the island-park. It includes a garden and beautiful views of the river, with spick and span rooms, with either air conditioning or fans, all with hot water, televisions and telephones. Book ahead for a room with a river view. In the same price range, **Hotel Internacional El Mol (** (06) 886808 FAX (06) 886215, Sucre 432, on the north side of town, boasts a pool and a restaurant, and some rooms have balconies with the same facilities as Los Yutzos. Good value, if somewhat soulless.

A cut above the budget options, the inexpensive **Hotel Pumarosa (**/FAX (06) 886320, on Orellana, has a range of rooms with either fans or air conditioning. They're all clean, decent and good value. With about the same rates, **Hostal Villa Belén (** (06) 886228, on the Baeza road near the airport, is a clean, modern hotel within an old hacienda with a garden and restaurant.

The aforementioned **Hostal Travelers' Lodging** (Amarongachi) ((06) 886372, on 15 de Noviembre, two blocks north of the bus station, is highly rated and popular, with a selection of rooms with private hot water bathrooms, all very acceptable for the inexpensive price. There's a view from the rooftop patio and the staff are friendly. The two good budget bets are **Hostal Limoncocha** ((06) 887583 E-MAIL welschingerm@yahoo.de, off Rosales on the hill south of the bus terminal, with four clean rooms sharing two hot showers, and **Hostal Camba Huasi** ((06) 886429, a block south of the bus terminal on Avenida del Chofer. It has several clean but Spartan rooms with cold showers.

The restaurants in most of these hotels are the best in Tena, the one at **Villa Belén** being particularly worth trying. **Cositas Ricas**, next to the Amarongachi, is a favorite haunt of travelers. Their vegetarian fare is carefully prepared and a big variety of juices is a feature. There's a decent pizza place next door. In the budget range, the restaurant at **Residencial Enmita**, on Simón Bolívar south of the airport, is also good, or try **Chuquitos** just off the plaza, which serves tasty fresh fish and has appealing river views.

Tena isn't famous for nightlife, but those with an ear to the ground will hear some salsa beats on weekends at **La Galera**, **Tattoo's** and the bar down by the river just north of the footbridge.

HOW TO GET THERE

Flight destinations are limited to Coca and Shell (Puyo), though a planned route to Quito might have started. Your best bet is to inquire with the local tour operators. The Terminal Terrestre bus station is just southeast of town, on the road to Puerto Napo. Bus destinations include Baeza, Quito, Ambato, Lago Agrio, Coca (a grueling, seven-hour, bone-shaking ride) and Puyo. All bus journeys in the Oriente are uncomfortable and unreliable.

MISAHUALLÍ

Misahuallí is either an over-touristy village, surrounded by despoiled rainforest and depleted wildlife, or a charming river port, conveniently situated for jungle excursions. Both views are valid. True, jungle tourism makes the place tick. Several agencies, guides, restaurants and a variety of accommodations cater to a steady stream of tourists and travelers who want to experience the thrills and adventures of the rainforest. Like Tena, Misahuallí is reasonably accessible from Quito and tours, if you shop around, are less expensive than in Quito.

Much of the primary forest in the area has been cut down for agriculture, destroying the natural habitat of large mammals such as jaguars, tapirs, monkeys, capybaras and ocelots. But on high escarpments, and in deep ravines that are inaccessible to the settlers, there are large tracts of virgin forest abundantly populated by birds, butterflies, insects and plants and flowers. The further east you go from the settled areas, the more prolific the wildlife. As for charm, it is also true that Misahuallí does have its attractions, with its picturesque location at the confluence of Río Napo and Río Misahuallí, its surrounding network of meandering waterways, river beaches, rapids, waterfalls and panning for gold along the shores of the Napo. In addition, there are several fine ecolodges down river, as well as a number of Quichua communities that welcome guests.

GENERAL INFORMATION

With a population of only about 4,000, Misahuallí isn't well endowed with urban amenities. Opposite the Hotel Albergue Español, there's a **telephone office**, with only two lines, and there are a few shops where you get basic supplies. There's also a **doctor** at the end of the Tena road, who runs the pharmacy near the main plaza.

There are plenty of travel agencies and guides in Misahuallí, though some are relocating up to Coca where jungle tourism is expanding. Consistently recommended is **Douglas Clarke's Expeditions** IN TENA ((06) 887584, close to the plaza. Douglas, who in fact speaks limited English but is knowledgeable, offers a variety of tours from day trips, to serious 10-day expeditions. Other com-

Just some of the numerous rainforest products found in the Oriente.

panies that have received favorable reports are **Misahuallí Tours** and **Ecoselva**, both on the plaza. Finding the right jungle tour may take two or three days if you want to save money by joining a group.

WHERE TO STAY AND EAT

For accommodation, Misahuallí is certainly no Saint-Tropez, but you are in the jungle after all.

Out of town, the best choice is the **Misahuallí Jungle Lodge** IN QUITO ((022) 520043 FAX (022) 255354 E-MAIL miltour@accessinter.net, Ramírez Dávalos 251. The lodge has comfortable cabins with private baths and hot water, electricity, a pool and a restaurant. Rates are expensive when booked through Quito, but moderate if you just turn up. Ask in town for directions. Close to the plaza, **France Amazonia** (/FAX (06) 887570 is about the most comfortable choice in town. The French-owned hostal includes six stone cabins with thatched roofs and hot water, all attractively laid out. Meals are also available; rates are moderate.

A good, clean choice in the inexpensive price range is the helpful **Hotel Albergue Español** ((09) 558360 IN QUITO (/FAX (022) 221626, by the river, a short walk from the plaza. Some rooms have river views, making them very good value. The owners run a lodge downriver with moderate prices for their cabins. With about the same rates, and also clean and helpful is **Hostal Dayuma Lodge**, owned by Douglas Clarke (see above). **El Paisano** (also known as Paleface Inn) on the Pununo road about 100 m (330 ft) from the central plaza, is popular with backpackers, has a garden restaurant with vegetarian food and hammocks. For jungle lodges, see below.

The best restaurants are in the hotels listed above. Beyond these, there are the usual *comedores* serving standard *desayuno* (breakfast), *almuerzo* (lunch) and *cena* (dinner).

JUNGLE LODGES

There are at least seven major jungle lodges downriver from Misahuallí, and several budget *cabaña* complexes. Eight kilometers (five miles) downriver is the famous **Jatun Sacha** (Big Forest) **Biological Reserve**, a 2,000-ha (5,000-acre) tropical wet forest, one of the most biologically diverse tropical areas on earth. No fewer than 532 bird species have been recorded in the reserve, along with 863 butterflies and more than 2,500 plant species. Scientific staff and student researchers from Ecuador and overseas help with reforestation and agroforestry projects, as well as working in the Amazon Plant Conservation Center. It's a race against time to save the surrounding forest from ill-conceived colonization. Donations to the foundation are welcome, and the lodge charges visitors about US$6.

Although the reserve and some of its facilities are open to the public, nonscientists aren't usually allowed to stay in the reserve's basic residential *cabañas*, but you can always ask if there's any space. Instead, they are directed to the spectacular **Cabañas Aliñahui** (Beautiful View) nearby, which is partly managed by the nonprofit Jatun Sacha Foundation. The cabins are comfortable and appealing, but combine two or four double rooms sharing one bathroom with heated water between them. The location on the bluff overlooking the river is superb, with shelters dotted about for relaxation and contemplation. Tours of villages and the forest with multilingual guides can be arranged, and accommodation with all meals lies in the expensive category. Jatun Sacha is commonly regarded as one of the best ecotourism operations in the Oriente. For more information about the foundation, contact **Jatun Sacha Foundation** (IN QUITO (022) 432240 or (022) 432173 FAX (022) 453583 E-MAIL jatsacha@jsacha.ecuanex.net.ec WEB SITE www.jatunsacha.org. For information about **Aliñahui**, contact (IN QUITO (022) 253267 FAX (022) 253266 E-MAIL alinahui@interactive.net.ec, Avenida Los Shyris 760 and República de El Salvador.

Continuing downriver for about 10 km (six miles), close to the mission village of Ahuano you come to the large and lavish **Casa del Suizo** on a bluff overlooking the river. This is about as good as you can get in rainforest luxury. Their expensive four-day package includes a full range of activities, including rafting and a visit to the **AmaZOOnica** animal rescue center, as well as very comfortable *cabañas* (for this neck of the woods), great food and landscaped tropical gardens. You can even have air conditioning in some cabins, in addition to an international phone line. The lodge is run by the same company as the Sacha Lodge (see JUNGLE LODGES BEYOND COCA, page 165 for reservation details).

Other jungle lodges further downriver are the rustic but comfortable **Cabañas Anaconda** (close to Casa del Suizo), **Dayuma Lodge** (at the confluence of the Puni and Arajuno rivers), and **Jaguar Lodge**, one of the oldest tourist facilities on the Napo, built in 1969 and essentially a modern hotel without the jungle charm. Inquire with Quito travel agents for more information on these lodges. At the AmaZOOnico animal rehabilitation center, some three kilometers (two miles) east Ahuano, the dedicated Swiss/Quichua owners have established a lodge called **Liana Lodge**, with double rooms with private baths (hot water) under six thatched cabins. Rates are in the expensive bracket and include all meals and tours. Contact **Selva Viva** (/FAX IN QUITO (022) 887304 E-MAIL amazoon@na.pro.ec.

The more-remote **Yachana Lodge**, in the village of Mondañam, is halfway between Misahuallí and Coca on the Río Napo. The lodge is part of a program of the nonprofit organization FUNEDESIN, which works with Indian groups. In a reciprocal arrangement, local people learn about things like beekeeping, while tourists learn about medicinal plants. The lodge ranks among the best in the country for interaction with local people on an equitable basis. It is also run on strict ecological lines, with some of the best multilingual guides in the region. Rates are about US$320 for a four-day package, and air transportation to Coca can also be arranged. For more information contact **FUNEDESIN/Yachana Lodge** (IN QUITO (022) 237133 FAX (022) 220362 E-MAIL info@yachana .com WEB SITE www.yachana.com, Andrade Marín 1888, Quito.

For an authentic experience staying in a Quichua community, contact **RICANCIE** in Tena (see TENA, page 168). The indigenous organization works with several Misahuallí communities, including **Capirona**, the first in the scheme and the model for subsequent communities. The Capirona tourism program emphasizes Quichua culture above all, but also includes jungle hikes highlighting medicinal plants and local mythology.

HOW TO GET THERE

The easiest and quickest way to get to and from Misahuallí is by bus. Buses depart several times a day from the main plaza to Tena, where there are onward connections. Buses also leave from Tena to the small downriver village of Ahuano, beyond Misahuallí on the north bank of the Napo. But the bus has to take the road on the south bank to La Punta (not marked on many maps), and passengers cross to Ahuano by dugout canoe. This is the best way to get to Casa del Suizo or Cabañas Anaconda unless the lodge has already arranged transport.

A more romantic and exciting way to travel up and down the Río Napo is by boat. There is usually a passenger boat in the morning from Misahuallí to downriver settlements and on to Coca, which costs about US$20. You might have to wait until the boat fills to keep the fare down. Passage in your own boat costs about 10 times more. Motorized dugout canoes make the six-hour journey between Coca and Misahuallí once or twice a week, but their schedules depend on demand and river conditions. Ask around the port to find out which boats are leaving and when, and register with the *capitanía* there before departure.

PUYO

As capital of Pastaza Province and with a population of some 25,000, the town of Puyo is one of the most important trade centers in the Oriente. But the town's significance to travelers and tourists is as a jumping-off point for trips deeper into the

selva (wet forest). Travelers mostly stay overnight in Puyo if they are waiting for a connecting flight or for a bus going back up into the highlands. Though human settlements existed here for many thousands of years, and Dominicans founded the town in 1899, Puyo is only just adapting to gringo travelers. The author Philippe Descola described its atmosphere succinctly as "a subtle blend of barbecued meat, overripe fruit and damp earth, sometimes overlaid with the pestilential exhaust fumes of a huge truck or jolting bus." That was in the 1970s, and it hasn't changed much since. Its name derives from the Quichua word for "cloudy," and if you spend any time here you'll soon understand why. If you're very fortunate you might spot both the incisors of El Altar and the dome of the Sangay volcanoes off in the distance.

GENERAL INFORMATION

The **Tourist Office** ((03) 855122 is on the first floor of the Municipio building, at the corner of 9 de Octubre and Francisco de Orellana. Open 9 AM to 12:30 PM and 2 PM to 5 PM, it won't blow you away with information, but can provide town maps and a selection of brochures, and the staff can answer most questions.

There is an **Andinatel** telephone office a block west of the market at Francisco de Orellana and General Villamil, and a **post office** on 27 de Febrero and Atahualpa. For money, change travelers' checks at **Casa de Cambio Puyo**, Atahualpa and 9 de Octubre, and get cash advances on Visa at the **Filanbanco** at Francisco de Orellana and 9 de Octubre. There are Internet cafés in the town center. Street signs are not Puyo's forte.

WHAT TO SEE AND DO

After walking around the Parque Central, with its bandstand, trees, cathedral and views, take a stroll northwards up Avenida 9 de Octubre for about half an hour until you get to a rope bridge over the Río Puyo. Cross the bridge into the grandly named **Parque Pedagógico Etno-Botánico Omaere** (open 8 AM to 6 PM daily). A botanical garden with medicinal plants and some traditional rainforest dwellings make up the attractive complex. You can also swim in the river by the park. Closer to town, the **Museo Etno-Arqueológico**, inside the Casa de la Juventud at 9 de Octubre and Atahualpa, showcases the traditional indigenous community quotidian life and utensils, as well as a small collection of pre-Hispanic ceramics and tools. The museum is open Monday to Friday from noon to 6 PM only.

Not to be missed in a suburb southeast of Puyo is the privately owned and run **Jardín Botánico Las Orquideas** ((03) 884855 or (03) 884854. Its creator, Omar Tello, takes guests around his wonderful collection of over 200 species of stunning orchids, imparting his knowledge with great enthusiasm as he leads you along forested paths. To do the gardens justice, allow two hours for the tour. Reservations are essential, and doors open 8 AM to 6 PM daily, with a US$5 entrance fee.

Another attraction close to Puyo is the **Centro El Fátima**, a small zoo 10 km (six miles) along the road to Tena. The wildlife is limited to indigenous Oriente species, including small and large mammals as well as various species of birds, so you can see the animals that you'll be extremely fortunate to spot in the wild when you visit the jungle. The zoo is open 8 AM to 6 PM daily and can be reached by taxi or by taking the Tena bus.

TOURS FROM PUYO

Although Puyo isn't yet a tourist town like Tena or Misahuallí, its importance is growing. If you haven't made travel arrangements in Quito or Guayaquil before coming, the Organización de Pueblos Indígenas de Pastaza (OPIP) has a tour operator called **Papangu Tours** ((03) 883875 E-MAIL papangu@a.ecua.net.ec, 9 de Octubre and Atahualpa. OPIP represents some 130 communities in Pastaza Province. Employing local guides, the organization feeds its profits back into the communities that are part of its tours, or helps increase awareness of the Pastazan indigenous

ABOVE: Forms of life you may never have seen or imagined are on display in limitless variety in the rainforest. RIGHT: Motorized launches are the most common means of transportation in the Oriente. Not all are as comfortable as this one.

people's plight on a national and an international level. Tours start from basic one-day trips visiting local sights and the forest of **Hola Vida** to the south, with longer tours of up to five days downriver by canoe or by plane to a number of remote communities. At the offices you'll find some fine crafts, including hammocks, weaving, jewelry and ceramics, on sale, as well as books about the Oriente.

WHERE TO STAY AND EAT

You shouldn't have a problem finding a room in Puyo, except perhaps during the town's annual fiesta in early May.

The most noteworthy choice in the area lies about five kilometers (three miles) along the road to Tena. **Hostería Safari** ((03) 885465 FAX (03) 851424 has appealing grounds, gardens with a pool, a Jacuzzi, a sauna and a good restaurant. Rooms come with private baths and hot water, but aren't air conditioned; moderate prices include breakfast and dinner.

At the top end of the inexpensive price range, **Hostería Turingia** ((03) 885180 FAX (03) 885384, out on Marín 294, has clean *cabañas* in a tropical garden and a good restaurant. The newer (better) rooms have fans, telephones and televisions. Closer to town, the new **Hotel Los Cofanes** (/FAX (03) 885560 or (03) 883772 E-MAIL loscofanes@yahoo .com, 27 de Febrero at Marín, represents excellent value. Ample rooms have fans, hot water, telephones and cable television, and are spotless. There's also a restaurant, which isn't up to much, but might fill a gap.

The travelers' choice is the clean and friendly inexpensive **Hotel Europa Internacional** ((03) 885220 FAX (03) 885120, on Avenida 9 de Octubre between Atahualpa and Orellana, which has a budget restaurant downstairs and a rooftop with fine views.

In addition to dining at the hotels mentioned, **El Mesón Europeo**, located near the bus station, has a good reputation. Just for its jazzy name it's worth trying **Cha-Cha-Cha Pollo a la Brasa**, which is near the Turingia.

HOW TO GET THERE

Terminal Terrestre bus terminal is on the west side of town, though after 6 PM most buses go into the center. Buses leave for the main Oriente towns as well as Guayaquil, Ambato and Quito. If the Baños road is closed, buses west have to go through Tena.

Flights from Quito and small airstrips in the jungle land at Puyo's airport, named Shell after the oil company that built it. Shell is about 10 km (six miles) west of Puyo near Mera on the road to Baños. The Ecuadorian Air Force (FAE) flies all around the Oriente every day, but getting on a

flight isn't easy. The best move is to ask at the nearest airbase, employing all powers of charm and persuasion. There are about three private companies, usually chartered by lodges for their guests. Contact operators in Quito, or OPIP in Puyo, for details and prices of these.

KAPAWI ECOLODGE AND RESERVE

Completed in 1996 after two years of construction, Kapawi Ecolodge in southwestern Ecuador represents the cutting edge of ecotourism. The architecture and building materials for the cluster of buildings, perched on stilts along the shore of a lake, are entirely in Achuar tradition, using

wood, palm leaves and twine. The long walkways connecting the individual huts are all made of materials from the rainforest. There's nary a nail in the place.

But there are also many twenty-first century conveniences in this luxury, environmentally friendly biosphere in the middle of the most remote rainforest: solar energy, biodegradable soaps, four-stroke outboard engines and specially made bags for shower water which are spread outside to heat in the sun. Also in evidence are electric lights, mosquito screens, kitchen utensils, computers, radios, walkie-talkies, refrigerators and outboard motors.

But the most ecotouristic element of this project is the role of the local Achuar. Canodros, the Guayaquil-based company that built and owns the lodge (and which has invested nearly US$3 million to date), has agreed to pay the local community a monthly rent for the use of the land. Rent currently stands at about US$2,500 a month, increasing by 16 percent every year. Come 2011, Canodros has agreed to hand the whole lodge over to the Achuar. The company will then assume a merely promotional role. Canodros is currently training the Achuar for their eventual management roles, and presently, between 60 and 70 percent of the employees at the lodge

are Achuar. For now, Kapawi is one of only three lodges in Latin America that have agreed to this hand-over policy.

For the tourist, Kapawi offers magic and mystery, not to mention sweat and a dose of fear. The magic comes when you paddle a canoe through a glassy lagoon listening to the jungle all around you: pipes and whistles, trills and drones, the jabbering of monkeys, the odd plop of fish and the soft kuala-kuala of the paddle in the water. There's magic too when you trek though shady glades under giant kapok trees and watch a troop of leaf-cutter ants going about their business, or when you sit back on your balcony, beverage in hand, overlooking the dark lake and listening to the high whine of jungle insects and the deep croak of frogs.

The mystery is all around you, too. What is that sound? What is this creepy creature? How do you see the spirits of the jungle, in which Achuar believe: the anaconda, the pink dolphin and the harpy eagle? What happens if you drink the hallucinogenic concoction they call *nataam* (commonly known as *ayahuasca*, or *Banisteriopsis caapi*)? Achuar and highly professional naturalist guides are on hand to decipher some of these mysteries. But others will remain as they are.

For more information on Kapawi Ecolodge and Reserve contact **Canodros** IN QUITO (/FAX (022) 442801 or (022) 256759 IN GUAYAQUIL (042) 285711 or (042) 280164 FAX (042) 287651 E-MAIL ecotourism @canodros.com.ec WEB SITE www.kapawi.com, Portugal 448 between Catalina de Aldaz and 6 de Diciembre, Quito.

MACAS

The capital of Morona-Santiago Province, Macas is an old Spanish town that was a trading and missionary post for some 400 years. But with a fast-growing population of 15,000 and more and more new buildings, the town is acquiring a modern face and is becoming important as a tourist center. At present Macas can only be reached from the north or south on Route 45, the southern Oriente highway, or by plane. But a new (dirt) road down the Sierra from Guamote on the Panamericana highway should be complete by the time you read this. The project will give an added boost to Macas, though there has been a lot of criticism because the road will pass through Parque Nacional Sangay, threatening the habitats of endangered species like the mountain tapir, of which only some 2,000 survive.

In line with the town's new image there is a large and relatively new Terminal Terrestre bus station, an airport with flights to and from Quito, a quite new main **plaza** and a **cathedral** that was completed way back in 1992. For international phone calls, the **Pacifictel** office is on Avenida 24 de Mayo between Cuenca and Sucre. Don't rely on banks in Macas for credit-card advances, but most tour operators should change travelers' checks. There's an **Internet café** on Soasti near Cuenca, if you're in need of a quick e-mail fix.

WHERE TO STAY AND EAT

The clean, modern highrise **Peñón del Oriente** ((07) 700124 FAX (07) 700450, found on Domingo Comin 837 and Amazonas, is everybody's nomination for best-value hotel in town. It offers a range of rooms with varying facilities at inexpensive rates. A short ride south of town on the road to Sucúa, the **Hostería del Valle** ((07) 700226 FAX (07)

700302 offers comfortable and clean bungalows with private baths, hot water, televisions and friendly owners in the same price category. Meals are available upon request. **Hostal Esmeralda** ((07) 700160, on Cuenca, is also clean, modern and good value. Recommended restaurants are **La Randimpa**, for Cuban food and music, and **Restaurant Café Bar**, for tropical atmosphere, music, *ceviche* and a strange name.

TOURS FROM MACAS

Though not as popular as a base for jungle exploration as Coca or Misahuallí, the vast Amazon Basin stretches out east of Macas, with all its potential for adventure. Visits to local **Shuar communities** can be arranged, as well as horseback riding, whitewater rafting, fishing and treks to remote caves, hot springs and waterfalls.

At **Miazal**, for example, 50 km (31 miles) southeast of Macas over the Cutucu mountain range, a hot spring bubbles from the earth and flows from a rock in a naturally hot waterfall, while next to it is a cold waterfall of pure mountain water. Where else can you find natural hot and cold waterfalls side by side in the middle of a tropical rainforest? There's no road to Miazal and it is a tough 50-km (31-mile) hike from Macas that takes a few days. Instead, visitors come by light aircraft and stay in the simple, but comfortable, Shuar-style **Miazal Lodge**. You can book this lodge through Tuntiak (see below). In the nearby Shuar community, visitors learn about the way of life of a people who live in close contact with their natural world.

In the vicinity of Miazal there are caves inhabited by colonies of the extraordinary **oilbird**. These huge, nocturnal, fruit-eating creatures live more like bats than birds and use a form of sonar navigation of audible clicks which keeps them from crashing into the walls in the pitch-black caves. Oilbirds have long been prized by the Indians because of their fatty flesh, which they boil down into oil and use for cooking and lighting. The best-known oilbird cave is **Cueva de los Tayos**, near Santiago between Méndez and Morona, but you'll need a guide to find them.

For more information about trips from Macas, including to the Parque Nacional Sangay (see page 131 in CENTRAL HIGHLANDS), contact **Ikiaam** ("jungle" in Shuar) ((07) 700497, by the Hotel Peñon del Oriente, run by helpful and knowledgeable Shuar guides. **Tuntiak** ((07) 700185, inside the Terminal Terrestre building, is also recommended as a reliable Shuar agent organizing shaman and "cleansing" tours. **Ecotrek** (IN CUENCA (07) 841927 FAX (07) 835387 E-MAIL ecotrek@az .pro.ec, at Larga 7-108 and Luís Cordero, Cuenca, arranges trips to Miazal.

HOW TO GET THERE

The airport is just east of town. **TAME** (/FAX (07) 701162 runs flights to and from Quito about three times a week, but check with them for latest times and fares. The other airline operating is **Austro Aéreo** ((07) 700939, which flies to Cuenca most days of the working week. There are also flights by the Air Force and missionary planes, which are hard to get on, but worth inquiring about.

The bus terminal is on 10 de Agosto at Amazonas, two blocks east of the main plaza. There are regular departures to points north and south. The bus can't cross the bridge on the road to Puyo, so another is employed on the other side of the roaring Río Pastaza.

OPPOSITE: Pink dolphins can sometimes be spotted breaking the surface of placid rivers in Ecuador's Amazonian forests. ABOVE: A handful of gold can make one rich for life.

SOUTH TO ZAMORA

The Oriente "Highway" continues south from Macas to the small town of **Sucúa**, a major center of Shuar Indians (also known as Jívaro) who are best known for their erstwhile habit of cutting off and shrinking the heads of their enemies. You can get information about Shuar culture and shop for handicrafts, but since the success of missionaries you won't see any *tsantsas* (shrunken heads) in the town's **Shuar Cultural Center**. The best place to see *tsantsas* is at the Municipal Museum in Guayaquil. Sucúa is also the location of the headquarters of the **Shuar Federation**, from whom you have to obtain permission to visit Shuar villages.

Carrying on southwards you pass through the small towns of **Méndez** and **Limón**. Unless you have some personal business, or you're on the run from the CIA, there's not much incentive to stop in either. From both of these towns you can branch off west on spectacular roads over the mountains to **Cuenca**. The narrow, unpaved roads in this area aren't always passable because of landslides, floods or other disasters, especially during the rainy months of April to June, so be prepared for delays.

The next town down the bone-shaking road is **Gualaquiza**, four hours from Limón. Its remoteness and its scenic setting in the hills are the town's main attractions, as well as nearby unexplored **Inca ruins**, deserted **caves**, and the **Salesian Mission** of Bomboiza. Further on, the village of **Yantzaza** is one of the fastest-growing towns in Zamora Chinchipe Province, because of mining. Nearby is the Wild West gold-rush town of **Nambija**, once a source of Inca gold, which you are unlikely to visit unless you want to live dangerously for a false vision of sudden riches.

If you have made your way all the way down the Southern Oriente Highway by bus, you'll be greatly relieved to reach the town of **Zamora**. There might not be much to do in this quiet provincial capital, but at least you shower or bathe away aches and pains from a stiff and shaken frame. You can also inquire about the Parque Nacional Podocarpus, which is accessible from Zamora, though more easily from Loja or Vilcabamba (see PARQUE NACIONAL PODOCARPUS, page 153). The best value hotel is the **Hotel Maguna (** (07) 605219 FAX (07) 605113, which is comfortable, popular and has rooms with great views from the balconies. From Zamora, take the scenic road up into the Sierra to **Loja**, only 64 (40 miles) — but over two hours! — away (see page 148). From there you can head off elsewhere by bus or plane, or make your way to Vilcabamba (see page 150 in CENTRAL HIGHLANDS) for some well-earned rest and recuperation.

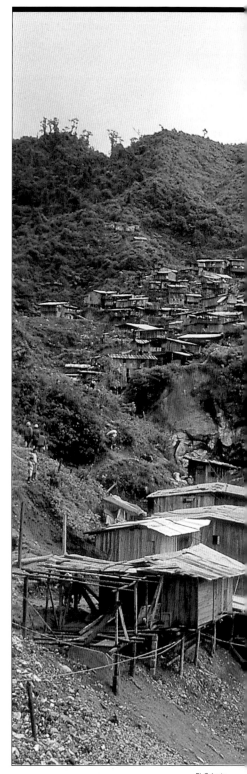

Shacks huddled on the hillside are home to miners seeking their fortune in the gold mines of Nambija.

The
Pacific
Coast

Though better known for its Andean mountains, Amazonian rainforest and the unique Galápagos Islands, Ecuador has a long, varied and fascinating coastline that until recently was underrated. Stretching some 1,500 km (932 miles) from the border with Colombia to Perú in the south, the Pacific coast embraces long expanses of deserted beaches, with warm swimming waters, busy fishing villages, luxury vacation resorts, ecolodges, and mangrove swamps, along with steamy ports, surfing beaches, wildlife sanctuaries and environmentally damaging shrimp farms.

The road-building projects along the coast were only recently completed, having been severely delayed by the impact of El Niño in 1997 and 1998. The new roads have opened up much of the coast, making it far more accessible. A coastal road to the northern border is now finished, bringing increasing numbers of Colombian tourists. In one sense, now is the time to visit the unspoiled Ecuadorian coastline, while it is still relatively undeveloped. On the other hand, development is bringing with it badly needed infrastructure, accessibility and tourist facilities.

Though it has no precise inland demarcation, Ecuador's coastal region generates the major part of the country's industrial and agricultural wealth, and is home to roughly half its population. Coastal farmers, called *montuvios*, are usually mixed-race black and Indian, or *negros de monte*, "blacks of the bush." But no love is lost between the coast and the Sierra. Coastal people call those from the Sierra *burros* (donkeys), while *serranos* say people from the *Costa* are *monos* (monkeys). Whatever these differences, many agree that *La Costa* is a state of being, a state of mind, and a place where people like to party and stay out late. Certainly it is where Ecuadorian vacationers go to relax and have fun.

SAN LORENZO

Ecuador's northernmost coastal town was once linked to Ibarra in the highlands by the extraordinary *autoferro* railway that took most of a day to descend from an altitude of 2,210 m (7,251 ft) to the coastal plains (see IBARRA, page 112 in NORTHERN HIGHLANDS). The rough road that linked the two towns has been gradually upgraded and now supersedes the railway, which was badly damaged by the El Niño floods of 1997 and 1998.

Whichever way you come, you may be mildly surprised when you arrive in this hot, tropical coastal town, where the streets are mostly unpaved, full of potholes and sprouting weeds. Most houses are ramshackle, and the inhabitants have a languid, easygoing air and never seem to be in much hurry. San Lorenzo isn't striking for its affluence or energy, especially during the heat of the day. Come nightfall, however, when the air

gets cooler, people saunter in the streets, sit in the park chatting with their friends, or just stand around watching the world go by. A salsa beat or marimba riff fills the air. "Walk and learn," they say here. "Walk and know."

BACKGROUND

San Lorenzo dates back to the sixteenth century, when a slave boat from Africa was wrecked off the coast. The escaped slaves, or maroons as they were called, established themselves around this estuary of islands and mangrove swamps. In their early days, the maroons allied with the freebooting British pirates, including Sir Francis Drake, and harassed Spanish galleons. The British supplied them with guns and cannon for use against their colonial masters, while the maroons gave the British food and a haven.

Cut off by inland forests and high mountains, the community of African expats retained its cultural traditions and independence. Some of these survive in the form of marimba music and the summoning of spirits with macumba voodoo. Its only lifeline being the sea, the community remained cut off from the rest of the country until the construction of the *autoferro* railway to Ibarra in 1959, enabling export of agricultural products to the Sierra. With the completion of the road linking Colombia in the north and the big city of Esmeraldas to the south, San Lorenzo will benefit from more traffic. Locals say that in 20 years it will become a real city, but at the same time San Lorenzo may lose some of its languid charm.

GENERAL INFORMATION

Gringos getting off trains, buses or boats are usually met by youths offering to find them hotels, introduce them to restaurants or even supply them with drugs. Be careful, and certainly don't fall for the drug scam. Another group, posing as plainclothed policemen, will accost and threaten to arrest the travelers who have bought marihuana from the first group of youths. A payoff is usually the only way out.

San Lorenzo doesn't have many facilities of use to tourists. Come with money. There is no tourist office, though there is a **Ministerio del Ambiente office** on the main square (with irregular hours), and an **Andinatel** office on the other side of the wide street from the Hotel San Carlos. Probably the best bet for tourist information is Jaime Burgos Echegaray, who runs La Estancia restaurant. He's very knowledgeable, and can

PREVIOUS PAGES: Coconut palm LEFT at a *hostería* near Río Verde on the coast of Esmeraldas Province. A natural abundance of the fruit RIGHT made Ecuador the original banana republic. OPPOSITE: A lonesome fisherman sings Latin-style blues near Chanduy.

THE PACIFIC COAST

Scale:
0 20 40 60 80 km
0 10 20 30 40 50 miles

COLOMBIA

ESMERALDAS

Mataje
Limones (Valdéz)
San Lorenzo
La Tola
Tambillo
Las Peñas
Borbón
Reserva Ecológica Cayapas Mataje
Carondelet
Río Verde
Colope
Montalvo
Lagarto
Urbina
Alto Tambo
Esmeraldas
Tonsupa
Vuelta Larga
Lita
Súa
Atacames
Chinca
Pta. Galera
Galera
Quingüe
Bislí
Cube
Tongorachi
Muisne
Río Muisne
Chucaple
Cube
Reserva Ecológica Cotacachi-Cayapas
Guadaul
Portete
Bolívar
Reserva Ecológica Mache-Chindul
Malimpia
Cojimíes
Salima
Quinindé (Rosa Zárate)

IMBABURA

Otavalo
El Limón
La Cieba
Cañaveral
Pedernales
La Independencia
La Vigencita
Reserva Biológica Maquipucuna
Reserva Geobótanica Pululahua
Otón
Ascáz
Tabuga
Santo Domingo de los Colorados

PICHINCHA

QUITO
Pifo
Pitagua
Novillo
Jama
Covento
El Carmen
San Raphael
Sangolqui
Muyoyal
Río Mariano
Flavio Alfaro
Aloag
Canoa
Patricia Pilar
El Mirador
San Vicente
Ricuarte
Guadual Gde.
Reserva Ecológica Antisa
Bahía de Caráquez
Boyacá
Chone
Parque Nacional Cotopaxi
Pta. Charapotó
San Clemente
Chugchilán

MANABÍ

Camarones
Guayacán
Crucita
Calceta
Palmar
Mangas
La Unión
Pujilí
Latacunga
Manta
Rocafuerte
Pueblo Nuevo
Pichincha
Guayas
Montecristi
Quevedo
San Lorenzo
La Pila
Pambilar

COTOPAXI

Santa Rosa
El Salto
San Carlos
Píllaro
Parque Nacional Llanganate
San José
Motete
Sucre
Balzar
La Reyesa
Zapotal
Ambato
Machalilla
Jipijapa
Olmedo
Salinas

TUNGURAHUA

Pto. Lopez
Salaite
Julcuy
Cerritos
Ventanas
Pondoa
Agua Blanca
La Unión
Colimes
El Altar
Parque Nacional Machalilla
Cascol
Palestina

LOS RÍOS

Guaranda
Riobamba
San José
La Cadena
Cañitas
Limonal
Pretoria
Balzapamba
Cajabamba
Parque Nacional Sangay
Montañita
Daule
Pimocha
Licto
Huámbo
Valdivia
Sabanilla
La Victoria

BOLÍVAR

San Pedro
Manglaralto
Guangalá
Guamote
Alao
Palmar
Simón Bolívar
El Tingo
San Pablo
Aguadita
Bellavista
Pascuales
Buijó
Milagro
Bucay
Alausí

GUAYAS

Salinas
Guayaquil
Chongón
Durán
Naranjito
El Triunfo
Compud
Chunchi
Pta. Carnero
Daular
La Esperanza
Reserva Ecológica Manglares Churute
La Troncal
Zhud
Maca
El Real
Caimito
Sabana Gde.
Tugaduaja
San Juan
San Lorenzo
Va. Nueva

CAÑAR

Engunga
San Antonio
Agua Piedra
La Reshalosa
Cañar
Amalzuna
Engabao
El Morro
Posorja
Taday
Patu
Playas
Puná
La Victoria
Chapurco
Azogues
Paute
Sevilla de Oro
Balao
Chordeleg
Indanza

AZUAY

Golfo de Guayaquil
Isla Puná
Cuenca
Pto. Grande
Tenguel
Baños
Cumbe
Sígsig
Girón
Machala
Pasaje
El Rosario

N

organize tours to the mangrove swamps, forests and communities on the Río Borbón.

WHAT TO SEE AND DO

The good news is the **marimba music**. The bad news is that you are unlikely to hear any unless you're in town on a Friday or Saturday night, or during a fiesta (the town's big marimba festival takes place during the last week of May). Ask around. It's a small town and if something is happening everyone knows. There's also a famous marimba school, where if you are lucky you might hear some marimba being played.

I spoke with marimba player Jackson, better known as El Potente (the Powerful One) because of his ability to play for hours nonstop. El Potente told me how the marimba came to San Lorenzo from Africa with the first castaways. The music is very similar to African marimba music, but there are subtle differences, he said. For example, resonators used on African marimbas are made of gourds, but in San Lorenzo they use bamboo. The most interesting experience in San Lorenzo is to see and hear it for yourself.

If you are interested in exploring the San Lorenzo area, check with the owner of the La Estancia restaurant, or ask around town. Locals organize various tours in motorized dugout canoes, including swimming trips to the deserted island of **San Pedro**. Also ask here about trips to **Borbón** and further up river. The local organization, **SUBIR**, runs projects with the communities of San Miguel and Playa de Oro upstream, as well as trips into the remote **Reserva Ecológica Cotacachi-Cayapas**. They have an office in Borbón (no phone) and in Quito ((022) 528696 FAX (022) 656990 E-MAIL subir@care.org.ec. On a tributary of the Borbón, the Cayapas, you can arrange to stay at the comfortable, moderately priced (full board) **Steve's Lodge** at the junction of the Cayapas and Onzole rivers, owned by English-speaking Hungarian Stephan Tarjanyi. For more information E-MAIL nagy@uio.satnet.net.

La Tolita

Another option is to take a boat across the estuary, and up the mangrove-banked Río Santiago to the small, impoverished riverside village of **La Tolita**, which has a small museum and an archaeological site. More than 2,000 years ago, shamans and chieftains of the Tolita culture were buried here in *tolitas* (small mounds), and people from far away came to worship and trade. Few travelers make this journey, despite the Tolita culture's notoriety—mostly due to the extraordinary Tolita gold and platinum jewelry found at this site, some of which can be seen in the Museo Nacional del Banco Central del Ecuador in Quito. The magnificent Sun God mask that is the bank's logo was found at La Tolita. The advanced gold- and platinum-working techniques used by craftsmen in the mangrove swamps of Tolita two millennia ago were not discovered in the western hemisphere until the nineteenth century.

Regrettably, there's not much to be seen in La Tolita except for the one-room museum attached to the school, where there are a number of burial jars. The bones of the dead were broken so the bodies could be squeezed into these less-than-life-size urns. When excavated, some of the urns also contained gold and platinum jewelry, serpent figures, and figurines representing supernatural spirits to help the dead in afterlife. No gold artifacts are displayed at La Tolita, because most of them have drifted away to big museums or private collections. One of the villagers, Antonio, can show you pits where archaeologists have been digging, but when I was there they were full of rainwater. Antonio has his own collection of Tolita figurines which he sells to visitors.

WHERE TO STAY AND EAT

As for hotels and restaurants, you won't lose much by accepting the offer of the self-appointed guides. It's easy enough to choose your own inexpensive hotel, because almost all are equally gruesome. The best of the uninspiring lot is the **Hotel Continental** ((06) 780125 or (06) 780304, Imbabura and Isidro Ayora, where most rooms have air conditioning and hot water, making it the most luxurious in town. The **Hotel San Carlos** (/FAX (06) 780284, on Imbabura, is unappealing from the outside, but better from the inside. It's simple, rooms coming with fans and cold water, but at least it's colorful. The best budget option is the **Hotel Tolita Pampa de Oro** ((06) 780214, Tácito Ortiz and 26 de Agosto, which has acceptable rooms for the price (some with air conditioning). Make sure your hotel provides mosquito nets.

For restaurants, probably your best bet is to follow one of your self-proclaimed guides, who of course will want a tip if you approve of their suggestion. Otherwise check out **La Estancia**, **La Red** or **Conchita**. There's excellent dining in San Lorenzo so it's worth looking around. Crabs, clams, conches, shrimp, oysters, crawfish and even turtle can be on the menu, all fresh. The best decor, ambience and food is at La Estancia.

HOW TO GET THERE

Most travelers come down to San Lorenzo from Ibarra by bus or train and then continue on down the coast. Motorized dugouts leave from the San Lorenzo waterfront to La Tola, from where you can travel on to Esmeraldas by bus or *ranchero*. Check with the *capitanía* on the waterfront for boat departure times. Early-morning boats to La Tola will connect you with a bus that will get you to Esmeraldas the same day. Alternatively, the bus service bumps its way to Borbón via Maldonado, from where the new road "whizzes" down to Esmeraldas. There are also boats to Tumaco in Colombia, though this is not an established tourist route and is said to be frequented by drug smugglers. Check with the police in San Lorenzo on border formalities and practicalities.

LIMONES

Most boats heading to La Tola go by way of the small island town of Limones, the next port down the coast from San Lorenzo. Arriving by motorized dugout, with mango forests on either side of the wide delta, your first glimpse of the town is a row of gray, sun-bleached shacks standing on stilts over the water. After disembarking at the wooden jetty, you pick your way though unpaved back streets with duckboards over stagnant, mosquito-breeding pools of water. Outside almost every meager house lies a dugout canoe, equivalent to a car in roadless Limones. Few gringos visit this dreamy town, which looks like a location in a novel by Gabriel García Márquez. Kids follow you about, laughing and pointing, delighted by the arrival of strangers.

Limones, a town of some 8,000 people, has seen better days. At one time it was an important port for the timber trade, where logs that had been floated down from the forests upriver were cut and loaded onto freighters. Now most of this is handled in Borbón, on the mainland. Although we saw mountains of shrimp by the waterfront, people say fishing isn't as good as it used to be. Without jobs, young people drift off to bigger cities, like Esmeraldas and Guayaquil down the coast.

In an effort to address some of the social and economic problems of this poor community, the privately funded **Fundación CIDESA (** (06) 789143 IN QUITO (022) 226303 or (022) 527119 E-MAIL cidesa2 @cidesa.org.ec has set up a project in Limones working with local groups. The foundation can arrange visits to the mangrove forests of the **Reserva Ecológica Manglares Cayapas-Mataje**, and to beaches and other places of interest in the vicinity. Limones offers a fascinating glimpse of life on the Pacific coast of Ecuador. But the hotel scene isn't one of the town's great assets. Aside from a bed at US$5 per night, the best hotel in town, **Hotel Mauricio Real (** (06) 789155, has nothing to commend it, not even running water.

THE ROAD TO ESMERALDAS

From La Tola, clapped-out buses run down to Esmeraldas, about 122 km (76 miles) west. Along the road west of Limones, you pass the **Reserva Ecológica Manglares Cayapas-Mataje**,

where we clumped in our boots along walkways over oozing black mud, and peered up in awe at what are thought to be the tallest and oldest mangrove trees in the world, 60 m (200 ft) high and 1,000 years old. This ancient, perfectly intact mangrove ecosystem is home to three-toed tree sloths, anteaters, ocelots, green iguanas, capybaras, small jaguars, parrots, kingfishers, herons, woodpeckers, storks, pelicans and the deadly poisonous fer-de-lance snakes. But you have to be patient to see these creatures; all we spotted were a few birds, numerous butterflies and a number of crabs scurrying into black holes in the mud.

Back at the research station, we sampled a rare and exquisite liqueur made by soaking the roots of black mangrove in a bottle of *aguardiente*. After years of maturation, the blood-red spirit has the smoothness of a fine cognac and is said to be a health tonic, but if you drink too much you might hallucinate. In the silence of the swampy, prehistoric forest wilderness, I would not have been surprised to see a pterodactyl flapping overhead, or a dinosaur lumbering through the mud.

ESMERALDAS

Esmeraldas, capital of the province, and with a population of about 250,000, is perhaps the opposite from the shining emerald ("esmeralda") of its name. If there is a jewel to be found there, it isn't obvious. Even before the 1997–1998 El Niño laid the town to waste, there wasn't much for the tourist to see. Things haven't changed much since. The town, the region's most important transportation and commercial hub, has also grown from the nearby oil refinery, the junction for the first trans-Andean oil pipeline from the Oriente.

Most travelers treat Esmeraldas as a stop-off point on their way to somewhere else.

GENERAL INFORMATION

The **tourism office (** (06) 714528 is on Bolívar and Mejía, open Monday to Friday 9 AM to 5 PM, and there's an Internet café, **Compunet**, on Bolívar and Cañizares. **Andinatel** is on Juan Montalvo and Malecón, above the post office. Useful banks are just south of the main square, on Bolívar.

WHERE TO STAY AND EAT

Most travelers tend to push south or north as soon as they can, but if you're stuck for the night, about the best moderately priced place to stay in the area is in Las Palmas district, just north of the city: the **Hotel Suites Costa Verde (** (06) 728714

Atacames is a rowdy, partying beach town.

FAX (06) 728716. Their suites are all very comfortable and well appointed, with balconies and cable television, as well as a good restaurant. In town, the best choices of a poor lot are **Hostal Costa Esmeraldas** ((06) 723912, Sucre 911 and Piedrahita, which is good value with private baths, some rooms with air conditioning; **Hostal Miraflores** ((06) 723077, Bolívar and 9 de Octubre, on the square (so take a room at the back), cheap and very clean; and **Hotel Diana** (/FAX (06) 723923, Cañizares 224 and Sucre, with decent-sized rooms and a welcoming courtyard.

The best restaurants in Esmeraldas are to be found in the Las Palmas district, notably along the Avenida Kennedy, such as **La Cascada**. In the town, there are plenty of inexpensive restaurants, serving mainly regional seafood dishes. Try **Tía Concha** on Piedrahita and Olmedo, or **Los Alamos** near the square on 9 de Octubre and Bolívar.

HOW TO GET THERE

Esmeraldas lacks a bus terminal, with companies scattered in the town. The drivers of **Aerotaxi** gather at Sucre and 10 de Agosto for the route to Quito and Ibarra, also served by **Trans Occidentales** on 9 de Octubre and Sucre. **Trans La Costeñita**, on Malecón and 10 de Agosto, has regular services for more local buses north and south along the coast.

ATACAMES

Atacames ranks among one of Ecuador's busiest beach towns. A row of round straw huts stretches along its long but narrow sands. Each has an identical framework with a palm-thatched roof, a circular bar inside, bamboo furniture and open walls to let in the warm night air. Hammocks are strung between palm trees or poles in the sand. The huts belong to municipal authorities, who lease them to operators of discos, clubs, bars and restaurants. Most feature loud Latin music and exotic cocktails made from cane liqueur and umpteen different Ecuadorian fruits. Try a Green Lady, a Forbidden Lover or a Coco Loco, the latter being a mixture of coconut water, cane spirit, grenadine and lemon served in a huge coconut shell with a straw. Too many of these will indeed make you *loco*.

Walking out onto the wide beach on a clear night, big white waves roll up the sand, while behind you the beach bars form a necklace of colored lights. Sexy, swinging salsa mingles with the booming song of the sea. Atacames is a party town, a place to let your hair down. At busy times of year, particularly during the rainy season vacations, the town heaves with revelers to the early hours. At other times it is still one of the Costa's busier resorts.

GENERAL INFORMATION

There's a small **tourism office** inside the Municipio building on Juan Montalvo, by the Parque Central, open Monday to Friday 9 AM to 5 PM. Also close to the park, are the **Banco de Pichincha**, for changing travelers' checks, the **Andinatel** office, the **post office**, and a console or two for the **Internet** at the stationers on Luís Tello. **Club Adventurs** ((06) 731409, run by the friendly Gilbert Tello, organizes tours to more remote beaches to the south, as well as hikes up into the Reserva Ecológica Mache-Chindul inland.

The town is divided between the beach-restaurant-hotel zone and the more residential and shopping part on the other side of the river. A small footbridge and the bridge on the main road connect them.

If you go out on the beach at night, keep close to the bars. Muggings and rapes happen in Atacames from time to time, even in daylight. Opportunistic theft is common. Also note that the sea is renowned for its strong undertow, so stay within your limits.

WHERE TO STAY AND EAT

If you're interested in a wild Atacames weekend, get there by Thursday evening, or make reservations in advance. Prices vary according to season, sometimes quite dramatically. During the week, bargaining with hoteliers for cheaper prices or longer stays will get results.

The only moderately priced hotel in town, **Villas Arco Iris** ((06) 731069 FAX (06) 731437 E-MAIL arcoiris@waccom.net.ec WEB SITE www.villas arcoiris.com, at the quieter northern end of the beach within a walled compound, comprises sets of attractive wooden cabins on two levels amongst plenty of greenery, some with kitchenettes. All have air conditioning and hot water, and there's also a swimming pool and modest restaurant.

Many of the inexpensive hotels are spread along the Malecón (embankment), the road that runs behind the row of beach bars. Many travelers head for this strip and check out what's available, though you have to enjoy noise to enjoy the rooms. **El Viejo Fritz** ((099) 451777 is above a recommended German-run restaurant of the same name. There are only three rooms available, but they're good value with sea views and air conditioning. Cheaper, and not as nice, **Hotel Galería** ((06) 731149 is nonetheless popular and central, though rooms are for four people and must be paid for as such in the high season. For something quieter, **La Casa de Manglar** ((06) 731464, on 21 de Noviembre just by the footbridge, is simple and friendly and has a relaxing terrace upstairs.

Though Atacames is better known for liquid than solid consumption, there are several reasonably good food stands and restaurants on the Malecón. Beef kebabs cooked over charcoal, fresh *ceviche*, hot dogs and burgers are standard beachside fare. There are several good **food stands** in the market near Discoteca Paradiso; **Marco's Restaurant** is good for ham-and-egg breakfasts; while **Restaurant No Name** serves good pizzas at the northern end of the strip. When you've partied out in Atacames, head down the coast for some rest.

HOW TO GET THERE

Coming in to town by bus, you're dropped at the Parque Central side of town. From there, it's a short walk down to the footbridge and over to the hotel and beach district. You can also hire an "ecological taxi" (a bike with seats) for the ride over. **Trans La Costeñita** and **Trans Pacífico** run up and down the coast every half hour or so. For longer rides to Quito or Guayaquil, there are two other companies close to the Parque.

SOUTH TO MUISNE

Tonsupa and **Súa** lie respectively just north and south of Atacames, like two younger brothers who haven't learned to party with the adults. Tonsupa is upmarket, with condos and timeshares, while Súa retains some fishing village charm, with pelicans and boats lying at anchor in its placid bay. Both are good places to relax in relative peace, and buses regularly run between Esmeraldas and these two smaller towns. In Tonsupa, the beachfront **Cabañas Turísticas Doña Emerita** ((06) 713226 is recommended, while in Súa, the best option is the hillside *cabañas* of **Hotel Chagra Ramos** ((06) 731006, also by the beach.

South of Atacames and Súa, small and exclusive, the town of **Same** (pronounced sah-may) faces a long, palm-fringed beach overlooked by some big modern condominiums and Florida-style beach houses. The beach is pretty and clean, and the town upholds a more upmarket reputation than its neighbors.

One of the best meals to be enjoyed on this part of the coast is at the whimsical **Seaflower** restaurant and hotel ((06) 733369, run by Margarita Lehmann, a German sculptor who has a great love for seashells and a gift for cooking fresh seafood meals. Her *cazuela* (mixed seafood stew) is highly recommended, as is her homemade sauerkraut and smoked pork chops. Though not cheap, the meals are excellent value by European or North American standards. Seaflower's three small rooms are pretty attractive and reasonably priced. Next door, **La Terraza** ((06) 733320 also has a good restaurant and more appealing *cabañas* on stilts. For something a lot cheaper, contact the friendly family at the southern entrance to the town: **Azuca** ((06) 733343. They rent two rooms with private bath and run a modest restaurant. Same is well recommended for a honeymoon, or a few days of therapeutic idleness.

Tonchigüe is the last little town on the coastal road going south from Same before it turns inland towards Muisne. Just beyond the town a rough ranch road leads out to the headland of **La Galera**, one of the most remote and dramatic parts of the Ecuadorian coastline. Out here are isolated beaches, cliffs, coves, caves, tunnels, forests and one or two small settlements only accessible from the sea.

Twenty-some years ago, a young Canadian adventurer, Judith Barrett, drove around the beaches in a jeep at low tide looking for a place to camp. She and her companion found a forested gully leading down to a small beach, where they camped for a month with only wild animals and birds for company. It was an idyllic, Robinson Crusoe experience, and Judith vowed she would return and set up her own wilderness retreat. Eighteen years later she had saved enough money to buy the land.

Today, some years after the purchase, **Playa Escondida** (Hidden Beach) is one of the most magical eco-refuges on the coast. A handful of rustic cabins and a camping ground look out over big billowing trees and the sea. An observation platform, where you can sleep overnight, nestles in the semitropical forest. Wildlife here includes parrots, seabirds, anteaters, guantas, iguanas, foxes and wild cats. Ebony and kapok trees grow here. Judith says that giant turtles regularly come to Playa Escondida between July and September because they have to find an inlet in the rocky coastline, just as she and her friend two decades earlier. "Sometimes when we are eating dinner a turtle will come right outside the restaurant," she says, "We get to see her lay her eggs."

Cabins at Playa Escondida are US$8 per person per night, and camping is US$5. A full meal service is US$10 to US$20 per day. For information and reservations call ((06) 733122 or (099) 733368 E-MAIL judithbarrett@hotmail.com WEBSITE www.ecuadorexplorer.com/playaescondida. You will need your own vehicle to get there, or you can rent a pickup truck or hire a taxi at Tonchigüe for the 14-km (nine-mile) rough road journey.

MUISNE

To get to Muisne Island itself, you have to take a short hop on a boat from the settlement called El Relleno (or Nuevo Muisne). At the island's quay, young men on tricycle rickshaws offer rides up the one-kilometer (half-mile) dirt road to the beach end of town. There are no cars in Muisne, bikes and horses being the popular form of transport.

Under bright stars and a big moon, the beach is wide and long with great rollers crashing on the sand in front of a scattering of beach bars and inexpensive hostels. Muisne makes no pretenses at being an upmarket resort, and is just about off the beaten track from Quito.

WHERE TO STAY AND EAT

The *hostales* at the dock end of town are very basic, but water shortages affect rich and poor in Muisne. At the beach end, the **Mapara Hostal (** (06) 480147 E-MAIL mapara@accessinter.net is the most upscale accommodation on offer, with an attractive wooden interior, and rooms with patio doors giving onto the sea. Two cheaper places line the beach: the **Hostal Playa Paraíso (** (06) 480192 is bright and breezy with plenty of room to relax and very clean rooms and shared bathrooms, and the equally appealing-for-the-price **Hotel Calade (** (06) 480279, a bright and friendly backpackers' joint with mosquito nets and shared showers. Most hotels can arrange tours of the nearby mangroves, or contact the nonprofit organization **Fundecol (** (06) 480167, which runs tours and projects to protect the mistreated ecosystem.

All the hotels boast good seafood and vegetarian dishes, but there's also good pizza and pasta to be enjoyed at **Restaurant Suizo-Italiano** back from the beach on the main road (Isidro Ayora), and tasty seafood at **Santa Martha** on the beachfront, by the entrance. **Habana Club** beach bar is the best in town.

HOW TO GET THERE

Buses running between Muisne and Esmeraldas are frequent throughout the day, and the main passenger boat for Cojimíes leaves at about 8 AM. You can also hire boats going south through one of the fishermen, but they're far more expensive. The seas can be very rough early in the year, so be prepared to hold on tight and waterproof your gear.

MOMPICHE

From the turnoff to the Galera headland, the new road linking Muisne to Pedernales loops inland. About 15 km (nine miles) after the crossroads, the main road passes the dirt track for Mompiche, which is impassable for parts of the rainy season. Mompiche ranks among the most idyllic, unspoiled beaches on the coast, little more than a sprinkling of huts and fishing boats. The best way to get there is on an early morning boat from Muisne or Cojimíes, but you can also walk the 12 km (seven and a half miles) at low tide, with the help of a fisherman to cross the odd river. There are two attractive places to stay just outside the village itself. **Casablanca (** (099) 496124 IN QUITO

(022) 726798 is the classier of the two, with four exclusive-feeling cabins sleeping four to six, with hot water and private baths. Prices are moderate, with horseback riding and transfers also available with advanced notice. The cheaper option is **Iruña (** (099) 472458, which lies on the other side of the bay. Colorful cabins, porches, hammocks and a peaceful atmosphere make up the friendly whole, with meals available.

NORTHERN MANABÍ

To head south, you can either take the boring overland route to Pedernales, via San José de Chamanga, or else the exhilarating boat ride to Cojimíes. The boat passes lines of pelicans flying in formation, skimming the tops of the waves looking for fish to snatch in their bulbous bills. From the sea, the deserted coastline of **Ensenada** (cove) **de Mompiche**, south of Muisne, looks

ever so tempting. Thick woods and bright green vegetation grow atop chunky cliffs overlooking secret, completely inaccessible bays and beaches. The only way to get to this wild stretch of coastline is by boat or on horseback.

Cojimíes is a barrio built on a sandbank. The foundation for this untidy assemblage of boats, shacks and shop-houses is continuously being worn away by the sea. The town has moved so many times that its cemetery is about to disappear under the water. But the shabby town is only of passing interest, unlike the wonderful stretch of beach running due south.

The main road to Pedernales is the beach, which can only be driven along at low tide. Trucks bump and rattle at high speed down the wide, endless stretch of sand, with pool-blue sea on one side and low cliffs and coconut groves on the other. No condos, no houses, no cottages, no tourists: there are few signs of humans on this wide, 30-km

(19-mile) stretch of seemingly virgin beach. Occasionally one passes a man on a horse, or another truck belting up the beach in the opposite direction. With a rising tide, this joyride can become a white-knuckle race against the sea. At high tide, the trucks use the more sedate and bumpy old road, slightly inland.

Developers have bought up most of this stretch of coastline, and in 20 years it might well become a long strip of beach resorts and vacation complexes. There is already one hotel halfway down the beach, hidden behind a screen of coconut palms. In splendid isolation for seekers of solitude and deserted beaches, **Hotel Coco Solo** ((099) 586952 has colorful cabins, a camping ground, a restaurant and horses for rent at reasonable prices. It ranks among the most isolated hotels on the Pacfic coast.

Trawling for shrimp larvae at Pedernales to supply the many shrimp farms along the coast.

PEDERNALES

Pedernales is a Wild West beach resort where *vaqueros* (cowboys) ride horses down the main street (racing them during the rodeo festival in August), and all motor vehicles, most of which are pickup trucks, sound like they have holes in their exhaust system, or none at all. It's a hot, dusty, gimcrack town with dirt roads and ugly concrete housing, which boomed in the 1990s from the expanding shrimping industry. Until a few years ago, Pedernales was only accessible by sea, and the town had a well-deserved reputation for its independent spirit. Within living memory, a police officer assigned to the district by Quito authorities was thrown out and not replaced for several years. Recently a road has brought the town within a four-hour drive of the capital. Most travelers employ it as a bus-change town, rather than a destination in itself, with the bus companies lining the main street, López Castillo.

Where to Stay and Eat

If you're coming through Pedernales and need somewhere to stay, about the best central location is the **Hotel América Internacional (** (05) 681321, on the road to the beach (López Castillo), which includes rooms with air conditioning and phones, or the slightly cheaper **Hotel Playas (** (05) 681125, on Juan Pereira and Manabí, still quite close to the main square, which has rooms with fans and private baths. The Hotel América has a decent restaurant, and there are a smattering of places close to the square, or down by the beach, none of which stand out particularly.

SOUTH FROM PEDERNALES

Heading south, the road sweeps by more long, semi-deserted beaches, where the only inhabitants are a few fishing families, before it climbs into the hills once again. Just over 30 km (19 miles) from Pedernales, a small sign points to the refuge of **Latitud 7 (** (099) 479914 E-MAIL artpri@hotmail .com, run by a friendly Frenchman. His ecologically run establishment is half for guests and half for visiting and resident artisans, with four eye-catching bamboo cabins spread over a hillside that leads down to a lovely beach. Prices are moderate but include all meals, the use of surfboards, and sailing trips and horseback rides.

After the uninspiring town of Jama, and just before Canoa, you pass the turnoff for the **Río Muchacho** area. Under the guidance of Guacamayo Bahíatours of Bahía de Caráquez (see below) and other nonprofit organizations, Río Muchacho has become a hotbed for sustainable development, involving both tourists and local communities. Visitors to the organic farm can take part in daily *montuvio* (as natives of the coast are called) activities such as grinding coffee or milking cows, but also enjoy the rivers, walks, fishing and horseback riding. Accommodation takes the form of an inspiring treehouse, or else more down-to-earth cabins, and tours are around US$30 per day per person, all-inclusive. A volunteer program for minimum stays of a month is also available.

Canoa is another long, wide beach with white-topped surfing waves and huge caves in cliffs at one end. The village is quickly becoming an *in* spot for the young beach crowd, but is yet to suffer any highrise developing. Its beach is clean and the waves best for surfing early in the year. From Canoa, the beach pretty much runs continuously for 17 km (over 10 miles) to San Vicente — great for off-roading.

The most appealing place to stay is the Dutch-owned-and-managed **Hotel Bambú (** (05) 616370, a building made of wood and bamboo that looks like a beachcomber's palace. They offer various rooms, from those with private bathroom through to communal rooms for five and a camping ground. Not all are of equal quality, so have a look around first. The hotel has a satisfactory restaurant, and rents windsurfers and surf boards. Back by the square, up from the beach, **La Posada de Daniel (** (099) 773276 or (05) 691201 is the other traveler's favorite, with a covey of *cabañas* set in pretty gardens. The cabins are a bit musty, and lack light, but there's a small swimming pool to compensate. There is also a new large, three-story hotel between the main road and the beach on the north side of town which looks to be an attractive alternative to the above places. Canoa also boasts some good and cheap seafood restaurants, among them **Costa Azul** and **Jixsy** on the beachfront, and **Torbellino** close to the square. For evening cocktails and light meals, head to **Arenabar**, one block back from the beach.

South of Canoa, the road continues alongside deserted beaches to the dusty town of **San Vicente**. Although some hotels and resorts have sprung up catering to Ecuadorians, San Vicente's main *raison d'être* is its airport and ferry, both of which service Bahía de Caráquez. The view across the **Chone estuary** to Bahía is a bit like an Ecuadorian version of Miami Beach — a gleaming white forest of modern highrise apartments, hotels and condominiums. Quite a shock after the wild and wooly shores of northern Manabí.

BAHÍA DE CARÁQUEZ

Bahía de Caráquez (which everyone calls Bahía) is the most upmarket playground of the Manabí coast, where politicians and a former president own vacation residences. "Bienvenidos a Bahía, Eco-Ciudad," trumpets a sign as you arrive by road or ferry. After the damage wrought by El Niño and later earthquakes, Bahía has attempted to reinvent itself as an eco-city: its market is the only one in Ecuador to recycle its waste, and there are many conservation and environmental-education programs underway. In the downtown area, the streets are clean, the roads well paved and the squares welcoming, and there are many smart new buildings. Expensive pleasure boats lie at anchor in the estuary, and even the road from Quito is relatively fast and well maintained. Unfortunately, the beach isn't up to much, and there isn't a whole lot to do in the town, but nevertheless Bahía is by far the most pleasant town on the coast for changing money, washing clothes and checking e-mail.

BACKGROUND

"Ecuadorian nationality was founded in Bahía with the balsa sailors," according to the proprietor of Bahía Dolphin Tours, Patricio Tamariz. "They were the Phoenicians of the Americas who sailed as far as Chile in the south and Mexico in the north." From prehistoric coastal cultures, our conversation moved on to the Incas, the Spanish conquistadors and the French astronomical expedition to Ecuador at the beginning of the eighteenth century. Not only was Bahía a focus of an ancient maritime civilization, but centuries later it became a base for Spanish ships exploring the Pacific coast of South America, and a base for their expeditions into the interior.

More recently, Bahía de Caráquez was an important banana-shipping center. Ecuador is still the world's leading banana producer, though most exports are now shipped through the bigger ports of Guayaquil and Machala down the coast. While still functioning as a port, tourism is increasingly important for Bahía. It is one of the country's leading and best-appointed resorts, even if it might seem a tad sedate for those who prefer the party mood and beach culture of hangouts like Atacames.

GENERAL INFORMATION

Bahía lacks a tourist office, but the two good tour operators can fill you in on all you need to know. For banks, **Filanbanco** (Visa ATM and travelers' checks) is on Aguilera and Malecón, and **Banco de Guayaquil** (Visa and MasterCard ATM and travelers' checks) is on Riofrío and Bolívar. The best place for the Internet is **Genesis** on Malecón, close to the ferry, and the **Pacifictel** office is at the corner of Alberto Santos and Arenas.

WHAT TO SEE AND DO

For a place with so much history there is surprisingly little heritage to be seen in the town itself. You can visit the Banco Central's **Casa de la Cultura** (open Tuesday to Friday 10 AM to 5 PM),

with its collection of pre-Columbian treasures found in the sea, and antique maps of the region. You can climb **La Cruz hill** for a panoramic view of the town and the coastline. Or you can stroll along the pleasant and peaceful **Malecón** with its riverside views and older housing. The beaches to the south of the town are best at low tide.

For close encounters with wildlife comparable to those on the Galápagos Islands, boat trips from Bahía to islands in the estuary can be arranged with tour operators. At the **Islas de Fragatas**, frigate birds can be observed and photographed at close range, along with pelicans, cormorants, herons, oystercatchers, spoonbills and blue-footed

boobies. The best time to see the magnificent frigate birds puffing up their red breast sacks is during mating rituals from August to January. Shrimp farms have destroyed most of the estuary's mangroves during the last 20 years, except those that are protected on the islands. For these and other excursions (to the mangroves of Isla Corazón for example), including fishing and bird-watching trips and visits to the coastal caves of Canoa, contact **Guacamayo Bahíatours** ((05) 690597 FAX (05) 691412 E-MAIL ecopapel@ecuador explorer.com WEB SITE www.qni.com/mj/ riomuchacho, Avenida Bolívar and Arenas. They also organize two-day horse trekking adventures to Río Muchacho, where you experience *montuvio* life on an organic coastal farm and sleep in a treehouse surrounded by birds and orchids.

Bahía Dolphin Tours ((05) 692097 or (05) 692086 FAX (05) 692088 E-MAIL archtour@telconet .net WEB SITE www.qni.com/~mj/bahia/bahia .html, on Calle Salinas, Edificio Dos Hemisferios, runs several tours, including visits to shrimp farms and villages where they make the misnamed panama hats. The company also runs a private ecolodge, archaeological site and small museum

Coastal craftsmen used advanced gold-working techniques long before they were discovered elsewhere.

farther down the coast at Chirije, which can only be reached from the beach at low tide. The site is thought to have been an important seaport at the time of the Bahía culture (BC 500–AD 500) and many ceramic, gold and copper relics have been found here. Staying in bungalows with private baths and hot water overlooking the sea, guests learn about the ancient culture of this area, while enjoying a long private beach and 160 ha (395 acres) of rare dry tropical forest, with numerous species of plants and wildlife.

WHERE TO STAY

Bahía claims a good selection of hotels, whose prices may fluctuate in season, but not wildly.

The most expensive place in town, **Casa Grande**, bookable through Bahía Dolphin Tours see above, commands beautiful sea views amid comfortable colorful rooms with private baths, hot water, cable televisions and air conditioning. Rooms are surrounded by lush tropical gardens with a terrace and pool. The interior of this beautiful residential house is decorated with some fine contemporary Ecuadorian art.

The moderately priced **La Piedra Hotel (** (05) 690780 FAX (05) 690154, on the Malecón at Bolívar, boasts great suites looking out over the sea from the northern end of town, beach access, a pool and a good restaurant. They also rent bikes. Next comes **Hotel La Herradura (** (05) 690446 FAX (05) 690265, Bolívar and Hidalgo, with some seafront rooms in an old house decorated with antiques. Staff are friendly and the restaurant recommended.

For somewhere less expensive, try **Hostal Querencia (** (05) 690009, on Velasco Ibarra and Eugenio Santos, a small, family-run place with plenty of character, or else the popular **Bahía Bed and Breakfast (** (05) 690146, run by a multilingual Ecuadorian and offering basic rooms and cheap breakfasts included in the rate.

WHERE TO EAT

Ceviche is what you eat in Manabí, and with all the shrimp farms in the Chone estuary, *ceviche camarón* (raw shrimp marinated in lemon or lime with onions and various spices) is what you have in Bahía. Like a Eurasian cross between Japanese sashimi and a shrimp cocktail, *ceviche camarón* at a waterfront restaurant on the Manabi coast is one of my ideas of heaven. Try one of the restaurants by the river, such as the **Restaurant Genesis**, which is popular and has a terrace on the water. As with restaurants all over the world, some of the humblest looking places can serve the most authentic cuisine.

For reasonable pizzas, try **Pizzería Donatello**, near the car ferry dock. The better hotels also have fine but rather expensive restaurants.

HOW TO GET THERE

All the buses for destinations south, north and east gather around the Malecón, close to the Hotel Bahía. There are plenty of services. The status of the airport across the estuary at San Vicente is still uncertain, so check with tour operators or travel agencies for the latest flights.

MANTA

Manta doesn't entice international visitors with many attractions, though it's popular with Ecuadorians. It's a busy, working port, second only to Guayaquil, handling shipments of pepper, sugarcane, fiber, cacao and other agricultural products of the region. Though less crime-ridden than the other big coastal towns, naval police patrol its less-than-pristine beaches. The main beach's seafront, **Playa Murciélago** (to the north), has been spruced up and renovated of late, although **Playa Tarqui** is calmer and quieter. If you come to town to change money or buses, the most pleasing area is around the **Parque Eloy Alfaro** and **Parque de la Madre**. The port around the *capitanía* has also been renovated, with some good restaurants from which to observe the comings and goings. The small but good **Museo del Banco Central** showcases archeological artifacts relating to the important Valdivian culture of the region, open Monday to Friday 9 AM to 4:30 PM.

GENERAL INFORMATION

The municipal **tourism office (** (05) 611471 is on Calle 9 and Avenida 4, open Monday to Friday 9 AM to 5 PM, and there's also a helpful booth at the entrance to Playa Murciélago. **Metropolitan Touring** has an office on Calle 13, and the staff can help with most travel questions. **Filanbanco** (Visa ATM and travelers' checks) is at Calle 7 and Avenida 4 and **Banco del Pacífico** at Calle 13 and Avenida 2. There's an Internet café at **Manta Cyber Café**, Avenida 1 between Calles 13 and 14. **Pacifictel** has an office at the Malecón at Calle 12.

Metropolitan Manta is divided by the Río Manta between the Tarqui area to the east and the Manta area to the west. Calles in Manta are numbered from the bridge, ascending as you go northwest, with numbers of Avenidas ascending from the Malecón as you go southwest. In Tarqui, *calles* start at 101 going east, and *avenidas* from 101 (Malecón) going inland south — don't ask me why.

The best panama hats are made in Montecristi, just inland from Manabí coast.

The Pacific Coast

WHERE TO STAY AND EAT

With its popularity with Ecuadorians, there are plenty of places to stay in Manta. The more budget places are south in Tarqui, while the up-market hotels cluster to the north close to Playa Murciélago.

Manta's most exclusive hotel, counterpart to its Quito outlet, is **Hotel Oro Verde** ((05) 629200 FAX (05) 629210, Malecón and Calle 23, which boasts all the amenities of a five-star hotel, including a casino, a swimming pool and a sports and sauna center (expensive). Service is excellent and rooms very comfortable. The restaurant also enjoys an excellent reputation, but isn't cheap.

Also in the northern part of town, **Cabañas Balandra** ((05) 620316 FAX (05) 620545, Avenida 8 and Calle 20, makes a welcome retreat from the hubbub of the town (moderate). The walkways, gardens and swimming pool are all eye-catching, with attractive, large cabins or rooms available, all with hot water, private bathrooms, phones, refrigerators and air conditioning.

In Tarqui, about the best bet for inexpensive accommodation is the **Hotel La Cascada** ((05) 622996, Avenida 105 and Calle 103, with decent, comfortable rooms, all with cable television, hot water and telephones, and with the plus of an outdoor pool. The nicest budget option is **Hostal Miami** ((05) 622055, Avenida 102 and Calle 107 (don't confuse it with the Hotel Miami), whose rooms with balconies are definitely good value; it also has friendly owners and private baths.

The Malecón at Playa Murciélago includes a series of identical seafood restaurants, all serving exactly the same thing at exactly the same prices. Take your pick for a cheap lunchtime meal. Playa Tarqui has more modest thatched restaurants. In town, the best restaurant, popular with business people for lunch, is **El Ejecutivo**, on the eleventh floor of the Edificio Banco Pichincha. The food and service are excellent and great value, and the views over the bay second to none. The best Chinese restaurant in town is the **Hotel Lun Fun**, while if you're missing your meat or steaks, the best choice is the **Beachcomber** on Calle 20 and Flavio Reyes.

HOW TO GET THERE

The airport is about three kilometers (two miles) east of Tarqui. **TAME** ((05) 622006, on the Malecón north of the plaza and theater, has flights every day to and from Quito, with flights to Guayaquil in the rainy season (December to June; check for other months). The main bus terminal is on Calle 7 and Avenida 8, used by the majority of bus companies, with good connections to main cities.

MONTECRISTI

About 16 km (10 miles) southeast of Manta and about 30 km (20 miles) west of Portoviejo lies Montecristi, spiritual home of the misnamed "panama" hat—misnamed because the hats originated centuries ago in Ecuador, still the biggest producer (see GET HATTED, page 21 in TOP SPOTS). Montecristi is a dusty town that lives on the income from its handwoven products. Concrete and cinderblock buildings are occupied by weavers and shops selling hats, hammocks, mats and tablecloths. There is a fine church and the grand former residence of Eloy Alfaro, liberal president and Montecristi's hero, whose father, Manuel, made a fortune trading in panamas. Thanks to Alfaro's efforts to modernize the legal code, his fight for women's rights and his efforts to separate church and state at the end of the nineteenth century, the panama hat is an icon of Ecuador's great liberal revolution. Sadly, in return for his vision, Eloy Alfaro was lynched in the streets by a mob incensed by his attempts to undermine the Church's power.

PORTOVIEJO

Portoviejo, with a population of 180,000, is one of Ecuador's oldest cities, founded in 1535. Capital of Manabí Province, the city forms the regional hub for commerce between the agricultural industry inland and the fishing industry of the coast. Despite its age, the busy town is of little interest to the tourist, and most travelers pass through on their way to and from the coast.

GENERAL INFORMATION

Filanbanco is on Pacheco and Gual, **Banco del Pacífico** on 9 de Octubre at Rocafuerte and **Banco de Pichincha** on the Parque Central changes travelers' checks. There is a pretty useless **tourist office** on Gual 234 at Montalvo, three blocks north and three blocks east of Parque Central. The **Pacifictel** office is at Pacheco and 10 de Agosto.

WHERE TO STAY AND EAT

The town's best hotel is the moderately priced **Hotel Ejecutivo** ((05) 632105 FAX (05) 630876, 18 de Octubre between Gual and 10 de Agosto, which includes comfortable and functional rooms with private baths, hot water, cable television and telephone. The restaurant serves good regional dishes. For something inexpensive, the **Hotel Conquistador** ((05) 631678 FAX (05) 633259, 18 de Octubre 407, is good value, with rooms with private bath and some air-conditioned rooms. **Hostal Paris** ((05) 652727, on Sucre and Olmedo, is a bit dilapidated, but makes up for it in charm, a balcony overlooking Parque Central, as well as friendly owners.

You won't find a great selection of restaurants in Portoviejo. Most serve lunchtime workers. **La Carreta**, close to the cathedral on Olmedo, serves fine set lunches, while **La Fruta Prohibida** is a haven of fruit salads, snacks and delicious juices. **La Crema** on the Parque Central is also passable.

HOW TO GET THERE

Portoviejo's airport lies about two kilometers (one and a quarter miles) northwest of the town center. Taxis are cheap. **TAME (** (05) 633600 or (05) 632429 has several flights a week to and from

tery and erotic sculptures, as well as weavings and wickerwork, are set up along the road to catch the eyes of passing motorists.

At **Jipijapa**, a road branches to the right into the mountains of **Parque Nacional Machalilla**, the tallest of which (at 750 m or 2,500 ft) is marked on some maps as **Cerro Perro Muerto** (Dead Dog Mountain). I don't know why it's so named. There are large tracts of rare **dry tropical forest** in this area, also known as the Sleeping Forest, because in July and August it turns into desert scrub, as brown, and dusty as southern Texas. In the winter the landscape is transformed by heavy rain into a green, glossy garden. Crossing the top of the range, one glimpses the gray Pacific Ocean in the distance.

Quito, although they fly more regularly to Manta. The bus terminal is southwest of the downtown area. There you'll find both local bus companies and long distance ones (Reina del Camino for Quito, for instance). To go south towards Puerto López, take a bus to Jipijapa and change there.

SOUTH FROM PORTOVIEJO

Driving south towards Jipijapa, one passes **La Pila**. Residents of this small village have found a unique niche in the country's economy: as makers of cunning archaeological counterfeits of pre-Columbian ceramics. With growing interest in the archaeological sites in the area, village craftsmen started making so-called "antiques," but are now better known for honest reproductions, though there are said to be workshops that still specialize in fakes. Stands selling figurines, decorated pot-

SOUTHERN MANABÍ

The most accessible, continuous stretch of beaches and bays in Ecuador begins at Puerto de Cayo in southern Manabí and ends at Salinas in Guayas Province. The 150-km (96-mile) sweep of this popular coastline, known as La Ruta del Sol, is dotted with towns and villages connected by reasonable roads and bus services.

Spread out on a long beach, **Puerto de Cayo** is a quiet, pleasant, unpretentious small fishing community with not many places to eat and stay. The most attractive hotel is **Hostería Luz de Luna** IN QUITO **(** (022) 407279 FAX (022) 400562, to the north of the town on the beach, whose complex of comfortable cabins (inexpensive for a double) includes

Young surfers make their own boards in some of the villages and towns along Ecuador's surf-fringed coastline.

a swimming pool and a good restaurant. Aside from eating excellent seafood and drinking beer, there are few tourist activities or sights, nor bars or discos, in Puerto de Cayo itself. Such is the place's charm that sitting on an empty beach and looking out on the ocean is one of its main attractions. On a clear day you'll see the misty outline of the mysterious Isla de la Plata.

PARQUE NACIONAL MACHALILLA

Isla de la Plata, named after the silver (*plata*) that Sir Francis Drake is reputed to have buried here after a successful raid on Spanish galleons, is part of the spectacular, 55,000-ha (135,850-acre) Parque Nacional Machalilla which also embraces regions of dry tropical forest and cloud forest, a beautiful coastline, islands and a number of archaeological sites. A more visible form of treasure on Isla de la Plata is its wildlife, almost as rich and varied as that of the Galápagos Islands, but with the advantage of being concentrated in one area. Frigate birds, waved albatrosses, occasional sea lions and iguanas and three types of boobies are just some of the stars of this insular animal kingdom. Dolphins and humpback whales can also be spotted between mid-June and early October.

The great curving beaches around **Los Frailes**, just south of Machalilla town but within the park itself, are some of the finest in Ecuador; they are the most likely to appear on travel posters. A trail from the main coastal road takes you to the first white-sand beach overlooked by green hills. A trail over the headland takes you to the other three beaches, each in its own isolated cove, one of which has black sand. Being part of the national park, there are no houses, the landscape is unspoiled, the water clear and clean for snorkeling, and often you have a beach or two to yourself.

Also within the park, the **archaeological site** and **museum** (open 8 AM to 6 PM daily) at the village of **Agua Blanca** are also worth visiting. Considered one of the most important in Ecuador, the site is about five kilometers (three miles) off the coastal road, just north of Puerto López. If you don't have your own transportation, you can hike up from the dirt road, or rent a truck or taxi in one of the nearby towns. For more strenuous hikes into the mountains — such as to the village of San Sebastián, 10 km (six miles) away at 600 m (1,968 ft) in altitude — local guides are available at Agua Blanca.

The museum is full of jewelry, pottery and other objects from the Manta culture that flourished in the area from BC 500 to AD 1500, the time of the Spanish conquest. There is evidence that the site was occupied by the much-older Machalilla, Chorrera and Salango cultures. A photography exhibit shows that people in the surrounding mountains and hills have the same features as figures appearing in ancient Machalilla pottery. It is thought that the area has been inhabited for at least 3,000 years, making it perhaps the longest continuously inhabited region of coastal South America. You can learn more about these ancient coastal cultures at another museum in the coastal village of **Salango**, south of Puerto López.

General Information

Most local tour operators can be found in the fishing town of Puerto López, just south of the park. Not all of them have great reputations, and there are many "unlicensed" operators also hustling for business. When weighing up costs, consider your safety too. The licensed operators employ boats with two outboard engines, use life jackets and radios, and have basic toilets. The standard of the guide will also be dependent on price. Tours require a minimum of four people, and you may have to proactively seek other people to make up numbers. Tours to Isla de la Plata can be arranged in Puerto de Cayo, or at Machalilla and Puerto López, but the latter is probably the easiest. Renting a five-passenger boat costs about US$100, or joining a group will cost about US$30 per person, not including the park entrance fee of US$20 from July to September and US$15 from October to June. Boats leave in the early morning and return in the afternoon for the one- to one-and-a-half-hour journey. The crossing is often very rough, so take seasickness tablets and bring waterproof gear. As well as the wildlife on the island, there are good walks, a pre-Columbian archeological site, coral reefs (the only ones on the coast of Ecuador) and great snorkeling. Dubbed the "Poor Person's Galápagos," Isla de la Plata is included by Quito travel agents in tours of this area of Manabí.

In Puerto López, recommended operators include **Bosque Marino Tours (** (05) 604221, General Córdova, **Machalilla Tours (** (05) 604154, Malecón and Julio Zuleta, and **Exploratur (** (05) 604128 E-MAIL explora1@uio.satnet.net, Malecón at General Córdova, which can also organize scuba diving trips with advance notice. A good tour operator employing local guides for trips up in to the hills around Agua Blanca is **Comuna Agua Blanca Tours (** (05) 604168, on General Córdova.

PUERTO LÓPEZ

The most convenient base for visiting Machalilla (unless you have your own transportation) is Puerto López, a down-at-heel fishing village just to the south. The town doesn't have a bank, and the Pacifictel office only manages national calls.

Where to Stay and Eat

The best choice among the town's inexpensive options is the **Hostería Mandala (**/FAX (05) 604181, a short walk along the beach to the north. The establishment is artistic and stylish, with artwork decorating the walls and colors washing through the airy main house, with its recommended beachfront restaurant, bar and library. Accommodation is set in 10 pretty simple but attractive thatched cabins at the back of the property, all with private baths with hot water. The friendly and efficient European owners speak various languages. With fine views over the town and the coast, **Hostería La Terraza (** (05) 604235 has a tranquil setting. Call the German owner, Peter, to get a lift up the hill. He offers half a dozen well-appointed and spotless cabins on the property, all with a double bed and a bunk bed, hot showers and a relaxing porch. Meals are served in the comfortable main house.

Café La Ballena, run by a knowledgeable and friendly American couple. **Restaurant Spondylus** is probably the next-best place for decent lunches and evening meals.

SOUTH OF MACHALILLA

Heading south, the next village along from Puerto López is Salango. Here you can stop by at the good **Museo Salango**, which, though modest, does a laudable job of displaying artifacts and providing information on the local archeological sites. The museum is only open Wednesday to Sunday, 9 AM to 5 PM, and includes a gift shop.

In town, the best hotel is the **Hotel Pacífico (** (05) 604147 FAX (05) 604133 E-MAIL hpacific@manta.ecua.net.ec, Malecón at Alejo Lascano, which is modern, charmless but clean and friendly, some rooms coming with air conditioning, and there's also a restaurant and garden. Cheaper, the **Hostal Los Islotes (** (05) 604108, Malecón at Cordova, is very clean again, but a bit bare. Both include private hot showers. The cheapest acceptable place is the IYH-chain **Albergue Cueva del Oso (** (05) 604124 FAX (05) 604128, Lascano 116, which offers a range of spotless rooms, with shared facilities.

For the best evening meal in the area, head to the Italian-run and predictably named **Bellitalia** just north of the center. The romantic candlelit garden setting is unbeatable, and the food freshly prepared and delicious. Back on the Malecón, good breakfasts, snacks and pizzas are served at

Ten kilometers (six miles) south of Puerto López you reach the small fishing village of Puerto Rico. Soon after, you'll see cabins on the hillside and, on the right, the entrance to the **Hostería Alandaluz (** / FAX (04) 780686 or (04) 780690 IN QUITO (022) 505084 FAX (022) 543042 E-MAIL booking@alandaluz.com WEB SITE www.alandaluz.com. The Ecuadorian-run Alandaluz has achieved both national and international fame for its ecologically sound building and management. It represents the cutting edge of "green-building" ecotourism for a coastal resort, with filtering or composting toilets, organic gardens, recycled water, sustainable building materials such as *caña gradúa* bamboo, and waste recycling and community-based programs. Besides all this praiseworthy stuff, its location and accommodation are also stunning.

Frigate birds make their nests on the islands of Islas de Fragatas and Isla de la Plata.

The *hostería's* complex has expanded over the years, and now includes a bed to suit all wallets. There is a camping area, older rustic cabins (but with electric lighting) which share hot showers and bathrooms, spacious brick-built family cabins with private baths and, the most appealing of all, new cane and bamboo two-story cabins right on the beach. Prices range from inexpensive to the top end of moderate and vary according to season. Meals are served in the soaring, cathedral-like main house, with mainly vegetarian or seafood dishes. Although backpackers have complained that prices have gone up of late, nearly everyone comes away with nothing but praise for the place, and the *hostería* plows profits back into the local community. Most people, as is the way of such places, stay much longer than they originally intended. The *hostería* is also a good base for exploring the surrounding area. Working with reputable local tour operators, they offer mountain biking, scuba diving, sea kayaking, whale-watching, bird-watching, and visits to a nearby wildlife sanctuary and ecological farm. A word of warning: the undertow on the beach is fearsome and definitely not suitable for children or inexperienced swimmers.

About another five kilometers (three miles) south, the small and sweet-sounding village of **Ayampe** nestles into a beautiful bay. A few places to stay have popped up in the last years. The friendly, family-run **Cabañas de La Iguana (** (042) 780605 lies a few streets back from the beach, with clean inexpensive cabins and meals on request. Also worth investigating is **Paraíso (** (099) 708329, a stunningly designed house on stilts tucked into the hillside at the south end of the village. Run by "party-on" surf dudes, the feel is chilled-out and arty, with four double rooms and great views, though little privacy.

THE GUAYAS COAST

As you push down the rest of the coastline to Salinas, the trees become fewer, and the landscape drier. From December to May, rainfall keeps the coast relatively lush, but the rest of the year, it can seem quite barren. The coast road runs parallel to the beach for the most part, passing small fishing villages and the vacation homes of rich *guayaquileños*.

MONTAÑITA

Montañita is Ecuador's most popular surfing town. When I first came to Ecuador as a backpacker in 1990, there were only two places to stay in the village, meals were what you got, and people didn't pretend to be surfers. Today, Montañita is transformed. I hardly recognized the place. There are well over two dozen places to stay, pizza

joints, swimming pools, granola breakfasts, surf shops and, of course, a bevy of Internet cafés. The village has earned its place in the gringo trail hall of fame, though its celebrity now rests more heavily on its chilled-out beach vibe than its original surfer's paradise status.

The best waves are along at **La Punta** (The Point), about a kilometer (just over a half mile) from the village, where surfers twist like ballet dancers on the crests of two-meter (six-foot), white-topped waves. "Ecuador is a fabulous place to surf, and Montañita is the best," one surfer told me. "From October to March the water is about 27°C (80°F). You get one to one-and-a-half-meter (four to five foot) waves, with a hollow right-hander at low tide and a real workable wall at high. I've had a couple of big days at three meters (ten feet). Down south at **Engabao** (south of Salinas) you get real thick hollow beasties." So now you know. The best surfing runs from December to May, and Montañita's annual international surfing competition takes place at Carnaval. At this time, the place is rammed and rocks till dawn.

General Information

There is a **Pacifictel** office by the square, and the best Internet café is **CyberSwell**, by the Casa Blanca hostel. There are no banks to date, but you can find people to change travelers' checks.

Where to Stay and Eat

Prices vary according to season, and reservations are essential for Carnaval time. For most visitors Montañita is a get-it-as-you-see-it place: you get what accommodation you see when you're here. However, the following will help you decide. Accommodation-wise, the town is split between the establishments at La Punta and the ones in the town itself. At La Punta, **Baja Montañita (** (042) 901218 E-MAIL marketing@ hotelbmontanita.com WEBSITE www.hotelb montanita.com, boasts a pool, air conditioning, telephones, televisions and hot water. The smart hotel and restaurant is the best in town, and the only moderately priced offer. There are comfortable doubles and rooms for up to six. Nearby, **Casa Del Sol (**/FAX (042) 901302 E-MAIL casasol@ecua.net.ec WEBSITE www.casasol .com is welcoming and very clean, though some rooms are a bit dark. The restaurant serves good international food. **El Pelicano (** (099) 316225 E-MAIL elpelicano@ hotmail.com is a funky little place with a cool bar and pizzeria, though rooms are bare-bones. The good Tex-Mex restaurant **Tres Palmeras**, also rents six modern rooms.

In town, I've whittled my selection down to three. **Hotel Montañita (** (042) 901296 E-MAIL hmontani@telconet.net commands the beach, with good, clean but unexciting rooms, a restaurant and pool tables. Close by, **La Casa Blanca (**(042) 901340 E-MAIL lacasablan@hotmail.com has two sections.

The first is cheaper, where rooms sharing bathrooms and showers are a bit beat-up but come with balconies. The second part has nice doubles with private baths and great views from their balconies. Finally, the friendly **Pakalolo** ((04) 901366 E-MAIL pakalolo88@hotmail.com is pretty much next door to the Casa Blanca. The French- and English-speaking owners only offer six rooms, but they're all comfortable and good value, and there are plans for a simple restaurant in the garden.

None of Montañita's restaurants stand out particularly, though **Doña Elena's** serves flapping-fresh fish, and **La Pizzería de María** big "beasties."

SOUTH TO SALINAS

The first fishing village after Montañita is **Manglaralto**, which has a popular beach. There's a welcoming place to stay called **Hostería Marakayá** ((042) 901294 at the north end of town; it has simple rooms. The knowledgeable owners can organize horse rides up into the cool hills of the Cordillera Chongón-Colonche, or you can contact the community-based foundation **Pro-Pueblo** ((042) 901208 or (099) 901195 E-MAIL propueb1 @propueblo.org.ec.

Further along, you pass **Valdivia**, **Ayangue** and **Palmar**, the latter two with appealing beaches. Site of the ancient Valdivian culture that flourished between 3000 and 2000 BC, the best of the Venuses of Valdivia sculptures, for which the culture is best known, are on display in the Museo Arqueológico del Banco Central in Guayaquil. The small museum in the village isn't really worth the effort.

After Valdivia, the next town of note is **Ballenita**. Just north of the village, look out for the signs to the moderately priced and thoroughly lovely **Farallón Dillon** ((042) 786643 or (099) 771746 E-MAIL ddillon@gu.pro.ec. Run by charming, English-speaking people, their property on a high bluff includes a small but fascinating nautical museum, an excellent restaurant, and comfortable rooms with artistic flourishes, French windows and unbeatable views. The best hotel in the area.

Sticking up like a rhino horn into the Pacific, the dry scrub land of the **Santa Elena Peninsula** supports the country's second-biggest oil refinery and a fishing industry with everything from fish and shrimp packing plants to meal manufacturers and ice-making factories. Most of this industry is around the city of **La Libertad**. Just a few kilometers west of Libertad, you come to the glitzy resort of Salinas.

SALINAS

The most westerly town on the Ecuadorian mainland, Salinas is totally dedicated to tourism, with a lavish array of condos, hotels, restaurants, bars, *discotecas*, water-sports facilities and the posh Salinas Yacht Club. Rich *guayaquileños* come to Salinas to show off their latest-model cars, play in their speedboats, gamble at the casino and perhaps indulge in a bit of deep-sea fishing. A four-lane highway carries you smoothly through an urban strip into the heart of town, where modern, 15-floor apartments on one side of the road face an attractive, white-sand beach on the other side. One eager tour guide told me "On weekends and holidays, the place goes nuts. Anything goes. Tequila-La and Nautica are the most popular rockin' party bars. On weekends they are wild, packed, dancing until dawn. The fashion scene is really hip. Women wear next to nothing in the bars, maybe high heels and a bikini. The guys all act big and bad. And cars are important. People come down in Porsches and Lamborghinis, like in Miami Beach." There you go. In the low season, however, Salinas is really pretty dead.

General Information

Salinas doesn't have a tourist office, but does have useful banks. **Filanbanco** at Calle 17 and Gallo and **Banco del Pacífico** at Calle 18 and Gallo. **Pacifictel** is on Calle 20 at Gallo. **Pesca Tours** ((042) 772391 WEB SITE www.pescatours.com.ec, close to the beach, can provide local information, and also organizes angling trips for swordfish, tuna and mammoth black marlin. The best times are from September to December.

Where to Stay and Eat

Many hotels can be booked solid in the high season, so reserve well in advance at these times. The cheaper hotels sometimes close in the off season. Salinas is not a budget traveler's port. Salinas' top hotel is the **Hotel Casino Calypsso** ((042) 772425 FAX (042) 773583 E-MAIL calypsso@gye.satnet.net, commanding great sea views from its comfortable but somewhat characterless air conditioned rooms, with telephones, televisions and refrigerators. The expensive to very expensive hotel has good service, and also provides a pool, Jacuzzi and sauna, as well as one of the town's poshest restaurants. After a meal, you can enjoy blowing more money at the hotel's casino. Not as plush as the Calypsso, but very much acceptable for the price, the moderate **Hotel El Carruaje** ((042) 774282 also enjoys a good seafront location. The popular hotel has a very good restaurant, and its rooms are bright and breezy with all mod-cons.

To the east of the center, on Enríquez at Calle 27, the **Hotel Salinas Costa Azul** ((042) 774268 is also popular, with good value air conditioned doubles, a restaurant and a swimming pool. Probably the best budget choice is the **Hostal Florida** ((042) 772780, which is a fair way down the Malecón at Avenida 2, but makes up for it with cheap, clean and decent rooms, some with sea views, and most with private baths.

Apart from the restaurants mentioned above, Salinas is an excellent place for *ceviche*. Try one of the stalls and modest restaurants along Calle 17 and Enríquez. Otherwise, a walk along the Malecón will yield plenty of places, including the popular **Oystercatcher Bar**, run by a Dutchman who also happens to be the coast's best birding guide.

WEST TO GUAYAQUIL

From Salinas, you have the choice of hugging the coastline of southern Guayas down to the beaches of Playas, or taking the inland road about 150 km (94 miles) straight to Guayaquil. Heading inland, you first come to the nondescript, hot town of **Santa Elena**. The town is worth avoiding, but it does host the intriguing archeological museum of **Los Amantes de Sumpa**. The well-presented museum, open every day except Wednesday, 9 AM to noon and 2 PM to 5 PM, is built around one of the oldest burial grounds on the continent, dating back to 6000 BC and the Las Vegas culture. The highlight are the "amantes" (lovers) themselves, the skeletons of an embracing couple of about 25, which must rank among the most haunting yet magical sights of the coast, and the country. From Santa Elena, you can loop back round to the coast at Chanduy.

Taking the less-traveled road on my last trip around the south, called Punta Pelada, we passed along the most deserted and forgotten corner of the coast. There is little public transportation, and foreigners are few and far between. On the 15-km-long (nine-mile), empty beach of **Punta Carnero** a sign stuck into the sand read "Dangerous waters, rip tides and whirl pools present" (in English, surprisingly). Out to sea, a couple of lone surfers braved the waves.

Cutting slightly inland, the road became no more than a cattle trail through scrub, cactus and brown dust. Nothing moved in the dry landscape except for a few goats and cows. We stopped in the small, poor village of **Chanduy**, on a cliff overlooking the sea, and listened to an old man in a shack playing guitar, singing local *pasillo* (passage) music. Most of his songs were about women who did him wrong and now were gone — Latin country music played by a Ecuadorian cowboy in a straw Stetson. Out in the bush, a man on a horse with a lasso attached to his saddle herded goats.

Rattling and rolling along the rough trail, we passed through hamlets with the indigenous names of **Tugaduaja**, **Engunga** and **Engabao**. Each settlement has a small church and a few blockhouses positioned seemingly at random on brown earth reminiscent of an aboriginal settlement in the Australian outback. The few people we saw were Asian-looking *indígenas* with slanted, roundish faces and flat features.

The road was paved after Engabao. As the sun was setting, we hurried to the broad beach of **Playas**, a slightly ramshackle resort town that fills with day-trippers from Guayaquil on weekends and during the December to April vacations. With all the beautiful places on the coast to chose from, I wouldn't opt for Playas as my destination. However, the beaches are good, and there is an appealing place to stay southeast of town, the Swiss-owned **Hostería Bellavista** (/FAX (042) 760600, which has large villas, some with kitchenettes, for rent, as well as surfboards and canoes.

About 15 km (nine miles) west of Guayaquil on the main road is the **Bosque Protector Cerro Blanco**, a private reserve set up and run the local cement works and the Fundación Pro-Bosque. The small reserve protects 3,500 ha (8,645 acres) of tropical dry forest, home to over 200 bird species and plenty of mammals, such as howler monkeys, kinkajous and jaguars. Contact **Fundación Pro-Bosque** ((042) 416975 or (042) 417004, Edificio Promocentro, Cuenca and Eloy Alfaro, in Guayaquil, for more information about the park and about guided tours.

GUAYAQUIL

Guayaquil doesn't enjoy the best reputation. People from other parts of Ecuador say their country's biggest city, with a population of some three million, is a steamy, smelly, malaria-infested seaport, ridden with crime, corruption and pollution. *Guayaquileños* might agree, to a point, but will also mention that theirs is the country's richest city, contributing the lion's share to the economy, where the hotels, nightlife, shopping and business opportunities are second to none. They may also add that nobody knows how to enjoy themselves better than lively *guayaquileños*, least of all staid, Sierran *quiteños*.

Guayaquil is on the way up, and the city is creating a new identity. Many gleaming new highrises have been built or are under construction, including a massive World Trade Center. Sweeping new highways and interchanges are creating a Los Angeles-style landscape. The new Malecón 2000 project along the Río Guayas rivals Barcelona's for slick and striking modern architecture, and the city's Museo Arqueológico del Banco Central ranks among the country's best.

The city is cleaning itself up, literally, by collecting trash three times a week, whereas before it was only once, if ever. Though there are still crumbling tenement blocks, slums and shanty towns resembling parts of Shanghai or Hong Kong, there are also smart and affluent suburbs in the north of the city. The state of emergency and nightly curfews imposed on the city in 1998 during an atrocious crime wave seems to have done the trick: the city's nightlife collapsed.

Guayaquil, despite the city's most powerful man and ex-president, Luís Febres Cordero believing otherwise — and attempting to ban the Spanish edition of this guide — still isn't perceived as a major tourist destination, notwithstanding its best efforts and improvements. Most tourists come here to change buses on their way elsewhere, or to hop on a plane to the Galápagos Islands. If you do come, enjoy it for what it is.

BACKGROUND

A tragic and heroic tale is the origin of Guayaquil's name. According to legend, the word is said to be the combination of the names of an Indian prince

played host to the meeting of two of the continent's greatest heroes, Simón Bolívar and José de San Martín.

With no stone in the area, the houses were built of wood and thus frequently destroyed in fires. A massive conflagration in 1896 ruined about three-quarters of the city, including many of its attractive, wooden colonial houses. In addition to floods, piracy and fire, the hot and humid location of Guayaquil has exposed its inhabitants to plagues and tropical diseases, especially malaria and yellow fever. For some hilarious quotes from embattled United States consuls in the nineteenth century, read Tom Miller's *The Panama Hat Trail*. Despite these challenges, *guayaquileños* have

Guaya and his wife, named Quil. Guaya fought bitterly against invasions of both the Incas and the Spanish conquistadors, but came to realize he could not resist any longer. To avoid capture, the couple committed double suicide, with Guaya first killing Quil and then drowning himself. The legend, though fanciful, is founded in fact: fierce fighting did occur between *indígenas* and the Spanish before and after Francisco de Orellana founded the city in 1537.

The story is an appropriate foundation-myth for a city that for 450 years has seen an abundance of tragedy and heroism. Situated on flat land at the mouth of the Guayas river, the town has had its share of floods, pirate raids and earthquakes (the last in 1942). It has also played a pivotal historical role: Sucre set out from the city in 1820 on his brilliant military campaign which concluded with Quito's liberation in 1822; later that year, it

shown heroic resilience and strength, capitalizing on the great banana boom of the 1950s and creating the industrial and commercial capital of the country.

Guayaquil's port is its *raison d'être*, the cornerstone of its economy, although the Guayas is in desperate need of dredging. Most of the vast agricultural riches of the fertile plains of the western lowlands, in particular bananas, cacao and coffee, pass through Guayaquil, as well as imports of cars, machinery, electrical goods, computers and other requisite consumer items. Powered by warehouse income, Guayaquil has also developed its own industries with oil and sugar refineries, food processing, breweries and many types of manufacturing. "We create the country's wealth," say the *guayaquileños*, "but the *quiteños* spend it."

Fishing still constitues the main *montuvio* economic activity.

GENERAL INFORMATION

Guayaquil is not likely, nor recommended, to be the first stop for first-time visitors to Ecuador. Those who do come here should already be comfortable with finding their way around Ecuadorian towns. The main square is Parque Seminario (also Parque Simón Bolívar) and the main avenue is 9 de Octubre. The Malecón Simón Bolívar runs all the way along the riverside.

The **tourist office** ((042) 568764 E-MAIL ecuainfo @turismolitoral.gov.ec, Pedro Icaza 203, is open Monday to Friday and gives out usable city maps and brochures. There are also unreliable booths at the airport and on the waterfront on the corner of the Malecón and Avenida Olmedo. Private travel agents and tour operators are likely to be of more assistance and speak better English. They are plentiful. **Metropolitan Touring** ((042) 320300 has an office at Hotel Hilton Colón, José de Anteparra 915 and 9 de Octubre, while **Guayatur** ((042) 322441 E-MAIL guayatur@ interactive.net.ec, Aguirre 108, is a reputable local tour operator for city tours and trips around Guayas Province.

The **Pacifictel** office is just off Parque Seminario, on Ballén at Chile, and there's an Internet café called **CyberTek** in the Unicentro mall, also on the Parque. **Banks** are plentiful, with a useful cluster around Pedro Carbo and 9 de Octubre, but also at the bus terminal and the airport.

Guayaquil has all the facilities and amenities one would expect of a major city, including a number of consulates. You'll find the **United Kingdom Consulate** ((042) 560400 at Córdova 625 and Padre Solano, the **United States Consulate** ((042) 323570 on 9 de Octubre 1571 and García Moreno; and the **Canadian Consulate** ((042) 563580 on Córdova 812 and Rendón, Edificio Torres de la Merced. Most Latin American and European countries have embassies and consulates, important for information if you are traveling onward in South America. See the telephone book or inquire at your hotel for further details.

There are a number of airline offices, both domestic and international: **American Airlines** ((042) 564111, **Air France** ((042) 221605, **British Airways** (Servemar agents) ((042) 325080 or (042) 323834, **Continental** ((042) 567241, **Ecuatoriana** ((042) 329299, **Iberia** ((042) 329558 or (042) 329382, **KLM** ((042) 692876, **Varig** ((042) 327082. **TAME** ((042) 560778, 9 de Octubre 424, or (042) 282062 at the airport, flies to most national cities.

For car rental, **Avis** is at the Hilton Colón ((042) 692884, or at the airport ((042) 287906; **Hertz** at the Hotel Oro Verde ((042) 327895, and at the airport ((042) 293011; **Budget** ((042) 288510 at the airport. There are also a number of national companies at the airport.

The city's biggest fiesta takes place around July 25, a combination of Bolívar's birthday and the founding of the city. Guayaquil then explodes in a riot of concerts, parades, beauty pageants, fireworks, and considerable hilarity and falling-down-drunkenness.

Guayaquileños aren't shy of a party, and you'll also find big celebrations for Carnaval, Easter Week, Christmas and New Year, and around October 9–12 for the Día de la Raza and the city's independence day.

WHAT TO SEE AND DO

A walk along the newly renovated, multimillion-dollar **Malecón**, by the wide Río Guayas, reveals the essence of the town's maritime history and its continental power at the beginning of the new century. The new Malecón is a symphony of polished stone and steel and glass, dotted with elegant trees, fountains, benches, fast-food chains and security guards. It's by far the most pleasant part of the city, and probably its safest, although you can't help wondering if the millions wouldn't have been better spent on social programs.

Where the Malecón crosses the end of the main thoroughfare, Avenida 9 de Octubre, **La Rotunda** is a statue commemorating the famous, but secret, meeting between Bolívar and San Martín in 1822. Following the encounter, Ecuador became part of Bolívar's long-fought after super-nation of Gran Colombia. The men are considerably out of proportion, if you ask me. Bolívar was only 1.65 m (5'6") but here looks like he plays in the NBA. Close to La Rotonda, two strikingly modern lookout towers rise above the river. There are great views from these across to the source of much *guayaquileño* pride, the Puente (bridge) de la Unidad Nacional. Further on, you come to one of the city's most famous sights: the cream-hued, Moorish **clock tower**, adorned with Islamic designs, and looking somewhat incongruous. Across the street from here, head down the beautiful glass-and-metal vaulted arcade of the ornate **Palacio Municipal**, with its Grecian statues looking down at passersby from on high.

Continuing north beyond the Malecón, you come to the historic **Las Peñas** district, where the city was founded. Because of its elevation, Las Peñas escaped floods and fires, and is the only area to have retained its cobbled streets and old wooden houses, some of them now occupied by artists. These back streets are not safe alone; go with a group or join a tour with a travel agent. The most picturesque street is Numa Pomplino Llona, where you'll find various artists' studios and galleries, of which the **Casa del Artista Plástica** is one of the best. While in Las Peñas, seek out the pretty **Iglesia de Santo Domingo**, the city's oldest church, restored in 1938.

For more history, Guayaquil has several good museums. In contrast to other more predictable exhibits pertaining to the city's history at the **Museo Municipal**, near Parque Seminario, you might be able to see the collection of *tsantsas*, Shuar shrunken heads, although they aren't always on display. The small **Museo del Banco del Pacífico** (9 AM to 7 PM Monday to Friday, 11 AM to 1 PM Saturday), a block up from La Rotunda on Paula de Icaza, has an excellent, well-presented and informative archaeological collection. Near the vast Parque Centenario, the **Casa de la Cultura** has a fine collection of gold items in its Sala de Oro, and some intriguing artifacts from the La Tolita culture. The museum is open from 10 AM to 5 PM (with a break from 1 PM to 2 PM) Monday to Friday, and from 10 AM to 1:30 PM Saturday. The **Museo Arqueológico del Banco Central**, where José de Antepara crosses with Avenida 9 de Octubre, has probably the best-presented collection in the city, with a wonderful display of gold masks and jewelry, as well as notable anthropological and archaeological displays from the Valdivian culture. The museum is due to move to the Malecón.

To experience the tangy side of Guayaquil's street life, go to **La Bahía black market**, on both sides of Avenida Olmedo towards the river, where you can buy goods that have somehow fallen off boats; prices are rock-bottom. You can save a fortune here on things like clothing, shoes, electrical goods, cameras, food and drink. Be warned: the market is rife with pickpockets and snatch thieves, mostly working in pairs, who might have the watch off your wrist as quickly as the flick of a snake's tongue.

To explore the modern side of Guayaquil, take a trip to the northern suburb of **Urdesa**, an almost self-contained community with many good shops, malls and restaurants and a vibrant nightlife. To get away from the crowds, visit the **Jardín Botánico**, also in the north of town in Urbanización Las Orquídeas, which has pleasant walks, a butterfly garden, gift shop, café and a wonderful collection of orchids, open 8 AM to 4 PM daily.

WHERE TO STAY

Reflecting its importance as a business city, Guayaquil is well appointed with first-class hotels, some even more expensive than those in Quito. Many new hotels have been built, leading to an oversupply, so it is worth trying to negotiate a discount.

Expensive

In the serious money-per-room range, the **Oro Verde** ((042) 327999 FAX (042) 329350 E-MAIL ov_gye @oroverdehotels.com WEB SITE www.oroverde hotels.com on 9 de Octubre and García Moreno,

has every facility you could expect, including a swimming pool, business center, disco and restaurants. The **Hilton Colón** ((042) 689000 FAX (042) 689149 E-MAIL ventas1@hiltonguayaquil .com WEB SITE www.hiltoncolon.com, on Avenida Francisco de Orellana-Manzana III, is also at the top of the range, but slightly less expensive than the Oro Verde.

Better value is the downtown, five-star **Hotel Continental** ((042) 329270 FAX (042) 325454 E-MAIL info@hotelcontinental.com.ec WEB SITE www .hotelcontinental.com.ec Chile at 10 de Agosto, known for its award-winning restaurants, friendly service and comfortable rooms. In the same luxury range, the **Gran Hotel Guayaquil** ((042) 329690

TOLL-FREE (800) 102030 FAX (042) 327251 E-MAIL granhot@gye.satnet.net www.grandhotel guayaquil.com, Boyacá at Clemente Ballén, has good sporting and sauna facilities, with a lovely swimming pool open to non-guests at a reasonable charge and excellent breakfasts. Even if you are staying elsewhere this is a good place for a morning swim and hearty breakfast to set you up for the day.

Moderate

Good, mid-priced hotels are scarce in Guayaquil. Two that have been recommended are **Hotel Palace** ((042) 321080 FAX (042) 322887, Chile and Luque, and the nearby **Hotel Doral** ((042) 327133 FAX (042) 327088, on Chile and Aguirre, where the "kingsize" rooms are the best value. **Hotel Sol de**

The fruit of the land in the western lowlands.

Oro ((042) 532067, Lorenzo de Garaicoa 1243, has well-appointed rooms, especially the large ones on the top floor that boast great views over the city, making it probably the best bet in this bracket.

Inexpensive

The best deal of all is the budget hostel **Ecuahogar** ((042) 248357 FAX (042) 248341, on Avenida Isidro Ayora, near the airport and bus terminal. Rooms in this pleasant house vary in price, but include a light breakfast. Laundry and storage facilities are available. If you're passing through Guayaquil but don't intend to stay, Ecuahogar is a convenient stopover. Downtown, the best inexpensive deal is the **Hotel Capri** ((042) 530093, Luque 1221, which has very clean rooms including cable television, air conditioning, refrigerators and good hot showers, although the interior rooms are dark, while the street ones are noisy. **Hotel Berlin** ((042) 524648, Sucre at Rumicacha, has cold showers and fans, but it's clean and roomy for the price.

WHERE TO EAT

As with hotels, good, mid-priced restaurants are also scarce in Guayaquil, though **La Canoa** at the Hotel Continental is a notable exception. This 24-hour eatery serves, in pleasant surroundings, beautifully prepared *típico* Ecuadorian dishes (try their *cazuela*) as well as gourmet burgers with French fries. For an expensive, but delicious, blow-out, head to the French restaurant, **Le Gourmet**, at the Oro Verde. The hotel also houses a cheaper sophisticated café-restaurant, and a restaurant serving Cajun and Oriental dishes. For more dining in style, don your best threads for an evening meal at the **Guayaquil Yacht Club**. The restaurant ostensibly isn't open to the public, but nor do they turn away tourists with dollars. The decor is elegant, the service excellent and the food delicious. The best deal for sushi in the city is the Unihotel's stylish **Sushibar**, off Parque Seminario, Clemente Ballén 406. Two good seafood restaurants can be found on the Malecón, at Muelle 4 and Muelle 5, north of La Rotonda.

Guayaquil, which has a large Chinese population, is well-known for its good Chinese *chifas*, **Gran Chifa** and **Chifa Amoi**, both on Pedro Carbo near Sucre, are the best. For a good cheap lunch while sightseeing, the **Coppelia** overlooks Plaza San Francisco.

NIGHTLIFE

For a taste of Guayaquil's famous nightlife (though much reduced following the curfew of 1998) take a taxi to **VE Estrada** in Urdesa. Popular clubs are **Infinity Club**, and **Tequila-la** in Urdesa Norte, and bars in the area include **El Manantial** and **Chappu's Bar**. The best *salsateca* in town is **El Jardín**

de Salsa, on the road between the bus terminal and the airport, which boasts the largest *pista* (dance floor) in the country.

If the club scene doesn't appeal, and you are more interested in a pint of English or Scottish draft beer (a change from the ubiquitous, though very good, Ecuadorian *Pilsner*), head for the **Rob Roy Bar** on Avenida Herradura 15 and Avenida Demetrio Agouilira, a popular gringo expat hangout. With more local character, the best place for an evening drink by a long shot is **Artur's Café**, on Numa Pompillo Llona in Las Peñas, which has several romantic patios, beautiful people and great views. They also serve delicious and simple local fare.

The best theater in the city is the **Centro Cívico**, on Avenida 25 de Julio, south of the city center. Classical music performances and visiting theater groups perform here. Check listings in the *El Universo* newspaper.

HOW TO GET THERE

Arriving by air, you'll land at **Simón Bolívar Airport**, on Avenida de las Américas, about five kilometers (three miles) north of the town center. There are good connections to all Ecuadorian cities. The chaotic and daunting Terminal Terrestre **bus station** lies about two kilometers (just over a mile) north of the airport. You can walk or take a taxi between the two. Taxis from the airport to the center of town shouldn't cost more than US$4 to US$5, but you might have to bargain. On the opposite side of the street from the airport terminals are buses to town. There are plenty of buses and taxis between the bus station and the center. The best buses to the Peruvian border are Ecuatoriana Pullman's, and there are numerous buses to most corners of the country.

The city's **train station** in the suburb of Durán, on the east side of the Río Guayas, is currently closed.

BEYOND GUAYAQUIL

If you've come along the coast, and fancy heading up back to the Sierra, take the bus to Bucay, and from there ride the train up the **Devil's Nose** (the most thrilling part), and onwards to **Alausí** and **Riobamba**. Check train schedules because they change often. Tickets go on sale at 6 AM on the day of travel. The bus ride up the Andes from Guayaquil to **Cuenca**, through Zhud, **Cañar** and **Azogues**, is also a spectacular journey.

If you are heading for Quito, there are frequent, daily walk-on flights, or you can take an eight-hour bus ride. If you want to see some banana, rice, coffee and fruit-growing areas in the western lowlands, you can take a bus north to **Quevedo** through **Los Ríos Province**, which, as the name implies, abounds in rivers. Quevedo is known as the "Chinatown of Ecuador" because of its many descendants of the Chinese laborers who helped construct the railway at the end of the nineteenth century.

Santo Domingo de los Colorados, further north, is the home of the **Colorados Indians**, but visitors are no longer likely to see them wearing their traditional bowl-shaped, bright-red hairstyles, dyed with achote plant, and faces painted with black stripes. A few kilometers southeast of the fast-growing town of Santo Domingo is the well-known **Tinalandia Hotel (** IN QUITO (022) 247461 FAX (022) 442638. Established by a Russian émigré many years ago, the hotel is surrounded by subtropical forests with many species of plants and birds. They also have a nine-hole golf course, one of the few in Ecuador.

The road south from Guayaquil passes through the **Reserva Ecológica Manglares-Churute**, one of the few areas of mangroves left on the coast. The reserve is home to some 200 species of bird, including flamingos from October to December, and also bottle-nosed dolphins between June and November. Boat rides can be arranged through the mangroves, and there are some great trails through the dry forest. The Centro de Visitantes is just off the main highway, and the reserve is open 8 AM to 2 PM (get there early to avoid the sapping heat). For more information, contact the **Ministerio del Ambiente** in Guayaquil (** (042) 397730, Avenida Quito 402 and Padre Solano.

Beyond the reserve, bananas, pineapples, citrus fruit and coffee take over. **Machala**, the capital of El Oro Province, 200 km (125 miles) south of Guayaquil, is known as the Banana Capital of the World, and a banana festival takes place in the town at the tail end of September. The town isn't big on tourism, though the island-beach of **Jambelí**, on a nearby island, is beautiful but primitive, treasured by birders searching for the rare rufous-necked wood-rail.

From Machala, a road branches southeast towards **Piñas** and the old mining town of **Zaruma**, 86 km (53 miles) inland. The journey, though beautiful, is rough and can take up to three hours. Though way off most travelers' paths, this is a picturesque area, and Zaruma, perched on a hill, has some charming old wooden buildings and a lovely timber church erected in 1912. White-skinned, blue-eyed descendants of Spanish colonialists still work old and exhausted gold mines, some dating back to pre-Columbian days. Recently discovered pre-Columbian ruins indicate the area was well populated before the Inca invasion. There's an enlightening **Museo del Banco Central** (open 9 AM to 5 PM Tuesday to Saturday) dedicated to the mining industry. The best hotel is the **Hotel Roland (** (07) 972703, with comfortable rooms and great views. From Zaruma,

you can bump your way up the mountains, via Catamayo, all the way to Loja.

Most travelers head directly south from Machala to the **Peruvian border**. The last Ecuadorian town is **Huaquillas**, 80 km (50 miles) south of Machala, an unkempt, dismal place with a reputation for smuggling and pickpockets. But inexpensive Ecuadorian goods have made it a shopping center for Peruvians who nip across the border for cut-price shopping. Travelers leaving Ecuador must get an exit stamp before crossing the **International Bridge** at the border. The immigration office is annoyingly located two kilometers (just over a mile) back up the road to Machala, open daily from 8 AM to noon and 2 PM to 6 PM.

If you're coming by bus, ask to be dropped off here, then take a taxi to the border bridge (bargain hard, because they'll try and rip you off). The Peruvian immigration office is just over the bridge. It's all pretty hectic and stressful, and keep your eyes on your belongings. Change little money here, since rates are far better in the first Peruvian town of **Tumbes**, 27 km (17 miles) south.

Riding the rails down the flanks of the Andes, passing along Devil's Nose en route.

The Galápagos Islands

Stepping onto a beach on one of the Galápagos Islands you could well find yourself surrounded by dozens of sunbathing sea lions lying about on the sand like so many sacks of potatoes. As you approach, they don't blunder off into the sea or shuffle behind a rock, as you might expect; they keep on sleeping in the sun or stare at you with studied indifference. If you stand within a meter or two they might snarl or bark with a sound that's a cross between a pig's oink and the klaxon of an antique car. But they are unlikely to be aggressive towards you, nor frightened.

Along rocky shorelines, you encounter blue-footed boobies laying eggs on the pathways; they show not the slightest concern at your presence. They don't bat an eye if you approach within a meter. Prehistoric marine iguanas, which look like miniature dragons or extras from a science fiction movie, eye you languorously from jagged lava rocks and hardly deign to move if you poke a lens within a few inches of their glistening heads.

The wildlife of these remote islands that straddle the equator in the Pacific Ocean, about 1,000 km (625 miles) off the coast of Ecuador, have charmed visitors for centuries. The absence of fear expressed by the animals in part explains why the Galápagos Islands have often been called the Garden of Eden. Protected by the 130,000-sq-km (51,793-sq mile) Galápagos Marine Resources Reserve, the islands are regarded as one of the great natural areas of the world, and possibly the greatest natural history show on earth.

Ecuador manages the islands through the Parque Nacional Galápagos parks service, which has offices in Puerto Ayora on Santa Cruz. Nearby is the Charles Darwin Research Station, run by the Charles Darwin Foundation. The Research Station carries out scientific research and assists the park service.

The Parque Nacional Galápagos parks service has designated more than 60 visitors' sites on the islands, enabling visitors to see all the interesting wildlife; the rest of the reserve is off limits to tourists. At each visitors' site a discreetly marked trail provides excellent views of wildlife, vegetation and landscape of the island. Most of the trails are less than one and a half kilometers (a mile) long but can be difficult underfoot, leading over rough lava or uneven boulders. There are also one or two longer hikes in the highlands.

The different sites are varied in their scenery and vegetation but some animals are common at nearly all of them. These include Galápagos sea lions, marine iguanas, lava lizards and a variety of coastal birds. In addition to the visitors' sites on land, the Galápagos Islands offer excellent scuba diving, though these aren't recommended for beginners. However, many snorkeling spots offer anyone the chance to see the colorful underwater life of the Galápagos.

Almost without exception, visitors are extremely impressed with what they see and do on the Galápagos Islands. "The trip of a lifetime," they say, "Like nowhere else on earth" or "Paradise on this planet." The only negative things you'll hear anyone say will be about increasing threats to the environment and wildlife, and fears that the fragile ecosystem will be further damaged.

BACKGROUND

Although they had no aboriginal human population, the Galápagos Islands have been a magnet for naturalists as well as a refuge for pirates, prisoners, castaways, rogues and eccentrics over the centuries. Potsherds examined by the Norwegian anthropologist and explorer, Thor Heyerdahl, suggest that the first sailors to the islands came from the coast of northern Perú. It is also thought that one of the great Incas, Tupac Yupanqui, sent an expedition to the islands at the end of the fifteenth century.

The bishop of Panama, Fray Tomás de Berlanga, who was blown off course onto the islands while on a mission to Perú in March 1535, made the first written record of the archipelago. In a letter to King Charles V of Spain, he wrote of finding seals and turtles, tortoises so big that each could carry a man, many serpents-like iguanas, and "birds so silly that they did not know how to flee." On one island there was "not even space to grow a bushel of corn because it was as if God had showered the land with very big stones." The bishop is credited for naming the islands Las Encantadas, the Bewitched or Enchanted Ones, because they seemed to move in the swirling mists. From his and the pilot's report of the voyage, the Flemish cartographer, Abraham Ortelius, learned of the islands and marked them as "Galápagos" on his *Orbis Terrarum* of 1574, the word *galápagos* being Spanish for turtles.

BRITISH BUCCANEERS

During the sixteenth and seventeenth centuries the Galápagos Islands were a refuge for British buccaneers pillaging the Spanish colonies on the western coast of South America and attacking Spanish galleons laden with Inca gold on their way back to Spain. One such ship, the *Bachelor's Delight*, made several visits to the islands in the 1680s. A member of the crew, William Ambrose Cowley, drew maps and named each island after leading personages of the day.

PREVIOUS PAGES Sunset/sunrise LEFT over Isla Santa Fé. Sea lions RIGHT inhabit most islands of the Galápagos and are generally not frightened of nor aggressive towards human visitors. OPPOSITE: Marine iguanas on Isla Española.

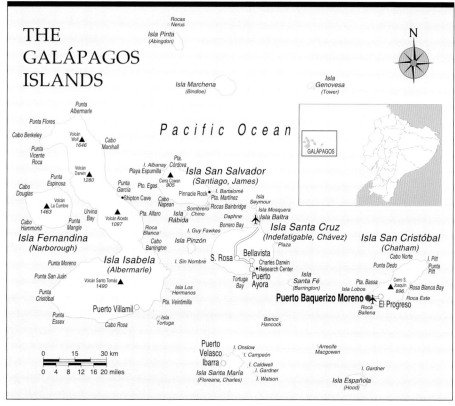

Thus these remote, uninhabited islands of the eastern Pacific acquired bizarre names like King James Island, the Duke of Albemarle's Island, the Earl of Abingdon's Island, the Duke of York's Island, Lord Cullpeper's Island, the Duke of Norfolk's Island, and Sir John Narborough's Island. Subsequently the islands were renamed by the British, United States officers and the Spanish, as well as by the government of Ecuador when it claimed sovereignty of them in 1832. The result has been a quaint confusion about names, so even modern maps show as many as three names for one island.

The Duke of Norfolk's Island, for instance, has been known variously as Indefatigable, Porter Island, Valdez, Chávez, San Clemente and finally Santa Cruz, by which it is now known. It is shown on maps as Santa Cruz, with Indefatigable and sometimes Chávez. Isla Santa María is usually known by its former name of Floreana and its even older name, Charles, is still shown on con-temporary maps. One island is simply called Sin Nombre, or Nameless.

To add to the confusion, the islands themselves were officially named Archipíelago de Colón by the National Assembly of Ecuador in 1892, to commemorate the 400th anniversary of Columbus's first voyage, Colón being the Span-

ish spelling of his name. But they are still called the Galápagos Islands in everyday usage.

THE FIRST RESIDENT

The first human resident of the Galápagos Islands on record was Patrick Watkins, an Irish castaway. According to the journal of Captain David Porter, a United States Navy officer, Watkins had no apparent desires aside from getting enough rum to keep himself intoxicated. Mostly he was found in a state of perfect insensibility, rolling around the rocks of the mountains.

After several years on Charles Island (now known as Isla Santa María or Floreana), where he supported his thirst by growing and selling vegetables to visiting ships, Watkins got some sailors extremely drunk and kidnapped them. He then stole a boat and embarked with these men. The boat arrived in Guayaquil on the coast of Ecuador with only Patrick Watkins on board. Watkins was thrown in jail in Perú and nothing more was heard of him.

During the nineteenth century there were various attempts to colonize the Galápagos Islands, none of them very successful. A General José Villamil tried to develop an enterprise to cultivate and export orchilla for the manufacture of dyes, for which he brought the first colonists to Charles Island. These were a group of 80 Ecuadorian soldiers who had been condemned to death for mutiny, but reprieved on condition they worked for the general. The islands were also used as a dumping ground for political exiles, common criminals and prostitutes deported from Guayaquil.

At the same time, whaling boats, naval ships and scientific expeditions regularly visited the islands. In 1825, the British Royal Navy's Captain Lord Byron, son of the poet, anchored off Albemarle Island. He wrote in his diary, "The place is like a new creation; the birds and beasts do not get out of our way; the pelicans and sea-lions look in our faces as if we had no right to intrude on their solitude; the small birds are so tame that they hop upon our feet; and all this amidst volcanoes which are burning round us on either hand. Altogether it is as wild and desolate a scene as imagination can picture."

CHARLES DARWIN

Ten years later, the naturalist Charles Darwin, another Englishman, spent five weeks in the archipelago as part of his five-year journey of exploration and scientific discovery aboard HMS *Beagle*. "Nothing could be less inviting than the first appearance," he wrote. "A broken field of black, basaltic lava… crossed by great fissures, is everywhere covered by stunted, sunburned brushwood… the many craters vividly remind me of parts of Staffordshire, where the great iron foundries are most numerous."

Notwithstanding those bleak first impressions, Darwin found the islands to be "infinitely strange, unlike any other islands in the world." And he recorded that the natural history of the archipelago was "very remarkable: it seems to be a little world within itself; the greater number of its inhabitants, both vegetable and animal being found nowhere else."

Despite intense heat and a shortage of drinking water, Darwin worked hard at collecting his specimens. Only later, during the years he spent examining his collection on his return to England, did he recognize the full significance of his work. He noted important differences between similar species collected on different islands, particularly in the shapes of the beaks of finches. He concluded that over the millennia, the finches had adapted to the varying conditions of the islands. One type of finch would have thick beaks for cracking nuts, for example, while another would be adapted for pecking at fruit or flowers, and yet another finch used twigs to dig insects from the bark of trees.

These and other observations eventually led Darwin to his theory of natural selection and that related organisms descend from common ancestors, in contradiction to the accepted ideas of divine creation. Darwin set forth his views in his controversial book, *On the Origin of the Species by Natural Selection*, which he published in 1859, nearly 25 years after his visit to the Galápagos Islands. The first edition of 1,250 copies sold out on the day of issue. Darwin's theories stimulated the most vigorous intellectual debate of the nineteenth century.

CURIOUS COLONISTS

Darwin's writings stimulated worldwide interest and further scientific expeditions to the Galápagos Islands. Wealthy Americans cruised down

on their yachts and in the 1920s American journalist William Beebe wrote a bestseller about the islands: *Galápagos: World's End*. The book sold particularly well in Norway, and inspired several Norwegians to come and live on the archipelago. In the 1930s, a German couple settled on Floreana and attracted international interest because of their curious lifestyles. Before leaving Germany, Dr. Friedrich Ritter and his companion took the precaution of having all their teeth removed and replaced with steel dentures, because they would be unable to obtain dental treatment on the island.

Three years later another German couple, Heinz and Margret Wittmer and their 12-year-old son, joined these two lone inhabitants of the 250-sq-km (96-sq-mile) island. The two families did not care for each other. The atmosphere on

Fishing boat off Isla Rábida, one of the best spots for snorkeling in the Galápagos Islands.

the island became more poisonous when a self-styled Austrian baroness arrived on the island with her three male lovers. The scene was set for one of the world's most intriguing true-life, unsolved mystery stories. First one lover, then the baroness with another lover disappeared. Dr. Ritter died in mysterious circumstances. Margret Wittmer, the last survivor, died on Floreana in the year 2000.

THREATS TO THE ENVIRONMENT

In the past two decades colonization of and tourism to the Galápagos Islands have increased rapidly. Although the national park accounts for 97 percent of the island's land area, there are serious problems with settler encroachment. In the 1950s, the population of the islands was just over 1,000, mostly concentrated on Santa Cruz, now the center of the tourist industry. According to official figures, the present population of the islands is 16,000, but it is in fact thought to be approaching 20,000, with an annual growth rate of some eight percent.

An even greater threat to the environment is the animals and plants human visitors and colonists have brought with them. Feral cats, dogs, rats, pigs, goats, donkeys, deer and cattle have contributed to the destruction of eggs, hatchlings and the vegetation, on which all the native species depend. On Española the tortoise population was almost extinct by the 1960s. A captive-breeding program for tortoises was started at Darwin Station, and the goats were eliminated. Young tortoises have now been returned to their ancestral island and the unique subspecies has been saved from extinction.

Served by nearly 100 cruise ships, the fast-growing tourist market also threatens the ecological balance. The national parks authority imposes strict control on where visitors are allowed to land, and all visitors are strongly requested to obey common-sense rules, such as not to stray from the paths, nor feed or touch the animals and birds. Touching a baby sea lion, for instance, will probably result in its death, as its mother will reject it. But no matter how diligently the tourist obeys the rules, his or her presence will impact on the islands' ecology in some way: Puerto Ayora, for instance, has yet to acquire a satisfactory wastewater treatment plant.

The disaster involving the small tanker *Jessica* in early 2001 brought the islands' vulnerability home to everyone involved in the Galápagos. The tanker was carrying fuel for the largest cruise ship of all, the *Galápagos Explorer II*, when the captain ran aground off San Cristóbal Island. By nothing short of a miracle, a major disaster was averted when strong currents kept the fuel away from the shore. The captain, the contracted company and the ministers of the environment and defense all face criminal charges. But some would say it's only a matter of time until a similar disaster occurs — this time with catastrophic consequences for the islands' fragile and unique species.

THE WILDLIFE

The Galápagos Islands, the world's greatest natural history museum, are one of the most exciting places on earth for wildlife watching and photography. Large numbers of species are endemic to (found only on) the islands, most of which are easy to see because they have not learned to fear humans. One piece of advice that every visitor should heed is to bring twice as much film as you originally intend to bring — and then to double that amount. The following are some of the more interesting species to watch for.

REPTILES

The Galápagos Islands are well known for their variety and abundance of various forms of primeval reptiles, most of which aren't found anywhere else on earth. Out of 22 species of tortoises, iguanas, snakes, lizards and geckos, 90 percent are endemic to the archipelago.

Giant Tortoises

Giant tortoises are the big stars in the pantheon on the Galápagos Islands. Numbering some 15,000 and weighing up to 250 kg (550 lb), these are the biggest tortoises in the world. It is estimated that in the eighteenth and nineteenth centuries, between 200,000 and 300,000 were killed or captured as sources of fresh meat by whalers and sealers or taken away by collectors.

Fourteen subspecies of giant tortoise inhabited the archipelago when it was discovered in 1535. Today, only five subspecies are numerous enough to be considered safe, five are threatened and three are extinct. One subspecies has just one surviving individual, Lonesome George, who lives at the Charles Darwin Research Station on Santa Cruz (see SANTA CRUZ AND PUERTO AYORA, page 229). Though it is known that tortoises once inhabited Santa Fé, no evidence remains to tell us what that particular breed was like.

There are two basic types of Galápagos tortoise. The first have shortish necks and high-domed carapaces, which come down low over both head and tail. These big beasts inhabit the lusher, thicker vegetation on the uplands of Santa Cruz and some of the Isabela volcanoes. The second, smaller type have longer necks and legs with carapaces shaped more like Spanish-style saddles, flatter on top and rising up at the front. They are able to reach up to cactus and high foliage and come from the arid zones. A continuum exists between the very pronounced saddleback shells, which come from the low, flat islands of Pinzón and Española, to the roundest dome-shaped shells from the lusher parts of Isabela.

Saving tortoises threatened with extinction through captive breeding and reintroduction to the wild is a major part of the work of the Charles Darwin Station on Santa Cruz (for more detail, see page 230).

Marine Turtles

Though not endemic to the islands, Pacific green sea turtles lay eggs and breed in the islands. At night during the breeding season from January to June, females waddle up island beaches above the high water mark, dig holes and bury dozens of

creatures seem to predate man by millions of years. Most are dirty black when wet and gray when dry, easily blending into their rocky environment.

Marine iguanas live on lava rocks on the water's edge, dine on seaweed, and can swim underwater for as long as an hour. Darwin discovered this by throwing them into the water with weights attached to their legs, and then pulling them back up at various intervals to see which ones survived. They are common on most Galápagos Islands and can often be seen in groups of similar age basking in the sun, all facing the same way, or even piled on top of each other.

In spite of their aggressive appearance, vegetarian marine iguanas won't bother humans

eggs. When hatched, baby turtles try to make their way to the sea, though they are vulnerable to predators such as rats, dogs, pigs and humans. If they make it safely, they disappear for years and travel huge distances. Incredibly, females are able to find their way back to the beach where they were born to lay eggs for the next generation. One of the big excitements of the Galápagos islands for snorkelers and divers is the sight of a turtle swimming nearby.

Marine Iguanas

Darwin called them "Imps of Darkness"... hideous looking creatures, stupid and sluggish in their movements. But he was fascinated by these endemic reptiles, the only seagoing lizards in the world. With long tails and spines like teeth running down their backs, and growing to a meter (three feet) in length, these fearsome-looking

unless provoked. After feeding on algae, these cold-blooded creatures sunbathe on the rocks to warm their bodies and digest their food. They even bask on hotel terraces in Puerto Ayora on Santa Cruz. With desalination glands in their heads to filter out salt from seawater, they snort out sprays of salt through their noses like Puff the Magic Dragon.

During their mating season, which varies from island to island, males become aggressive and territorial, fighting head to head and mating with several females. Their scaly skin becomes blotchy red and green at these times, though marine iguanas on Española are colorful all the year round. Females lay two to four eggs in sandy nests and defend them until they hatch, but don't pay much attention to their young after that.

A giant Galápagos tortoise on Isla Isabela.

Land Iguanas

Thought to have the same ancestors as marine iguanas, land iguanas are now totally different in habit and habitat. At one time the Galápagos land iguana lived on almost all the islands of the archipelago, but hunting and competition with introduced animals, such as pigs, goats, dogs and rats, have confined them to Isabela, Santa Cruz, Fernandina, Seymour and South Plaza islands. This yellowish lizard, slightly bigger than its aquatic cousin, has a tough, leathery mouth, enabling it to feed on the spiky prickly pear cactus. A second species of land iguana, the Santa Fé land iguana, is bigger and more yellow than the Galápagos land iguana and is confined to Santa Fé island.

Snakes, Lizards and Geckos

Though rarely seen by visitors, two kinds of snake inhabit the archipelago: the Galápagos land snake and the yellow-bellied sea snake. The constricting but inconspicuous brown or gray land snake, with yellow spots or stripes, grows to about a meter (three feet three inches) in length. It asphyxiates insects, lizards and hatchlings, but isn't dangerous to humans. The black and yellow sea snake is rare, though its venom can be stronger than a cobra's. Harmless lava lizards can be seen scurrying around most of the islands, as can the equally harmless nocturnal geckos, who climb vertical walls and walk upside down on ceilings hunting for insects.

MAMMALS

There are few native species of mammals on the Galápagos, because of the islands' separation from the mainland and the difficulty for land mammals to survive an ocean crossing. Aside from two species of seals, the only mammals not introduced by man are some species of rats and bats. Animals brought to the islands by man include dogs, cats, goats, donkeys, horses and the black rat (*Rattus rattus*).

Sea Lions

These sleek, blubbery, playful creatures are one of the main attractions of the Galápagos. Close relatives of this endemic subspecies exist in the Sea of Japan, on the California coast, and in sealife aquariums all over the world, but on the beaches of the archipelago the Galápagos sea lions are abundant, easily approachable and not intimidated by humans.

Landing on some beaches you might find yourself in a colony of scarred and tired males, exhausted after fighting off male rivals and looking after their harems of cows. On another beach there may be families of cows with their pups and a sea lion bull patrolling the nearby waters,

trying to keep his females to himself. In practice, a jealous male may guard his females for up to a month, until hunger and lack of sleep exhausts him. At this point a rival male takes over the harem and the old bull skulks off back to the bachelor colony.

Male sea lions are easily distinguished from females: they are generally much bigger, growing up to 250 kg (550 lb), and they have a high, bulging foreheads in contrast to the flatter female skulls. Mothers give birth to one cub at a time and nurse them for up to two years. Females are tamer than the males and can be approached to within a meter or so. Be careful of bull sea lions, especially when they are guarding their cows.

Fur Seals

Although about as numerous as sea lions, endemic fur seals aren't as easy to see because they don't lie around sunning themselves on the sand and rocks, preferring instead the cool of caves and grottoes. They are more timid towards humans than towards other animals, but were still almost hunted to extinction for their luxuriant, cinnamon-brown fur, made of two layers of hair. They are smaller than sea lions, broader headed, and they emit a bovine lowing sound rather than a canine bark. Thanks to conservation efforts their numbers have increased and the fur seals are no longer in danger of extinction.

Whales and Dolphins

One of the great thrills of cruising the islands is when somebody shouts: "Dolphins on the bow!" Everybody rushes to lean over the rails and watch these streamlined torpedoes racing along at the sharp end of the boat, breaking surface for a split second in a shower of spray. There are so many dolphins in the Galápagos waters that if you take a boat cruise you're almost certain to have this exhilarating experience. If you're lucky you'll see a mother swimming at high speed with cubs who keep so close that they seem to be joined by an invisible cord. Suddenly, as quickly as they've come, the playful dolphins disappear, leaving you wondering where they've gone and what they will do next.

Several species of dolphins have been sighted here, but the ones that play with the ships are the bottle-nosed variety. Several whale species are

ing eggs under their webbed feet. Even within a few feet they appear as indifferent to you as you might be to a passing stranger on a street. Blue-footed boobies frequently lay eggs right in the middle of a path, their nest being nothing more than a circle of guano defining a boundary for their young chicks. Masked boobies also lay their eggs on the ground, while red-footed boobies make primitive nests in bushes or low trees. Each of the booby species has carved out its ecological niche, with the blue-footed birds feeding from the shore and the red-footed variety diving for fish away from the breeding colonies.

The friendly Galápagos penguin is one the world's smallest, rarest and least-studied pen-

also sighted regularly, including the common rorqual, sei, sperm, killer, humpback and blue. Whale sightings are usually so brief and distant that it's difficult to identify the species.

BIRDS

The attraction of bird life in the Galápagos isn't only the abundance of rare and interesting species (nearly 60 resident species on the islands of which some 28 are endemic). It is also the fact that many birds are unafraid of humans and therefore easy to see close up. There are also dozens of migrant birds that can almost always be spotted.

The comical boobies are likely to be among the first birds you'll meet on the islands. As you wander along pathways through their nesting colonies, they continue on with their rituals and activities, such as courtship dancing or incubat-

guins, and lives further north than any other species. These flightless birds charm all as they hop about the rocks and plop feet-first into the sea. Aside from penguins, the world's only other flightless seabird is the flightless cormorant, another rare and endemic species. Its small, atrophied wings are thought to be the result of evolution, where swimming and hunting became more important than flight. The tallest of the world's 29 species of cormorant, it is curiously ungainly on land but is a powerful swimmer. It's also one of the few seabirds that don't keep the same mate from one nesting to the next.

Of special interest among seabirds, the waved albatross, one of the rarest and by far the largest

OPPOSITE: The small, dark lava heron, seen here on Isla San Salvador, is endemic to the Galápagos. ABOVE: Sea lions are one of the main attractions in the Galápagos Islands.

bird in the archipelago, is endemic to Española, aside from some pairs on Isla de la Plata, off the mainland coast. Albatrosses spend their first few years at sea before returning to breed, and all are at sea from mid-January to mid-March. One of the most spectacular sights on the Galápagos is their courtship dance, when they bow and sway, honk and whistle, point to the sky and fence with their long, yellow bills.

Various species of petrel are common on many of the islands of the archipelago but the dark-rumped petrel has been in danger of extinction. Also known as the Hawaiian petrel, this shy, nocturnal seabird, which mates for life, is nearly extinct on those islands. Early settlers found these petrels in immense numbers. Reports say that during nesting season, the night air was filled with their howls and weird cackling calls. By the 1960s very few young were surviving long, because rats and pigs were eating their eggs and dogs and cats were killing chicks and adult birds. An intensive predator-control program run by the Darwin Station and the park service has had promising results.

One of the most spectacular seabirds of the Galápagos is the frigate bird, of which there are two difficult-to-distinguish species: the augustly named great and magnificent frigate birds. With deep, forked tails and long pointed wings spanning over two meters (six and a half feet), they have the highest wingspan-to-body ratio of any other bird. Elegant and streamlined, they can be seen cruising thermals above many parts of the islands on the lookout for prey. Frigate birds aren't hawks; they are air pirates, or cleptoparasites. Their technique is to harass other birds such as boobies to drop or regurgitate their food. With atrophied preening glands, they are unable to secrete enough oil to waterproof their wings. This is why frigate birds cannot dive or land in the water, though they can fish on the surface with their hooked beaks. The male frigate bird has an enormous red pouch of skin under his beak, which he inflates almost to the size of a football to attract females. Another extraordinary sight of the Galápagos is that of a courting male frigate bird sitting in a tree, or even flying overhead, with a big, bright red balloon puffed up on his chest. Frigate birds are opportunistic breeders and mate all year-round. The females lay one egg annually because feeding the chick until it can fly and getting food for itself means another year of hard-line aerial piracy.

Other special, mostly endemic seabirds to watch for on the Galápagos islands include the beautiful swallow-tailed gull, with its crimson eye-ring (which travels great distances out to sea and is the only gull to feed only at night); the lava gull, considered to be the rarest gull in the world; the splendid red-billed tropical bird, with its two elongated tail streamers; and the brown pelican, with its huge "scoop-fishing" bill and prehistoric appearance.

Among shorebirds, the stately but shy greater flamingo is literally head and shoulders above other birds in its habitat of salty lagoons, though it's slightly shorter than the more ubiquitous common egret, also known as the great egret or the American egret, which favors the rocky coastline. Though flamingos breed in other parts of the world, the Galápagos subspecies is rare. They don't like to be disturbed, and are likely to desert their mud nest if disturbed. Birdwatchers are advised to be especially sensitive. On the shorebird watch you may also spot oystercatchers, sandpipers, plovers, turnstones, whimbrels and stilts.

Of the land birds, the most scientifically important are the 13 species known as Darwin's finches, so-called because these birds were a key in the development of the scientist's theory of evolution by natural selection. By studying the sizes and shapes of their beaks, Charles Darwin observed how the finches had adapted themselves and survived in the harsh habitats of the volcanic Galápagos islands. His belief that all the finches shared a common ancestry was a major factor in the formulation of his theories about the origins of species and the beginning of life itself.

Since Darwin's visit in 1835, many scientists have studied his famous finches in great detail, researching the mechanisms of evolution. As an indication of the number of such studies, *The Beak of the Finch,* by Jonathan Weiner, lists some 300 bibliographical references.

On the Galápagos islands, the 13 species of finches can be classified into four subspecies. There are those that live in trees and eat fruits and bugs; those that also live in trees but are vegetarians; birds that live in trees, but look and act like warblers; and birds who spend much of their time hopping on the ground. Among these species there are great differences in behavior. The woodpecker finch, for example, has the extraordinary ability to break a cactus spine or a twig to make a tool, which it uses to dig for insects in a tree, while the sharp-beaked ground finch picks at the tail feathers of molting boobies and drinks their blood.

On most of the Galápagos Islands you see finches flying about, picking up crumbs, bathing in puddles. They are all small, black or gray-brown birds, no bigger than sparrows, with short wings and tails. Their differentiating characteristics are the shapes and sizes of their beaks. Unless you are an expert bird watcher it's unlikely you'll be able to distinguish one species from another. As one field guide states: "It is only a very wise man or a fool who thinks he is able to identify all the finches which he sees."

Ninety-seven percent of the land area of the remote and isolated Galápagos Islands is designated parklands.

Like the finches, the Galápagos mockingbird, of which there are four endemic species and six subspecies, has been the subject of painstaking scientific research. These noisy, curious, sociable birds are on all the islands except Pinzón.

There is thought to be just a hundred pairs left of the endemic Galápagos hawk, the only raptor that breeds on the islands. The birds practice co-operative polyandry, in which female mate with two or more males and all the adults help raise the young. There are also two subspecies of owl found on the islands: the short-eared owl and the Galápagos barn owl.

FISH

The wealth of marine life makes the Galápagos waters a paradise for divers and snorkelers. Within the 70,000-sq-km (27,000-sq-mile) Galápagos Marine Reserve more than 300 species of fish have been identified; with further research, the number is expected to go beyond 400. About 50 of those identified are endemic. With water often as clear as glass, you can see many sorts of colorful tropical fish when you dive. There's a good chance these will include one or more of about 12 species of sharks that swim in these waters, the most common being the white-tipped reef shark, the black-tipped reef shark, the gray reef shark and the Galápagos shark. In some areas hammerheads and tiger sharks are also common. Fortunately there have been no serious sharks attacks in Galápagos waters, and the dangerous great white shark is not an inhabitant of the archipelago. Several marine life guidebooks, available in Quito or Puerto Ayora on Santa Cruz, list most of the fish to be seen in the Galápagos.

Commercial fishing is permitted within the archipelago, though illegal fishing threatens the environment. Local and Japanese fishing pirates have seriously depleted shark, lobster and sea cucumber stocks, upsetting established ecosystems. Some islanders see fishing regulations as a threat to their livelihood. In 1995, local fishermen occupied the Charles Darwin Station and threatened to kill tortoises and beat up staff, protesting a government ban on fishing for sea cucumbers and other creatures. The situation was defused, but the tensions between the conservationist and fishing lobbies remain high. The Ecuadorian navy has stepped up its presence within the archipelago, but overfishing continues.

INVERTEBRATES

Among the wide variety of anemones, chitons, corals, jellyfish, sponges, snails, sea slugs, shrimps, starfish, lobsters, sea urchins, sea cucumbers, barnacles and crabs, the most eye-catching is the bright red-topped, blue-bottomed Sally lightfoot

crab (*Grapsus grapsus*), which can be seen scurrying over almost every rock in the archipelago. On beaches and in rock pools you can see many ghost crabs and hermit crabs. For divers, there's not as much living coral as in other top diving spots, like the Red Sea or the Maldives, but the abundance and variety of other marine life is stunning.

PLANTS

Far from being lush, tropical islands of coconut palms and ferns, like others in the Pacific, much of the Galápagos is dry, desert-like and covered with cactus. Formed from the tips of submerged volcanoes, and never joined to the mainland, the islands host a plant life which has developed according to the ability of seeds to survive winds and waves and the curious microclimates of the islands. Lack of suitable terrain and absence of pollinating insects limits the numbers of some

plant species, such as orchids, of which there are only 11 species on the archipelago, compared with over 3,000 on the mainland. At the same time, many unique species flourish on the islands because they adapted to the harsh conditions. The oppuntia cactus, for example, with its pretty yellow flowers, is unique to the archipelago, and is also the most common cactus.

Including subspecies and varieties, some 900 plants have been recorded on the archipelago, of which a quarter are endemic, and another quarter introduced by man. For classification purposes, the archipelago is usually divided into seven vegetation zones.

The sea level Coastal Zone is home to salt-tolerant plants such as mangroves and saltbush. The Arid Zone, 80–120 m (264–396 ft) above sea level, hosts the ghostly and ubiquitous, gray-barked palo santo tree, which has leaves only in wet season, as well as plentiful acacia, various thorny plants and cacti. Slight rainfall in the Transition Zone, up to 100–200 m (330–660 ft) in elevation, makes for richer vegetation, including perennial herbs and the zone's characteristic plant, the pega pega, or "stick stick" tree, so named because its leaves stick to your fingers.

During the dry season, from June to September, a thick fog, or *garuha*, creates a moist cloud forest in the Scalesia Zone, up to 500 m (1,640 ft) (named after the ubiquitous and endemic scalesia tree). Growing to a height of 10 m (33 ft), this beautiful "sunflower" tree has white, daisy-like flowers and is usually covered with mosses, vines and bromeliads. Scalesias are also common in the higher Brown Zone, named after the color of the moss that forms on the tree's branches at altitudes of around 500 m (1,640 ft).

A stand of giant opuntia cactus lines the shore on Santa Fé. The island is also home to a unique subspecies of giant land iguana.

Above this level is the Miconia Zone, named after leafy miconia bushes, up to four meters (13 ft) tall, with pink or violet flowering heads. Vegetables, coffee and fruit are grown in this belt. At the top level, from about 650 m (2,133 ft) to the peaks of the volcanoes, the tallest being over 1,600 m (5,249 ft), is the Pampa Zone. Ferns, grasses and sedges grow in this misty climate but there are few trees except the giant Galápagos fern tree.

GENERAL INFORMATION

The park entrance fee is currently US$100 per passenger, payable in cash at the airport. Children under 12 and students under 26 (with a valid

the **Charles Darwin Foundation** WEB SITE www .galapagos.org; the **Galápagos Coalition** (of biologists, lawyers and scientists) at WEB SITE http:// serv1.law.emory.edu.sites/galapagos/; and the author and guide **Michael Jackson**'s WEB SITE www.islandnet.com/~mjackson/homepage .html. Another enjoyable site is **Terraquest**'s WEB SITE www.terraquest.com/galapagos/. Good travel, tour information and last-minute-deals web sites include **www.go2galapagos.com** and **www.galapagosislands.com**. For suggested books to enrich your trip, see RECOMMENDED READING, page 259 in TRAVELERS' TIPS. The SAE in Quito sells a useful and up-to-date information pack about the islands.

student card) pay half price. Travelers' checks and credit cards are *not* accepted. Ninety-five percent of this fee is retained by the Galápagos: 40 percent goes to the park (more than in mainland parks), 40 percent to local authorities and the rest to other local organizations.

The sun on the equator is extremely fierce, so slather yourself with high-factor suncream, wear a sun hat and sunglasses, and snorkel wearing an old T-shirt or long-sleeved shirt. Although mosquitoes aren't generally a problem, if the wind drops on some islands they can appear in force. Carry repellent and sting relief cream with you in your day bag. It's unlikely to rain during your visit, but pack a lightweight waterproof jacket just in case. Don't forget to bring your passport.

Useful and informative web sites for the islands include the **International Galápagos Tour Operators' Association** WEB SITE www.igtoa.org;

When to Go

The high seasons in the Galápagos are mid-June to end-August, December to mid-January and around Easter Week. But these tourist periods are dictated more by vacation opportunities than by climate. In fact, the warmest months are December to April. If you like snorkeling or diving, these two months are the most pleasant time of year to visit. The water is warm, the sea is calm and the air tends to be clear, even though this is theoretically the wet season. In May the sea is still calm, but getting cooler. By July the weather has become almost cold, and snorkeling isn't pleasant without a wetsuit. In August the sea tends to be rough and the weather becomes misty until October. The coldest month is September, when many boats stay in dock and many *galapagueños* go on vacation. The weather in the Galápagos is just as fickle as it is in most other places in the world and you can be lucky or unlucky any time of year.

GETTING AROUND

If you're planning on traveling the islands independently, you should pack patience along with sun-block. Inter-island boat services are run by **INGALA** ((05) 526151 or (05) 526199 in Puerto Ayora. You should check boat times and destinations with them, as well as asking around in the port for private yachts that might be going your way. There is also a small seven-seat airplane operated by **EMETEBE** ((05) 526177 in Puerto Ayora, or (05) 520615 in San Cristóbal. Currently, they fly three times a week between Baltra and Puerto Villamil on Isabela; Baltra and San Cristóbal; and San Cristóbal and Puerto Villamil. Another airline, **Aerogal**, might also be serving the islands by the time you read this.

SPORTS AND OUTDOOR ACTIVITIES

WHALE WATCHING

Whale watching is on the rise in the Galápagos waters, where several species of large whales can sometimes be seen. With the exception of the bottlenose dolphin, no species is predictable enough to be reliably sighted, but boats cruising between the islands encounter them occasionally. Whales avoid boats that approach aggressively, and the most exciting encounters and opportunities to swim with them occur when the whales approach stationary boats themselves.

The most frequently seen baleen whale is the 12- to 15-m-long (40- to 50-ft) Bryde's whale. The 18-m (60-ft) finback and the 8-m (27-ft) minke whale have also been sighted, and there are occasional reports of 10-m (33-ft) humpback whales. Aside from baleen whales, the other most commonly sighted whales are 9- to 17-m (30 to 57-ft) sperm whales. Beaked whales and orcas (killer whales) are occasionally seen. Several species of dolphin live around the islands, but the only species consistently sociable with boats is the bottlenose dolphin. There's no point in approaching these dolphins; if they wish to swim with your boat, they will. **Galasam** (see below) runs recommended whale-watching tours.

SCUBA DIVING

The waters around the Galápagos offer some of the world's best scuba diving. Unpredictable conditions and a rich variety of underwater environments make for a constantly fascinating and exciting underwater environment. Offshore pinnacle reefs rise from submerged volcanoes, supporting rich sea life and big oceanic creatures. The Devil's Crown, a sunken volcano near Isla Santa María, is a marine wonderland of sea lions, turtles, rays, morays, garden eels, whitetip reef sharks, hammerhead sharks and thousands of tropical fish. Hydrothermal vents in these submerged volcanic peaks heat the waters to temperatures as high as 30°C (86°F). Scientists are particularly interested in these places because of the creatures that have adapted to live in such conditions. The northerly islands of Darwin and Wolf are regarded as the best islands for serious divers, with the chance of swimming alongside huge whale sharks.

Though diving can be straightforward, strong currents, sometimes-low visibility, large marine animals and cold water can be quite challenging. There are some good dive sites for beginners, but the Galápagos are *not* the place for beginning divers. There have been several fatalities (mainly off Darwin and Wolf) over the years, and there isn't a decompression chamber to be found on the islands (or in Ecuador, one worthy of the name). Even though the archipelago straddles the equatorial line, its waters are cooler than you might expect. Cold-water currents and upwellings can bring water temperatures as low as 10°C (50°F), though the average is 18°C (65°F) most of the year.

Charles Darwin was fascinated by the only sea-going lizard in the world, the marine iguana, which can swim underwater for up to an hour.

Galápagos Sub-Aqua (/FAX (05) 526350 IN QUITO (/FAX (022) 565294 E-MAIL sub_aqaua@ga .pro.ec WEB SITE www.galapagos-sub-aqua.com, on Avenida Charles Darwin at Puerto Ayora, offers a full range of diving services, including introductory diving, full certificate courses, daily and live-aboard diving tours and full equipment rental. Prices from US$80 per day for introductory diving, with two boat dives, to first-class, seven nights, live-aboard diving tours for up to US$2,000. Staff speak German and English. **Scuba Iguana** (/FAX (05) 526497 E-MAIL info@scubaiguana.com WEB SITE www.scubaiguana.com, based at Hotel Galápagos, operates similar courses and dive trips. They also offer discounts for divers at the hotel. Both organizations are highly recommended, and prices come down if you form a group. Some cruise boats also carry diving equipment on board.

SEA-KAYAKING, WINDSURFING AND MOUNTAIN BIKING

Although mainly confined to Santa Cruz island, challenging sea-kayaking and windsurfing trips around the islands can be arranged through the Red Mangrove Inn in Puerto Ayora (see WHERE TO STAY, page 232 in PUERTO AYORA). They can also rent excellent mountain bikes, as can one or two other operators in the town.

GALÁPAGOS TOURS

The best way to see the Galápagos is as Charles Darwin did, by boat. You sleep through the hours covering the considerable distances from island to island. Although expensive, most people book their tour of the Galápagos as a complete package with a travel agent in their home country. This usually includes international flights, hotels and transfers on the mainland, flights out to the Galápagos, and the complete cruise around the islands. Insurance, tips, alcoholic drinks and entrance fee to the Parque Nacional Galápagos aren't usually covered. Most packages fly you to Quito, and then on via Guayaquil to either Baltra or San Cristóbal, where you embark immediately on your boat.

Boat tours are mostly a week long, but larger boats often offer three- to four-day cruises as well. Most people visit two visitors' sites a day, one in the morning and another in the afternoon, and return to the boat to eat, sleep and relax. Be aware that you will rarely be the only group at a particular site. Some believe three or four days is enough time to spend on a boat and see the islands and the wildlife. But if you spend longer you will have a much deeper experience and discover the differences among the islands. Another plus is that you will encounter few other visitors on the more remote islands. Serious wildlife enthusiasts should consider going on a two-week tour to

some of the even more distant and less visited islands, as well as the central sites.

It is also possible to make your own arrangements to visit the Galápagos. You can buy your flights yourself and book your cruise when you arrive in Quito, Guayaquil or Puerto Ayora. You can save money this way, although in the high season (July, August, December, January and Easter Week) you risk not finding a vacancy on a cruise that suits you. If you have the time, a good plan is to make your way to Puerto Ayora outside the high season and shop around for a trip. This will give you a few days in Puerto Ayora, which itself is worthwhile and enjoyable. If you decide not to buy a cruise you can set up at Puerto Ayora or at Puerto Baquerizo Moreno on San Cristóbal and take day trips to the nearer islands.

About 100 vessels operate Galápagos cruises, ranging from simple, converted fishing boats to luxurious cruise ships. All rely on engine power

although some also have sails. Which you choose depends on your budget and the style of trip you prefer. The large, comfortable cruise ships offer private bathrooms, air conditioning, bars and sundecks, and carry up to 100 passengers. The smaller boats vary greatly from fairly simple six-passenger vessels to comfortable, modern yachts and catamarans carrying 12 to 16 passengers.

A guide licensed by the national parks service accompanies each cruise ship and, except in limited areas, no tourist is allowed on land in the park without a guide. A good guide who knows the Galápagos and its wildlife, and speaks your language, will immeasurably enrich your trip. Since the Galápagos is a "once-in-a-lifetime" destination, in my opinion, it's worth investing in a good ship and a good guide. Guides are rated by the national parks service as "Naturalist I, II or III" — III being the most qualified and experienced. Before booking a tour confirm that it will include

a fully qualified guide who is fluent in the language of your choice. They are responsible for enforcing national park rules, which stipulate among other things that visitors must stay on set trails and that no animals may be touched.

From your newspaper travel sections at home you can see how many tour operators offer Galápagos journeys. Prices can range from US$50 to over US$300 per day (excluding airfares) depending on the boat, facilities, season and how far in advance you reserve it. In general, the further you are from the islands when you buy a tour, the higher the cost, although with some of the most expensive cruises the cost will be the same in Quito, London or New York. Don't forget that the crew and the guides aren't paid well and are very dependent on tips. Each passenger is expected to

The stark beauty and incredible wildlife of the Galápagos Islands make a cruise around the archipelago one of the world's best travel experiences.

pay about US$4 per day for the crew and US$5 per day for the guide. The following is a selection of operators in Ecuador based on experience or strong recommendations. Exclusion of any company doesn't imply poor service.

Kleintours ((022) 430345 or (022) 461235 FAX (022) 442389 or (022) 469285 E-MAIL ecuador@ kleintours.com.ec WEB SITE www.galapagos ecuador.com, Avenida Shyris 1000 and Holanda, Quito, is one of the top operators in Ecuador. Kleintours' flagships are *Coral I* and *Coral II*, equipped to the highest standards. With room for only 20 passengers, *Coral I* just has the edge over her sister ship, which takes 26 on board. Both ships serve excellent food and the guides are first class. One week per person in a standard cabin in high season costs US$2,090.

Beluga, the best boat run by **Angermeyer's Enchanted Expeditions** ((022) 569960 FAX (022) 569956 E-MAIL angermeyer@accessinter.net WEB SITE www.angermeyer.com, Foch 726 and Juan León Mera, Quito, is a spacious and comfortable yacht that holds 16 passengers and has first-class guides and food. One week in a standard cabin costs US$1,900 per person. They also have two attractive sailing yachts, the *Cachalote* and the *Suledae*.

Latin Tour ((022) 508800 or (022) 508811 FAX (022) 568657 E-MAIL latintour@galapagos-tours.com WEB SITE www.galapagos-tours.com, Edificio Blanquius, Diego de Almagro 1219 at La Niña, Quito, own the beautiful 23-m (75-ft) catamaran *Freedom*, with an excellent crew, food and guides; they also run the cheaper motor-yacht *Pelícano*. They are one of the few operators to combine scuba diving with land tours. Weekly rates for the *Freedom* are around US$1,700 per person.

Metropolitan Touring ((022) 464780 FAX (022) 464702 E-MAIL info@metropolitan.com.ec WEB SITE www.ecuadorable.com, with a main office at Avenida República de El Salvador N36-84, Quito, is one of the longest-running and reliable operators in Ecuador. Its luxury boats include the *Santa Cruz*, the *Isabela II* and the *Delfín*. The latter combines stays at the Hotel Delfín on Santa Cruz for passengers who aren't keen on spending nights at sea. Bookings for the *Beagle III*, a former Darwin Research Station vessel, can also be made through Metropolitan. Get in touch with them for their rates, which start around US$1,600.

Quasar Nautica ((022) 441550 FAX (022) 436625, Avenida Shyris 2447, Edificio Autocom, Quito, is a high-quality operator of sail and power yachts, arranging diving cruises. They operate the luxury and impressive trimaran *Lammer Law* among others such as the *Alta, Resting Cloud* and *Parranda*. Prices on request; they run US$2,000 and up.

Canodros (/FAX (022) 442801 or (022) 256759 E-MAIL eco-tourism@canodros.com.ec WEB SITE www.canodros.com, Portugal 448 between Catalina de Aldaz and 6 de Diciembre, Quito, owns and operates the largest, and possibly most luxurious, vessel in the Galápagos, the *Galápagos Explorer II*.

Andes Discoveries ((022) 236446 FAX (022) 506293, Paraguay 229 and Selva Negra, Quito, is recommended for various boats excursions, from economy upwards, with rates beginning around US$1,000.

TRANSCORD ((022) 467441 FAX (022) 467443 E-MAIL admin@transcor.ecx.ec, Avenida República de El Salvador 112 and Avenida Shyris, Edificio Onix, Of. 9C, Quito, or PO Box 17-21-1062, Quito, has a good reputation for Galápagos cruises, either with their boat *Reina Silvia* or through other well-tested operators. Prices begin at under US$1,000.

Safari Tours ((022) 234799 or (022) 552505 FAX (022) 223381 E-MAIL admin@safari.com.ec WEB SITE www.safari.com.ec, Pasaje Roca, off Calle Roca (between Amazonas and Juan León Mera), Quito, is not a Galápagos operator, but keeps a database of boats with current vacancies and offers trips at wholesale price, plus a US$30 reservation fee. They are very useful for last-minute reservations.

In Puerto Ayora, you'll find quite a few companies vying for last-minute, cheaper trips. Among the established and reputable agencies are: **Galasam**, close to the dock, IN QUITO ((022) 507080 or (022) 507081 FAX (022) 567662 E-MAIL galapagos @galasam.com.ec WEB SITE www.galasam.com.ec, Pinto 523 and Amazonas, IN GUAYAQUIL ((042) 306289 or 313724 FAX (042) 313351 or 562033, Avenida 9 de Octubre 424, Edificio Gran Pasaje, Eleventh Floor, Guayaquil; and **Moonrise Travel Agency** (/FAX (05) 526403 or 526348, Avenida Charles Darwin (facing Banco del Pacífico), an excellent agent for last-minute reservations, as inexpensive as dealing with boat captains directly.

HOW TO GET THERE

By Air

TAME flies from Quito to the Galápagos via Guayaquil twice every morning, except Sundays in the low season. Sometimes flights are added in the high season. Flights leave Quito and stopover in Guayaquil before the 90-minute flight to the Galápagos. TAME either flies to Baltra airport (north of Santa Cruz island), or to San Cristóbal island. If you're joining a cruise, make sure you fly to the island from which your boat will depart (Baltra for Puerto Ayora, and San Cristóbal for Puerto Baquerizo Moreno).

The cost of a Quito–Galápagos–Quito ticket is US$378 (including taxes). In the low season

The frigate bird, one of the most spectacular species in the Galápagos. Though they cannot land in water themselves, they harass other seabirds for their prey.

(January 16 to June 14, and September 1 to November 30) it's US$323. You can also fly from Guayaquil at a reduced price or depart Quito and end your journey in Guayaquil. Student discounts are available with an international student ID card. Less expensive fares can be obtained in some countries if the Galápagos leg is added on to your ticket to Ecuador.

Flights to the islands are often overbooked, so you should arrive at the airport at least an hour before departure. Agencies often block-book seats, so even if TAME says the flight is fully booked, hunt around the agencies in Quito. The agencies often release their tickets on the day of departure, so it's still worth getting on a waiting list and trying your luck at the airport anyway. Tuesdays are said to be best for same-day ticket purchases.

If you are on a tour, your boat's representative will meet you when you arrive at Baltra. He or she will then make sure you board your boat, either at the port in Baltra or at Puerto Ayora. If you are traveling independently, immediately buy a bus ticket from the counter inside the terminal. The bus will take you to the ferry to Santa Cruz. Another bus carries you on to Puerto Ayora. The whole complicated procedure can take up to two hours. On departure, the procedure is reversed, with buses leaving Puerto Ayora or from your hotel in the morning to enable you to catch flights from Baltra that leave at about 11:30 AM. Arrangements on San Cristóbal are much simpler, as the airport is a 10-minute walk from the town of Puerto Baquerizo Moreno. At either place, make sure you reconfirm your return ticket at least two days ahead (most agencies do this for you). You must bring your passport with you to enter the Galápagos. For a nice, free souvenir, ask the official to give your passport a unique "Parque Nacional Galápagos" stamp upon entry or exit.

BY BOAT

Most believe it's not worth trying to save money buying an inexpensive passage from Guayaquil. Cargo boats, military boats and expensive cruise ships make the crossing, but never on a schedule. If you have an aversion to flying, your best plan is to check with shipping agents in Guayaquil or go to the harbor and ask the port *capitán* if there's a boat about to head off to the islands. The M/V *Piquero* leaves on the 25th of each month, or thereabouts. More information on this tramp steamer can be obtained from Johnny Franco of **Acotramar** ((042) 401004 or 404314 FAX (042) 444852. The crossing takes three-and-a-half days and costs US$150, one way. Passengers are advised to bring their own rations, sleeping bags or hammock (and seasickness tablets!). If you happen to own a yacht,

you pay a mooring fee at the ports, and the parks entrance fee. The permit to cruise the islands costs thousands of dollars, and most people therefore join a tour arranged in Puerto Ayora.

THE CENTRAL ISLANDS

In rough terms, there are about a dozen major, a dozen minor and 50 small islands and islets in the Galápagos chain. Of these only five are inhabited: Santa Cruz, Baltra, San Cristóbal, Santa María (usually known as Floreana) and Isabela. The capital of Ecuador's Galápagos Province is Puerto Baquerizo Moreno on Isla San Cristóbal, although the largest town is Puerto Ayora on Santa Cruz.

BALTRA

Most visitors land at the airport on the small, flat island of Baltra, just north of the main tourist island of Santa Cruz, where they are confronted by a dry, desert-like moonscape of brown lava rock and tall cactus plants and windblown trees. American forces built the runway to defend the Panama Canal in World War II. The airport was given to Ecuador after the war, and is now the main entry point for tourists to the islands. There is an Ecuadorian naval base to the west of the island and a small port for cruise ships and cargo boats. The Ecuadorian army supervises the island. On landing, visitors have to pay a national parks entry fee of US$100. There are no visitors' sites on the island.

NORTH SEYMOUR

This small island, close to the airport on Baltra, is a popular stopping point for cruise boats because it has one of the most active nesting colonies of frigate birds. Here visitors can see the splendid male frigate bird puffing up its big red chest pouch in a flamboyant courtship display to attract females. Blue-footed boobies, marine iguanas and sea lions are also plentiful on the island. North Seymour is often the last stop on a cruise before passengers fly out from Baltra, formerly known as South Seymour. The nearby islet of **Mosquera**, only 600 m (2,000 ft) long, has a sandy beach with a sea lion colony, and is sometimes the first stop on a boat tour of the islands.

DAPHNE MAJOR AND MINOR

These two small, barren tips of submerged volcanoes are surrounded by steep cliffs, undercut by waves, making it very difficult to land. The main claim to fame of Daphne Major is that for nearly two decades it's been the site of a major scientific research program. Peter and Rosemary Grant and their assistants have been investigating and measuring the characteristics of the island's varying population of Darwin's finches over some 20 generations. The results of their work show an intimate and fascinating portrait of evolution as it happens in real time. Jonathan Weiner, author of a book about this research, *The Beak of the Finch*, which won the 1995 Pulitzer Prize, described the Grants' project as "one of the most remarkable works in progress on this planet."

SANTA CRUZ AND PUERTO AYORA

Most visitors get to know Santa Cruz better than the other islands. Unless a cruise boat meets them, passengers arriving at Baltra take a bus from the

For people used to living in big cities, Puerto Ayora, with a population of some 10,000, is a peaceful, pleasant, fishing port. Big-billed pelicans dive for fish in Pelican Bay, while sea lions and marine iguanas sunbathe on the rocks by the shore and on the terraces of seaside cafés. Bicycles, pickup trucks and motor scooters make up most of the traffic around the waterfront, and there are only two sets of traffic lights in town. Most visitors board boats here for island cruises, while others simply enjoy a few day's break onshore, availing themselves of a choice of bars, restaurants, hotels, dive shops, souvenir shops, travel agents and banks.

Many residents and others who have known the island for decades are shocked by the devel-

airport (no taxis are available) before transferring to a small ferry to cross the Itabaca Channel to Santa Cruz. Another bus then takes them on a 40-km (25-mile), one-hour ride over the top of the island and down to the small town of Puerto Ayora. This empty, straight, narrow road cuts through vegetation zones of the island, from arid north shore to wet, green highlands. Some tour buses stop in the highlands so passengers can stretch their legs and look at the twin craters, known as **Los Gemelos**, one each side of the road, outside the village of **Santa Rosa**. These 30-m-deep (100-ft) holes in the earth look as if they were caused by volcanic explosion or blasted by meteorites, but in fact are thought to be caved-in magma chambers. Dense scalesia forest surrounding the craters abounds with wildlife. Birders should watch out for vermilion flycatchers and the diurnal short-eared owl.

opment of Puerto Ayora in recent years. In 1980 the population was less than a quarter of what it was in 2000. A former Galápagos tour guide told me there was only one car on the island when he first came to Santa Cruz in the 1970s. Jimmy Perez, owner of Hotel Sol y Mar, arrived in the early 1960s as a beachcomber, when there were only 120 inhabitants on the whole island, most of them farmers.

The main concern of Señor Perez and others is that the rising population, mostly from mainland Ecuador, is harming the archipelago's ecosystem through illegal fishing and encroachment on national parks. Insufficient electricity, fresh water, garbage disposal services, education and medical facilities are also problems caused by population pressure and the increasing number

Puerto Ayora on Isla Santa Cruz, the largest town on the Galápagos with a population of 10,000.

of tourists. Proposals are now being considered on limiting the number of tourists, and the number of immigrants from the mainland who come to the archipelago hoping to make a living from tourists, but the issue remains extremely thorny, to say the least.

General Information

Orientation is pretty easy in town. The two main avenues are the shoreline Avenida Charles Darwin (winding northeastwards from the docks) and Avenida Padre Julio Herrera, which runs northwest from the traffic circle close to the docks at the southern end of town. Although there is a **tourism office** on Charles Darwin, better maps and

local information is available from the **Galápagos Chamber of Tourism (** (05) 526206 FAX (05) 526609 WEB SITE www.galapagoschamberoftourism.org, a few doors down. To date, there is only one bank in Puerto Ayora, **Banco del Pacífico**, which only has a MasterCard ATM. In general MasterCard is preferred to Visa by shops and hotels. Most hotels, shops or tour operators will change travelers' checks. The **Pacifictel** office is three blocks up Avenida Padre Julio Herrera. The **TAME office** is unmissable for its ugliness on Avenida Charles Darwin. The best supermarket is **Proinsular** by the dock, with the **Post Office** nearby. You're better off sending postcards or letters on the mainland (or from the post barrel on Floreana — see SANTA MARÍA, page 237). There are now several expensive Internet cafés. The best is Casvernet, by the tortoise traffic circle on Charles Darwin. Prices will come down once the island acquires its own server.

Hotels, restaurants and bars open, close and change hands frequently on Santa Cruz so it's worth asking fellow travelers and agents for the latest recommendations.

What to See and Do

Aside from the warm climate and the vacation atmosphere, the main attractions at Puerto Ayora are the **Charles Darwin Research Station** and the headquarters of the **Parque Nacional Galápagos**, a 15-minute walk northeast from town. At the Darwin Station giant tortoises are born and bred in captivity.

Visitors see how hatchling giant tortoises are incubated in dark boxes for the first two weeks of their lives, then transferred to outdoor corrals for two or three years. Then they are released into bigger, adoption corrals, which simulate natural conditions of the islands, where they learn to walk on lava rocks and how to find water. At four or five years old their shells are hard enough to protect them from predators, and they are released into the wild.

The last dozen or so remaining tortoises on Española island were taken into the center, where some 200 offspring were brought up in captivity before being taken back to their island. A similar scheme for the Pinzón tortoise has been equally successful. The center has returned nearly 3,000 tortoises to their native islands throughout the archipelago.

One tortoise who will probably never leave Darwin Station is Lonesome George, the sole survivor of the Pinta breed. Found unexpectedly on Pinta in 1971, he is now a resident of Santa Cruz. In spite of thorough searches of his birthplace, no mate has been found for George. There is a US$10,000 reward for anyone who does—a tricky proposition for a bounty hunter because only qualified scientists are allowed on the island.

George, who is from the biggest of the saddle-back subspecies, shares his corral at the Darwin Station with two females from Volcán Wolf on Isabela. Although from a subspecies that is very similar to George's, the old man doesn't show interest in mating. Scientists have taken the precaution of extracting and deep-freezing George's sperm for possible use in the future.

The chance to say good-bye to a dying breed is one of the high points of a visit to the Darwin Center, but also interesting is the walk-in tortoise enclosure for almost face-to-face meetings with other incredible, armor-plated hulks, though visitors should refrain from touching them. In addition there's a museum, an exhibition center, a souvenir shop selling T-shirts to support the research station, and trails through salt bush, mangrove and cacti plantations populated by Darwin's finches and other birds.

A visit to the Darwin Station can be a hot and exhausting experience, after which a swim might be very welcome. The best place for this is **Tortuga (Turtle) Bay**, three kilometers (just under two miles) southwest of Puerto Ayora. The bay has a fine white beach, one of the best on the archipelago, beautiful blue sea and a lagoon protected by a spit of land. Sea turtles come to lay their eggs here, but you're more likely to spot pelicans, marine iguanas and flamingos. Although the wildlife is protected you don't need to be accompanied by a guide and you could well have the beach to yourself.

Most visitors don't spend much time, if any, in Puerto Ayora because they are on cruises from the beginning to the end of their island stay. And it's true that the best way to see the wildlife is by boat. Some people make reservations when they get to Puerto Ayora, which means they usually get a cruise for a lower, last-minute price (in the low season), though they might have to spend a few days on Santa Cruz. This is no hardship. Aside from relaxing in the warm sunshine, there are plenty of places to explore and things to do on Santa Cruz.

The fit and adventurous go hiking or horse riding in the highlands. A bus from Puerto Ayora takes you to the inland villages of **Bellavista** and **Santa Rosa**. Check departure times with a local travel agent or at the CITTEG (bus company) because service isn't frequent. From Bellavista you can climb the cinder cone of **Media Luna**. The base of the tallest peak of Santa Cruz, **Mount Crocker** (864 m or 2,835 ft), is three kilometers (nearly two miles) further on. The view from the peak of

Mount Crocker is spectacular, taking in the scalesia forest pushing up the lava slopes of the barren volcano and some surrounding islands studded in the emerald sea.

From Santa Rosa, you can visit the wild **Tortoise Reserve** — wild because of the dense, unruly vegetation, and because the tortoises aren't tame like those at Darwin Station. The best way to see the reserve is with a guide and atop a horse. Guides can be hired and horses arranged through travel agents in Puerto Ayora. There are also a couple of private farms in the area, which supply refreshments and allow you to watch tortoises drinking at a watering hole for a small fee. Another place to watch the lumbering giants in the wild is on Volcán Alcedo on Isabela.

From Bellavista, it's a short walk to the nearby **Lava Tunnels**, long tubes of rock formed by the solidification of a lava flow during a volcanic eruption. There are several such tubes on the island but these are the most impressive, one of which is about a kilometer (just over a half mile) long and as high and wide as a subway tunnel. It is known as "The Tunnel of Endless Love," because of a heart-shaped hole in its roof. Guides with torches can be hired at Bellavista to explore these dark labyrinths.

Several coves and beaches cut into the isolated and rarely visited northwestern shore of Santa Cruz. The most interesting of these is **Caleta Tortuga Negra** (Black Turtle Cove) where green turtles can sometimes be seen during the breeding season, from September to February.

An ethnographic museum for the islands, **Museo Galápagos**, on Charles Binford up from Banco del Pacífico, might be up and running by the time you read this. Its web site address will be www.galapagosmuseum.com.

Shopping

Nearly every house between the wharf and the Research Station seems to sell souvenirs from the Galápagos, including the famous "I love boobies" T-shirts. If you're not going to have any time in Quito, then buy things here, but otherwise they're considerably cheaper on the mainland. For a purchase above the run-of-the-mill trinkets or T-shirts, two places stand out. One is the gallery of resident British painter Sarah Darling, called **Angelique Art Gallery**, close to the dock, which sells her wonderfully vivid oil paintings of the islands and their animals, as well as colorful mirrors and silk scarves. See Sarah's work at WEB SITE www.sarahdarling.com. The other place is **Bambú**, on Charles Darwin, beyond the tortoise traffic circle by the Media Luna restaurant.

Carl Angermeyer, seen on the right in his house on Isla Santa Cruz, is a pioneer of tourism in the Galápagos.

Where to Stay

Santa Cruz is the only one of the five inhabited islands that has a decent choice of land-based accommodation ranging from budget to almost first class. During the popular vacation times of June, July, August, December, early January and Easter it's advisable to make reservations. Prices are much higher compared to the mainland. At the time of writing, a five-star luxury hotel was under construction up in the hills of Santa Cruz, called the Royal Palm and run by the Millennium Group. For more details, contact Furio Balvonesi ((05) 526018.

At the top end of the price scale (very expensive) is the well-established **Hotel Galápagos (** (05)

526296 FAX (05) 526330 E-MAIL jack@hotelgalapagos .com WEB SITE www.scuba-iguana.com. Although the gardens are attractive and tranquil, the bungalow-style rooms have about as much charm as a telephone directory, and the furniture is pretty dated. All 14 rooms have baths, hot showers and wide ocean views over Academy Bay. The American owner, Jack Nelson, also part-owns the adjoining scuba school, and is very knowledgeable and friendly. Also in the top league for both price and quality is the **Hotel Delfín (** (05) 526297 FAX (05) 526283 E-MAIL rsievers@ecuanet.net (or book through Metropolitan Touring — see GALÁPAGOS TOURS, above), on the opposite side of Academy Bay, reached only by boat. The biggest draws are the hotel's peaceful beach, hidden location and its decent-sized swimming pool. The 21 rooms are comfortable if unimaginative, with beach views and private bathrooms, but no hot water. The owner, Rolf Sievers, also owns the luxury yacht *Reina Silvia* for island cruises or day trips.

The most appealing and original choice in Puerto Ayora is the chic but informal **Red Mangrove Inn (**/FAX (05) 526564 E-MAIL redmangrove @ecuadorexplorer.com WEB SITE www.ecuador explorer.com/redmangrove, whose rates range from expensive to very expensive. The hotel

commands fine views across Academy Bay from its wide, wooden terrace (or from its sunken Jacuzzi), and each room is decorated individually in bright colors. Prices depend on whether they have sea views or not, and on the season. If he's home, affable owner Polo Navarro will help with any travel arrangements. The hotel rents sea kayaks, windsurfers and mountain bikes, as well as organizing fishing, diving or camping trips. The hotel has a tasty but pricey restaurant on request.

Close to the Red Mangrove on Charles Darwin at Piqueros, the **Hotel Angermeyer (** (05) 526186 includes nearly 30 clean and comfortable rooms, as well as a swimming pool and room service, but lacks character (expensive). The restaurant enjoys a good reputation. At the time of writing, the hotel was closed and its future uncertain, but likely to reopen.

Moderately priced hotels are in short supply at Puerto Ayora. For individuality and a splendid location on the waterfront in sight of fishing boats and diving pelicans, **Hotel Sol y Mar (** (05) 526281, owned by the somewhat eccentric Jimmy Perez, is recommended. Marine iguanas eye you calmly as you breakfast on the terrace. Prices depend on the season and whether the room overlooks the sea. Accommodation is clean and functional, if not wildly comfortable, but the restaurant and bar are recommended.

Further down the price scale, the next best bet with sea views is the **Hotel Lobo del Mar (** (05) 526188 or (05) 526569. Most rooms have balconies and cold-water showers. The only decent budget option with hot showers is the **Estrella del Mar (** (05) 526427. Both of these are down the road by the TAME offices. **Hotel Darwin (** (05) 526193, Avenida Padre Julio Herrera, has a pleasant courtyard and relaxed atmosphere, but also worn paintwork and old beds and plumbing. Other hotels and hostels worth checking out are **Residencial Los Amigos (** (05) 526265, with shared cold showers, and the friendly **Bed and Breakfast La Peregrina (** (05) 526323.

Where to Eat

None of Puerto Ayora's restaurants are outstanding, and most are expensive compared to the rest of the country. If you can, refrain from eating lobster here since it's been dangerously overfished. For good seafood and meat dishes, **La Garrapata**, on Charles Darwin, has a pleasant atmosphere and is popular with locals in the evening. Also good in the evening is **Limón y Café** serving lighter snacks with a good bar. Further along, the best set-lunch in town is probably at **Espondylus**, tucked in close to Galápagos Sub-Aqua. Close-by is the **Trattoria de Pippo**, serving Italian staples including risotto and tasty pizzas. Keep going, and **Kathy's Kitchen** serves good meals and snacks in the high season, and **Media Luna** also comes recommended for its international dishes and friendly service (closed Tuesdays). By the docks, **Restaurant Salvavidas** has been going for years and is reliable for a quick bite. The nearby **Rocky's** bar and grill is a more pleasant, but expensive, option. The road leading up from the harbor, Avenida Padre Julio Herrera, has a number of good-value bars and restaurants including **Restaurante El Sabrosón**, which serves excellent grilled meats (*parrilladas*) and seafood.

The best and liveliest bar in town is the **Bongo Bar**, upstairs from the popular **La Panga** *discoteca*, by the La Garrapata on Charles Darwin.

NORTH AND SOUTH PLAZA

The twin islands of North and South Plaza lie just off the east coast of Santa Cruz. North Plaza is reserved for scientific research and is closed to visitors, while South Plaza has plentiful wildlife and makes an excellent day trip from Puerto Ayora. If you are on a cruise boat it's better to visit South Plaza in the early morning or late afternoon to avoid other day-trippers. South Plaza's best-known resident is a huge, bad-tempered gentle-man sea lion by the name of Charlie who jealously guards his harem. Charlie sometimes sits on the landing dock in an attempt to keep visitors away, but a few loud handclaps should be enough to make him let you pass. Charlie's entourage of females and pups are a playful, frolicsome bunch who play chicken with snorkelers by swimming up close to them underwater and veering off at the last minute. Such an encounter makes for one of the most breathtaking Galápagos experiences, but isn't dangerous unless Charlie himself mistakes you for a competing male. Sea lions from a bachelor colony live above the cliffs on the other side of the island, sharing their rocky home with a host of seabirds from blue-footed and masked boobies to frigate birds, tropic birds, pelicans and swallowtail gulls. Large, brown-yellow land iguanas lumber over the lava rocks in search of fruit from colossal prickly pear cacti.

SANTA FÉ

This small island, just 24 sq km (just over nine square miles) and only 20 km (12 miles) south-east of Santa Cruz, is home to a unique subspecies of land iguana which is bigger than its cousins on other islands of the archipelago, sometimes growing up to 120 cm (four feet) in length. These un-friendly looking, cactus-guzzling reptiles with long tails, clawed feet, spiny dorsal crests and bloodshot eyes look like mythical creatures from the medieval traditions.

There are two marked paths on the island. One is a steep trail of about one and a half kilometers (nearly a mile), which heads for the iguana colony

in the highlands. The other is a short walk from the landing point to a stand of giant cacti. Popular with day visitors from Santa Cruz, the island includes a sea lion colony and a pleasant blue lagoon, though swimmers should keep an eye out for stingrays. Santa Fé's unique subspecies of giant tortoise was exterminated about 100 years ago by American and European whalers and sealers, who hunted them for meat.

PINZÓN

At the end of the nineteenth century the Pinzón tortoise was dangerously near extinction because of depredations by whalers, sealers and scientific collectors. However, a captive breeding and rein-troduction program at the Darwin Center, and the eradication of black rats that eat tortoise eggs and young hatchlings, has rescued this saddleback breed. Visits to this cliff-ringed, 12-sq-km (four-and-a-half-square-mile) island, also known as Duncan, are usually restricted to scientists.

RÁBIDA

Formerly known as Jervis, this five-square-kilo-meter (two-square-mile) island is one of the best snorkeling spots of the Galápagos, as well as the best place to see nesting pelicans. The ubiquitous sea lions lounge on a red sand beach and pink flamingos can occasionally be seen wading in a brackish lagoon.

SAN SALVADOR

The fourth-largest island of the archipelago, San Salvador (often referred to by one of its former names, Santiago or James) is also the largest un-inhabited island. In the 1920s, and again in the 1960s, salt was mined from the inside of a volca-nic crater on the western end of the island. When the Parque Nacional Galápagos was created in 1968, all property and mining rights were annulled and the island lost its small human population. San Salvador is overpopulated by feral goats and other animals left behind, despite the national park authorities' attempts to control them. A few abandoned buildings are all that can be seen of the old salt mine.

What to See and Do

San Salvador is a popular destination for cruise boats, and there are four sites where visitors are allowed to land. The most impressive is the black sand and lava shoreline of **Puerto Egas** in **James Bay** on the west coast, with its eroded rock forma-tions, caves and inlets, which are home to a vari-ety of wildlife including fur seals and a large colony

A giant opuntia cactus on South Plaza, off the east coast of Santa Cruz.

of marine iguanas. Rock pools in the area known as **Grottoes** abound with anemones, hermit crabs and tiny fish that are a feast for oystercatchers, herons and other seabirds.

Energetic hikers can take a rocky, two-kilometer (just over a mile) trail from Puerto Egas to the peak of Sugarloaf Volcano for a magnificent view of the island. A less demanding hike goes to the crater with the old salt mine. At the north end of James Bay, best reached by boat, is **Playa Espumilla (Foam Beach)** where the swimming is good and the sand is golden.

Beautiful **Buccaneer Cove**, further northwards along the coast from James Bay, was a popular haven for pirates in the seventeenth and eighteenth centuries. On the red beach below the dramatic palisade of cliffs the mariners tilted the hulls of their boats. In search of food supplies, they hunted for giant tortoises and the island's now-extinct land iguanas. Today, Buccaneer Cove is better known for its sea lions, seabirds and snorkeling.

Instead of a sandy beach, **Sullivan Bay**, on the eastern tip of San Salvador, boasts a wide moonscape of solid black lava, which might be the most extraordinary coastline you will ever see. In the middle of this enormous field of ropy lava formations are two imposing tuff cones, rocks that were surrounded by the flow of molten lava about 100 years ago.

BARTOLOMÉ

Bartolomé's popularity is way out of proportion to its size. Just over a square kilometer (less than half a square mile) in area, the island is not much more than a stone's throw from San Salvador. A short walk to the 114-m (374-ft) peak of the island is rewarded by magnificent views of the archipelago. Looking westwards towards San Salvador, you see one of the most photographed views in the Galápagos with **Pinnacle Rock** on the northern shore of Bartolomé standing like a finger pointing defiantly to the sky. Galápagos penguins swim the waters below this rock. This is the best place to see these comical creatures, unless you have the time to visit colonies on Fernandina and the western side of Isabela. Bartolomé is truly a lunar landscape, with twisted lava formations, sparse plant life, but plenty of sea creatures, including nesting turtles (late December until early March) and great blue herons.

SOMBRERO CHINO

Also just off the coast of Bartolomé lies the tiny, conical island whose name means "Chinese Hat." A beautiful blue lagoon separates it from the larger island, where there are some good snorkeling spots. A small colony of sea lions inhabits a beach on the north shore, where there is a visitor site.

ISABELA

Isabela, at 4,588 sq km (1,771 sq miles), is by far the largest island and boasts the tallest point of the archipelago, the 1,646-m (5,400-ft) Volcán Wolf. Stretching 132 km (82 miles) from north to south and 84 km (52 miles) at its widest, the island includes more than half the land area of the Galápagos. A wild and inaccessible place of rumbling volcanoes, the island supports a population of about 1,000.

The main settlement, **Puerto Villamil** on the southeast coast, has a grim history, and some visitors feel a dismal, end-of-the-world feeling

hanging in the air. Not many cruise boats visit Puerto Villamil because of its distance from the main tourist areas and because of the difficulty entering the bay in rough weather. A few kilometers west of the village is the site of a penal colony, now destroyed, which had a reputation for cruelty. Little remains except an enormous basalt wall, known as the **Wall of Tears**, which was built from lava blocks by prisoners. Further on from here there's an airport, which had to be abandoned because the runway was badly positioned.

Despite its size, Puerto Villamil has a few shops, one or two excellent budget hotels, and the odd bar and disco. A short walk from the village is the white sand **Lover's Beach** and a lagoon, said to be the best place to see water birds in the Galápagos. Puerto Villamil might well turn into a major tourist area like Puerto Ayora.

What to See and Do

From Puerto Villamil, visitors can take a bus or a rental truck to the little hamlet of **Santo Tomás** on the slopes of the volcano of the same name (but also called **Sierra Negra**). From there it's a nine-kilometer (five-mile) hike or horse ride (horses can be rented in the hamlet) to the rim of the volcano. The views here are magnificent — weather permitting. It's a further eight-kilometer (five-mile) hike around the rim to see the belching fumaroles.

Isabela is well known for its population of several thousand giant Galápagos tortoises. Tortoise subspecies on the island have developed over hundreds of years around each volcano. Intervening fields of jagged lava rocks has pre-

vented tortoises lumbering from one volcanic area to another, intermingling the species. Feral goats, descendants of domestic animals brought by humans, are more agile and able to cope with the rugged terrain. Goats eat cactus, the staple diet of the tortoises, and thus threaten the older inhabitants with extinction. In an attempt to prevent such an ecological tragedy, shooting parties regularly venture to Isabela to control the goat population.

The best place to see giant tortoises is on **Volcán Alcedo**, home to the biggest population on the island. It isn't a quick and easy journey. The usual procedure is to join a boat in Puerto Ayora that takes you to **Shipton Cove**, halfway down the eastern coast of Isabela. From the beach, a three-to five-hour hike takes you to the rim of the volcano, the last steep haul being particularly difficult because of loose volcanic scree. The slopes of Alcedo become very hot in the middle of the

day so it's advisable to start your climb before dawn. With little shade en route, you must bring water and other supplies with you. If possible, arrange to camp for one or two nights on the rim of the volcano, from where there are wonderful views across the island and down 200 m (656 ft) into the immense lava field of the seven-kilometer-wide (four-and-a-half-mile) caldera itself.

Walking around the rim for another three or four hours, you will come to fumaroles of spewing vaporous gases. Tortoises tend to hide under bushes or in burrows in hot season to avoid the sun, but during rainy season, from June to December, hundreds of giant tortoises can be seen in or around the caldera wallowing in muddy pools.

Isabela is also a breeding ground for the world's only flightless cormorant. Occasionally these rare birds can be seen around **Punta Garcia**, further northwards up the coast from Shipton Cove, but the birds may have deserted this area for the more populous and inaccessible colonies in the west of the island. Moving up to the northern tip of Isabela, **Punta Albemarle** is a remote and seldom-visited promontory that was an American radar base during World War II.

Unless you spend a few weeks in the Galápagos Islands, you are unlikely to have time to discover the desolate charm and teeming bird life of western Isabela. But if your heart is set on seeing the unique flightless cormorant, you can find several colonies along the coast. The other

There are some 28 endemic and 60 resident bird species and in the Galápagos. LEFT TO RIGHT: A hawk, a brown pelican, and a blue-footed booby.

flightless bird, the Galápagos penguin, also resides here. One of the best places to see them is from a boat off the cliffs of **Tagus Cove**. Some of the cliffs and the rocks of the cove are covered with names of boats and people inscribed by sailors who used the bay for refuge. If you land here you can take a wooden stairway to a viewpoint overlooking **Darwin Lake**, a circular, lagoon that was raised above sea level by tectonic movements. Walking on further, you come to another panoramic viewpoint. So jagged are the lava rocks here you could lose the soles of solid boots if you walked over them for more than four kilometers (two and half miles). Wild dogs in the area have adapted to their environment by growing extrathick pads on their feet and acquiring the capacity to drink seawater.

Other visitors' sites on the west coast of Isabela include **Urvina Bay**, **Elizabeth Bay** and **Punta Moreno**. Giant tortoises can sometimes be seen at Urvina Bay, along with iguanas, pelicans and flightless cormorants. A short walk after landing on a white sand beach is the bizarre sight of coral reef stranded on land, tectonically uplifted from the ocean floor in 1954. Further down the coast, an inlet on **Elizabeth Bay** penetrates deep into an aquatic mangrove forest before opening up into a maze of convoluted channels and lagoons inhabited by green turtles, rays and an array of seabirds. There is no landing site at Elizabeth Bay. At Punta Moreno visitors can land on a lava flow where there are pools and small lagoons, the feeding grounds for a variety of birds, including pintails, flamingos and great blue herons. Feral dogs prowl the area on the lookout for a tasty morsel of baby sea lion or marine iguana.

Where to Stay and Eat

Though limited to the budget end of the market, accommodation in Puerto Villamil is surprisingly good for such a small town. **La Casa Marita ℂ** (05) 529238 FAX (05) 529201 E-MAIL hcmarita@ga.pro.ec includes attractive beachfront rooms sleeping up to four people, with kitchenettes and hot showers. Well-known and highly recommended is **Hotel Ballena Azul ℂ**/FAX (05) 529125, with large airy rooms, mosquito nets, ocean views: excellent value. Hostess Dora Gruber enjoys chatting with her guests in several languages. On the road to the highlands, **Hotel Tero Real ℂ** (05) 529106, with its triangular, red-roofed bungalows, has friendly management and is also very good value. Also recommended and slightly less expensive is **Posada San Vicente**, where the owner can arrange horse rides up the volcano.

Ballena Azul also has a good reputation for fine food at reasonable prices. Breakfast is particularly scrumptious, but it's advisable to let Dora know in advance if you would like lunch or dinner. On the beach, the restaurant at **Hotel Loja**

is recommended. Other restaurants in town worth checking out are **Costa Azul**, **Restaurant Iguana** and **Ruta**. Don't expect a wide choice of fare at any of these establishments.

How to Get There

Most people come to Isabela on cruise ships, but the adventurous who want to spend more time on this beautiful island should travel independently. There are occasional flights on a five-seat plane from Baltra. Check with your travel agent or call Dora at the Ballena Azul for more information. Alternatively, the government-run transportation service INGALA (Instituto Nacional Galápagos) operates weekly ferries that leave Santa Cruz for Isabela on Thursdays at 8 AM and return on Fridays at 10 AM. There's also a private ferry, the *Estrella Mar,* which leaves Isabela to Santa Cruz on Tuesdays at 10:30 AM and returns the next day at the same time. Be sure to double check these schedules and buy your ticket at least a day in advance. Fares are around US$30 each way. Ask around for passages on private boats and yachts.

FERNANDINA

Fernandina is the third largest, the geologically youngest and the most volcanically active of the Galápagos Islands. This uninhabited island is also the most remote and least visited of the main islands. **Volcán La Cumbre** (1,463 m or 4,800 ft) erupts regularly, most recently in 1995, when lava flowed into the ocean for over a month, and the cone of the volcano shifted and changed in shape. Columns of sulfurous smoke and steam rose 4,000 m (13,120 ft) into the air, with extremely loud echoing explosions and a cacophony of hissing and popping and low-level thumps. Dead mesopelagic fish from the depths floated on the steaming and bubbling surface of the water, which reached a temperature of 60°C (140°F). Biology was in confusion.

Exactly 170 years earlier the captain of the American schooner *Tartar,* which was off the coast one night in February 1825, wrote this account of an eruption on Narborough, as the island was then called. "The heavens appeared to be one blaze of fire, intermingled with millions of falling stars and meteors; while flames shot upwards from the peak of Narborough to the height of at least two thousand feet in the air... the boiling contents of the tremendous cauldron had swollen to the brim, and poured over the edge of the crater in a cataract of liquid fire. A river of melted lava was now seen rushing down the side of the mountain, pursuing a serpentine course to the sea... the demon of fire seemed rushing to the embraces of Neptune; and dreadful indeed was the uproar occasioned by their meeting. The ocean boiled and roared and bellowed…" The captain also recorded that when the temperature of the sea rose to 65°C (150°F), melted pitch ran from the vessel's seams and tar dropped from the riggings. Had not a lucky breeze helped its escape, the *Tartar* would certainly have fallen apart and sank.

In addition to being one of the world's most volcanically active islands, Fernandina is also considered one of the most pristine for lack of nonnative plants and animals. There are no feral dogs or donkeys on Fernandina, nor goats, rats, pigs and cats. With such an environment to protect it is easy to understand why the national parks service insists on precautions to avoid transportation of seeds or any animal forms to the island

— visitors are required to wash their shoes before landing. Because of these measures, neither flightless cormorants nor marine iguanas have predators on the island and are left to multiply in safety. In this sense Fernandina is the only place in the Galápagos where you can travel back in time and see the island before arrival of humanity.

Fernandina has been associated with illegal harvesting and smuggling of protected sea cucumbers. Encouraged by Japanese fishermen, Ecuadorians have harvested huge quantities of these creatures off the coast of Fernandina for shipment to Asia.

What to See and Do

Fernandina has only one visitors' site, at **Punta Espinosa** on the northwest coast, opposite Isabela. Here thousands of marine iguanas lie about in the sun, digesting their dinners and shooting sprays

of salt water into the air in fits of iguanic sneezing. There are also sea lions, flightless cormorants and a few Galápagos penguins. Snorkelers swimming in the clear waters of the lagoon will see rays, whitetip sharks, turtles and plenty of brilliantly colored tropical fish.

THE SOUTHERN ISLANDS

SANTA MARÍA (FLOREANA)

Usually known as Floreana, sometimes called Charles, Santa María was colonized by convicts in the nineteenth century, the first of the Galápagos islands to sustain a human population. The island has since acquired a reputation for murder, mystery and curious goings-on. The best known murder mystery is that of the Germans who came to the islands in the 1930s and then disappeared one by one, as in Agatha Christie's story, *The Ten Little Niggers*. Margret Wittmer, the last survivor, died in 2000, aged 95. Up until then she was still in charge of the island's only guesthouse and restaurant. Several books have been written about this unsolved mystery, including Margret Wittmer's own fascinating account of life on the island, *Floreana,* though she leaves many questions unanswered. The full story of what happened died with Señora Wittmer.

Floreana boasts one of the most charming curiosities of the Galápagos Islands: the mail box of **Post Office Bay**, perhaps the most unusual in the world. In the days before radio and air travel, when whaling ships cruised the Pacific for years on end, a thoughtful English captain established a "post office" barrel on Floreana. The idea was that mail could be deposited in the barrel, which ships heading home would pick up. The system worked so well that during Anglo-American hostilities at the beginning in 1812, information obtained from letters stolen from the mail barrel helped an American captain destroy more than half the British whaling fleet. The original barrel is long gone, but a replacement box is still used in the same way. A Canadian visitor recently sent a letter from the Floreana mail barrel that arrived before a letter to the same address in Canada, which had been sent a few days earlier through the regular Ecuadorian mail.

What to See and Do

Though there are more imported plants and animals here than on other islands, descended from those brought by early inhabitants, Santa María has some fine visitors' sites with a wealth of fascinating Galapagean wildlife. The best site is **Punta Cormorant**, on the north shore, where the beach has a green tinge because of olivine crystals in the

Plant life on Isla Santa María.

sand. There are plenty of sea lions on the beach, and the swimming is good. Walking eastwards over a small isthmus, you pass a lagoon, where there are often flamingos and other water birds, before coming to another pleasant beach. There are a number of stingrays here so it's important to shuffle your feet in the sand as you wade out to sea. Just off the coast is one of the best snorkeling spots in the Galápagos Islands, the tip of a submerged volcano known as the **Devil's Crown**, where you will see big cast of glittering tropical fish of all colors, shapes and sizes, and perhaps sea lions and sharks. Take heart that it is said that nobody has been killed by a shark in the Galápagos Islands — yet!

Where to Stay and Eat

If you do find your way to the island's small port of **Puerto Velasco Ibarra** (population not more than 100) you're not spoiled for choice; in fact, you have none at all. The only place to stay and eat is the small, moderately priced guesthouse and restaurant ((05) 520250 run by the Wittmer family. Margret's son Rolf was born on Santa María in January 1933, and his was the first historically documented birth on the Galápagos Islands. Rolf now runs a travel company and his charter boat, *Tip-Top III*, regularly anchors off his birthplace. At the guesthouse, rooms are on the beachfront, and include hot water and fans, with all meals available upon request.

How to Get There

Few independent travelers stay overnight on Santa María. Visitors usually come by cruise boat for a short visit. However INGALA ferries stop in Floreana on their way from Puerto Ayora to Isabela on Thursdays, or from Isabela to Puerto Ayora on Fridays. Check with INGALA ((05) 526151 in Puerto Ayora to confirm.

ESPAÑOLA

Despite its small size, the southernmost island of Española, formerly known as Hood, has a rich variety of wildlife, making it popular with cruise boats. Ninety kilometers (55 miles) from the main tourist center of Puerto Ayora, this uninhabited island is often the first stop of a one-week itinerary after an overnight crossing. The visitor site of Punta Suárez, a long, low headland of twisted volcanic rock, is a popular haunt of prehistoric marine iguanas, which Darwin called "Imps of Darkness." They lounge on black rocks while sleek sea lions sun themselves on the beach. We spotted a rare Galápagos hawk and several endemic Española mockingbirds at close range. About a kilometer's walk (just over a half mile) from landing at Punta Suárez, one comes to the edge of a high cliff where breakers crash on the rocks

below, where a lava-tube blowhole shoots out a 30-m (100-ft) fountain of white spray.

What to See and Do

The usual cast of Galápagos wildlife takes the stage on Española. Always hiding in the wings, however, is the reclusive Española subspecies of the giant saddleback tortoise, some 700 of which have been reintroduced to the island during the last 25 years after captive breeding at the Darwin Station on Santa Cruz.

The bird most closely associated with the island is the waved albatross, a creature famous for its elegant flight, elaborate courtship display and its size — it's the biggest bird of the archipelago. It's also the most monogamous. Birds mate for life, though they repeat their courtship ritual each year. Only a few thousand of these white-necked, yellow-billed beauties exist on the planet, all from Española, except for a few that breed on Isla La Plata, off the mainland. Breeding season, from about April to mid-December, is the time to see them. The rest of the year they spend at sea.

In the afternoon there is often a snorkeling expedition around **Gardner Rock**, off the northeast shore and then time to relax with sea lions on the long, golden beach of **Gardner Bay**. Life isn't all sun, sea and sleep for the sea lions. Many big scars on the sleek fur of the males are evidence of fights with other males to dominate the female herd. We saw one youngster who was rejected by the group. Perhaps a shark had eaten its mother, but there was evidently no hope for this little one. It would die of starvation a couple weeks.

SAN CRISTÓBAL AND PUERTO BAQUERIZO MORENO

Small and somnolent, San Cristóbal's main town has a big name: Puerto Baquerizo Moreno. Such an elegant appellation is appropriate for a place that boasts a naval base, a radio station and is the provincial capital of Ecuador's Galápagos Province. Most of the basic utilities are available in Puerto Baquerizo Moreno, including a Pacifictel telephone office, a hospital, an airline office, a police station and a bank (Banco del Pacífico, with MasterCard ATM only, but does change travelers' checks). Nevertheless, the town (population 3,000) has a rundown, backwater atmosphere, and from a tourist's point of view isn't as pleasant as its sister, Puerto Ayora, over on Santa Cruz. This might change, however, because Puerto Baquerizo Moreno boasts a new airport, which makes it a second gateway to the archipelago.

What to See and Do

One of the town's few tourist attractions is the small **natural history museum** full of dusty stuffed birds, iguanas, sea lions and dolphins as well as whalebones, tortoise shells, corals and crabs. The sole living exhibit in the museum is a tortoise named Pepe, who lives in an enclosure behind the main building. Included in the admission to the museum is a fistful of green leaves to feed the gentle giant. Nobody knows how old Pepe is because scientists haven't found a way of determining the age of tortoises, though it's known that they often live well over 150 years. It's possible that Pepe was around when Charles Darwin visited these islands.

A notice on the wall of the museum gives a short version of the horrendous story of one Manuel J. Cobos, who operated a sugar plantation and refinery up in the hills of Chatham, as San Cristóbal was then called, at the end of the

lake of **Laguna El Junco**, where you can walk around the rim, which is rich in plant and bird life. From the crater you can look out over most of the island, including the 896-m (2,940-ft) peak of **Cerro San Joaquín**. To the northeast you can also see the cliffs of **Punta Pitt**, the most spectacular visitors' site on San Cristóbal.

As with most visitors' sites on the Galápagos, the only way to reach Punta Pitt is by boat. Disembarking onto the small beach, visitors are confronted by the strong stench and cacophony of barking sea lions. At certain times of the year there are as many of these beautiful beasts are as bodies on West Palm Beach on spring break. This is a bachelor colony, and most are exhausted from

nineteenth century. Cobos was a dreadful tyrant with a taste for flogging his convict laborers to death. Rebellious workers murdered him in 1904. In recording the story of Cobos, author of *The Enchanted Islands*, John Hickman writes: "These stories — and there must be many similar unrecorded incidents — show the Galápagos archipelago as a sinister backdrop against which all human dramas are doomed to tragedy. There seems to be something inimical to human life or at least to human happiness in the very atmosphere."

In spite of a dire history, the island of San Cristóbal has plenty to offer visitors. **El Progreso**, as Cobos' small plantation village was ironically called, still exists and can be reached by truck or bus from Puerto Baquerizo Moreno, or by walking eight kilometers (five miles). Ten kilometers (six miles) further up the road is the beautiful crater

fighting and mating. They won't budge an inch as you approach so you have to step around their basking bodies while being careful to avoid the source of the strong stench. A steep gully leads up the cliff to a breeding ground for boobies of all three varieties: red-footed, blue-footed and masked. It's the only place in the Galápagos where you can see all three species nesting together.

The view from the top of the cliff over the beach of sea lions is magnificent, as are the contours of the barren, wind-eroded peaks of the island. The trail across the Punta Pitt site offers a closer look at the hardy vegetation that manages to thrive in this volcanic wasteland. From saltbush and spiny shrubs by the beach the trail leads up to an area of palo santos trees, big yellow-green shrubs,

Margaret Wittmer on Santa María was the last survivor of a remarkable band of expatriate islanders.

tiny cacti and, in the dry season, carpets of red sesuvium. A short distance westward along the coast from Punta Pitt is the new visitors' site of **Galapaguera**, where giant turtles can sometimes be seen. Getting there involves a long hike so it's advisable to go with a guide.

Off the coast of San Cristóbal are a number of steep, rocky islets that rise almost vertically from the sea. There's good snorkeling around the islet opposite Punta Pitt, but the most impressive of these solitary, sea-girt towers is **León Dormido** (Sleeping Lion). Also known as **Kicker Rock**, this twin-peaked cathedral of stone looks as if it had been split by a divine karate chop. Huge, cackling colonies of sea birds nest in its vertiginous walls, and it's a popular spot for scuba diving.

Where to Stay and Eat

Accommodation in the town is uninspiring but passable. The top of the range accommodation (which isn't saying much) at Puerto Baquerizo Moreno is the moderately priced **Hotel Orca** (/FAX (05) 520233, the island's largest. It has a good restaurant, and rooms include private bathrooms, hot water and fans. Similarly priced, the **Hostal Galápagos** (/FAX (05) 520157 has spick and span rooms with air conditioning.

The best inexpensive hotel is the **Mar Azul** ((05) 520139, which has pleasant, shady courtyards, hot water showers and equally pleasant prices. The well-recommended budget bet is **Hotel San Francisco** ((05) 520304 on the waterfront where a single room with fan, television and cold water bathroom is good value.

Restaurante Rosita behind Hotel San Francisco has legendary status because of Rosita's skill at cooking fish. Prices are reasonable and you can dine inside or out. For evening meals, the restaurant **Genoa** is more expensive but enjoys a good reputation and is popular with locals. Otherwise follow your nose and trust your judgment. *Ceviche* lovers can choose from a number of *cevicherías* well supplied by local fisherman. One of the best is **Langostino**. Also recommended for snacks and light meals are **Casa Blanca** (by the dock).

Though not the most swinging of provincial capitals, Puerto Baquerizo Moreno does have a couple *discotecas* near the center of town, **Blue Star** and **Neptunus**, which are most lively Friday and Saturday nights.

How to Get There

After Baltra, San Cristóbal is the second entry point to the Galápagos Islands from Quito and Guayaquil. There is also passenger boat service between San Cristóbal and Puerto Ayora on Santa Cruz run regularly by INGALA. Ask around for the latest schedules. Most tourists visit Puerto Baquerizo Moreno for just a few hours from their cruise boats.

THE NORTHERN ISLANDS

GENOVESA

Seldom visited by tourists, the remote northern island of Genovesa, also known as Tower Island, is a paradise for bird lovers. The avian abundance is a strong incentive to endure a sometimes rough 10- to 12-hour boat ride from Puerto Ayora. The island has a thriving red-footed booby colony, as well as plentiful masked boobies, swallow-tailed gulls, red-billed tropical birds, storm petrels and great frigate birds. There are two visitors' sites. A path through woods and nesting colonies to the top of a cliff is known as Prince Philip's Steps after the prince's 1964 visit, which helped stimulate international interest in the Galápagos' survival. The second site is Darwin Bay, a collapsed caldera filled with sea water, surrounded by a ring of cliffs, where there's a coral beach and several seabird colonies.

MARCHENA

This desolate island is the seventh-largest in the archipelago and the biggest island lacking an official visitors' site. Though landings are possible on the black sand beach on the southwest of the island, Marchena is best known for scuba diving. The 343-m (1,125-ft) volcano in the center of the island erupted in 1991.

PINTA

Though tourists rarely visit the ninth-largest of the Galápagos islands, it has had one celebrated resident. He is the solitary survivor of the Pinta breed of tortoises, Lonesome George, who now lives at the Darwin Research Station on Santa Cruz, as mentioned above. There are no visitor sites on Pinta and anyone wishing to go there for research has to obtain special permission.

DARWIN AND WOLF

These two small, remote islands, about 100 km (63 miles) northwest of the central islands, are seldom visited except by scuba divers. They are regarded as the most challenging and exciting of the archipelago's dive sites, with the chance of swimming with whalesharks. Though plenty of seabirds make their homes here, steep cliffs encircling the islands make landing difficult from a boat. A rare expedition to Darwin in 1964 landed by helicopter.

The beaches of the Galápagos Islands are alive with colonies of sprawling sea lions.

Travelers'
Tips

GETTING THERE

BY AIR

Information about flights, fares and tours to Ecuador can be obtained from South American travel operators in the United States and most European countries. Some of these operators also have information about specialist tours, such as bird watching, climbing or adventure travel. For my recommendations, see SPECIAL INTERESTS, page 56, and TAKING A TOUR, page 57, in YOUR CHOICE.

Several international airlines fly in and out of Quito's Aeropuerto Mariscal Sucre. The airport, which includes national and international terminals, is a short ride from the modern, northern end of town. Most taxis won't cost more than about US$5. There are plenty of them. Since many flights tend to be overbooked it's a good idea to reconfirm at least 72 hours before your flight, and to get to the airport two hours before departure. Ensure your travel agent gives you a local contact number for your airline. Don't forget there is a US$25 per person departure tax for international flights, payable in dollars, cash only.

Quito's airport is the gateway to Ecuador for almost all international tourists. Otherwise, visitors fly into the country's second international airport at Guayaquil, especially those going straight on to the Galápagos Islands. Few people arrive by boat these days unless cruising in a yacht or working their passage on a cargo boat.

Quito is relatively well served by international airlines, all with main offices in Quito, and some with subsidiary offices in Guayaquil (which are listed in that chapter, see page 204). Major airlines include: **AeroPerú** ((02) 561699, Jorge Washington 718; **Air France** ((02) 527374 E-MAIL airfranc@impsat.net.ec, World Trade Center, 12 de Octubre and Luís Cordero; **American Airlines** ((02) 260900, Amazonas 4545 and Pereira; **British Airways** ((02) 540000 or (02) 540902, Amazonas 1429 and Colón, office 5; **Continental** ((02) 261487, World Trade Center, 12 de Octubre and Luís Cordero; **Iberia** ((02) 566009, Edificio Finandés, Eloy Alfaro 939 and Amazonas; **KLM** ((02) 986828, 12 de Octubre and A Lincoln; **Varig** ((02) 437137, Portugal 794 and República de El Salvador.

BY LAND

Overland travelers enter Ecuador either from Colombia, crossing to Tulcán, or from Perú to Huaquillas or Macará. Minibuses, taxis and trucks run between border points for a small fee and the immigration offices in both countries are open seven days a week during office hours. There are frequent buses to and from both sides of both borders (see pages 117 and 176).

ARRIVING AND LEAVING

A passport valid for at least six months from your arrival date is all that is usually required to enter Ecuador. Citizens of some countries should obtain a visa in advance from their local Ecuadorian consulate. The list of these countries varies according to diplomatic relations, but at time of writing they included France, China, Guatemala, Cuba, Costa Rica, Vietnam and North and South Korea.

The normal tourist visa obtained from immigration on entry is good for 60 or 90 days. If you want to stay longer, obtain a different visa from your local Ecuadorian consulate before traveling. If you are only given one or two months on entry you will be able to extend your visa up to 90 days at the Jefatura Provincial de Migración in the state provinces, or at the office in Quito at Isla Seymour 1152 and Río Coca, open Monday to Friday 8 AM to noon and 3 PM to 5 PM. Occasionally visitors are required to show evidence of financial independence when they arrive, in the form of a return ticket and/or sufficient funds to support themselves during their stay.

EMBASSIES AND CONSULATES

If you get into serious trouble in Ecuador you will need your embassy or consulate. Also, if you are going to be in the country a while, or take part in adventurous activities, it's a good idea to register with your consulate and leave photocopies of your passport so they can issue you a new one quickly.

The following addresses of embassies in Quito may be of use (other embassies are listed in the telephone directory): **Canadian Embassy** ((022) 506162, Avenida 6 de Diciembre 2816 and Paul Rivet; **French Embassy** ((022) 560789 FAX (022) 566424, General Plaza 107 and Patria; **United Kingdom Embassy** ((022) 970800 E-MAIL britemq @impsat.net.ec, Edificio Citiplaza, Fourteenth floor, Naciones Unidas and República de El Salvador; **United States Embassy** ((022) 562890 FAX (022) 502052 WEB SITE www.usis.org.ec, Patria and 12 de Octubre. The **Australian Consulate** is in Guayaquil: ((042) 680823 or (042) 680800 FAX (042) 682 008, Kennedy Norte, Calle San Roque y Avenida Francisco de Orellana, Edificio Tecniseguros. The nearest **New Zealand** consulate is in Perú ((51-1) 442-1757 FAX (51-1) 442-8671 E-MAIL 2012527@pol.com.pe, Camino Real 390, Oficina 601-602, (Torre Central) Lima 27, Perú, and **South Africa**'s nearest representation is the

PREVIOUS PAGES: Paddling through the backwaters LEFT in a dugout canoe, one of the great rainforest experiences. A Cuencan gentleman RIGHT. OPPOSITE: Catedral de la Inmaculada Concepción in Cuenca, sporting its curvacious cupolas.

embassy in Venezuela (**(** (58-212) 991-4622/6822 E-MAIL rsaven@eldish.net).

Information about travel in Ecuador can also be obtained from Ecuadorian embassies and consulates abroad. These include: **Australia (** (02) 6262-5282 FAX (02) 6262-5285, The Law Society Building, 11 London Circuit, Canberra, ACT 260; **Canada (** (613) 563-8206 FAX (613) 235-5776, 50 Connor Street, Office 316, Ottawa, ON K1P 6L2; **United Kingdom (** (020) 7584-1367 FAX (020) 7823-9701, Flat B, Hans Crescent, London SW1X 0LS; **United States (** (202) 234-7200 FAX (202) 667-3482, 2535 15th Street NW, Washington, DC 20009.

TOURIST INFORMATION

The Ministerio de Turismo offices aren't particularly helpful for individual travelers. This organization's role seems to be to keep an eye on Ecuadorian tourism in general rather than to answer individual tourists' specific needs. You are likely to get better and more relevant information from private tour companies. Fellow travelers are also good sources of information, and comment books found at hostels, cafés and restaurant often have valuable tips as well as hilarious stories. Another good source of travel tips are the trip reports filed by members of the South American Explorers in Quito (see GENERAL INFORMATION, page 82 in QUITO). The staff of the club is well informed about most aspects of Ecuador. You might also want to look out for the booklet *This is Ecuador*, published monthly and available in most hotels and restaurants in Mariscal.

GETTING AROUND

BY AIR

The local carrier with the widest choice of flights is **TAME** (Transportes Aeros Militares Equatorianos) **(** (022) 509382, (022) 509384 or (022) 509386 to 8 E-MAIL tame1@tame.com WEB SITE www .tame.com, which flies to all major cities and the Galápagos Islands. The main office is at Amazonas 13-54 and Rábida, Sixth Floor, Quito. **SAN-SAETA (** (022) 564969, (022) 550291 or (022) 565005, at Colón and Amazonas, Edificio España, Quito, also has flights to the Galápagos, Guayaquil and Cuenca. Domestic flights are relatively inexpensive, but often overbooked, so always try to reconfirm and arrive early at the airport.

BY BUS

Unless you are on an organized tour where transportation is arranged, you will almost certainly use buses to get around. Squashed in a little seat in a crowded bus on a dangerous mountain road, with soft porn or kung-fu on the video and a driver who seems to be falling asleep, might not be everybody's idea of fun. But you have to get used to it: traveling by bus to remote areas is the price of enjoying Ecuador to its fullest.

There are a number of private bus companies, some better than others. Recommended companies include **Reina del Camino** (Queen of the Road), which has a good safety record and fast buses; **Coaltur**, good for service from Quito to Guayaquil and the coast; **Panamericana** (especially for night buses); and **Manglaralto** for coastal services. **Trans Loja** has the worst safety record in Ecuador. Instead use **Cooperativo Viajeros** for journeys between Cuenca and Loja. Traveling by bus at night is discouraged by most embassies.

A word of warning about taking buses, especially the smaller ones in Quito: they are often so crowded that if you get stuck in the back you won't be able to get out when you want to. And the driver will not wait as you push your way to the door.

BY BICYCLE

As an alternative to buses, some intrepid souls bring bikes to Ecuador. Cyclists enjoy biking in the mountains, although the coastal areas are said to be rather uninteresting. Mountain bikers from all over the country bring their bikes to Jefferson at **Bici Sport** on Avenida 6 de Diciembre, out past the stadium in Quito: the best bicycle mechanic in Ecuador.

The United Kingdom-based **Cyclists'Touring Club** has an informative WEB SITE at www.ctc .org.uk.

BY TRAIN

Trains are not as fast or practical as buses for getting around the country. The rail network is limited and trains don't run often. However, there are some spectacular train journeys, and passengers can have the unusual and exciting experience of riding on the roof of an ancient coach. For more details, see RIDE THE RAILS, page 17 in TOP SPOTS.

BY CAR

Although very few overseas visitors arrive in Ecuador by car, some do rent cars when they get to Ecuador. These are the adventurous travelers, willing to put up with poor roads, bad signs and erratic driving. A small saloon car is adequate for most of the country's roads, but a high-clearance model is preferable for more rural driving. A four-wheel-drive jeep is pretty essential in the Oriente, particularly in the rainy season.

To rent a car, you should be over 25, have a valid (preferably international) driver's license and a credit card with sufficient funds for the deposit (which, be warned, can be up to US$3,000). A small car costs about US$40 per day including mileage, or about US$260 a week. Four-wheel-drive vehicles are also available, but are more expensive. Check insurance, tax, drop-off and other charges, particularly mileage, carefully. The cost of gasoline in oil-producing Ecuador is low and gas stations pretty frequent. If taking an unleaded car into the wilds of the Oriente, it would be wise to carry a jerry can of fuel. Check your car over for scratches and dents before signing, and also have any four-wheel drive or spare tire practicalities explained. If possible, never travel at night, since road markings are virtually nonexistent and night accidents common. Never leave valuables visible in a car, and always try to park your vehicle in an inexpensive guarded parking lot, never on the street.

The best road maps for the country are the *Guía Vial de Ecuador*, a blue, fold-out booklet published yearly (but not amazingly accurate) and available in many hotels and bookshops, or the *Hojas de Ruta* maps of the most popular routes, published by the Instituto Geográfico Militar (IGM) (see GENERAL INFORMATION, page 82 in QUITO).

The big international car rental companies, such as Budget, Avis and Hertz, have offices in Quito and Guayaquil, and Hertz also has an office in Cuenca. Rental prices are no less than Europe and the United States, though local Ecuadorian car rental companies are less expensive than the international ones. Although you can book your car rental from abroad before you arrive, probably the best way to do it is upon arrival by shopping around the companies clustered near the airport. This way, you can take advantage of their frequent promotional offers.

Most of the major car rental companies (including **Hertz** ((02) 254258, **Budget** ((02) 240763 and **Avis** ((02) 550238) have offices at the airport and downtown. Local rental companies include **Localiza** ((02) 249294, **Sicorent** ((02) 432858 and **Expo** ((02) 260487.

FINDING YOUR WAY

Ecuadorian addresses refer to the nearest intersection. For example the main Andinatel office in Quito New Town is given as Avenida Amazonas

and (y) Avenida Cristóbal Colón, which means that it is on or near the intersection between these two streets. In this guide, we have dispensed with the "Avenida" part for main and known avenues.

Street numbers are sometimes included in the address, as in Amazonas 1646 and Orellana for the British Council in Quito. In recent years, a new system of street numbers has been introduced, though it's still not employed by everyone. The new addresses have N for north of the Old Town, and east–west streets (depending upon their position in relation to the large arterial Avenida 10 de Agosto) have E for *este* and O for *oeste* (west) prefixing them. After the letter comes the block number, then a dash and the house number itself. Thus the British Council address is also Amazonas N26-146 and Orellana.

OPPOSITE: Plaza de Ponchos in Otavalo.
ABOVE: Quito residents on Avenida Amazonas.

Sometimes there are a number of streets with the same name in an address, which makes it difficult to find the location on a map. Often only the last name is given, without the first name, so that a street given as Carrión could be Baltazar Carrión, Eudoro Carrión, Jerónimo Carrión, José Carrión, or Miguel Carrión, etc.

The best way of finding your way around Quito is to buy the pocket-sized Quito book of street maps by Nelson Gómez called *Guía Informativa de Quito*. It has an A–Z index of street names referenced to excellent maps.

The best general map of the country is the **Map of Ecuador** (No. 278) 1:1,000,000, published by International Travel Maps WEBSITE www.itm.com,

345 West Broadway, Vancouver, BC, Canada. These maps are available from better map sellers overseas, at some bookshops in Quito and from the South American Explorers (see GENERAL INFORMATION, page 82 in QUITO).

ACCOMMODATION

There is accommodation in Ecuador to suit all pockets, from the true budget traveler to the most prosperous vacationer. The less expensive the lodging (and there are some *very* inexpensive places) the less likely they take reservations. Many of these places don't even own a phone, let alone a fax machine. However, there are also plenty of medium-priced hotels and hostels that can't take reservations simply because of their remoteness. Don't despair. Except over public holidays, chances are that even these more upmarket hostelries will have a bed or two.

Note that the better hotels add 10 percent sales tax (*IVA*) and a 10 percent service charge to your bill, so check whether this has been included or not. If you're staying in budget accommodation (called *hotel*, *residencia*, *hostería*, or *pensión*), always ask to see the room before committing, and check on the noise level of the air-conditioning unit — they are often very loud.

These hotels will always ask for payment up-front, nearly always in cash. Note that most hotels will charge a small percentage extra for payment by credit card.

A single room is a *habitación sencilla*, while double rooms come as *habitación doble* (twin beds) and *matrimonial* (double bed).

Prices brackets used in this guide are based on two people sharing, include all taxes, and are as follows:

Very Expensive	over US$100
Expensive	$51 to US$100
Moderate	$25 to US$50
Inexpensive	under US$25

EATING OUT

Unless you're planning dinner for a dozen, or you want a table in the most elite of restaurants, and you speak fluent Spanish, you wouldn't consider phoning for a reservation. Besides, many of the best and most interesting places won't have a number to offer you. In Ecuador, take our recommendations, or follow your nose and choose a spot that looks popular. If you have to wait, grab a beer or an aperitif and enjoy the atmosphere. You should be aware that most restaurant prices don't include a service and sales tax (*IVA*), and this will be added on to the end of your bill.

Prices brackets used in this guide are based on one person dining, including service and tax, but excluding drinks, and are as follows:

Expensive	over US$15
Moderate	US$6 to US$15
Inexpensive	US$1 to US$5

BASICS

ELECTRICITY

Ecuador operates on 110 volts (60-cycle), and uses standard United States flat, parallel, two-prong plugs. If you're traveling from a country not compatible with this shape, purchase an adapter *before* you leave. Some jungle lodges may use their own generators, in which case you should check with the managers before plugging in an appliance.

MONEY

You can **cash travelers' checks** and **change money** at most banks and *casas de cambio* (money changers), and the rates aren't significantly different. Most banks are open between 9 AM and 1:30 PM on weekdays. Money changers are usually open until about 6 PM. Some major hotels will cash travelers' checks for nonresidents, which can be very helpful if you are strapped for cash on a weekend, but usually not very cost-effective.

The Hilton Colón International at Amazonas and Patria has a good service but it's wise to dress neatly if you want to use their facilities.

Automated Teller Machines (ATMs) are becoming more common in cities throughout the country. They are about the most economical way of using cash abroad. For Visa, head to Filanbanco, and for MasterCard to Banco del Pacífico. Check with your home bank before leaving about any charges you might incur. My advice would be to bring a mix of dollars in cash, some travelers' checks and a Visa or MasterCard.

If you're bringing dollars in cash (or changing travelers' checks), make sure you ask for **small denominations** (no bills larger than US$20). Many

paper basket where you deposit your toilet paper. Flushing it often blocks the pipes. Toilets are *baños*.

WATER

Avoid drinking tap water in Ecuador, and stick to bottled water, which is widely available. Three-star and up hotels provide mineral water and ice, and most hotels will supply them on request.

WEIGHTS AND MEASURES

Ecuador operates on the metric system. Liquids are sold in liters, vegetables and fruits by the kilogram.

stores and small businesses won't accept US$100 or US$50 bills, and it can be frustrating attempting to get them changed.

TIME

Mainland Ecuador is five hours behind Greenwich Mean Time, and thus the same as Eastern Standard Time. The Galápagos are six hours behind GMT. When it's noon in Quito, it's noon in New York, 9 AM in Los Angeles, 5 PM (depending on British Summer Time) in London, and 2 AM in Sydney.

TOILETS

Always have toilet paper or tissues with you. Plumbing tubes are narrow and water pressure is often low in Ecuador. Many toilets have a waste-

Distance
1 km = .625 (⅝) miles
1 meter = 3.28 feet

Weight
1 gram =.035 ounces
1 kilogram (kilo) = 2.2 pounds

Volume
1 liter = 2.1 United States pints = 1.76 United Kingdom pints

Temperature
To convert Fahrenheit to centigrade, subtract 32 and multiply by ⅝. To convert centigrade to Fahrenheit, multiply by 1.8 and add 32.

OPPOSITE: Craft items made by the Cofán Indians. ABOVE: Hacienda Hualiagua de Jijon, an oasis of graceful living.

COMMUNICATION AND MEDIA

TELEPHONES

Fifty years ago, writer Christopher Isherwood described the Ecuadorian telephone system as "about as reliable as roulette." Remarkably, the system wasn't much better a few years ago. However, leaps and bounds have been made of late, and today the phone system is pretty good by Latin American standards.

The two main telephone companies are Andinatel and Pacifictel. This may well change in the future. All offices in the big cities have

facilities for sending and receiving faxes. They are generally open from 8 AM to 10 PM seven days a week. Calling is straightforward: you ask for a numbered chit, stating whether your call is *nacional* or *internacional*, and then make the call from a numbered cabin. You can ask for a top limit to your call, or *sin limite* (unlimited).

There are also two companies for street phones, Porta and BellSouth, which use phone cards. These cards can be purchased at most convenience stores, and I suggest you buy one of each. From BellSouth phones, you always have to dial the city code, even if you're in the city already. All cell phones are prefixed (09) and are pretty expensive to call. The country code for Ecuador is 593.

MAIL

Letters and small parcels (up to two kilograms or five pounds) can be sent from any post office (*oficina de correos*), although it's advisable to check that your stamps are properly postmarked since officials have been known to steam off unmarked stamps. Bigger parcels should be sent from the post offices at Ulloa and Dávalos in Quito (see GENERAL INFORMATION, page 82 in QUITO). You can receive *poste restante* mail at Lista de Correos, Correos Central, Quito. Your mail will be filed

under whichever name is printed in capitals. American Express customers can also receive mail care of American Express, Apartado 2605, Quito. The office is in the Ecuadorian Tours building on Amazonas 339.

INTERNET CAFÉS

Internet and e-mail cafés are now common throughout Ecuador, and you'll find terminals in all big cities and most stops on the gringo trail. Connections, speed, reliability and prices vary from town to town. You will find cafés listed in the GENERAL INFORMATION sections of this book. Many Internet cafés offer **"net-phone"** services, which are the cheapest means of calling abroad (dialing the United States for instance costs about 30 to 40 cents a minute). These are practicable for calling "Western" countries, but pretty impossible for other countries in South America.

NEWSPAPERS AND MAGAZINES

Ecuador's two main national newspapers are the Quito-based *El Comercio* WEB SITE www.elcomercio .com and the Guayaquil-based *El Universo* WEB SITE www.eluniverso.com. They have good national and international reporting, as well as cinema and events listings, and weekend travel sections. There isn't an English-language newspaper currently available, but English-language magazines (such as *Time* or *Newsweek*) are available in posh hotels and good bookshops. In Quito, you'll find many tourist booklets and small magazines (*The Explorer* and *This is Ecuador* are the best) aimed at foreign travelers. The best weekly Ecuadorian current affairs magazine is *Vistazo*, while there are two good monthly magazines called *Diner's* and *Terra Incognita* which always run interesting travel and wildlife features.

ETIQUETTE

Ecuadorians are generally polite and courteous people and they appreciate these qualities in others. They are also curious about visitors' views about their country, and even though they might modestly demur, they are delighted to hear praise of its finer aspects. Some Ecuadorians feel that their country is rather small and remote and are interested in news and views from the wider world.

Hand shaking is an important part of the social ritual. Shake hands when you meet somebody for the first time or when you meet an old friend. Shake hands again when you say good-bye. A greeting kiss is usually a single peck on the right cheek. Most people employ the *"tú"* form of address (the familiar "you"), as opposed to the more polite *"usted"* used on the Spanish mainland. However, it's usually best for tourists to begin by using *usted*, changing to *tú* once the other person has begun to employ it. In general, you should always address a member of the police or armed forces, or a person of authority, as *usted*.

Ecuadorians are keen on their greetings, so always enter an office, elevator or hotel by saying *"con permiso"* (with permission), or by greeting *"buenos días"* or *"buenas tardes"* (good morning and good afternoon).

Ecuadorians are proud of their families and will be interested in yours. Family talk and family photos are always a good conversational starting point. If you are invited to an Ecuadorian house a small gift will be appreciated. People tend to dress smartly and believe that how well you dress is a measure of how importantly you are treating the occasion. Try to wear a suit when meeting with government officials. Scruffy travelers are frowned upon in general.

Concepts of "personal space" differ from the West — particularly on buses, where you will have to get used to reduced privacy and comfort, or a chicken on your lap.

HEALTH

Check with your doctor or a travel clinic about vaccinations well before starting your journey. Several transmittable diseases and conditions occur in Ecuador, especially in rural areas. Vaccinations for yellow fever, polio, rabies, Hepatitis A, typhoid and tetanus are usually recommended. The risk of cholera is low enough that vaccination isn't usually prescribed.

Most doctors also advise a course of malaria tablets if you will be on the coast or in the rainforest. If you are only going to the highlands you don't need to worry about malaria pills because malaria-carrying mosquitoes don't live above 2,500 m (8,330 ft). Mosquitoes aren't usually a problem on the Galápagos Islands either, especially on a cruise, but bring insect repellent and relief cream anyway.

The best precaution against malaria is to prevent mosquitoes from biting in the first place. When mosquitoes are about, particularly between dusk and dawn, wear long trousers, socks and a long-sleeved shirt. Apply repellent to exposed areas of skin, not forgetting the ears, and rub some in your hair. Sleep under a mosquito net if your room isn't sealed against mosquitoes.

Malaria is a serious illness and it isn't worth being casual about preventative measures. If you develop a fever and flu-like symptoms after returning from a malarial region, you need to be aware of the possibility of a malaria infection and should see a doctor as soon as possible.

Contaminated food and water are another common source of disease in tropical countries. Drink only bottled water and make sure the seal

has not been broken. Avoid drinks that come in little plastic bags. If you are going to be traveling around extensively, bring water-purifying iodine tablets in case bottled water isn't available, or else a portable water-purifying pump. Avoid ice cubes, which are usually made from unpurified water, and use bottled water for brushing your teeth. Unless you are eating in a smart hotel, avoid salads and uncooked vegetables and confine yourself to peelable fruits, of which there are many in Ecuador. Make sure eggs are well cooked.

However careful you are, stomach upsets are a hazard of traveling; studies have shown that diarrhea occurs with 40 to 50 percent of overseas travelers. Come prepared with anti-diarrhea pills,

such as Imodium or Pepto-Bismol, and toilet paper. If the nasties strike, get plenty of rest, drink plenty of liquids, such as herbal tea or soda water, and don't eat much, except yogurt and a some dry bread or toast. You should recover in a day or two.

Another health hazard of travel in Ecuador is heat exhaustion and sunburn. With a little common sense these conditions are easily avoided. Don't over exert yourself, drink plenty of fluids, stay in the shade and use sun block.

Many people, regardless of age or fitness, suffer from mild altitude or mountain sickness, even in Quito, at 2,850 m (9,500 ft), in the form of shortness of breath, headaches and general lassitude.

OPPOSITE: Ambulant salesmen are a common sight throughout the country. ABOVE: Known as "vegetable ivory," tagua nuts, which come from a rainforest palm, are used for making buttons and a variety of decorative objects.

The best way to avoid these symptoms is to drink plenty of water, take aspirin for the headache, moderate or eliminate alcohol and tobacco intake, breath deeply and slow down. You should acclimatize in two or three days. The traditional and effective Andean remedy for mountain sickness is to make a tea by boiling coca plant leaves (the basis of cocaine) and drinking it through a straw. The leaves can be bought from the Indian women on the streets of the Old Town in Quito.

At higher altitudes climbers may suffer more acute symptoms such as loss of appetite, inability to sleep, rapid pulse and irregular breathing. In extreme cases thinking and judgment may become impaired and, very rarely, a potentially fatal complication called high altitude pulmonary edema, caused by fluid buildup in the lungs, can occur. Oxygen intake and descent to lower altitudes relieve the symptoms.

Wherever you are traveling, it is sensible to pack a small medical kit. If you are on medication, bring enough to last your stay. Bring tape, scissors, bandages, gauze, topical antibiotic ointment to prevent infection of minor wounds, and an antiinflammatory drug such as aspirin. An antihistamine relieves itching from insect bites, while a steroid cream is helpful in treating skin rashes or relieving sunburn. Ask your doctor about antibiotics and also ask about medications for malaria, such as quinine sulfate or Fansidar.

Don't forget to bring enough strong sunblock, as the sun's rays are very powerful close to the equator. For the same reason it is also important to wear a good pair of sunglasses, especially in the mountains As for those stomach pills, don't leave home without them.

A useful source of information is WEB SITE www.cdc.gov/travel.

SECURITY

Although Ecuador is considered to be the safest South American country for traveling, it is important to exercise caution and watch your valuables at all times. Snatch thieves operating in crowded streets and markets are the most common criminals. Often they work in pairs, one of whom distracts you, while the other relieves you of your bag, your camera and your watch. If a woman carrying a baby trips up in front of you in a market, watch your back. Other scams include contrived fights and pretend drunks.

In one classic scam, "Misdirected Man" gets on a bus carrying lots of bags and looking all confused. He sits next to you, claiming it's his seat. Then he realizes he's on the wrong bus. He jumps up and off the bus in a hurry, taking his and one of your bags with him.

The languid tranquility of the jungle hides thousands of species of living creatures.

Also watch out for people who claim to be plainclothes policemen. This is often just an excuse for some form of extortion. If they ask you to get in a car because they want your help in investigating a crime, or they claim you've been seen talking to drug dealers, do not do so in any circumstances. Instead, insist that they go with you on foot to the police station. Chances are they are hassling you, hoping you'll give them some money to go away.

Although taxi drivers are generally safe and honest, you might encounter a troublesome one. Taking taxis late at night, especially if you are alone and have had a few drinks, can be hazardous. For safety, pick up a cab from a stand outside one of

ceipt for anything you hand over. Keep an emergency phone card on you. On a slip inside your passport, write "en caso de emergencia, llamar a:" and insert the details of at least one relative or friend to be contacted in case of an accident. Include your blood type *(tipo de sangre)*, and any allergies *(alergias)* you might have.

The nearest police station to the Mariscal district is at the corner of Reina Victoria and Roca.

WHEN TO GO

Any time of year is a good time to visit Ecuador, but each region has some months that are better than others.

the better hotels. If you don't like the look of a driver don't get in the cab.

Common sense is your best sense in any city. The first rule is to avoid dangerous neighborhoods, especially with valuables. In Quito, the narrow market street of Ipiales near the Church of San Francisco in the Old Town is notorious for its pickpockets, as is 24 de Mayo for general vice and danger. The roads leading up to the Virgin Statue on the hill known as El Panecillo in the Old Town is known for assault and robbery. The Terminal Terrestre bus station is a hangout for petty thieves. And stay out of all city parks after dark, especially Carolina and Ejido.

Always carry a photocopy of the first pages of your passport, police sometimes make spot identification checks. Photocopy all your documents, and try to keep them separate from your person. Use hotel safes where possible, insisting on a re-

December to June are the best months for the Galápagos Islands because the weather is warm and the sea tends to be calm. Although this is wet season, skies are generally clear except during downpours. March and April are often the very best months.

During the dry season in the Galápagos, from July to November, the weather tends towards overcast and the sea is just below pleasant swimming temperatures. The worst months can be August and September, when temperatures tend to be quite cool and waters rough. Because of overseas vacation periods, the busiest tourist seasons in the Galápagos are around Christmas and in July and August.

On the coast, the warm, but wetter months from January to April are popular with Ecuadorians and Colombians, who take vacations during this period. Many gringos visit the coast during their

own vacation periods from June to August. For the Oriente, it's wise to avoid the wettest and hottest months from June to August. In the Sierra the climate is pleasant throughout the year.

If you want your visit to coincide with popular festivals, see FESTIVE FLINGS, page 53 in YOUR CHOICE. December is the best time for seeing bullfights in Quito.

National holidays not included in FESTIVE FLINGS include:

January 1 *New Year's Day*. Most of the excitement will have taken place on New Year's Eve so this tends to be a quiet day.

January 6 *Epiphany*, also known as The Festival of the Three Kings.

padlocks, light chains and mosquito nets if backpacking, sealable ("Ziploc") plastic bags, foam earplugs, sanitary products, contraceptives, sun hat and sunglasses (good ones), sandals and rain jacket, a fleece and warm clothes (hat, gloves, scarves, socks, etc.) for the highlands, photos of your house and family to show, small presents for people (crayons, needles and threads, balloons, etc.), a travel pillow. Binoculars and strong sunblock are particularly useful for the Galápagos Islands.

Camping gear is generally expensive, so if you intend to do a lot of camping out, come prepared. If you plan to do a lot of hiking, bring gaiters.

February 27 *National Unity Day* commemorates the Battle of Tarqui.

Easter Holy Thursday, Good Friday and Easter Saturday are all public holidays

July 24 *Birthday of the Liberator, Simón Bolívar.*

August 10 *Quito Independence Day.*

October 9 *Guayaquil Independence Day.*

October 12 *Anniversary of Columbus' Discovery of the Americas, called El Día de la Raza.*

November 1 *All Saints' Day.*

WHAT TO TAKE

Although you can purchase most things once in Ecuador, goods are usually of low quality. A brief checklist of things to bring looks like this: a penknife, a flashlight (with spare batteries), needle and threads, duct tape for repairs, a small alarm clock or inexpensive watch, a first-aid kit, small

PHOTOGRAPHY

Humidity, dust, sand and water are the greatest enemies of photographic equipment. For the former, acquire plenty of bags of silica gel for your camera bag. For the latter, bring sealable or "Ziploc" plastic bags. In general, avoid flashy camera bags, which will attract attention (roll them around in the mud a bit before you come). I usually carry my camera bag inside an innocuous-looking one, and wander city streets with my camera wrapped in a magazine. You might consider bringing a disposable waterproof camera for river-trips and very wet conditions, while you can

OPPOSITE: Masked boobies on Isla Española. These comical creatures became known as boobies because human visitors mistook their tameness for stupidity. ABOVE: Milk shortages are not a problem in the fertile Andean Highlands.

also buy "canoe bags" or "Pelican cases" which will seal your camera completely underwater.

If you have a 35mm, SLR camera, a UV filter and a polarizing filter are absolutely essential. Bring fast films (200 or 400 ASA) for low light conditions in forests, churches and dawn or dusk shots. You might also want to invest in a large zoom lens (with a macro function) for capturing wildlife (essential on the Galápagos) and for more discreet portraiture. In general, film is widely available in Ecuador, but it's always best to bring your own — particularly if you take slides. Always check the use-by date (*fecha de vencimiento*). For developing, I would suggest you wait until you get back home to avoid any

disasters, although the Ecuacolor stores are generally reliable.

Light on the equator casts very dark shadows, so it's best to take photos in the first and last hours of the day. Fill-in flash will also help remedy this.

Photography etiquette requires that you ask the permission of the person you're taking a photo of before shooting away. If they ask for money, you decide if you want to give them something.

LANGUAGE BASICS

A little Spanish goes a long way in Ecuador, even if it's just a few words. Words ending in a consonant, except "n" and "s," are stressed on the last syllable, while words ending with a vowel (and with "n" and "s") are stressed on the second to last syllable. For exceptional cases an accent is written over the vowel in the stressed syllable, as in *delegación* for delegation.

VOWELS

Vowels are pronounced very "purely" as short phonetic sounds, not the diphthong drawn out version that we mostly use in English:
"A" — as in apple
"E" — as in bet
"I" — "ee" as in seek
"O" — as in occupy
"U" — as put
"Y" — is considered a vowel when it stands alone or appears at the end of a word. When alone it means "and" and is pronounced like our name for the letter "e."

CONSONANTS

Consonants are pronounced as follows:
"B" and "V" are almost interchangeable. Both sound like an English "b." In writing, "b" may replace what would be a "V" in English, like "sabana" for savanna.
"C" is sibilant as the "s" in sea, but hard like a "k" before "a", "o" or "u" as in "carrito."
"CH" is plosive as in "church."
"-ción" the very common ending as in "nación" is "sion" not the English "shun" sound of nation.
"D" is hard, as in "dog."
"G" is guttural like a strongly aspirated "h" in "hat" before "e" and "i," but hard as in "go" before "a" or "o," as in "gato" or "gol." "G" before "u," followed by a consonant, is hard like "guru," but becomes like the English "w" when placed before "ua," as in "guava." "G" before "ue" or "ui" is hard except when you see the umlaut on the "u" as in "güinche" (a winch).
H is always silent.
J is always a guttural aspirated "h" sound, not like our "dj" as in "jump." "Jugo" meaning juice sounds like "hoogo."
"LL" is pronounced "y" as in "yam."
"Ñ" sounds like the "ny" of "canyon."
"Q" is always pronounced like the English "k," unless adapted from an English or Latin word as in "quórum."
"R" is rolled, a double RR even more so.
"Z" is like the "s" in "bass."

GREETINGS AND PHRASES

Hóla   Hello (note the "h "is always mute).
Hasta luego   See you later and *Chao* (less formal).
Buenos días   Good morning (used from midnight to midday).
Buenas tardes   Good afternoon (from midday to 6 PM).
Buenas noches   Good evening/night (from 6 PM to midnight) or *Hasta mañana*.
¿Cómo está?   How are you? (formal).
¿Cómo estás?   How are you? (informal).
Muy bien, gracias   Very well, thank you.
Yo me llamo…   My name is…
¿Como se llama Usted?   What is your name?
Mucho gusto conocerle   Pleased to meet you.
¿Puede Usted ayudarme?   Can you help me?
¡Ayúdame!   Help!
Por favor   Please.

Gracias Thank you.
De nada It's nothing, you're welcome.
Con mucho gusto It's a pleasure.
¿De dónde es usted? Where do you come from?
¿Habla inglés? Do you speak English?
No entiendo I don't understand.
No hablo español I don't speak Spanish.
Lo siento I'm sorry.
Puede repetir más despacio por favor Please repeat more slowly.
Perdone Excuse me, or *Con permiso* to get past someone.
¿Cómo? How, or come again?
¿Dónde está/están…? Where is/are…?

SOME USEFUL WORDS

sí yes
no no
bueno good
malo bad
grande big
pequeño small
caliente hot
frío cold
bien well
bastante enough
izquierda (ees-key-er-dah) left
derecha right
todo recto or *derecho* straight ahead
cerca near
lejos (leh-hohs) far
muy very
más more
menos less
arriba up
abajo down
baños toilets
¿Dónde? Where?
¿Qué? What?
¿Cuándo? When?
¿Por qué? Why?
aquí here
allí or *allá* there
hoy today
abierto open
cerrado closed
mañana tomorrow
por or *en la mañana* in the morning
entrada entrance
salida exit
banco bank
aeropuerto airport
ciudad city
pueblo town or village

HOTEL BASICS

habitación room
habitación individual single room
habitación doble double room
habitación matrimonial double-bed room
¿Hay una habitación libre? Do you have a room?
cabaña cabin
con dos camas with two beds
con baño with bath
ducha shower
ventilador fan
aire acondicionado air-conditioned
llave key

RESTAURANT BASICS

comedor informal local restaurant
chifa Chinese restaurant
cantina canteen, drinking establishment
borracho/a drunk
una mesa a table
mesonero/a waiter/waitress
la cerveza beer
el vino blanco white wine ("v" is pronounced "b")
el vino tinto red wine
un vaso a glass
una botella (boh-tey-yah) a bottle
el té tea
el café coffee
con leche with milk
el azúcar sugar
el agua mineral mineral water
sin gas/con gas still/sparkling
la carta menu
buen provecho have a good meal
el desayuno breakfast
la comida/el almuerzo lunch
la cena dinner
un cuchillo a knife
un tenedor a fork
una cuchara a spoon
el plato del día dish of the day
la sopa soup
el pan bread
las tostadas toast
la mantequilla butter
el pollo chicken
los mariscos seafood
las gambas prawns
el pescado fish
ceviche fish or shellfish marinated in lemon juice and herbs
la carne meat
la ternera beef
el chorizo sausage
hervido boiled
al horno baked
asado/hornado roast
frito fried
el huevo (weh-voh) egg
soy vegetariano/a I'm a vegetarian

"Petroleum and there's no progress." Some of urban Ecuador's ubiquitous graffiti.

la menestra   vegetable stew
las patatas (also *papas*)   potatoes
arroz   rice
la cebolla   onion
la sal   salt
la salsa   sauce
el postre   dessert
el queso   cheese
la fruta   fruit
el helado   ice cream
la cuenta por favor   the bill, please

SHOPPING BASICS

supermacado   supermarket
tienda   shop, store
¿Qué desea?   What would you like?
Quiero…   I want some…
Aqui tiene   Here it is
¿Algo más?   Anything more?
Nada más   No more
¿Cuánto es?   How much is it?

NUMBERS

0   *cero*
1   *uno*
2   *dos*
3   *tres*
4   *cuatro*
5   *cinco*
6   *seis*
7   *siete*
8   *ocho*
9   *nueve*
10   *diez*
11   *once*
12   *doce*
13   *trece*
14   *catorce*
15   *quince*
16   *dieciseis*
17   *diecisiete*
18   *dieciocho*
19   *diecinueve*
20   *veinte*
21   *veintiuno*
22   *veintidós*
30   *treinta*
40   *cuarenta*
50   *cincuenta*
60   *sesenta*
70   *setenta*
80   *ochenta*
90   *noventa*
100   *cien*
101   *ciento uno*
102   *ciento dos*
200   *doscientos*
300   *trescientos*

400   *cuatrocientos*
500   *quinientos*
600   *seiscientos*
700   *setecientos*
800   *ochocientos*
900   *novecientos*
1,000   *mil*
100,000   *cien mil*
1,000,000   *un millón*

TIME

un minuto   one minute
una hora   one hour
¿Qué hora es?   What time is it?
Son las tres   It is three o'clock
mediodía   noon
medianoche   midnight
domingo   Sunday
lunes   Monday
martes   Tuesday
miércoles   Wednesday
jueves   Thursday
viernes   Friday
sábado   Saturday
enero   January
febrero   February
marzo   March
abril   April
mayo   May
junio   June
julio   July
agosto   August
septiembre   September
octubre   October
noviembre   November
diciembre   December

RECOMMENDED WEB SITES

There are several good web sites aimed at travelers that are useful for before-trip browsing and up-to-date information. These include the first-class **www.ecuadorexplorer.com**, **www.ecuadorial.com** and **www.travelecuador.com**. These have good practical advice, as well as links to dozens of operators and places to stay. The **www.ecuaventura.com** site is officially sponsored by the Ministry of Tourism and has lots of information in English, while the Ecuador Ecotourism Association has a site at **www.ecoturismo-ecuador.com**. Most of Ecuador's museums and cultural institutions are online in Spanish at **www.cultura.com.ec**. Other useful sites are the Ecuadorian Embassy in Washington's site, **www.ecuador.org** and About.com's South America pages at **http://gosouthamerica.about.com**. For up-to-the-minute travel advice, see the United States Department of State site at **http://travel.state.gov/travel_warnings.html**.

For Galápagos web sites, see GENERAL INFORMA-TION, page 222 in THE GALÁPAGOS ISLANDS.

For general news, in Spanish, see the newspaper sites **www.elcomercio.com** and **www.eluniverso.com**. For English-language news on the Americas, see the *Washington Post* WEB SITE **www.washingtonpost.com** or the *International Herald Tribune* WEB SITE **ww.iht.com**. Other good continent-wide sources of information for travelers include the Latin American Travel Advisor **www.amerispan.com/lata** and the excellent Planeta site, **www.planeta.com**, for all things in eco- and travel-related.

Recommended Reading

For the best background the Inca conquest, dive straight into John Hemming's great narrative, *The Conquest of the Incas* (1987), followed by the somewhat denser, but still readable *Historical Dictionary of Ecuador* by A.W. Bork and G. Mayer (1973).

Probably the best overview of more recent politics and economics is the brief *Ecuador in Focus*, by Wilma Roos and Omer van Renterghem, published by the Latin American Bureau and updated in 2000. An insightful and provocative analysis of current Ecuadorian identity and politics is available in *Remaking he Nation: Place, Identity and Politics in Latin America* by Sarah Radcliffe and Sallie Westwood (1999). For recent events chronicled from an indigenous perspective, as well as some history and culture, seek out *We Will Not Dance on Our Grandfathers' Tombs* by Kintto Lucas (Latin American Bureau, 2000). An enlightening overview of the weaving, costumes and customs of highland Indians is found in *Costume and Identity in Highland Ecuador*, edited by Ann Rowe and Lynn Meisch (1998). More culturally specific is Lynn Meisch's *Otavalo: Weaving, Costume and the Market* (Libri Mundi, Quito, 1987).

Tom Miller's *The Panama Hat Trail: A Journey from South America* (1988) makes for an entertaining read, covering good historical and geographical ground, though a bit stretched at times. Other recommended "foreigners abroad" books include Richard Poole's *The Inca Smiled: The Growing Pains of an Aid Worker in Ecuador* (1993) and Moritz Thomsen's *Living Poor* (1989) (and his other books). If you're interested in Vilcabamba's old people, and Andean life in general, David Davies' *The Centenarians of the Andes* (1995) makes for interesting reading.

Travelers heading to the Oriente would do well to read Joe Kane's first-class, if depressing, *Savages* (1995), which chronicles the struggle of the Huaorani against oil development on their lands. Randy Smith's *Crisis Under the Canopy* (1993) also deals with the Huaorani, but focuses particularly on tourism. For an overview of eco- and community-based tourism in Napo Province, seek out Rolf Wesche et al., *The Ecotourist's Guide to the Ecuadorian Amazon, Napo Province* (1995), which is a bit out of date, but still useful. French anthropologist Philippe Descola's *The Spears of Twilight: Life and Death in the Amazon Jungle* (1996) is a fascinating account of his time among the Achuar in the early 1970s, with Michael Harner's *The Jivaro: People of the Sacred Waterfall* (1984) also good. For a clear and concise overview of shamanism and hallucinogens, see Mircea Eliade's *Shamanism: Archaic Techniques of Ecstasy* (1989), while one of my all-time favorite books about the Amazon, which touches on Ecuador and the Huaorani, is Wade Davis' *One River* (1996), a beautifully told story of three generations of ethnobotanists.

Climbers wanting to step into the shoes of the intrepid Edward Whymper can acquire his wonderful *Travels Amongst the Great Andes of the Equator*, originally published in 1891 and reprinted by Peregrine Books in 1990. Richard Snailham's *Sangay Survived: The Story of the Ecuadorian Volcano Disaster* (1978) is a harrowing account of a tragic climb of Volcán Sangay. The best practical information for climbers and trekkers is available in Rob Rachowiecki and Mark Thurber's *Climbing and Hiking in Ecuador* (latest edition 2000).

There is a wealth of books on the Galápagos Islands. For some historical background and a look into the bizarre murder-mystery on Floreana Island see Johanna Angermeyer's *My Father's Island* (1989), Margret Wittmer's *Floreana* (1961), or John Treherne's *The Galápagos Affair* (1983). There are several editions in print of Darwin's *Voyages of the Beagle*, which include captivating chapters on the islands. For more on Darwin and evolutionary theories, both Alan Moorehead's *Darwin and The Beagle* (1969) and Jonathan Weiner's Pulitzer Prize-winning *The Beak of the Finch* (1994) are excellent. For a more general book, see John Hickman's *The Enchanted Islands; The Galápagos Discovered* (1985). Michael Jackson's *Galápagos — A Natural History* (1985, second edition 1993) is regarded as the best naturalist guide. You can find out more at Jackson's web site, www.islandnet.com/~mjackson/homepage.html. The best birding guide is *A Field Guide to the Birds of the Galápagos* by Michael Harris (1992).

The two pocket guides that are useful for Quito and the country are Nelson Gómez's *Guía Informativa de Quito*, authorized by Instituto Geográfico Militar (1996), and *The Pocket Guide to Ecuador*, updated yearly. *A Neotropical Companion* (paperback, second edition 1999) by John Kricher provides the best introduction to the flora, fauna and ecosystems of South America.

The excellent Libri Mundi bookshop in Quito has a web site where you can order books online: www.librimundi.com. The South American Explorers also have a comprehensive list of books available to order at www.samexplo.org.

Quick Reference A–Z Guide
to Places and Topics of Interest

Photo Credits

All photographs were taken by **Robert Holmes**, with the exception of those on pages 42, 62, 83 and 101, by **Dominic Hamilton**.